Nutshell Series

of

WEST PUBLISHING COMPANY

P.O. Box 64526

St. Paul, Minnesota 55164–0526

Civil Procedure, 2nd Ed., 1986, 306 pages, by Mary Kay Kane, Professor of Law, University of California, Hastings College of the Law.

Civil Rights, 1978, 279 pages, by Norman Vieira, Professor of Law, Southern Illinois University.

Commercial Paper, 3rd Ed., 1982, 404 pages, by Charles M. Weber, Former Professor of Business Law, The Wharton School of Finance and Commerce, University of Pennsylvania and Richard E. Speidel, Professor of Law, Northwestern University.

Community Property, 2nd Ed., 1988, 432 pages, by Robert L. Mennell, Former Professor of Law, Hamline University, and Thomas M. Boykoff.

Comparative Legal Traditions, 1982, 402 pages, by Mary Ann Glendon, Professor of Law, Harvard University, Michael Wallace Gordon, Professor of Law, University of Florida, and Christopher Osakwe, Professor of Law, Tulane University.

Conflicts, 1982, 470 pages, by David D. Siegel, Professor of Law, St. John's University.

Constitutional Analysis, 1979, 388 pages, by Jerre S. Williams, Professor of Law Emeritus, University of Texas.

Constitutional Federalism, 2nd Ed., 1987, 411 pages, by David E. Engdahl, Professor of Law, University of Puget Sound.

Constitutional Law, 1986, 389 pages, by Jerome A. Barron, Professor of Law, George Washington University, and C. Thomas Dienes, Professor of Law, George Washington University.

Consumer Law, 2nd Ed., 1981, 418 pages, by David G. Epstein, Dean and Professor of Law, Emory University, and Steve H. Nickles, Professor of Law, University of Minnesota.

Contract Remedies, 1981, 323 pages, by Jane M. Friedman, Professor of Law, Wayne State University.

Contracts, 2nd Ed., 1984, 425 pages, by Gordon D. Schaber, Dean and Professor of Law, McGeorge School of Law, and Claude D. Rohwer, Professor of Law, McGeorge School of Law.

NUTSHELL SERIES

Corporations—Law of, 2nd Ed., 1987, 515 pages, by Robert W. Hamilton, Professor of Law, University of Texas.

Corrections and Prisoners' Rights—Law of, 2nd Ed., 1983, 386 pages, by Sheldon Krantz, Professor of Law, University of San Diego.

Criminal Law, 2nd Ed., 1987, 321 pages, by Arnold H. Loewy, Professor of Law, University of North Carolina.

Criminal Procedure—Constitutional Limitations, 4th Ed., 1988, 461 pages, by Jerold H. Israel, Professor of Law, University of Michigan, and Wayne R. LaFave, Professor of Law, University of Illinois.

Debtor-Creditor Law, 3rd Ed., 1986, 383 pages, by David G. Epstein, Dean and Professor of Law, Emory University.

Employment Discrimination—Federal Law of, 2nd Ed., 1981, 402 pages, by Mack A. Player, Professor of Law, Florida State University.

Energy Law, 1981, 338 pages, by Joseph P. Tomain, Professor of Law, University of Cincinnatti.

Environmental Law, 2nd Ed., 1988, about 348 pages by Roger W. Findley, Professor of Law, University of Illinois, and Daniel A. Farber, Professor of Law, University of Minnesota.

Estate and Gift Taxation, Federal, 3rd Ed., 1983, 509 pages, by John K. McNulty, Professor of Law, University of California, Berkeley.

Estate Planning—Introduction to, 3rd Ed., 1983, 370 pages, by Robert J. Lynn, Professor of Law, Ohio State University.

Evidence, Federal Rules of, 2nd Ed., 1987, 473 pages, by Michael H. Graham, Professor of Law, University of Miami.

Evidence, State and Federal Rules, 2nd Ed., 1981, 514 pages, by Paul F. Rothstein, Professor of Law, Georgetown University.

Family Law, 2nd Ed., 1986, 444 pages, by Harry D. Krause, Professor of Law, University of Illinois.

Federal Jurisdiction, 2nd Ed., 1981, 258 pages, by David P. Currie, Professor of Law, University of Chicago.

Future Interests, 1981, 361 pages, by Lawrence W. Waggoner, Professor of Law, University of Michigan.

Government Contracts, 1979, 423 pages, by W. Noel Keyes, Professor of Law Emeritus, Pepperdine University.

Historical Introduction to Anglo-American Law, 2nd Ed., 1973, 280 pages, by Frederick G. Kempin, Jr., Professor of Business Law, Wharton School of Finance and Commerce, University of Pennsylvania.

Immigration Law and Procedure, 1984, 345 pages, by David Weissbrodt, Professor of Law, University of Minnesota.

Injunctions, 1974, 264 pages, by John F. Dobbyn, Professor of Law, Villanova University.

Insurance Law, 1981, 281 pages, by John F. Dobbyn, Professor of Law, Villanova University.

Intellectual Property—Patents, Trademarks and Copyright, 1983, 428 pages, by Arthur R. Miller, Professor of Law, Harvard University, and Michael H. Davis, Professor of Law, Cleveland State University, Cleveland-Marshall College of Law.

International Business Transactions, 3rd Ed., 1988, about 484 pages, by Ralph H. Folsom, Professor of Law, University of San Diego, Michael Wallace Gordon, Professor of Law, University of Florida, and John A. Spanogle, Jr., Professor of Law, State University of New York, Buffalo.

International Human Rights, 1988, about 275 pages, by Thomas Buergenthal, Professor of Law, Emory University.

International Law (Public), 1985, 262 pages, by Thomas Buergenthal, Professor of Law, Emory University, and Harold G. Maier, Professor of Law, Vanderbilt University.

Introduction to the Study and Practice of Law, 1983, 418 pages, by Kenney F. Hegland, Professor of Law, University of Arizona.

Judicial Process, 1980, 292 pages, by William L. Reynolds, Professor of Law, University of Maryland.

Jurisdiction, 4th Ed., 1980, 232 pages, by Albert A. Ehrenzweig, Late Professor of Law, University of California, Berkeley, David W. Louisell, Late Professor of Law, University of

California, Berkeley, and Geoffrey C. Hazard, Jr., Professor of Law, Yale Law School.

Juvenile Courts, 3rd Ed., 1984, 291 pages, by Sanford J. Fox, Professor of Law, Boston College.

Labor Arbitration Law and Practice, 1979, 358 pages, by Dennis R. Nolan, Professor of Law, University of South Carolina.

Labor Law, 2nd Ed., 1986, 397 pages, by Douglas L. Leslie, Professor of Law, University of Virginia.

Land Use, 2nd Ed., 1985, 356 pages, by Robert R. Wright, Professor of Law, University of Arkansas, Little Rock, and Susan Webber Wright, Professor of Law, University of Arkansas, Little Rock.

Landlord and Tenant Law, 2nd Ed., 1986, 311 pages, by David S. Hill, Professor of Law, University of Colorado.

Law Study and Law Examinations—Introduction to, 1971, 389 pages, by Stanley V. Kinyon, Late Professor of Law, University of Minnesota.

Legal Interviewing and Counseling, 2nd Ed., 1987, 487 pages, by Thomas L. Shaffer, Professor of Law, University of Notre Dame, and James R. Elkins, Professor of Law, West Virginia University.

Legal Research, 4th Ed., 1985, 452 pages, by Morris L. Cohen, Professor of Law and Law Librarian, Yale University.

Legal Writing, 1982, 294 pages, by Lynn B. Squires and Marjorie Dick Rombauer, Professor of Law, University of Washington.

Legislative Law and Process, 2nd Ed., 1986, 346 pages, by Jack Davies, Professor of Law, William Mitchell College of Law.

Local Government Law, 2nd Ed., 1983, 404 pages, by David J. McCarthy, Jr., Professor of Law, Georgetown University.

Mass Communications Law, 3rd Ed., 1988, 538 pages, by Harvey L. Zuckman, Professor of Law, Catholic University, Martin J. Gaynes, Lecturer in Law, Temple University, T. Barton Carter, Professor of Public Communications, Boston University, and Juliet Lushbough Dee, Professor of Communications, University of Delaware.

Medical Malpractice—The Law of, 2nd Ed., 1986, 342 pages, by Joseph H. King, Professor of Law, University of Tennessee.

Military Law, 1980, 378 pages, by Charles A. Shanor, Professor of Law, Emory University, and Timothy P. Terrell, Professor of Law, Emory University.

Oil and Gas Law, 2nd Ed., 1988, about 402 pages, by John S. Lowe, Professor of Law, Southern Methodist University.

Personal Property, 1983, 322 pages, by Barlow Burke, Jr., Professor of Law, American University.

Post-Conviction Remedies, 1978, 360 pages, by Robert Popper, Dean and Professor of Law, University of Missouri, Kansas City.

Presidential Power, 1977, 328 pages, by Arthur Selwyn Miller, Professor of Law Emeritus, George Washington University.

Products Liability, 3rd Ed., 1988, 307 pages, by Jerry J. Phillips, Professor of Law, University of Tennessee.

Professional Responsibility, 1980, 399 pages, by Robert H. Aronson, Professor of Law, University of Washington, and Donald T. Weckstein, Professor of Law, University of San Diego.

Real Estate Finance, 2nd Ed., 1985, 262 pages, by Jon W. Bruce, Professor of Law, Vanderbilt University.

Real Property, 2nd Ed., 1981, 448 pages, by Roger H. Bernhardt, Professor of Law, Golden Gate University.

Regulated Industries, 2nd Ed., 1987, 389 pages, by Ernest Gellhorn, Former Dean and Professor of Law, Case Western Reserve University, and Richard J. Pierce, Professor of Law, Southern Methodist University.

Remedies, 2nd Ed., 1985, 320 pages, by John F. O'Connell, Dean and Professor of Law, Southern California College of Law.

Res Judicata, 1976, 310 pages, by Robert C. Casad, Professor of Law, University of Kansas.

Sales, 2nd Ed., 1981, 370 pages, by John M. Stockton, Professor of Business Law, Wharton School of Finance and Commerce, University of Pennsylvania.

NUTSHELL SERIES

Hornbook Series

and

Basic Legal Texts

of

WEST PUBLISHING COMPANY

P.O. Box 64526

St. Paul, Minnesota 55164–0526

Admiralty and Maritime Law, Schoenbaum's Hornbook on, 1987, 692 pages, by Thomas J. Schoenbaum, Professor of Law, University of Georgia.

Agency and Partnership, Reuschlein & Gregory's Hornbook on the Law of, 1979 with 1981 Pocket Part, 625 pages, by Harold Gill Reuschlein, Professor of Law Emeritus, Villanova University, and William A. Gregory, Professor of Law, Georgia State University.

Antitrust, Sullivan's Hornbook on the Law of, 1977, 886 pages, by Lawrence A. Sullivan, Professor of Law, University of California, Berkeley.

Civil Procedure, Friedenthal, Kane and Miller's Hornbook on, 1985, 876 pages, by Jack H. Friedental, Dean and Professor of Law, George Washington University, Mary Kay Kane, Professor of Law, University of California, Hastings College of the Law, and Arthur R. Miller, Professor of Law, Harvard University.

Common Law Pleading, Koffler and Reppy's Hornbook on, 1969, 663 pages, by Joseph H. Koffler, Professor of Law, New York Law School, and Alison Reppy, Late Dean and Professor of Law, New York Law School.

Conflict of Laws, Scoles and Hay's Hornbook on, 1982, with 1986 Pocket Part, 1085 pages, by Eugene F. Scoles, Professor of Law, University of Illinois, and Peter Hay, Dean and Professor of Law, University of Illinois.

HORNBOOKS & BASIC TEXTS

Constitutional Law, Nowak, Rotunda and Young's Hornbook on, 3rd Ed., 1986, with 1988 Pocket Part, 1191 pages, by John E. Nowak, Professor of Law, University of Illinois, Ronald D. Rotunda, Professor of Law, University of Illinois, and J. Nelson Young, Late Professor of Law, University of North Carolina.

Contracts, Calamari and Perillo's Hornbook on, 3rd Ed., 1987, 1049 pages, by John D. Calamari, Professor of Law, Fordham University, and Joseph M. Perillo, Professor of Law, Fordham University.

Contracts, Corbin's One Volume Student Ed., 1952, 1224 pages, by Arthur L. Corbin, Late Professor of Law, Yale University.

Corporations, Henn and Alexander's Hornbook on, 3rd Ed., 1983, with 1986 Pocket Part, 1371 pages, by Harry G. Henn, Professor of Law Emeritus, Cornell University, and John R. Alexander.

Criminal Law, LaFave and Scott's Hornbook on, 2nd Ed., 1986, 918 pages, by Wayne R. LaFave, Professor of Law, University of Illinois, and Austin Scott, Jr., Late Professor of Law, University of Colorado.

Criminal Procedure, LaFave and Israel's Hornbook on, 1985 with 1986 pocket part, 1142 pages, by Wayne R. LaFave, Professor of Law, University of Illinois, and Jerold H. Israel, Professor of Law University of Michigan.

Damages, McCormick's Hornbook on, 1935, 811 pages, by Charles T. McCormick, Late Dean and Professor of Law, University of Texas.

Domestic Relations, Clark's Hornbook on, 2nd Ed., 1988, 1050 pages, by Homer H. Clark, Jr., Professor of Law, University of Colorado.

Economics and Federal Antitrust Law, Hovenkamp's Hornbook on, 1985, 414 pages, by Herbert Hovenkamp, Professor of Law, University of Iowa.

Employment Discrimination Law, Player's Hornbook on, 708 pages, 1988, by Mack A. Player, Professor of Law, Florida State University.

HORNBOOKS & BASIC TEXTS

Environmental Law, Rodgers' Hornbook on, 1977 with 1984 Pocket Part, 956 pages, by William H. Rodgers, Jr., Professor of Law, University of Washington.

Evidence, Lilly's Introduction to, 2nd Ed., 1987, 585 pages, by Graham C. Lilly, Professor of Law, University of Virginia.

Evidence, McCormick's Hornbook on, 3rd Ed., 1984 with 1987 Pocket Part, 1156 pages, General Editor, Edward W. Cleary, Professor of Law Emeritus, Arizona State University.

Federal Courts, Wright's Hornbook on, 4th Ed., 1983, 870 pages, by Charles Alan Wright, Professor of Law, University of Texas.

Federal Income Taxation, Rose and Chommie's Hornbook on, 3rd Ed., 1988, 923 pages, by Michael D. Rose, Professor of Law, Ohio State University, and John C. Chommie, Late Professor of Law, University of Miami.

Federal Income Taxation of Individuals, Posin's Hornbook on, 1983 with 1987 Pocket Part, 491 pages, by Daniel Q. Posin, Jr., Professor of Law, Catholic University.

Future Interest, Simes' Hornbook on, 2nd Ed., 1966, 355 pages, by Lewis M. Simes, Late Professor of Law, University of Michigan.

Insurance, Keeton and Widiss on, 1988, about 1050 pages, by Robert E. Keeton, Professor of Law Emeritus, Harvard University, and Alan I. Widiss, Professor of Law, University of Iowa.

Labor Law, Gorman's Basic Text on, 1976, 914 pages, by Robert A. Gorman, Professor of Law, University of Pennsylvania.

Law Problems, Ballentine's, 5th Ed., 1975, 767 pages, General Editor, William E. Burby, Late Professor of Law, University of Southern California.

Legal Ethics, Wolfram's Hornbook on, 1986, 1120 pages, by Charles W. Wolfram, Professor of Law, Cornell University.

Legal Writing Style, Weihofen's, 2nd Ed., 1980, 332 pages, by Henry Weihofen, Professor of Law Emeritus, University of New Mexico.

Local Government Law, Reynolds' Hornbook on, 1982 with 1987 Pocket Part, 860 pages, by Osborne M. Reynolds, Professor of Law, University of Oklahoma.

New York Estate Administration, Turano and Radigan's Hornbook on, 1986, 676 pages, by Margaret V. Turano, Professor of Law, St. John's University, and Raymond Radigan.

New York Practice, Siegel's Hornbook on, 1978 with 1987 Pocket Part, 1011 pages, by David D. Siegel, Professor of Law, St. John's University.

Oil and Gas Law, Hemingway's Hornbook on, 2nd Ed., 1983, with 1986 Pocket Part, 543 pages, by Richard W. Hemingway, Professor of Law, University of Oklahoma.

Property, Boyer's Survey of, 3rd Ed., 1981, 766 pages, by Ralph E. Boyer, Professor of Law Emeritus, University of Miami.

Property, Law of, Cunningham, Whitman and Stoebuck's Hornbook on, 1984 with 1987 Pocket Part, 916 pages, by Roger A. Cunningham, Professor of Law, University of Michigan, Dale A. Whitman, Professor of Law, University of Missouri, Columbia, and William B. Stoebuck, Professor of Law, University of Washington.

Real Estate Finance Law, Nelson and Whitman's Hornbook on, 2nd Ed., 1985, 941 pages, by Grant S. Nelson, Professor of Law, University of Missouri, Columbia, and Dale A. Whitman, Professor of Law, University of Missouri, Columbia.

Real Property, Moynihan's Introduction to, 2nd Ed., 1988, 239 pages, by Cornelius J. Moynihan, Late Professor of Law, Suffolk University.

Remedies, Dobbs' Hornbook on, 1973, 1067 pages, by Dan B. Dobbs, Professor of Law, University of Arizona.

Secured Transactions under the U.C.C., Henson's Hornbook on, 2nd Ed., 1979 with 1979 Pocket Part, 504 pages, by Ray D. Henson, Professor of Law, University of California, Hastings College of the Law.

Securities Regulation, Hazen's Hornbook on the Law of, 1985 with 1988 Pocket Part, 739 pages, by Thomas Lee Hazen, Professor of Law, University of North Carolina.

Sports Law, Schubert, Smith and Trentadue's, 1986, 395 pages, by George W. Schubert, Dean of University College, University of North Dakota, Rodney K. Smith, Professor of Law, Delaware Law School, Widener University, and Jesse C. Trentadue, Former Professor of Law, University of North Dakota.

Torts, Prosser and Keeton's Hornbook on, 5th Ed., 1984 with 1988 Pocket Part, 1286 pages, by William L. Prosser, Late Dean and Professor of Law, University of California, Berkeley, Page Keeton, Professor of Law Emeritus, University of Texas, Dan B. Dobbs, Professor of Law, University of Arizona, Robert E. Keeton, Professor of Law Emeritus, Harvard University, and David G. Owen, Professor of Law, University of South Carolina.

Trial Advocacy, Jeans' Handbook on, Soft cover, 1975, 473 pages, by James W. Jeans, Professor of Law, University of Missouri, Kansas City.

Trusts, Bogert's Hornbook on, 6th Ed., 1987, 794 pages, by George T. Bogert.

Uniform Commercial Code, White and Summers' Hornbook on, 3rd Ed., 1988, about 1200 pages, by James J. White, Professor of Law, University of Michigan, and Robert S. Summers, Professor of Law, Cornell University.

Urban Planning and Land Development Control Law, Hagman and Juergensmeyer's Hornbook on, 2nd Ed., 1986, 680 pages, by Donald G. Hagman, Late Professor of Law, University of California, Los Angeles, and Julian C. Juergensmeyer, Professor of Law, University of Florida.

Wills, Atkinson's Hornbook on, 2nd Ed., 1953, 975 pages, by Thomas E. Atkinson, Late Professor of Law, New York University.

Wills, Trusts and Estates Including Taxation and Future Interests, McGovern, Rein and Kurtz' Hornbook on, 1988, about 924 pages by William M. McGovern, Professor of Law, University of California, Los Angeles, Jan Ellen Rein, Professor of Law, Gonzaga University, and Sheldon F. Kurtz, Professor of Law, University of Iowa.

Advisory Board

MASS
COMMUNICATIONS LAW
IN A NUTSHELL

Third Edition

HARVEY L. ZUCKMAN
Professor of Law, The Catholic University
of America
Director, Institute for Communications
Law Studies, Washington, D.C.

MARTIN J. GAYNES, ESQ.
Member, Wilkes, Artis, Hedrick and Lane
Washington, D.C.

T. BARTON CARTER
Associate Professor of Mass Communication
College of Communication
Boston University

JULIET LUSHBOUGH DEE
Assistant Professor of Communication
College of Arts and Science
University of Delaware

ST. PAUL, MINN.
WEST PUBLISHING CO.
1988

Library of Congress Cataloging-in-Publication Data

Mass communications law in a nutshell/by Harvey L. Zuckman ... [et al.].

   p. cm.—(Nutshell series)

  Rev. ed. of: Mass communications law in a nutshell/by Harvey L. Zuckman and Martin J. Gaynes.

  Includes index.

  ISBN 0–314–62943–2

  1. Mass media—Law and legislation—United States. I. Zuckman, Harvey L. II. Zuckman, Harvey L. Mass communications law in a nutshell. III. Series.

KF2750.Z9M37   1988   343.73'099—dc19   [347.30399]

87–28013
CIP

(Z., G., C. & D.) Mass.Comm. 3rd NS
1st Reprint—1989

For Charlotte, Barbara,
Greg and Richard

*

PREFACE

To appreciate the interrelationship of law and mass communications look at a daily newspaper. There, one is likely to find news of important court decisions, perhaps even of concern to the newspaper itself, news of new legislation having great impact on the citizenry as well as news about the judiciary. Even the sports page may contain as much news about law suits between team owners, unions and players as about team performance. There has been a veritable explosion in media coverage of legal issues since the early 1960s. At the same time their increasing influence and complexity have resulted in increased problems for the mass media, particularly in the areas of First Amendment protection and Federal Communication Commission regulation and deregulation of broadcasting and cable.

In attempting to meet what we perceive as a continuing need for a basic text in communications law, not only for law students but journalism and communications students as well, the original authors, a full-time law professor and a practicing communications lawyer, decided to add two superbly qualified communication school instructors as co-authors of this third edition. T. Barton Carter is an associate professor of mass communication in the College of Communication of Boston University. His scholarly work includes co-authorship of two well received casebooks in the field as well as shorter articles in law reviews. He also brings to this work a practical understanding of electronic media gained from his ownership of broadcasting properties. Juliet Lushbough Dee is an assistant professor of communication in the College of Arts and Science at the University of Delaware. She is the author of a major study of media responsibility for stimulating real life violence recently published in the Journal of Communication.

These two young scholars bring fresh perspectives to this text which are displayed particularly in the chapters on First Amendment theory, restraint of the press for reasons of national security and cable television and the new technologies.

While we continue to avoid change merely for the sake of change, some structural modifications have been made to enhance logical continuity and to accommodate growth of the law in certain areas. Because of highly publicized continuing government threats of criminal prosecutions against the press for disclosures of allegedly sensitive information about national security and of civil actions for injunctions to prevent such disclosures, this area of restraint of expression is now treated in a separate chapter (V).

Certain topics included in Chapter V of the second edition, *i.e.,* media access to copyrighted material and the effect on newsgathering of searches and seizures in the newsroom, seemed, on further reflection, to fit more logically elsewhere.

The limited discussion of copyright and the First Amendment has been moved to Chapter I of this edition, and newsroom searches and seizures are now treated in the chapter (VIII) dealing with newspersons' legal rights and responsibilities.

Reflecting some of the new realities of the electronic media that have emerged since the second edition, including deregulation of broadcasting and the substantial judicial and legislative attention paid to cable television, the second edition chapters on the functions of the Federal Communications Commission and the FCC's licensing policies have been merged into one chapter here (X) and the chapter on "emerging technologies" has been transformed into one emphasizing cable television (Chapter XII). A select number of other "emerged" technologies are also discussed in Chapter XII, while a few technologies that failed to emerge, for one reason or another, have been dropped from discussion.

The reader will note that the authors have made every effort to achieve gender neutral exposition in this edition. We believe the time has long since passed when we might ignore the need for equality of opportunity and the achievements of both sexes in the fields of law and communications. In this regard, Professor Zuckman is proud to report that his daughter recently entered the ranks of professional journalists as a reporter for a large midwestern newspaper. Our only regret is the need to resort to the awkward "he or she" and "him or her" pronoun construction in order to reflect that belief. We trust the reader will understand.

We wish to acknowledge our heavy debt to the following individuals and organizations in the preparation of this text: Professors Donald M. Gillmor and Jerome A. Barron, authors of the casebook, "Mass Communication Law," for allowing their organizational scheme to be followed here; Professor Thomas I. Emerson, whose many writings greatly influenced our thinking on First Amendment issues, and the editorial board of Law and Contemporary Problems for permitting us to reprint material from Professor Emerson's article "The Doctrine of Prior Restraint," appearing in a symposium on Obscenity and the Arts in Law and Contemporary Problems (Vol. 20, No. 4, Autumn, 1955), published by Duke University School of Law, Durham, North Carolina, copyright 1955, by Duke University; the late Dean William L. Prosser, founding author of the Handbook of the Law of Torts, whose works greatly shaped our thinking in Chapters II and III on the law of defamation and privacy; Professor Dan B. Dobbs, author of the Handbook of the Law of Remedies for his guidance on the law of damages in defamation actions; Earl W. Kintner, Esquire, author of "A Primer on the Law of Deceptive Practices," (copyright 1971 by Mr. Kintner, all rights reserved) whose thinking on the regulation of advertising greatly influenced the approach taken in Chapter VIII; the late Professor Melville B. Nimmer, without whose brilliant thinking on the law of copyright infringement actions no rational discussion of those subjects could be presented; the editorial board of the Texas Law Review for permission to paraphrase portions of the article by Donna Murasky, Esquire, "The Journalist's Privilege: Branzburg and Its Aftermath," 52 Texas Law Review 829 (1974); the editorial board of the Washington Law Review for permission to paraphrase portions of the article by Professors Don R. Pember and Dwight L. Teeter, Jr., "Privacy and the Press Since Time, Inc. v. Hill," 50 Washington Law Review 57 (1974); Charles B. Blackmar, distinguished jurist and former teaching colleague and cherished friend of Professor Zuckman for his insights into First Amendment problems engendered by lawyer advertising (he argued and won In re Matter of R_____ M.J. _____ in the United States Supreme Court); West Publishing Company for its new computerized storage and retrieval system that made the progression from galley to page proof to publication so much easier for the authors and helped keep typographical errors to a minimum; Kristine Snow for her dedicated work in preparing the index for this edition; Myrna Hoffman, office coordinator and Laura Sowers, secretary in the University of Delaware Communication Department for their administrative support, and Karin Thurman, Head of Public Services, and Mary Jane Mallonee, reference librarian at the Delaware Law School Library for their research assistance.

HARVEY L. ZUCKMAN
MARTIN J. GAYNES

Washington, D.C.
October, 1987

*

OUTLINE

PART ONE. THE FIRST AMENDMENT AND MASS COMMUNICATIONS

PART TWO. REGULATION OF THE ELECTRONIC MASS MEDIA

OUTLINE

*

TABLE OF CASES

References are to Pages

TABLE OF CASES

TABLE OF CASES

TABLE OF CASES

*

MASS COMMUNICATIONS LAW
IN A NUTSHELL

Third Edition

*

PART ONE

THE FIRST AMENDMENT AND MASS COMMUNICATIONS

CHAPTER I

THE FIRST AMENDMENT IN PERSPECTIVE

A. INTRODUCTION

The development of mass communications throughout the western world and particularly in the United States in the twentieth century is a product of both science and law. Science has given us the technology by which individuals may communicate information, ideas and images across time and space to other individuals. And for this we owe a debt of gratitude to scientists and inventors such as Edison, Bell, Marconi, DeForest, and Zworykin.

But technology does not exist in a vacuum. It operates in organized societies governed by laws. These societies may be open ones in which the members are relatively free to express themselves and to communicate with others by whatever means available or they may be relatively closed, with the modes of communications tightly controlled by a very few persons. Gutenberg's invention of moveable type gave promise of spreading both literacy and ideas to the masses, but in Elizabethan England and beyond, licensing acts severely limited access to the printing press to a few printers considered "safe" by the ruling authorities. It was this legal restriction on the utilization of the first technology of mass communication that led the great poet John Milton to make his stirring call for a free press in "Areopagitica." In our own time the vast promise of cable television was retarded for years because of the complex of statutes and Federal Communications Commission regulations designed to reign in this new technology in order to protect existing economic interests.

Thus, while technology is the necessary antecedent to mass communication, a society's laws ultimately determine how the technology will be developed and how "mass" will be its reach.

In our country the fountainhead of the law governing mass communication is the First Amendment to the Constitution which says in spare but sweeping language "Congress shall make no law . . . abridging the freedom of speech or of the press; . . ." The way this mandate is carried out tells us much about the kind of society we have. For as that giant of electronic journalism Edward R. Murrow once noted, what distinguishes a truly free society from all others is an independent judiciary and a free press.

B. BACKGROUND, THEORIES AND DIRECTION OF THE FIRST AMENDMENT

1. Background

At the time Madison was directed by Congress to draft the amendment to the Constitution expressly protecting free speech and press from governmental encroachment, he and the other founders of the Republic were acutely aware of the long history of suppression in England and the Colonies of free expression, particularly that concerning the affairs of government. Even after Parliament refused to renew the last of the licensing acts in 1695, the Crown was largely able to retain its control over the press by the imposition of heavy taxes on periodicals in England, by the refusal to permit the introduction of printing presses in many of the American colonies and, most importantly, by vigorous enforcement of the criminal law of seditious libel everywhere.

Under that law printers and publishers who offended the government and its ministers could be severely punished even when their statements were true. The maxim at common law was "the greater the truth the greater the libel." The journalistic exposure of a Watergate or Teapot Dome style scandal would have been virtually impossible under that law. Worse yet for the defendant, it was the Crown's judges who determined whether the utterance or writing was defamatory to the government. Needless to say, the prosecutors won nearly all of their cases, including one against Daniel Defoe for a satirical essay "Shortest Way with Dissenters." For his efforts Defoe was fined, pilloried and imprisoned.

Much the same fate befell a number of colonial printers and publishers until the royal governor of New York, William Cosby, instituted a prosecution for seditious libel against a New York printer, John Peter Zenger. Zenger had had the temerity to criticize Cosby's administration of the colony in the pages of his Weekly Journal. In the face of the uncontested fact of publication by Zenger and the common law of libel previously described, the jury refused to convict and the seed of a free press was planted in America.

Doubtless, then, with this history in mind, the press guarantee of the First Amendment was aimed at the very least at the abuses of licensing, censorship and punishment of political expression. Indeed, when Alexander Hamilton raised the question what was meant by freedom of the press, Madison responded that it meant freedom from despotic control by the federal government. Beyond this, the drafters failed to hand down to us any clear theory of the Amendment.

Only after the outbreak of World War I and the consequent increase in radical agitation in the country, did the Supreme Court and constitutional scholars begin to search for coherent theories to explain the allowance or suppression of expression

in specific cases. This search for theory was further encouraged by the ruling in Gitlow v. New
York, 268 U.S. 652, 45 S.Ct. 625, 69 L.Ed. 1138
(1925) that the constraints of the First Amendment
applied to the states through the operation of the
due process clause of the Fourteenth Amendment.

2. Theories and Tests of the First Amendment

Over the years a number of general theories
have been espoused to justify the existence of the
First Amendment guarantees of free speech and
free press. The most famous of these is the "free
trade of ideas" espoused by Justices Holmes and
Brandeis in their dissenting opinion in Abrams v.
United States, 250 U.S. 616, 630, 40 S.Ct. 17, 22, 63
L.Ed. 1173, 1180 (1919) and their concurring opinion in Whitney v. California, 274 U.S. 357, 375–77,
47 S.Ct. 641, 648–49, 71 L.Ed. 1095, 1105–06 (1927).
By this theory the First Amendment stands as a
protector of truth emerging from the public discussion of competing ideas.

Another major theory is the so-called Meiklejohn
interpretation of the First Amendment. Named
after its leading proponent, Professor Alexander
Meiklejohn, this interpretation, broadly stated,
holds that ours is a self-governing society and the
First Amendment protects the freedom of thought
and expression directed to the process by which we
govern ourselves. Thus, it is concerned with the
need for the citizenry to acquire such qualities of
mind and spirit and such information as will make

possible responsible self-governance. Implicit in
this form of government is the idea that while the
people delegate certain responsibility to their elected representatives, they reserve for themselves the
means to oversee their government and that the
elected representatives may not abridge the freedom of the people in maintaining this oversight.
Thus, in the Meiklejohn view, the central meaning
of the First Amendment is the protection it affords
to the public power of the people collectively to
govern themselves. See Meiklejohn, "The First
Amendment is an Absolute," 1961 Sup.Ct.Rev. 245,
253–263.

Practically, what this thesis translates into is
absolute protection for all thought, expression and
communication which bears on the citizen's role of
self-government. Major emphasis is placed on political expression: punishment for seditious libel
becomes an impossibility. But Meiklejohn would
also include within the coverage of the First
Amendment all aspects of educational, philosophical, scientific, literary and artistic endeavors because sensitivity to humanistic values and rational-
ity in judgment are dependent upon these pursuits.
Other expression not directly or indirectly related
to the process of self-government would be beyond
the pale of the First Amendment, as perhaps hor-
ror comic books.

While no Supreme Court decision has completely
accepted the Meiklejohn thesis, it has been embodied to some extent in New York Times Co. v.

Sullivan, 376 U.S. 254, 84 S.Ct. 710, 11 L.Ed.2d 686 (1964). There, a civil rights group purchased a full page advertisement in the New York Times, entitled "Heed Their Rising Voices." The advertisement set out certain facts concerning private as well as governmental action in Alabama violative of the civil rights of black citizens and asked for contributions to continue the fight for racial justice in the South. Many of the statements asserted as fact were incorrect, including allegations concerning the police department of Montgomery, Alabama. The elected city commissioner of Montgomery, whose responsibility it was to supervise the operation of the police department, sued the New York Times Company and four individual signatories of the advertisement claiming that he had been libeled. The commissioner obtained a jury award of $500,000, the full amount sought, against the defendants. The Alabama Supreme Court affirmed the judgment under ordinary common law rules of defamation, rejecting the contention that the expression involved in the advertisement was protected by the First and Fourteenth Amendments. The Alabama court asserted that libelous publications were beyond the scope of such protection.

In reversing the judgment because the state's common law of libel was constitutionally deficient in failing to provide safeguards for freedom of speech and press in libel actions brought by public officials against critics of their official conduct, the

United States Supreme Court drew support from the history of the controversy over the Sedition Act of 1798. That statute made it a crime punishable by a $5,000 fine and five years in prison for anyone to print or publish any false, scandalous and malicious writing against the government or certain of its officials with intent to defame. In declaring that the "central meaning" of the First Amendment was the protection of public discussion of government and its officials and that in the court of history the Sedition Act was unconstitutional, Justice Brennan, speaking for the Court, quoted James Madison's argument against its passage. "If we advert to the nature of Republican Government, we shall find that the censorial power is in the people over the Government, and not in the Government over the people." Id. at 275, 84 S.Ct. at 723, 11 L.Ed.2d at 703. This idea is, of course, at the heart of the Meiklejohn interpretation. If the New York Times case retains its vitality, the idea of seditious libel will have been relegated to the scrap heap of history and "uninhibited, robust, and wide-open" debate on the public issues will be encouraged. See also Near v. Minnesota, 283 U.S. 697, 713–718, 51 S.Ct. 625, 630–632, 75 L.Ed. 1357, 1366–1369 (1931) for an earlier Supreme Court expression of the same idea.

Other general theories of the First Amendment include the somewhat cynical "safety valve" idea of permitting individual members and groups in society to "let off steam" without seriously affect-

ing the status quo, and the more idealistic belief
that free expression is a necessary aspect of individual development and growth.

a. Absolutism

But these general theories and principles do not
resolve hard cases. Thus, the quest has been for
operative or functional tests permitting reasonably
consistent decisions in the field of free expression.

The most extreme approach is the idea that the
First Amendment provides a central core of protection for expression in all circumstances—the so-
called absolutist approach. While this approach
has been characterized as holding that the "no
law" injunction of the First Amendment *means* no
law, the absolutist schools of thought are more
complex than that.

The absolutists agree that the First Amendment
does provide a central core of protection, but to
determine whether particular expression is protected in the face of governmental efforts at regulation, the broad language of the First Amendment
must be defined. What does "no law" mean?
What constitutes abridgment? And what is the
expression that is to be protected? "No law" is
defined generally to include not only statutes but
administrative regulations promulgated pursuant
to statutes, municipal ordinances, executive orders
and court orders. Insofar as abridgment is concerned, the absolutists would permit limitations on
free expression incidental to reasonable regulation

promulgated pursuant to a "law" directed solely to controlling the time, place and manner of expression. In determining whether a challenged regulation is reasonable, the absolutists would reject any regulation based on a law that does not contain appropriate safeguards to limit administrative discretion. If such safeguards are present the absolutists would then look to see whether the regulation has created a sufficient inroad on expression by its nature, degree and impact so as to constitute an "abridgment" of free expression.

The key to understanding the absolutist's view of abridgment is recognition that regulation must relate only to time, place and manner of the presentation of expression and that such regulation must not be so restrictive as to interfere with the *substance* of expression. See, e.g., Saia v. New York, 334 U.S. 558, 68 S.Ct. 1148, 92 L.Ed. 1574 (1948), in which Justice Douglas, an adherent of absolutism, while conceding that some narrow regulation of sound trucks to prevent abuses would be constitutionally permissible, held unconstitutional a local ordinance which forbade the use of sound amplification devices except with the permission of the chief of police. The grant of such permission was placed in the chief's sole discretion and thus under the ordinance he was in a position to determine not only the time, location and volume of operation but the kind of speech that might be amplified and the particular groups that might use amplification equipment.

Of the various absolutist views of the scope of the First Amendment, perhaps the most celebrated is that held by the late Justice Hugo Black. Justice Black was an adherent of the Holmes-Brandeis view of the First Amendment as primarily a protector of the free market in ideas. But he was wary of their "clear and present danger test" discussed below, because judges could hold that certain expression in certain circumstances failed the test for First Amendment protection. Rather, Justice Black came to believe that all ideas and their expressions, including the libelous and the obscene, are to be given absolute protection. This view of the scope of the First Amendment is, of course, more expansive than that taken by Meiklejohn and has never commanded majority adherence on the Court.

While Justice Black was an implacable foe of any infringement of free expression except the most incidental occasioned by reasonable "time, place and manner" regulation, "speech" and "press" were to him technical terms and only expression encompassed within those terms was to be protected. Justice Black normally defined "speech" and "press" more broadly than anyone else on the Court, but in the context of public demonstrations he defined "speech" very narrowly so as to exclude expression bound up with essentially physical conduct. For instance, in Adderley v. Florida, 385 U.S. 39, 87 S.Ct. 242, 17 L.Ed.2d 149 (1966), he spoke for the Court in upholding the convictions of 32 students who demonstrated in a nonviolent manner on a nonpublic jail driveway to protest the arrests of fellow students and local segregation policies. The 32 were among 200 students who had apparently blocked the driveway and had engaged in singing, clapping and dancing to protest what they believed to be an unjust situation. Among the dissenters in the Adderley case were Justice Black's usual allies in First Amendment cases, Justices Douglas and Brennan and Chief Justice Warren.

At bottom, whatever their differences as to the reach of the First Amendment, the late Justice Black and the other absolutists were attempting to remove from the judiciary the power to balance the interest in free expression against the exigencies of the times. For them, the balance was struck once and for all in favor of freedom of speech and press by the drafters of the Bill of Rights and that balance may not be disturbed.

b. The "Clear and Present Danger" Test

Another approach reflective of the free trade of ideas approach, was the "clear and present danger" test. Proposed by Justice Holmes in Schenck v. United States, 249 U.S. 47, 39 S.Ct. 247, 63 L.Ed. 470 (1919), the test permitted the punishment of expression when "the words used are used in such circumstances and are of such a nature as to create a clear and present danger that they will bring about the substantive evils that Congress has a right to prevent. It is a question of proximity and degree." Id., at 52, 39 S.Ct. at 249, 63 L.Ed. at 473–474.

In Schenck, the expression was in the form of a leaflet authorized by the American Socialist Party attacking the Conscription Act of World War I and urging recent conscripts to resist serving in the armed forces by asserting their alleged rights under the Thirteenth Amendment. Defendant, an officer of the party, was indicted, inter alia, for conspiracy to violate the Espionage Act of 1917 by causing and attempting to cause insubordination in the military forces and obstruction of the recruiting and enlistment service during a period of war. In the circumstance of war time, Holmes, who had himself been an officer in the Union Army during the Civil War, found that the leaflet created a danger of disruption of the war effort of sufficient proximity and magnitude to permit punishment in the face of the sweeping guarantees of the First Amendment.

Aside from the problem that it frankly permits the Congress in certain circumstances to legislate punishment of expression, the test is vague and difficult to apply. As Brandeis and Holmes admitted in their concurring opinion in Whitney v. California, 274 U.S. at 374, 47 S.Ct. at 648, 71 L.Ed. at 1105 (1927), the Supreme Court had not yet "fixed the standard by which to determine when a danger shall be deemed clear; how remote the danger may be and yet be deemed present; and what degree of evil shall be deemed sufficiently substantial to justify resort to abridgement of free speech and assembly as the means of protection."

Moreover, even if there were a common understanding of the meaning of the test, the results of its application to challenged legislation directly or indirectly prohibitive of expression would vary according to extrinsic circumstances such as war or peace, cold war or detente, and prosperity or depression. Expression that might be afforded First Amendment protection from legislative repression in one social context might be denied it in another, and the speaker or publisher would not know whether his particular expression was safeguarded until the courts passed upon it. Thus, the test might have the effect of discouraging borderline writings or utterances.

In recent years, doubts about the test by civil liberties oriented justices and constitutional scholars and the hostility of those more state security oriented, have sapped "clear and present danger" of its vitality as constitutional doctrine. For instance, Brandenburg v. Ohio, 395 U.S. 444, 89 S.Ct. 1827, 23 L.Ed.2d 430 (1969), involved a prosecution for violation by certain members of the Ku Klux Klan of the Ohio criminal syndicalism statute. While this prosecution was much like earlier prosecutions in which the "clear and present danger" test had been employed (compare Whitney v. California, 274 U.S. 357, 47 S.Ct. 641, 71 L.Ed. 1095 (1927) involving a similar state criminal syndicalism statute), the per curiam opinion of the Supreme Court striking down the state law as an infringement of the First Amendment did not mention the test. Rather, the Court simply drew a distinction between advocacy of forcible or illegal political action in the future and advocacy directed to inciting *imminent* lawless action and likely to produce just such action. Only the latter is unprotected speech.

In the field of political speech akin to seditious libel, the test now appears to be inoperative. But it may retain vitality in the narrow area of criminal contempt of court. Beginning with Bridges v. California, 314 U.S. 252, 62 S.Ct. 190, 86 L.Ed. 192 (1941), the Supreme Court applied the test to determine whether out-of-court utterances or writings attempting to influence the outcome of pending judicial matters or to criticize or ridicule members of the judiciary for their conduct on the bench could be punished through contempt of court proceedings. The substantive evil to be guarded against by the judiciary's exercise of the contempt power in these cases was the subversion of the fair administration of justice. The question in each case then was whether the out-of-court expressions created a clear and present danger to the proper administration of justice. The Supreme Court held that under the circumstances of the cases the out-of-court attacks on the judiciary and their handling of pending matters did not pose the requisite danger and thus the contempt citations were violative

of First Amendment guarantees. See Bridges v.
California, supra; Pennekamp v. Florida. 328 U.S.
331, 66 S.Ct. 1029, 90 L.Ed. 1295 (1946); Craig v.
Harney, 331 U.S. 367, 67 S.Ct. 1249, 91 L.Ed. 1546
(1947); Wood v. Georgia, 370 U.S. 375, 82 S.Ct.
1364, 8 L.Ed.2d 569 (1962). An important theme in
these cases is that judges are made of sturdy stuff
and will not be affected by such expression. It
must be borne in mind, however, that the last
explicit application of the "clear and present danger" test in a contempt case was in 1962.

c. Ad Hoc Balancing of Interests

In Justice Frankfurter's dissent in Bridges is the
seed of another general approach to First Amendment cases. In his opinion Justice Frankfurter
emphasized that other interests protected by the
Bill of Rights were also at stake—the interests of
due process of law and fair trial. He would not
give any special deference to the interests protected by the First Amendment. "Free speech is not
so absolute or irrational a conception as to imply
paralysis of the means for effective protection of all
the freedoms secured by the Bill of Rights. . . .
In the cases before us, the claims on behalf of
freedom of speech and of the press encounter
claims on behalf of liberties no less precious."
Bridges v. California, 314 U.S. at 282, 62 S.Ct. at
203, 86 L.Ed. at 213.

Frankfurter would resolve competing claims by
weighing their relative importance in each case.

In *Bridges*, he came to the conclusion that the interest in the impartial administration of justice outweighed the competing interest in allowing the Los Angeles Times through its editorial pages to attempt to prevent a judge from granting a request for probation from several labor organizers convicted of strong arm tactics, or in allowing Harry Bridges, a Pacific Coast longshoremen's union leader, to proclaim in the newspapers his threat to tie up the entire Pacific Coast shipping business if a court order of which he disapproved was enforced.

Frankfurter's approach formed the basis for the ad hoc balancing of interests. This balancing of First Amendment interests was embraced by a majority of the Court in *American Communications Association v. Douds*, 339 U.S. 382, 70 S.Ct. 674, 94 L.Ed. 925 (1950), in which certain labor unions attacked a provision of the Labor Management Relations Act barring unions from access to procedures important to the collective bargaining process unless their officers executed affidavits declaring, among other things, that they were not members of or affiliated with the Communist Party. The unions contended that the provision violated union leaders' fundamental rights guaranteed by the First Amendment such as the right to hold and express whatever political views they choose and to associate with whatever political groups they wish. In concluding that the section of the act was compatible with the First Amendment, Chief Justice Vinson weighed First Amend-

ment interests against the interest to be fostered
by the statute in question, i.e., interstate commerce
free from the disruption of political strikes.

Perhaps the most explicit statement of this approach was made by Justice Harlan in Konigsberg
v. State Bar of Cal., 366 U.S. 36, 81 S.Ct. 997, 6
L.Ed.2d 105 (1961). There Konigsberg, a candidate
for admission to the California Bar, was denied a
license to practice law because he had refused to
answer questions put to him by a bar committee
(acting as a state agency) concerning his alleged
membership in the Communist Party. Konigsberg
challenged the state's action on several grounds
including violation of protected rights of free
speech and association. In rejecting this challenge
Justice Harlan said, "Whenever . . . these constitutional protections are asserted against the exercise of valid governmental powers a reconciliation
must be effected, and that perforce requires an
appropriate weighing of the respective interests
involved [citations omitted]. . . . With more
particular reference to the present context of a
state decision as to character qualifications, it is
difficult, indeed, to imagine a view of the constitutional protections of speech and association which
would automatically and without consideration of
the extent of the deterence of speech and association and of the importance of the state function,
exclude all reference to prior speech or association
on such issues [concerning bar membership] as
character, purpose, credibility or intent." Id. at

51, 81 S.Ct. at 1007, 6 L.Ed.2d at 117. Following this standard, a majority of the Court found that the state's interest in safeguarding the bar from possible subversive influence outweighed interests protected by the First and Fourteenth Amendments.

The ad hoc balancing approach has the virtue of pragmatism. It recognizes the importance of First Amendment interests but permits the making of pragmatic judgments as to when those interests should prevail over other and conflicting interests, often of a state security nature. But this virtue may also be a vice, for the protections afforded by the First Amendment are stated in absolute terms and the Amendment makes no provision for restricting freedom of speech and press when other interests are in conflict. This approach also suffers from vagueness. Because it is ad hoc, no consistent weight can be given to conflicting interests and the lower court judges are left on their own to determine when First Amendment interests are outweighed. Under such an approach a judge's predilections either for state security or individual liberties may be easily rationalized and, as with the "clear and present danger" test, the individual can never have any advance notice whether his interest in freedom of expression will outweigh some competing interest of the state expressed in its legislation. See Frantz, "The First Amendment in the Balance," 71 Yale L.J. 1424, 1440–1443 (1962).

d. Definitional Balancing

Another approach to the balancing of government and speech interests was first enunciated in Chaplinsky v. New Hampshire, 315 U.S. 568, 62 S.Ct. 766, 86 L.Ed. 1031 (1942), which addressed the constitutionality of a New Hampshire statute construed to ban "words likely to cause an average addressee to fight."

In upholding the statute, the Court stated that certain classes of speech had never been thought to raise a constitutional problem. They included the lewd and obscene, the profane, the libelous and insulting or "fighting words."

At first glance this approach, placing entire classes of speech outside the protective ambit of the First Amendment, gives much more guidance for future decisions than the ad hoc approach. Often however, it creates a different uncertainty due to the difficulty of defining these classes of speech. Thus, the court has struggled for more than thirty years to define obscenity, a struggle that reduced Justice Stewart to declaring in Jacobellis v. Ohio, 378 U.S. 184, 197, 84 S.Ct. 1676, 1683, 12 L.Ed.2d 793, 804 (1964), that he couldn't define hard core pornography but he knew when he saw it. Similar problems exist with the definition of commercial speech. See, e.g., Central Hudson Gas & Electric Corp. v. Public Service Commission of New York, 447 U.S. 557, 100 S.Ct. 2343, 65 L.Ed.2d 341 (1980) (Justice Steven's concurring opinion).

The other problem with definitional balancing is that there is a danger of overreaching. Essentially, definitional balancing is a finding that the societal interest in restricting a certain type of speech always outweighs the value of that speech, regardless of context or circumstances. Thus, prior to 1964, there was no constitutional protection for libel, even for discussions of the performance of public officials. This, of course, was changed by New York Times Co. v. Sullivan.

The preceding approaches or tests have not been consistently applied by their proponents to all First Amendment problem areas and when they are applied the competing approaches do not always yield results in conflict with each other. But, again with the caveat that tests or theories cannot always be relied upon to predict the outcome of specific cases, an understanding of them is useful in predicting the direction of the Supreme Court in relation to the First Amendment.

3. Present Direction of the Supreme Court

The transition from the Burger Court to the Rehnquist Court should not present anywhere near the radical change in direction that occurred between the Warren and Burger courts. Thus, it is possible to make some tentative judgments about the direction of the current Supreme Court regarding First Amendment philosophy.

It appears that the entire Court has embraced an ad hoc balancing approach, some justices perhaps more completely than others. This ad hoc balancing approach has produced a more limited view of the First Amendment than existed in the Warren era.

Often, as part of its attempt to balance the particular interests at stake, the Court will apply a "test" or set of guidelines to the specific facts of the case. For example, in Central Hudson Gas & Electric Corp. v. Public Service Commission of New York, 447 U.S. 557, 100 S.Ct. 2343, 65 L.Ed.2d 341 (1980), Justice Powell enunciated a four-part test to determine the constitutionality of restrictions on commercial speech. First, is the commercial speech protected by the First Amendment? (At a minimum, it should not involve illegal activity, nor should it be false or misleading.) Second, is there a substantial government interest in restricting the speech? Third, does the regulation directly advance the asserted government interest? Fourth, is the regulation no broader than necessary to serve the asserted government interest?

This "test" is typical of the Court's approach in that it forces the government to articulate a competing public interest that justifies restricting First Amendment rights, recognizes that such competing interests can outweigh First Amendment rights, and requires the government to tailor its restrictions as narrowly as possible. See, also, Press Enterprise Company v. Superior Court (II), 478 U.S. ____, 106 S.Ct. 2735, 92 L.Ed.2d 1 (1986).

Obviously, whenever ad hoc balancing is used, one of the keys is the weight given to the First Amendment interest involved. In the Court's eyes all First Amendment rights are not created equal. Rather, the Court has established at least three distinct hierarchies of speech that are used to determine the degree of First Amendment protection involved.

One hierarchy is based on the actual content of speech. In what is essentially a refined version of definitional balancing the Court has taken the position that protected expression is not monolithic but divisible into categories with the extent of First Amendment protection dependent upon the intrinsic worth of the expression in each category. See Young v. American Mini Theatres, 427 U.S. at 50, 66–71, 96 S.Ct. at 2450–52, 49 L.Ed.2d at 323–26 (1976); Federal Communications Commission v. Pacifica Foundation, 438 U.S. 726, 744–47, 98 S.Ct. 3026, 3038–3039, 57 L.Ed.2d 1073, 1090–92 (1978) (opinion of Justice Stevens joined by Chief Justice Burger and Justice Rehnquist); Posadas de Puerto Rico Associates v. Tourism Company of Puerto Rico, 478 U.S. ___, 106 S.Ct. 2968, 92 L.Ed.2d 266 (1986). This position raises some very thorny questions for the courts: what criteria should they use in categorizing protected speech; how will individual judges be able to cast aside their own personal value systems in determining objectively the comparative worth of particular expression; and finally, what degree of First Amendment protection will be afforded each of the categories of expression?

The mode of transmission of speech is also used to determine the degree of First Amendment protection available. The Court has long held that differences in the characteristics of new media justify the application of different First Amendment standards. Thus, in Miami Herald Publishing Company v. Tornillo, 418 U.S. 241, 94 S.Ct. 2831, 41 L.Ed.2d 730 (1974) the Court declared unconstitutional a statute granting an individual attacked by a newspaper the right to have a response printed in that newspaper; yet the Court upheld a similar regulation applying to broadcasters in Red Lion Broadcasting Company v. FCC, 395 U.S. 367, 89 S.Ct. 1794, 23 L.Ed.2d 371 (1969). The Court recently reaffirmed its support of different standards for different media in City of Los Angeles v. Preferred Communications, Inc., 476 U.S. 488, 106 S.Ct. 2034, 90 L.Ed.2d 480 (1986) (a case involving the constitutionality of cable franchising rules), but left the determination of the standard for cable to a future case. As new communication technologies proliferate, the Court may find it more and more difficult to differentiate them in terms of appropriate First Amendment standards.

Finally, recognizing that the right to publish news can be seriously restricted by limitations on the right to gather news, the Court has extended some First Amendment protection to newsgathering, often under the rhetoric of a right of access.

See Branzburg v. Hayes, 408 U.S. 665, 92 S.Ct. 2646, 33 L.Ed.2d 626 (1972); Richmond Newspapers, Inc. v. Virginia, 448 U.S. 555, 100 S.Ct. 2814, 65 L.Ed.2d 973 (1980). However, the degree of protection afforded newsgathering is nowhere near as extensive as that given dissemination of news, a situation unlikely to change given Chief Justice Rehnquist's strong opposition to protection for newsgathering. See Gannett Co., Inc. v. DePasquale, 443 U.S. 368, 99 S.Ct. 2898, 61 L.Ed.2d 608 (1979).

The good news for advocates of strong First Amendment protection is that the decisions produced by the ad hoc balancing approach tend to make small adjustments in the law as opposed to sweeping changes.

The bad news is that because the ad hoc approach depends so heavily on the value that each Justice attaches to the government interest asserted, as well as to the speech involved, there is much less guidance for the lower courts. In addition, several of the Justices are increasingly evincing a willingness to accept state assertions as to the validity and importance of its interest without any requirement of proof. The increasing deference to the state's judgment clearly tilts the scales in favor of the restrictions at issue. See Posadas de Puerto Rico Associates v. Tourism Company of Puerto Rico, 478 U.S. ___, 106 S.Ct. 2968, 92 L.Ed.2d 266 (1986).

Further, predicting Supreme Court decisions has become very difficult. It appears that there now exists considerable reluctance upon the part of important segments of the media to chance litigation in the Supreme Court because of the Court's embrace of the ad hoc balancing philosophy. See, e.g., Street v. NBC, 645 F.2d 1227 (6th Cir.1981), in which NBC successfully defended a libel action in which a central issue was whether the rape prosecutrix in the famous "Scottsboro Boys" case of the 1930s was still a public figure more than 30 years later. The Sixth Circuit answered affirmatively, but when the Supreme Court granted Mrs. Street's petition to review that ruling, NBC, which had prevailed below, settled the suit, paying her a substantial sum of money, rather than face the Burger Court.

Other trends in the Court's approach to the First Amendment include a continued departure from the idea that time, place and manner restrictions on protected expression may not be influenced by the content of the expression except where captive or juvenile audiences are involved, i.e., the restrictions must be "content neutral." In Young v. American Mini Theatres, Inc., 427 U.S. 50, 96 S.Ct. 2440, 49 L.Ed.2d 310 (1976), a five-justice majority upheld a Detroit zoning ordinance that required dispersal of "adult" bookstores and motion picture theatres but not other bookstores and theatres in order to protect established commercial and residential neighborhoods. This "place" restriction was justified on the basis of the type of books sold and the motion pictures exhibited. In other words, the majority "peeked" at the content of the expression here and, having peeked, upheld the place restriction embodied in the ordinance because of the content. See, also, City of Renton v. Playtime Theaters, Inc., 475 U.S. 41, 106 S.Ct. 925, 89 L.Ed. 2d 29, rehearing denied 475 U.S. 41, 106 S.Ct. 1663, 90 L.Ed.2d 205 (1986).

Finally, in the past, the Court, perhaps to conserve judicial energy, occasionally avoided the philosophical struggle over the proper approach to the First Amendment by nullifying statutes, ordinances and governmental regulations infringing free expression simply on the basis of their "vagueness" or "overbreadth." See, e.g., Erznoznik v. Jacksonville, 422 U.S. 205, 95 S.Ct. 2268, 45 L.Ed. 2d 125 (1975) (ordinance making it a public nuisance and a criminal offense for a drive-in movie theater to exhibit any film containing nudity if the screen is visible from the street held overbroad and struck down as violative of the First Amendment). But the Court now seems to be narrowing the application of the "vagueness" and "overbreadth" devices. See, e.g. Young v. American Mini Theatres, Inc., 427 U.S. 50, 96 S.Ct. 2440, 49 L.Ed.2d 310 (1976) (all opinions); New York v. Ferber, 458 U.S. 747, 102 S.Ct. 3348, 73 L.Ed.2d 1113 (1982) (statute prohibiting the promotion of a sexual performance by a child by distributing material which depicts

such performances held not substantially overbroad).

C. THE DICHOTOMY BETWEEN PRIOR RESTRAINT AND SUBSEQUENT PUNISHMENT OF EXPRESSION

On one point adherents of all schools of thought
appear to agree. At a minimum the First Amendment was adopted to prevent the federal government—and later the state governments through
the Fourteenth Amendment—from instituting a
general system of prior restraint on speech or press
similar to that employed in England and the Colonies in the seventeenth and eighteenth centuries,
i.e., licensing of the press and censorship of expression.

There were those, including Blackstone in his
Commentaries on the Laws of England, who believed that freedom of the press consisted only in
proscribing prior restraints upon publication and
that once publication was made the publisher had
to accept the consequences which might be imposed upon him by an offended government or
individual. That First Amendment protection extended also to attempts by government to punish
completed utterances and publications through imposition of criminal sanctions was not fully settled
until the formulation of the "clear and present
danger" test in Schenck v. United States, 249 U.S.
47, 39 S.Ct. 247, 63 L.Ed. 470 (1919). And that the
Amendment further provided the publisher or

speaker some protection against subsequent civil defamation actions was not recognized until New York Times Co. v. Sullivan, supra.

Despite the fact that the threat of subsequent criminal punishment and civil judgments for damages may have a substantial deterrent effect upon free expression, the Supreme Court has not, as indicated in the preceding sections, achieved anywhere near the consistency of doctrine that it has regarding the condemnation of administrative and judicial prior restraints.

There are many reasons besides the historical for the Court's hostility toward governmental action smacking of prior restraint. Professor Emerson in his classic article "The Doctrine of Prior Restraint," 20 Law and Contemporary Problems 648 (1955) provides us with a modern catalogue of these reasons. A system of prior restraint is broader in its coverage, more uniform in its effect and more easily and effectively enforced than subsequent punishment. Everything which is published or publicly uttered would be subject to scrutiny. Then, too, expression which is banned never sees the light of day and that which is not banned may be so delayed in the administrative mill that it becomes superfluous or obsolete when it is "cleared." The procedural safeguards of the criminal judicial process, including public scrutiny, are not present to the same degree in the administrative censorial process. Finally, the entire process

is geared toward suppression and the censor will be
impelled to find things to suppress. Id. at 656–59.

The landmark case recognizing the dangers of
prior restraint is Near v. Minnesota, 283 U.S. 697,
51 S.Ct. 625, 75 L.Ed. 1357 (1931). There, a state
statute provided for the abatement as a public
nuisance of "malicious, scandalous, and defamatory" publications. The statute further provided
that all persons guilty of such a nuisance could be
permanently enjoined from further publication of
malicious, scandalous and defamatory matter. A
county attorney brought an action under the statute to enjoin The Saturday Press on the ground
that it accused law enforcement agencies and officials of the city of Minneapolis with failing to stop
vice and racketeering activities allegedly controlled by a "Jewish Gangster." In the face of the
publisher's claim that his activities were protected
by the First and Fourteenth Amendments, the trial
court perpetually enjoined him from conducting a
public nuisance under the name of The Saturday
Press or any other name. The state supreme court
affirmed the injunctive order. The United States
Supreme Court reversed. Cutting through the peculiar procedures of the statute, the Court indicated that its object and effect was to suppress further
publication. This they equated to prior restraint
of the press. Moreover, if the person enjoined
were so bold as to resume his or her publishing
activities, he or she would have to submit the
material to the appropriate judicial officer for

clearance prior to publication in order to avoid being held in contempt of court for violation of the injunctive order. To the Court this constituted effective censorship prohibited by the due process clauses of the First and Fourteenth Amendments.

This decision stands out for many reasons. It was the Court's first definitive statement concerning the constitutionality of prior restraint on expression. More than this, it made clear that what was important was not the form governmental action took but its effect on speech and press. And because it indicated that the constitutional ban on prior restraints was not absolute and did permit certain narrow exceptions, it opened up the question of the precise limits of the First Amendment in this area. Finally, it made the point very clearly that while expression was generally protected from prior restraint, it might subsequently be punished if it were determined that the expression was unlawful. This dichotomy drawn by the Court in Near persists today. It was relied upon expressly by four of the Justices in their separate opinions in New York Times Co. v. United States, 403 U.S. 713, 91 S.Ct. 2140, 29 L.Ed.2d 822 (1971) (the "Pentagon Papers" case). See also Vance v. Universal Amusement Co., Inc., 445 U.S. 308, 100 S.Ct. 1156, 63 L.Ed.2d 413 (1980).

D. INFORMATION AS PROPERTY

As the United States moves further towards an information-based economy, there is an increasing conflict between the property rights in information and the free flow of ideas protected by the First Amendment.

1. Conflict Between Economic Interests and Information Flow

The primary motivation for information owners restricting others' First Amendment rights is an economic one. Often it is simply a question of seeking compensation for what is seen as the use of someone else's property. In other words, anyone who is willing to pay can disseminate the information. Other times the purpose is to obtain a competitive edge through exclusive coverage of a news or entertainment event. For example, ABC originally claimed exclusive rights to some of the July 4, 1986 Statue of Liberty festivities.

Sometimes, however, the primary motivation is not an economic one. For example, a Boston cable news channel attempted unsuccessfully to prevent Congressional candidate James Roosevelt from using an unauthorized tape of its interview with his opponent, Joseph Kennedy, in his campaign advertisements. The cable channel claimed that this particular use of its programming would damage its credibility as a news organization.

In another recent case author J.D. Salinger sought to enjoin a biography of him containing excerpts from personal letters that he had donated to various school libraries. Here, the issue was not who would get to distribute the information or profit from it, but whether it would be distributed at all.

The conflict between information rights and First Amendment values can take place within the framework of many different areas of the law including right of publicity, trademark law, trade secret law, and contract law. However, copyright law is probably the best illustration of the problems raised by the conflict and attempts to strike an accommodation between these competing interests.

2. Copyright and the First Amendment

The legal concepts of American copyright law and the provisions of the Copyright Act of 1976, 17 U.S.C.A. § 101 et seq., 90 Stat. 2541 (1976) are summarized in another volume of the "Nutshell" series and will not be generally repeated here. It is enough to say that the Congress, pursuant to constitutional authority can and does protect the owners of intellectual property in fixed form such as writings, photographs, and sight and sound recordings from having their creations copied and appropriated by others. Such copying and appropriation of copyrighted works constitutes infringement for which the copyright holder may seek civil remedies and the federal government may in certain cases seek criminal sanctions.

While the aim of copyright law to encourage the production of intellectual property is laudable, it can have the effect of limiting distribution of copyrighted material even in the face of First Amendment claims by the newsmedia.

Thus in Roy Export Co. v. Columbia Broadcasting System, Inc., 672 F.2d 1095 (2d Cir.1982), CBS's claim of First Amendment protection in the use, on the occasion of Charlie Chaplin's death, of a special compilation of excerpts from Chaplin's motion pictures in which Roy Export Co. held the copyright was rejected by the United States Court of Appeals. In affirming that CBS had been guilty of copyright infringement in using "the compilation" originally prepared for the 1972 Academy Award Presentations during which Chaplin received a special "Oscar," the Second Circuit made clear that it would be a very rare case in which copyrighted material was so imbued with news value as to subordinate the copyright holder's protection to First Amendment claims.

It should be noted, however, that raw news and information are not subject to copyright and are in the public domain for anyone to disseminate. See International News Service v. Associated Press, 248 U.S. 215, 39 S.Ct. 68, 63 L.Ed.2d 211 (1918) in which the Supreme Court recognized that the substance of the news of the day was not copyrightable because of the obvious public policy that such history should be made freely available to all. But the way news or information is organized, including the words used and the manner chosen by the reporter or publisher to express the news or information gathered, is copyrightable.

Sometimes, the line between the news and someone's expression of the news is a difficult one to draw. The determination of when two descriptions of an event are similar enough to constitute copyright infringement is not governed by any clear guidelines.

It should be obvious that copyright protection provides a serious limitation on the use of existing material by the news media. But the nonconstitutional "fair use" defense to copyright infringement suits provides at least limited protection for First Amendment values by affording journalists some right to publish copyrighted material.

This defense is not statutory in origin but was created by the courts, apparently in the belief that public policy requires persons other than the copyright owner to be able to use the owner's work under strictly limited conditions in certain contexts in which it will be of value to the public. This defense has often been misunderstood by the courts and has not been defined with any great precision. Nevertheless, certain features of the defense can be discerned. One may be protected in copying another's copyrighted work where the copying is not likely to hurt the present and potential markets for the copyrighted work and where the copying is likely to be of substantial benefit to the public. In determining whether the use of another's creation is a "fair use," the purpose of the defendant's work, the amount of copying involved, the public interest in the copyrighted material, the nature of the media involved and the effect of the copying on the market value of the plaintiff's work are all factors to be considered. An example of the balancing of these factors is Time, Inc. v. Bernard Geis Associates, 293 F.Supp. 130, 144–146 (S.D.N.Y.1968), in which a book publisher reproduced several frames of the Zapruder home movie of the Kennedy assassination in a book about the assassination. In holding the reproduction of the frames a fair use the court balanced the great public interest in information concerning the assassination against the doubtful effect of the reproduction on the market value of Time, Inc.'s copyright in the entire film.

These principles have now been given explicit statutory recognition in § 107 of the 1976 Copyright Act which states that in determining whether the use made of a work in any particular case is a fair use, the following four factors shall be considered:

    1. the purpose and character of the use, including whether such use is of a commercial nature or is for nonprofit educational purposes;

    2. the nature of the copyrighted work;

    3. the amount and substantiality of the portion used in relation to the copyrighted work as a whole; and

    4. the effect of the use upon the potential market for or value of the copyrighted work. 17 U.S.C.A. § 107.

The public interest is central to a successful invocation of the fair use defense. Statutory protection of expression encourages authors and artists to continue to produce original works; continued production and dissemination of these works aids the flow of ideas throughout society. But statutory protection can also retard the flow of ideas, offering a work so much protection that the ideas contained therein are no longer free to enter the marketplace. The fair use defense moderates this overprotection, thus stimulating the circulation in society of the ideas and information that the copyrighted work contains. This rationale for the defense explains some of the more common examples of fair use, such as the quotation or paraphrase of passages from books in book reviews and the limited quotation of copyrighted materials in news stories.

At bottom, then, two elements predominate in determining the availability of the fair use defense: (1) the intensity of the public interest in the free dissemination of portions of particular copyrighted works (e.g., the desire of the public for as much opinion and information about the Kennedy assassination as possible); and (2) the effect such free dissemination will have on the property value of or income from the particular copyrighted work (e.g., parody of a literary work or motion picture in such detail that an audience exposed to the parody will have little desire to pay for the privilege of reading or viewing the original).

Harper & Row Publishers, Inc. v. Nation Enterprises, 471 U.S. 539, 105 S.Ct. 2218, 85 L.Ed.2d 588 (1985) is a good example of the difficulty of applying the fair use defense in a "news" context. Harper & Row had contracted for various exclusive rights to President Gerald Ford's memoirs, "A Time to Heal," including the right to license prepublication excerpts. Harper & Row had then granted Time Magazine the right to excerpt 7,500 words from President Ford's account of his decision to pardon President Nixon in return for $25,000 (half in advance), such publication to take place one week before the publication of the book. Prior to Time's scheduled publication, Victor Nevasky, editor of The Nation Magazine, obtained an unauthorized copy of "A Time to Heal." Working directly from this manuscript, he produced a 2,250 word article consisting exclusively of quotes, paraphrases and facts drawn from the Ford manuscript. This article appeared before the scheduled publication of the Time article. As a result Time did not publish its article and refused to pay Harper & Row the remaining $12,500.

In the ensuing copyright action, The Nation relied on fair use and the First Amendment to defend its actions. In a 6–3 decision the Court held that The Nation's excerpt was not a fair use. In applying the four factors of fair use, the Court first held that the general purpose was indeed news reporting, but that the more specific purpose was to supplant "the copyright holder's commercially valuable right of first publication."

In examining the nature of the copyrighted work, the Court acknowledged that it was a factual work and that the need to disseminate factual works is greater than that for fictional works. Having done so, however, the Court then focused on the unpublished nature of the work and decided that fair use has a more limited application to *unpublished* works.

A key issue was the amount and substantiality of the portion used. Here, although there was some dispute as to exactly how much of The Nation's article consisted of infringing material, it was clear that overall it was a very small amount when compared to the entire text of "A Time to Heal." The Court, however, viewed this as a qualitative as well as a quantitative issue, and found that the material on the Nixon pardon was the heart of the book and that the quotes used in The Nation's article were the essence of that article. In that sense the portion used was substantial.

For the Court, the easiest part of the test was the effect on the market for the copyrighted work. Harper & Row had lost $12,500 when Time cancelled its projected article as a result of The Nation's article. When considered in conjunction with the analysis of the other three factors, the finding against fair use was clear.

Justice Brennan wrote a sharp dissent accusing the majority of extending copyright protection to

information and ideas. In his view the purpose of
the work—news reporting—and the nature of the
copyrighted work—historical and factual—supported a fair use defense. He found the amount
taken not to be excessive even though it dealt with
the most important part of the book. Because he
believed that the cancellation by Time was as
much a result of information contained in The
Nation article as expression appropriated from
Ford's book, he did not find that the infringement
had any serious effect on the market for the copyrighted material.

The significance of this case is in some ways
difficult to determine. Some would argue it is
limited to the rather unusual facts of the case.
Although there was no proof the manuscript was
stolen, the Court appeared to assume that it was.
Also, the infringing work was published prior to
the copyrighted work, a fact emphasized by the
Court. Given that most fair use cases involve
someone copying an already published work, it
may be relatively easy to distinguish Harper &
Row.

On the other hand, if it operates, as Justice
Brennan suggests, to restrict the fair use defense to
a point where information itself acquires some
copyright protection, then it presents a serious
threat to the free flow of information protected by
the First Amendment.

The limitations of fair use as a vehicle for First
Amendment protection have become even more ap-

parent with the recent decision by the court of appeals in Salinger v. Random House, Inc., 818 F.2d 252 (2d Cir.1987), cert. denied ___ U.S. ___, 108 S.Ct. 213, ___ L.Ed.2d ___ (1987). Author J.D. Salinger sought to restrain the publication of a biography of him on the grounds that it contained excerpts from copyrighted letters that he had written. The biographer, Ian Hamilton, had obtained copies of the letters from various college libraries to which they had been donated by their recipients. As in Harper & Row the case was treated strictly as a copyright case with no real First Amendment issues. For the court of appeals, the key question was whether or not the use of the excerpts from the letters constituted fair use.

The court of appeals relied heavily on Harper & Row for its fair use analysis because it was "the court's first delineation of the scope of fair use as applied to unpublished works."

In considering the application of the four fair use factors to Hamilton's use of the Salinger letters, the court started by categorizing the purpose of the use alternatively as "criticism," "scholarship," or "research." All of these categories are viewed as appropriate to a fair use. The court went on, however, to specifically reject the idea that a biographer is entitled to an especially generous application of the defense.

The court noted that as long as the biographer took only the factual content of the letter, there was no copyright problem. But the court did not recognize any need to take the expression contained in the letter.

Turning to the second factor, the court focused on the unpublished nature of the work as being of critical importance. In essence, the court viewed it as creating a heavy presumption against a finding of fair use.

With regard to the amount and substantiality of the use, the court of appeals found that copyrighted expression was used on at least 40% of the book's 192 pages.

Finally, the court found that due to the substantial amount taken by Hamilton and his extensive use of the phrases "he wrote" and "he said" that at least some members of the public might be misled into believing that they had read the essence of Salinger's letters, thus reducing the potential market for a book of his letters. This led the court of appeals to conclude that the fourth fair use factor—effect on the potential market for the work—weighed slightly in Salinger's favor. Based on this analysis the court ordered an injunction prohibiting the sale of the biography.

Perhaps the most important conclusion that can be drawn from Salinger is that courts appear to be unwilling to examine any copyright case for First Amendment problems. The assumption is that the idea-expression dichotomy and the defense of fair use provide a proper accommodation between the sometimes competing interests.

Thus in Salinger the court was not concerned that the expression contained in Salinger's letters will not generally be available to the public until 50 years after his death. Nor did the court address the fact that the remedy it granted—an injunction—is a prior restraint. The dichotomy between prior restraint and subsequent punishment recognized by the Supreme Court in Near and the "Pentagon Papers" case does not seem to apply to copyright cases.

As illustrated by these recent copyright cases there is an increasing conflict between property rights in information and the free flow of ideas protected by the First Amendment. When asked to balance these sometimes competing interests, the courts appear strongly to favor property rights over First Amendment interests.

———

In the chapters that follow, the First Amendment will be considered in several specific contexts. These include the permissible scope of defamation and invasion of privacy actions in tort, the efforts of government to suppress pornography, the possible conflict between protection of a free press and the Fifth and Sixth Amendment guarantees of a fair and impartial trial, the existence, or non-existence of a newsperson's privilege not to reveal his or her sources of information when compelled to do so, and the permissible limits of governmental regulation of advertising.

Traditionally, these First Amendment problem areas have involved questions concerning the limitation on the power of government or its agencies to act in certain ways, e.g., the power of courts to enter judgments in defamation actions. But we will also advert to a theory largely developed by Dean Jerome A. Barron that the First Amendment actually compels the government to act affirmatively to insure freedom of expression by requiring citizen access to the mass media. While this theory has been rejected by the Supreme Court with regard to the print media, it has been instrumental in forcing a wide ranging re-examination of the nature of the First Amendment in the late twentieth century.

CHAPTER II

DEFAMATION AND MASS COMMUNICATION

A. INTERESTS IN CONFLICT

One of the interests which has competed with the interest in freedom of expression down through the centuries is that of reputation, both personal and proprietary. The importance of this interest should not be minimized. As Justice Stewart said in his concurring opinion in Rosenblatt v. Baer, 383 U.S. 75, 92, 86 S.Ct. 669, 679, 15 L.Ed.2d 597, 609 (1966), "The right of a man to the protection of his own reputation from unjustified invasion and wrongful hurt reflects no more than our basic concept of the essential dignity and worth of every human being—a concept at the root of any decent system of ordered liberty."

The early common law courts considered reputation to be an interest deserving of protection by recognizing an action for money damages to compensate for injury resulting from defamatory communications. This action has evolved into the complex (some would say "confused and confusing") twin tort actions of libel and slander. There is no doubt that the ever present fear that one may have to respond in damages for what one publishes has a limiting effect on the work of the modern

45

journalist or public speaker. It has been reported that one of the reasons for the demise of Pulitzer's New York World was the drain on its resources from numerous libel actions brought against the paper.

The thrust of the recent significant cases in the field of defamation has been the recognition of the unavoidable conflict between these two interests and the attempt to provide a measure of legal protection for both.

B. COMMON LAW DEFAMATION

1. Definition and Elements

Defamation has been defined as the injury to reputation by words which tend to expose one to public hatred, shame, contempt or disgrace, or to induce an evil opinion of one in the minds of right-thinking persons and to deprive one of their confidence and friendly intercourse in society. Kimmerle v. New York Evening Journal, 262 N.Y. 99, 102, 186 N.E. 217, 218 (1933). While this definition provides a good starting place for understanding the nature of defamation, it fails to place any emphasis on loss of reputation in one's business or profession. Moreover, the loss of reputation need only be with regard to a small but significant segment of the community, whether "right-thinking" or not. Finally, as the late Dean William L. Prosser pointed out, one may be defamed by imputations of insanity or poverty, which would instead arouse pity or sympathy—feelings, however, that diminish esteem and respect. Prosser, Handbook of the Law of Torts 739 (4th Ed. 1971). An example of this would be a false statement that an individual was a hopeless alcoholic.

In the past, defamation actions have been either criminal or civil in nature. But in recent years, with the notable exception of the state's prosecution of New Orleans district attorney James Garrison for his verbal attacks on certain sitting criminal court judges (Garrison v. Louisiana, 379 U.S. 64, 85 S.Ct. 209, 13 L.Ed.2d 125 (1964)), the criminal action has largely fallen into disuse. Perhaps this is because of its odious historical association with prosecutions for political sedition. In any event, the focus of this chapter will be the modern civil actions of libel and slander.

The essential elements common to both libel and slander actions are (1) the making by the defendant of a defamatory statement; (2) the publication to one other than the plaintiff of that statement; and (3) the identification in some way of the plaintiff as the person defamed.

a. The Defamatory Statement

The words complained of must be such as will injure the reputation of a living person or existing organization because only the injured party may sue for defamation. Some words such as "thief," "cheat," "murderer" or "whore" are almost universally understood to affect adversely the person referred to. Other words may have that effect in relation to the times and the victim's position. Falsely labeling one a communist during the World War II period of United States-Soviet cooperation was not actionable. But the same false label was considered defamatory after the commencement of the "Cold War."

The plaintiff's situation in life may also give a damaging effect to otherwise innocent words. The selling of pork is normally a respectable occupation, but suggesting that a kosher butcher sells bacon has been considered defamatory, for clearly it would cause religiously oriented customers to think less of the butcher and to take their business elsewhere. See Braun v. Armour & Co., 254 N.Y. 514, 173 N.E. 845 (1930).

Defamatory words can be presented in numerous ways. One need not attack with a verbal axe. The stiletto of ridicule may suffice. The communication complained of, however presented, must be understood by those hearing or seeing it as having a defamatory meaning, regardless of whether they personally believe it to be true. Thus, it is incumbent on a plaintiff in a defamation action to establish that someone other than himself understood the words or image as an attack on his or her reputation. The defendant, on the other hand, may attempt to show that the communication had at least one nondefamatory meaning and others understand it in that sense or that the communication was made in jest and could not reasonably be taken seriously. But if only one person other than the plaintiff understands the communication to be defamatory and such understanding is reasonable, given its content and context, the improper nature of the communication is made out.

b. Publication

Publication is a legal term of art meaning that the defamatory communication, whatever its form, has been perceived by someone other than the person defamed. Publication in the sense of printing and distribution of printed matter is not required. For example, publication occurs if a patient makes a serious statement in a loud voice in a crowded waiting room directly to a licensed physician that he or she is a "quack" and the statement is overheard by one or more of the other patients.

In this situation, it is clear that the communicator either intends that others overhear his or her accusation or is so uncaring whether it is overheard as to be deemed reckless in his or her conduct. But where one does not intend the communication to be conveyed to anyone other than the target of his or her attack, and the means chosen to convey the communication will in the normal course prevent reception by third persons, there is no publication. For instance, Able writes his former business partner Baker a letter in which he accuses Baker of causing the downfall of their business by "stealing the company blind." Able places the letter in a sealed envelope, marks it "personal," addresses it to Baker and mails it to

his house. Baker's son, curious about the letter
from his father's former associate, opens and reads
the letter prior to Baker and without authority.
There is no publication here and, hence, no actionable defamation.

Moreover, since it is the *defamer* who must intentionally or recklessly promote publication, the
requirement is not met by the victim himself or
herself publicizing the communication to others.
If in the above hypothetical, Baker opened the
letter and then showed the letter to his son, the
result would be the same—no publication. Where
there is publication, however, repetition of the
original defamation by persons other than the victim constitutes republication for which the original
communicator will also be held liable provided the
republication is foreseeable. Of course, the person
who does the republishing may also be held liable.

A question of special significance to the print
media is whether the distribution of each copy of a
press run is a separate publication providing the
basis for multiple defamation actions or whether
the press run is to be viewed as constituting one
publication. The early English cases suggested the
first alternative but they were decided before the
advent of high speed presses, large press runs and
mass distribution. Shortly before World War II
American courts began to move toward what has
become known as the "single publication rule."
The rule provides that only one cause of action for
defamation arises when the product of a press run

or printing is released by the publisher for distribution, no matter how many separate transactions may result. A corollary is that the statute of limitations for defamation commences to run from the moment of first release. See Gregoire v. G.P. Putnam's Sons, 298 N.Y. 119, 81 N.E.2d 45 (1948), the leading case for the single publication rule holding that a libel action based on the sale of a single copy of a book whose last printing was more than two years prior to the sale was barred by New York's one-year statute of limitation. Reinforcing this judicial trend is the Uniform Single Publication Act promulgated by the National Conference on Uniform State Laws in 1952. This model legislation extends the single publication concept to radio, television and motion pictures. The act has been adopted by the legislatures of seven states, including California, Illinois and Pennsylvania.

c. Identification

Published defamation is not actionable unless the complaining party can establish that it was he or she who was defamed. Very often the target of a defamatory communication is not clearly named therein and thus the identification of the complaining party with the communication becomes a problem of analyzing extrinsic circumstances. An example of this problem is the celebrated case of New York Times Co. v. Sullivan, 273 Ala. 656, 144 So.2d 25 (1962), reversed 376 U.S. 254, 84 S.Ct. 710, 11 L.Ed.2d 686 (1964). There, the defendants published a paid advertisement which made allegations, among others, that the police of Montgomery, Alabama had improperly "ringed" a black college campus to put down a peaceful demonstration for civil rights and that certain unnamed "southern violators" had bombed Martin Luther King's home, had physically assaulted him, arrested him seven times for "speeding," "loitering" and similar "offenses;" and finally charged him with "perjury." Some of these statements were erroneous in whole or part.

While no "southern violator" was named in the ad, L.B. Sullivan, the Commissioner of Public Affairs for Montgomery, Alabama, filed suit for libel. Sullivan persuaded the jury that he had been referred to in the advertisement because he was the city commissioner in charge of the police at all times in question and thus would have been responsible for the "ringing" of the campus and the multiple arrests of Dr. King for minor infractions as part of the alleged lawless campaign of harassment and intimidation. Sullivan also contended that being identified as a "southern violator" in conjunction with the arrests had resulted in his further identification in the public mind with the other lawless acts listed. Several Montgomery residents so testified. The United States Supreme Court reversed a judgment for Sullivan, holding, among other things, that the identification of Sullivan with the advertisement was inadequate.

Identification may also be difficult when a group is defamed. Generally, the courts will not entertain an action when the complainant is a member of a large group which has been defamed. In the case of defamation of small homogeneous groups, the courts will permit actions by the individual members of the group. And some courts will allow individual actions by certain members of small groups when the defamatory communication is directed to a segment of the group. Of course, in this last case the plaintiff must convince the finder of fact (normally the jury) that he or she was a member of the segment attacked. See Neiman-Marcus Co. v. Lait, 107 F.Supp. 96, 13 F.R.D. 311 (S.D.N.Y.1952) for an application of these rules regarding civil actions for group defamation.

d. *Economic Loss*

In addition to establishing the defamatory nature of the communication, its publication and the necessary identification, the plaintiff in certain cases must also plead and prove that he suffered actual pecuniary or economic loss (special damages). In determining when this additional requirement must be met, we are confronted with the herculean task of sorting out libel from slander, libel per se from libel per quod and slander per se from all other slander.

2. The Contrast Between Libel and Slander

Broadly differentiated, the tort of libel includes defamatory communications of a more or less permanent sort such as printed material, photographs, paintings, motion pictures, signboards, effigies and

see p. 55 top

even statuary, while slander includes more ephemeral communications such as the spoken word, gestures and sign language. The distinction arises out of the historical development of common law court jurisdiction. In wresting jurisdiction from the ecclesiastical courts of England, which heard cases of slander, and in succeeding to the jurisdiction of the notorious Star Chamber over printed defamation, the common law courts kept the two types of defamation separate. See Donnelly, "History of Defamation," 1949 Wis.L.Rev. 99.

While classification of communications as slander or libel might not have been too difficult in the late seventeenth century with the limited communications then available, it becomes troublesome in an electronic age with its dependence on telephones, radio, television and even computers for communication. Indeed, the courts have never agreed on the taxonomy of radio and television defamation. At least one court has classified defamation by radio as slander while a number of others have labeled it libel. Still others, seeking greater discrimination, classify it as libel if read from a script and slander if the remark is ad libbed. And finally, a few courts try to avoid the classification problem by calling radio defamation a new tort.

What too many courts appear to do when they are confronted with defamation via a new medium is to fix their gaze on the medium rather than on the interest the law is trying to protect and the reasons supporting the libel-slander dichotomy. The interest is, of course, reputation and the sting of defamation is its injury to reputation. Initially, the main justification for labeling writings as libelous, with concomitantly more serious consequences, including fine or imprisonment, was the greater permanence of the defamation and the correspondingly greater potential for wider distribution and greater injury to the victim. Today, no medium surpasses radio and television in wide distributive power. The potential injury to reputation from electronic defamation is devastating and on principle justifies the libel classification whether the defamation is read from a script or made extemporaneously.

There is no real way to avoid the troublesome task of classifying defamation since the requirement of special damages rests upon that classification. Generally, if the defamatory communication is held to constitute libel, the complaining party is not required to plead and prove as part of his or her case actual pecuniary loss resulting from the libel. On the other hand, if the communication is categorized as a slander, the complaining party generally has to establish such loss. As a practical matter many slander suits are quashed in the law office when the angry prospective plaintiff is informed by his or her own attorney to forget a lawsuit because he or she has no out-of-pocket loss. There is, however, a qualification to the requirement of financial sting in slander actions.

a. The Special Cases of Slander

As another matter of jurisdictional development, the common law courts established three special categories of slander which were to be actionable without regard to the existence of special damages: (1) imputation of crimes recognized by the common law courts; (2) imputation of certain loathsome diseases (limited to venereal disease, leprosy and the black plague); and (3) imputations affecting the victim in his or her business, trade, profession or office. Later, by statute or common law decision a fourth category was created, i.e., the imputation of unchastity to a woman. These four categories of slander continue to be recognized by most courts as permitting a plaintiff to sue his or her slanderer without establishing special damages, though the fourth category will almost surely be modified under state equal rights amendments. The scope of the categories has not changed greatly over the years. However, the present day test for the imputation of criminal conduct is whether the conduct involves moral turpitude. Thus, today a false oral allegation to a third party that "X" embezzles from his employer, would be actionable in most American jurisdictions without the need for "X" to establish pecuniary loss.

While from a plaintiff's perspective the existence of these special categories provides a liberalizing force in the law of slander, a somewhat parallel development in the law of libel has had the opposite effect.

b. Libel Per Se and Per Quod

As the tort of libel developed, the rule became fixed that in contrast to slander actions, special damages need not be pleaded and proven by the plaintiff in order for him or her to recover. An explanation often given for this distinction is that the written communication once had greater potential for mischief because of its more permanent form. Therefore, some injury to the victim could be conclusively presumed.

No distinction was drawn by the courts between those libelous communications plain upon their face (libel *per se*) such as "John Doe is a bastard" and those which require reference to extrinsic circumstances to give them the necessary defamatory meaning (libel *per quod*). The classic example of libel per quod is the erroneous newspaper story stating that Mary Doe of 1234 Shady Lane had just given birth to twins at a local hospital. The story was libelous because of the extrinsic fact that Mrs. Doe had been married only one month before and several persons reading the story knew this fact.

clear ex.

Originally, then, if the defamatory communication was broadly classified as libel, special damages were not essential to a successful action. This is still stated to be the majority rule by the American Law Institute's Restatement of the Law of Torts Second, Section 569. But the late Dean William L. Prosser stated flatly that some thirty-five American jurisdictions draw a distinction between libel per se and per quod and hold that libel per quod is to be treated like slander, i.e., actionable only with the pleading and proving of special damages unless the libel falls within one or more of the four special categories associated with slander. W. Prosser, Handbook of the Law of Torts (4th ed. 1971) 763. Moreover, the presumption of damage required by libel per se is now constitutionally suspect with regard to libelous communication of public concern not made with actual malice. See Gertz v. Robert Welch, Inc., 418 U.S. 323, 94 S.Ct. 2997, 41 L.Ed.2d 789 (1974); W. Prosser and W. Keeton, Handbook of the Law of Torts (5th ed. 1984) 796, 843. A major reason for this apparent change in the common law appears to be the reluctance of courts to hold newspapers and other media broadly liable for communications which they may not even be aware are defamatory.

To summarize:

1. Slander is actionable only with a showing of special damages . . .

2. . . . unless the slander imputes to the complaining party (1) criminal conduct recognized as involving moral turpitude; (2) infection with venereal disease, leprosy or the plague; (3) misconduct or mismanagement in business, trade, profession or office; or (4) unchastity (if the victim is a female).

3. Libels per se in all jurisdictions and libels per quod in a large number of jurisdictions (including New York) are actionable without the need for special damages.

4. Libels per quod in other jurisdictions are now actionable only with a showing of special damages unless they fall into one of the four special categories established originally for slander.

The above rules and the proper classification of defamation cases under them are extremely important since the establishment of special damages, i.e., pecuniary loss, as a result of the defamatory communication, is often very difficult for the plaintiff.

3. Theories of Liability

At common law, so long as the defendant intended to publish to a third person that which is ultimately adjudged to be defamatory toward the plaintiff, the defendant is strictly liable in tort, absent a valid defense. The plaintiff need only establish the intention of the defendant to publish and need not establish that the defendant intended the publication to be defamatory. Peck v. Tribune Co., 214 U.S. 185, 29 S.Ct. 554, 53 L.Ed. 960 (1909). Thus, a publisher under this rule "published at his own peril" and would be held liable for coincidences and honest errors as well as for intended defamatory attacks. Strict liability for the media was ended by the Supreme Court decisions in New York Times Co. v. Sullivan, 376 U.S. 254, 84 S.Ct. 710, 11 L.Ed.2d 686 (1964) and Gertz v. Robert Welch, Inc., 418 U.S. 323, 94 S.Ct. 2997, 41 L.Ed.2d 789 (1974), discussed supra at pp. 79, 89.

4. Remedies

Once the plaintiff has established his cause of action and assuming the defendant has not interposed any valid defense (see infra, pp. 63–73), the focus of the defamation suit shifts from the question of liability to the question of remedies available to the defamed person. The major remedy for injury to reputation is the award of monetary damages.

a. Damages

We have already seen that in cases of libel per quod in perhaps a majority of jurisdictions and in cases of slander, excluding the four special categories, proof of special damages is necessary for liability. Of course, such damages may be established in any defamation action. Such damages require rather specific pleading and proof by the plaintiff of pecuniary or economic loss actually resulting from the defamatory communication and reasonable foreseeability of the plaintiff's loss by the defendant. Obvious cases are the loss of one's employment, the loss of opportunity for business profits and impaired credit rating because others are influenced by the defamation.

The existence of special damages may influence the jury's award of general damages. These are damages awarded for actual losses to the plaintiff from the defamation and cover both proven and unproven pecuniary and nonpecuniary loss for such injuries as hurt feelings, embarrassment,

mental and emotional distress and physical consequences. Unless the action is one which specifically requires the showing of special damages, such
damages are not a prerequisite for the award of
general damages.

Many factors may be considered by the jury in
attempting to determine reasonable and appropriate general damages. These are catalogued by a
leading authority as including (1) the nature of the
defamation (e.g., irrational name calling or insinu-
ation of serious wrongdoing); (2) the form and
permanency of the publication (oral conversations
between individuals or communication by the mass
print or electronic media); (3) the degree of dissemination; (4) the degree to which the defamatory
communication is believed; (5) the nature of the
plaintiff's reputation; (6) in certain cases, the good
faith of the defendant in publishing the defamatory matter and (7) the defendant's subsequent conduct in retracting the complained of communication or in making apology. D. Dobbs, Handbook on
the Law of Remedies, 514–520 (1973).

In awarding these compensatory damages jurors
are instructed that they are to consider both past
injury suffered by the plaintiff and likely future
injury. Prospective future injury is to be estimated and made an element of the total award of
damages.

Occasionally, a jury may determine that a plaintiff has suffered no actual damage to his or her
reputation either because his or her good reputa-

tion was left unimpaired by the defamation or because his or her reputation was worth little or nothing to begin with. In that event, unless the plaintiff has established special damages (meaning out-of-pocket financial loss) the jury will award only nominal damages, ordinarily six cents or one dollar, depending on the jurisdiction.

If spite, evil motive or reckless disregard for the truth is present, the jury will be instructed that it may, but need not, award the plaintiff <u>punitive</u> <u>damages</u>. As the term implies, such damages <u>are</u> <u>designed to punish the defamer and are not com-</u> <u>pensatory in nature.</u> If such damages are to make the defendant "smart" for his or her indiscretion and deter him or her in the future, the jury must be entitled to know the defendant's net worth and to reduce it to where it hurts.

Punitive damages may have too great a deterrent effect. One lower court has suggested that when First Amendment interests are balanced against the interests of the state in punishing defamers, the "chilling effect" of punitive damages on freedom of expression is too great a price for a free society to pay in attempting to rid itself of defamation. Maheu v. Hughes Tool Co., 384 F.Supp. 166 (C.D.Calif.1974). This suggestion was rejected, however, when the Ninth Circuit reviewed the case. Maheu v. Hughes Tool Co., 569 F.2d 459, 480 (9th Cir. 1977). And the United States Supreme Court recently upheld the imposition of punitive damages in a case involving an erroneous private credit report containing no matter of public concern. Dun and Bradstreet, Inc. v. Greenmoss Builders, Inc., 472 U.S. 749, 105 S.Ct. 2939, 86 L.Ed.2d 593 (1985).

C. THE COMMON LAW DEFENSES

Once the plaintiff has provided sufficient evidence of the elements necessary to establish a prima facie case of defamation and the consequent award of damages, the defendant is put to his or her defense. He or she may, of course, deny one or more aspects of the plaintiff's case such as the defamatory nature of the communication or the publication of the offending communication. In addition or alternatively, he or she may attempt to establish one or more of the complete common law defenses of truth, privilege and fair comment in order to defeat liability or to attempt to establish certain incomplete defenses to reduce the award of damages. In resorting to these defenses, the defendant accepts the burden of pleading them in his or her answer and then proving them by a preponderance of the evidence at trial.

1. Truth or "Justification"

As we have seen in Chapter I, truth was not a defense to criminal libel prosecutions at common law. But in civil actions for defamation the rule was to the contrary. Truth was recognized as a complete bar to liability. This is the rule followed in a large majority of American jurisdictions. Behind this rule are the ideas that one is not entitled to a greater reputation than he or she in fact merits and that the public is served by knowing as much as possible about those in their midst with whom they may deal. Therefore the motives of the communicator are irrelevant to the availability of truth as a defense. A minority of states legislatively qualified the common law defense of truth in civil actions by requiring that the defendant establish his or her good motives or the justifiable ends to be served or both. As we shall see below, this requirement has been largely nullified by the Supreme Court.

Whether qualified or not the defense of truth is a risky one. Knowing something to be true and proving it in a court of law are, of course, two different things. In many situations only the plaintiff will have access to the necessary proof and, understandably, he or she will not make it easy for the defendant to establish the defense.

Moreover, the defense must be as broad in its reach as the communication complained of. The defense will fail if only a portion of the allegation is verified. For example, a newspaper charge that X is a habitual vice law offender is not justified by the paper establishing one conviction of X for a gambling violation. And a statement that a reliable source has informed the communicator that X is guilty of tax evasion is not justified by establishing only that someone informed the defendant about X and that someone is indeed a reliable source. The truth of the charge itself must be established even though the defendant was not the originator of the story. But this does not mean that the defendant will have to verify every detail of his communication. The defense is available if the substance of the communication can be established. An individual who publicly accuses his or her neighbor, the treasurer of the local homeowners association, of embezzling $1500 from the association, will escape liability by proving embezzlement of $150 and a news service report that volume beef sellers were ordered by a state court to make restitution to customers that could total $700,000 is not actionable when the actual amount of money obtained by the sellers as a result of unfair and deceptive practices was substantially less than $700,000.

2. Privilege

As with most intentional torts, the common law recognizes the defense of privilege in certain cases of defamation. Despite the fact that the plaintiff suffers harm to his or her reputation from the defamation, the defamer may be shielded from liability because the law accords supremacy to conflicting interests of the defendant in communicating the defamation or of third persons in receiving the communication or of the public generally in encouraging free expression of matters of general concern. The defense, which is relatively narrow in scope, is divided into two aspects: the absolute privilege to defame and the qualified privilege.

a. Absolute Privilege

One who possesses an absolute privilege to defame or, perhaps more accurately, an absolute immunity from suit is not required to establish his or her good faith in making the defamatory communication. Motivation is immaterial.

[handwritten margin note: more accurate wording]

Only the most compelling interests of society justify this license to injure or destroy reputations, and it is properly conferred almost exclusively on those directly involved in the furtherance of the public's business. So long as the defendant is so involved and the expression complained of is relevant to the public business at hand, he or she will, for the most part, be accorded the absolute privilege. While earlier cases imposed strict evidentiary standards of relevancy, the modern trend is to protect any expression which is at all related to the public proceeding. This trend accords with one of the major purposes for granting absolute immunity, i.e., insuring the independence and fearlessness of those participating in the public's business. If participants are forced to analyze their remarks for strict legal relevance and risk civil liability should they be in error, their fearlessness and independence may be impaired and their actions on the public's behalf inhibited. The public proceedings in which the absolute privilege may be available are divided into the judicial, legislative, executive and administrative.

There are a few instances aside from governmental activity in which the absolute privilege obtains.

These include communications between husband and wife, defamatory communications either expressly or impliedly invited by the party defamed and the carriage of communications required by law where the carrier is not permitted to control the content of the material. From a mass communications perspective the last situation is the important one.

The principle that absolute immunity attaches to those required by law to publish, without editorial control, communications which may be defamatory was established in Farmers Educational and Cooperative Union v. WDAY, Inc., 360 U.S. 525, 79 S.Ct. 1302, 3 L.Ed.2d 1407 (1959). There, a radio station licensee required by the so-called "equal time provision" of Section 315 of the Federal Communications Act of 1934 to carry a speech by a political candidate and barred by the same provision from controlling the content of the speech, was held absolutely immune from suit by those allegedly defamed by the speech.

b. *Qualified Privilege*

In contrast to the absolute privilege previously discussed, the qualified privilege to communicate defamatory matter is defeated by the plaintiff establishing malice on the part of the defendant. This entails proving a publication was motivated chiefly by some consideration other than furthering the interest for which the law accords the privilege in the first place. The law's recognition

of this lesser privilege reflects the idea that some
of the interests competing with that of reputation,
while not as compelling as those which justify an
absolute privilege or immunity for the publisher,
are still sufficiently important to justify a lesser
degree of protection.

In the case of the media, the interests supporting
the existence of the qualified privilege in reporting
the proceedings of government and some private
institutions and organizations are those of public
oversight of governmental activity and legitimate
public desire for information about matters affecting the public generally or a substantial segment
thereof. And even when the oversight function is
not involved the public may have some legitimate
interest in being informed of public proceedings of
both governmental and private organizations in
order to prepare for or guard against the consequences of those proceedings.

(1) Limitations on the Scope of
the Privilege

The courts have placed certain limitations on the
scope or availability of the privilege to the media
in reporting public proceedings. A majority of
courts, for instance, led by Massachusetts, takes
the position that the privilege does not extend to
reporting allegations or statements contained in
complaints, affidavits or other pretrial papers unless and until such papers are brought before a
judge or magistrate for official action. See, e.g.,

Sanford v. Boston Herald-Traveler Corp., 318 Mass. 156, 61 N.E.2d 5 (1945). Thus the reporter must be alert to the law of his or her state and, if it follows the majority view, must be wary of the content of court papers filed with the clerk of court but not yet acted upon by a judicial officer vested with discretionary authority. The minority view, exemplified by the New York case of Campbell v. New York Evening Post, Inc., 245 N.Y. 320, 157 N.E. 153, 52 A.L.R. 1432 (1927), is that the report of the contents of papers properly filed and served on the required parties may be privileged since the filing and serving of pleadings or other papers authorized by the rules of court are public and official acts done in the course of judicial proceedings.

Then, too, reports of the activities of executive officers or administrative agencies are generally not privileged until the officer or agency has taken some definite final action, as a district attorney filing a criminal information or obtaining an indictment. The report of a district attorney's preliminary investigation would not in most jurisdictions be privileged. As Professors Nelson and Teeter point out, police proceedings are especially dangerous for the newsperson to report because of the significant variations from state to state regarding the point at which the privilege attaches. The status of the police blotter, the record of arrests and charges and the oral reports of police officers concerning their preliminary investigations varies according to the jurisdiction involved.

H. Nelson and D. Teeter, Jr., Law of Mass Communications 175 (5th ed. 1986).

With regard to the legislative process, so long as
the particular proceeding reported upon is authorized, the report itself will be privileged, assuming
conformity with the general requirements discussed below.

The proceedings subject to the privilege must
normally be public in nature unless a statute provides otherwise. Thus, a report of secret grand
jury deliberations would not be considered privileged though such deliberations are official proceedings. Exceptions to the "public proceeding"
requirement are occasionally recognized such as in
Coleman v. Newark Morning Ledger Co., 29 N.J.
357, 149 A.2d 193 (1959), where a fair and accurate
report of Sen. Joseph McCarthy's press conference
summarizing the secret proceedings of his subcom-
mittee's investigation into alleged communist activity at Fort Monmouth, New Jersey, was held to
be privileged despite the fact, pointed out in the
dissenting opinion, that there was no verification
of whether Sen. McCarthy's report of the secret
legislative proceeding was itself fair and accurate.
Such exceptions are rare and the reporter should
not assume from them that there is legal justification for publishing reports of secret governmental
proceedings.

(2) General Requirements of the Privilege

As indicated by the Coleman case, if the qualified privilege is to attach the report must be fair and accurate and motivated by a sense of duty to make disclosure to those receiving the report. The privilege will be unavailable if it is held to be either an unfair or inaccurate account of that portion of the proceeding covered. The report need not, of course, be verbatim, but its condensation, abridgment or paraphrasing must accurately and fairly reflect what transpired. An erroneous detail will not destroy the privilege so long as it does not affect the essential accuracy or fairness of the report. A report may, of course, be literally accurate so far as it goes and yet unfairly portray the proceedings and the complaining person's involvement in them because the report ends at a critical point or omits important facts favorable to that person.

Moreover, if the defamatory report is made chiefly for a purpose other than to inform those who have a "need to know," the publication will be considered malicious and the privilege will be destroyed. Malice is found when the main reason for the publication is not the proper one of informing those the law recognizes as having a legitimate interest in the contents of the report. A fair and accurate account of a proceeding containing defamatory matter given to a friend at a party to make idle cocktail conversation could be considered mali-

cious because the proper motivation for making
the account is missing. And the privilege will not
obtain if the communication is motivated mainly
by some selfish objective of the reporter or publisher such as enhancing their business interests at the
expense of a competitor who is unfavorably referred to in the public proceeding reported.

3. Fair Comment

The fair comment privilege was the most popular of the common law defenses. It is now made
largely unnecessary by the holding in New York
Times Co. v. Sullivan, 376 U.S. 254, 84 S.Ct. 710, 11
L.Ed.2d 686 (1964) and by dictum in Gertz v. Robert Welch, Inc., 418 U.S. 323, 94 S.Ct. 2997, 41
L.Ed.2d 789 (1974). The constitutional privilege
found in New York Times Co. regarding public
figures is broader than traditional fair comment
and the dictum in Gertz providing First Amendment protection for expressions of opinion makes
the common law privilege superfluous. Therefore,
its treatment here will be quite summary.

As traditionally viewed fair comment involved
the honest expression of the communicator's opinion on a matter of public interest based upon facts
correctly stated in the communication. Such expression had to be free of speculation as to the
motivation of the person whose public conduct is
criticized unless such discussion was warranted by
the stated facts. See, e.g. Foley v. Press Publishing
Co., 226 App.Div. 535, 235 N.Y.S. 340 (1929). Chief

among the unique characteristics of this defense were (1) its emphasis upon opinion based upon fact rather than the reporting of the facts themselves and (2) its broader scope, permitting comment on all matters of public interest rather than simply proceedings of a public nature. It was these characteristics which made possible political and artistic criticism by the media prior to New York Times v. Sullivan.

The courts gave broad meaning to fair comment. Commentaries containing exaggeration, illogic, sarcasm, ridicule and even viciousness were protected if at all justified by the underlying facts.

Malice would negate the defense but it could not be inferred merely from the words chosen by the publisher or speaker. Malice could only be found from an examination of the communicator's motives in publishing. The defense was also negated in a majority of the jurisdictions if the comment or opinion were based on a major error of fact.

4. Incomplete Defenses

Certain defenses in defamation actions are labeled incomplete because they do not bar liability even if successful but only reduce the amount of damages recoverable by the plaintiff. Chief among them is that of retraction. If the defamer publishes a retraction of the defamatory communication punctually and with essentially the same prominence as he or she gave to the defamation, the danger of a punitive damages award will be negated and compensatory damages may be reduced.

The theory behind this mitigation of damages is that a true retraction of the defamation evidences the good faith of the communicator, thereby rebutting the existence of ill will, spite or evil motive and likely reducing the actual damage done to the plaintiff's reputation. However, the retraction cannot erase the defamation entirely because the plaintiff's legally protected interest in his or her reputation has already been violated, the cause of action arising with the original publication. Therefore, at least nominal damages and special damages, if any, must be awarded if there is no complete defense available to the defendant.

It should be emphasized that the retraction must be complete and unequivocal. Less than full retraction or a veiled continuance of the defamation will not mitigate damages but, in fact, may increase them. It will not do to state that "John Doe hasn't the morals of a tom cat" and then be willing to "retract" by stating that "John Doe does have the morals of a tom cat." It should also be noted that the availability of the partial retraction defense, the effects of retraction and the consequences of a refusal to retract are governed in a number of states such as California by statute. The California retraction statute figured prominently in the celebrated libel suit by comedienne Carol Burnett against the National Enquirer. The statute by its terms applies to and provides partial protection for newspapers. In the Burnett case the trial court ruled that the National Enquirer was a magazine and thus, although it had published a retraction of the libelous material about Miss Burnett, it was not protected against the imposition of punitive damages.

Somewhat akin to retraction is the idea of allowing the defamed party the right to reply to personal attack. The voluntary agreement by the defamer to allow use of his facilities by the victim to reply to the attack does not necessarily establish the defamer's good faith and the award of punitive damages remains a possibility. But the actual injury to the defamed party may be reduced because of the opportunity afforded to reach and favorably influence those whose good opinion of him or her has been affected. However, any effort by government to mandate the right of reply insofar as the print media are concerned would appear to be violative of the First Amendment. See Miami Herald Publishing Co. v. Tornillo, 418 U.S. 241, 94 S.Ct. 2831, 41 L.Ed.2d 730 (1974). But as of this time, a distinction is made by the Supreme Court with regard to broadcasters, and they may be compelled to extend the right to reply, in certain narrow circumstances, to those personally attacked over their facilities. Red Lion Broadcasting Co. v. Federal Communications Commission, 395 U.S. 367, 89 S.Ct. 1794, 23 L.Ed.2d 371 (1969). The distinction between print and electronic media is a doubtful one in this context and may eventually be eliminated. See the discussion of the "Fairness Doctrine" infra Chapter XI, pp. 455–469.

———

This completes the discussion of common law defamation, a law in many respects quite favorable to the defamed party's interest in reputation. Witness, for instance, its theory of strict liability. Conversely, this law imposes many restrictions upon and dangers for those who seek to exercise their right of free expression under the First Amendment.

No more graphic illustration of the dangers posed to a free press by the common law can be suggested than the decision of the Alabama Supreme Court in New York Times v. Sullivan, 273 Ala. 656, 144 So.2d 25 (1962), reversed 376 U.S. 254, 84 S.Ct. 710, 11 L.Ed.2d 686 (1964). That decision was, in almost all respects, in accord with accepted common law principles concerning the elements of libel, malice, compensatory and punitive damages and the recognized defenses.

The effect of that litigation in the state courts was to cause the New York Times Company to halt distribution of its newspaper in Alabama for a time and to saddle the company with a massive judgment for $500,000 damages which, if not reversed, would (along with a potential $2,500,000 more in damages claimed in other pending related suits) have caused a weakening of its financial position, with all the implications that that might have had for the Company's continued ability to adhere to its motto "all the news that's fit to print."

The common law principles which were applied by the Alabama courts and which have been considered at length in this chapter are still applied in whole to communications that do not involve public figures or matters of public concern and in part to communications which do. See Dun and Bradstreet, Inc. v. Greenmoss Builders, Inc., 472 U.S. 749, 105 S.Ct. 2939, 86 L.Ed.2d 593 (1985). They are, therefore, worthy of continued discussion. But the very serious question posed to the Supreme Court by the New York Times case was whether the application of all aspects of the common law of defamation to newspapers and other media is consistent with the guarantees of the First Amendment. The answer to that important question and its qualifications is the subject of the next section of this chapter.

D. THE NEW CONSTITUTIONAL LAW OF DEFAMATION

1. New York Times Co. v. Sullivan

The facts of New York Times v. Sullivan are set out in detail in Chapter I at pp. 7–8. It is sufficient to say here that the paid advertisement in question in the case did contain erroneous information which if satisfactorily identified with the plaintiff police official would be considered defamatory toward him at common law. However, the United States Supreme Court held that there was not adequate proof of identification of the plaintiff to support liability of the defendants for defamation and reversed the state court judgment for the plaintiff.

It seemed clear to the Court that, at most, the New York Times Company was guilty of negligence in publishing the advertisement without checking the facts alleged therein against its own news files to verify the accuracy of the advertisement. Money judgments against newspapers and other media for honest mistake or negligence in publication of defamatory material concerning public officials, interfered with debate on public issues. In the Court's understanding, the encouragement of such debate was part of the central meaning of the First Amendment. The court therefore laid down the rule that a public official may not recover damages for a defamatory falsehood relating to his official conduct unless he proves with "convincing clarity" that the statement is made with actual malice. "Actual malice" was defined by the Court as publication with knowledge that the statement in question is false or with "reckless disregard" of whether or not it is false.

Thus, for the first time in the long history of this country, certain false and defamatory communications were accorded constitutional protection if not maliciously made. This historic ruling represents a corollary to Barr v. Matteo, 360 U.S. 564, 79 S.Ct. 1335, 3 L.Ed.2d 1434 (1959), in which the Court accorded government officers an absolute privilege to make defamatory communications within the bounds of their offices. Critics of official conduct are given an equivalent privilege in order to encourage public oversight of these same officers.

2. Effects of the New York Times Case

The effects of the New York Times 376 U.S. 254 case on common law defamation are many and wide-sweeping. Briefly summarized they include the following:

1. The idea of "fair comment" is broadened to include facts and to permit the communication of erroneous facts, and is raised to a constitutional privilege when the comment concerns conduct of public officials relating to their office.

2. Strict liability for the making of defamatory communications concerning public officials is eliminated and a new fault standard of intentional or reckless conduct is substituted.

3. The definition of actual malice to mean evil motive, spite or ill will is rejected and a new definition of knowing falsehood or reckless disregard for the truth is substituted when public officials and public figures are complaining parties. Even hard-hitting investigative reporting begun with a preconceived point of view and an "adversarial stance" does not indicate actual malice where the reporter conducts a detailed investigation and writes a story therefrom that is substantially true. Tavoulareas v. Washington Post Co., 817 F.2d 762 (D.C.Cir. 1987), cert. denied ___ U.S. ___, 108 S.Ct. 200, ___ L.Ed.2d ___ (1987).

4. Under common law the defense of privilege, including lack of actual malice, was for the defendant to establish; after New York Times the plaintiff public official has the burden of negating the defendant's constitutional privilege by proving that the defendant acted with actual malice in publishing the false and defamatory material, i.e., intentionally or recklessly. Implicit in this is the shifting of the burden of proof on the issue of truth to the plaintiff. He or she must now establish falsity as part of his or her prima facie case. See Philadelphia Newspapers, Inc. v. Hepps, 475 U.S. 767, 106 S.Ct. 1558, 89 L.Ed.2d 783 (1986).

5. The plaintiff's proof of malice and his or her identification as the party defamed must now be made with convincing clarity; at common law the normal standard of proof for defamation is mere preponderance of the evidence.

Another important effect is somewhat more indirect. As a practical matter, plaintiff public officials have had, since the New York Times Co. case was decided, a very hard time in making out their defamation cases against media defendants because of the difficulty of establishing actual malice under the convincing clarity standard. Responsible media organizations rarely traffic in known falsehoods or act recklessly in disseminating news or information. Very often then when there is no real dispute as to the material facts, defendants are able to obtain summary judgments on the basis of preliminary papers, documents and affidavits showing insufficient proof of actual malice and thus do not have to defend themselves at trial. See, e.g., Anderson v. Liberty Lobby, Inc., 477 U.S. 242, 106 S.Ct. 2505, 91 L.Ed.2d 202 (1986).

3. The New York Times Progeny

As great a charter as the New York Times case is for the mass media, it raised more questions than it answered, and only the existence of two decades of subsequent court decisions permits an assessment of the true boundaries and impact of that case. One of the questions raised was as to the meaning of "reckless disregard." In the New York Times case itself the facts pointed so strongly to honest mistake in publication, that no real clue was given as to the boundaries of the concept.

see p. 82 middle

Considerable light is cast on this issue in St. Amant v. Thompson, 390 U.S. 727, 88 S.Ct. 1323, 20 L.Ed.2d 262 (1968). There, the defendant, a candidate for office, made a television speech in the course of which he read questions which he had put to a local Teamsters Union member and the member's responses. The member's answers falsely charged the plaintiff, a local deputy sheriff, with corruption and the deputy sued. The defendant had no personal knowledge of the deputy's alleged corrupt activities, had relied solely on what the Teamster told him though the candidate had no apparent reason to accept his informant's veracity, had failed to make his own investigation of the charge, had given no heed to the seriousness of the charge and had rather cavalierly assumed that he had no responsibility for his conduct because he was merely quoting someone else. In reversing the Louisiana Supreme Court's affirmance of the trial court's judgment for the deputy sheriff, the Supreme Court held that the facts proved fell short of proving the candidate's reckless disregard for the accuracy of the quotations. Analyzing cases following New York Times Co. v. Sullivan, supra, the Court concluded that reckless conduct is not measured by whether a reasonable person would have investigated before publishing. Rather, the Court generalized, "[t]here must be sufficient evidence to permit the conclusion that the defendant in fact entertained serious doubts as to the truth of his publication." 390 U.S. at 731, 88 S.Ct. at 1325, 20 L.Ed.2d at 267. See also Herbert v. Lando, 441 U.S. 153, 156, 99 S.Ct. 1635, 1639, 60 L.Ed.2d 115, 122 (1979). This comes very close to requiring the public official to prove knowing publication of falsehood and appears to protect those publishers who deliberately avoid discovering the truth.

Another question expressly left open in New York Times Co. is the meaning of "official conduct." This concept now appears to parallel closely the boundaries of an executive or administrative officer's duties and responsibilities in office set forth in Barr v. Matteo, supra. As long as the defamatory material is published within the constitutional and statutory bounds of his or her office,

the public official would be bound by the New York
Times Co. rule. Cf. Butz v. Economou, 438 U.S.
478, 98 S.Ct. 2894, 57 L.Ed.2d 895 (1978). In addition, erroneous charges of criminal conduct on the
part of public officials and candidates for public
office, no matter how remote in time or place, are
protected by the constitutional privilege because
such charges are always relevant to the question of
fitness to hold or seek office. Monitor Patriot Co.
v. Roy, 401 U.S. 265, 91 S.Ct. 621, 28 L.Ed.2d 35
(1971); Ocala Star-Banner Co. v. Damron, 401 U.S.
295, 91 S.Ct. 628, 28 L.Ed.2d 57 (1971). On the
other hand, even public officials are entitled to
private lives and false and defamatory communications relating thereto would not be protected by
the privilege established in the New York Times
case. For instance, a defendant who publishes a
negligently erroneous accusation that a county as-
sessor owns an extensive collection of pornographic
films would not be entitled to such protection since
possession does not constitute a crime and is hardly relevant to the conduct of his or her office.

The Court in New York Times v. Sullivan also
declined to provide a general definition of "public
official." The cases that followed New York Times
have established that "public official" includes at
least those in governmental hierarchies who have
or appear to have substantial responsibility for the
conduct of government business, including judges
(Garrison v. Louisiana, 379 U.S. 64, 85 S.Ct. 209, 13
L.Ed.2d 125 (1964)); county clerks (Beckley News-

papers Corp. v. Hanks, 389 U.S. 81, 88 S.Ct. 197, 19 L.Ed.2d 248 (1967)); chiefs and deputy chiefs of police (Henry v. Collins, 380 U.S. 356, 85 S.Ct. 992, 13 L.Ed.2d 892 (1965); Time, Inc. v. Pape, 401 U.S. 279, 91 S.Ct. 633, 28 L.Ed.2d 45 (1971)); mayors (Ocala Star-Banner Co. v. Damron, 401 U.S. 295, 91 S.Ct. 628, 28 L.Ed.2d 57 (1971)); and even deputy sheriffs (St. Amant v. Thompson, 390 U.S. 727, 88 S.Ct. 1323, 20 L.Ed.2d 262 (1968)). The term also included former office holders who exercised substantial responsibility while in office and who are attacked for their past official conduct (Rosenblatt v. Baer, 383 U.S. 75, 86 S.Ct. 669, 15 L.Ed.2d 597 (1966)).

While the term "public official" is thus an expansive one, it covers only a small percentage of public personages. Recognizing this, the Court subsequently extended the reach of the New York Times Co. decision to public figures and their non-official but public acts, such as famous college athletic directors and football coaches and resigned Army generals who, by their public conduct, thrust themselves into the limelight (Curtis Publishing Co. v. Butts, 388 U.S. 130, 87 S.Ct. 1975, 18 L.Ed.2d 1094 (1967); Associated Press v. Walker, 388 U.S. 130, 87 S.Ct. 1975, 18 L.Ed.2d 1094 (1967)); a prominent real estate developer involved in a land dispute with a local city council (Greenbelt Cooperative Publishing Association v. Bresler, 398 U.S. 6, 90 S.Ct. 1537, 26 L.Ed.2d 6 (1970)); and candidates for public office (Monitor Patriot Co. v. Roy, 401 U.S. 265, 91 S.Ct. 621, 28 L.Ed.2d 35 (1971)).

But what of persons who are neither public officials nor public figures but who are caught up in matters of public interest? Should the media have the same constitutional privilege regarding communications about private persons who may be less able to defend themselves against false and defamatory allegations because of less access to the corrective mechanisms of the mass media? In other words, should the focus be shifted from public persons to matters of public interest, regardless of the status of the participants involved? These are extremely important questions. Affirmative answers might so alter the balance between the interest in free speech and press and the interest in individual reputation as to destroy the latter. Whomever the media deemed newsworthy might be regarded by the courts as being bound by the New York Times rule when they sought legal redress.

Initially, a plurality of the Supreme Court in Rosenbloom v. Metromedia, Inc., 403 U.S. 29, 91 S.Ct. 1811, 29 L.Ed.2d 296 (1971), answered this question in the affirmative, deeming the distinction between public and private individuals to be artificial in relationship to the public's interest in a broad range of issues, including, in that case, the arrest of an obscure distributor of nudist magazines on obscenity charges and the confiscation of his magazines as pornographic.

4. The Basic Public Figure-Private Person Distinction of Gertz v. Welch

Strong dissent was registered in Rosenbloom to this extension of the constitutional privilege, and in Gertz v. Robert Welch, Inc., 418 U.S. 323, 94 S.Ct. 2997, 41 L.Ed.2d 789 (1974), a majority of the Court rejected that plurality decision, holding that the privilege recognized in New York Times Co. v. Sullivan was applicable only to cases involving defamation of public officials and public figures.

In Gertz, a reputable lawyer not generally known to the public and not then associated with any particular causes, was retained by the family of a youth killed by a police officer to bring a civil suit against the officer. Perceiving that the state's successful criminal prosecution for murder and the family's civil suit was part of a nationwide conspiracy to discredit local law enforcement agencies, the corporate defendant, publisher of the magazine, "American Opinion," commissioned one of the regular contributors to the periodical to write an article about the case. Under the title "FRAME–UP: Richard Nuccio And The War on Police," the published article asserted that the police had a huge file on Gertz. The article also claimed that he had been an official of the "Marxist League for Industrial Democracy," which advocated the violent seizure of the government, and that he was a "Leninist" and a "Communist-fronter." Finally, the article stated that Gertz had been an officer of the National Lawyers Guild, described as a Communist organization which "probably did more than any other outfit to plan the Communist attack on the Chicago police during the 1968 Democratic convention." These statements contained many serious inaccuracies, especially the implication that Gertz had a police record and the express assertions that he was a "Leninist" or a "Communist-fronter" and that he supported violence against duly constituted authority. The editor had made no effort to verify or substantiate the author's charges.

Gertz brought suit for libel against the corporation and obtained a jury verdict for $50,000. Following the verdict, the United States District Judge concluded that the privilege afforded by New York Times Co. v. Sullivan, supra, should be extended to cover discussion of any public issue without regard to the status of the person defamed. Accordingly, the court entered judgment for respondent notwithstanding the jury verdict and Gertz appealed. The United States Court of Appeals affirmed the judgment, citing Rosenbloom v. Metromedia, Inc., supra.

In a 5 to 4 decision, the Supreme Court, speaking through Justice Powell, reversed, limiting the New York Times Co. doctrine to cases involving defamation of public officials or public figures and rejecting the plurality opinion in Rosenbloom.

According to the majority the private person is more in need of judicial redress and the state has a greater interest in providing it because he or she has not voluntarily invited public comment, thus choosing to put his or her reputation at risk. Moreover, the private person will normally have less access to the channels of effective communication (the media) to correct the record than will the public person. Therefore, while the media's First Amendment interest in matters of public or general concern is a constant factor regardless of the plaintiff's status, the plaintiff's interest in achieving legal redress for injury to his or her reputation varies according to whether he or she is a private person. By its decision the majority in Gertz was attempting to restore the balance between protection of expression and protection of reputation which it perceived had been upset in New York Times Co.

The Court's reasoning was vigorously criticized by Justice Brennan in his dissenting opinion. He suggested that the social interaction in a society which places primary value on freedom of speech and press necessarily exposes all of its members to some degree of public exposure. As for the assumption that public persons have greater access to the media for non-judicial redress Brennan argued that empirically this is often not the case. The main concern expressed by Brennan, the author of the plurality opinion in Rosenbloom, is that anything less than the constitutional privilege will result in self censorship by the media in handling matters of public concern when the participants are not clearly public persons.

This concern was recognized by the majority and, aware of the dangers of leaving the media subject to the unreconstructed common law in suits by private persons, they directly modified the common law in two fundamental respects. First, they abolished strict liability for the publication of defamatory material and left to the individual states the determination of the appropriate fault standard of liability. This means that while the states may no longer impose liability on the media where there is no fault in the communication of defamatory material, they may impose it on one of the following bases (listed in ascending order of protection for the media): unreasonable publication (negligence), extremely unreasonable publication (gross negligence) or knowingly false or reckless publication (New York Times standard).

Second, when liability is imposed on the basis of a lower standard of fault than that of New York Times Co., i.e., negligence or gross negligence, recovery is to be limited to compensation for proved actual injury caused by the defamation. The Court thus ruled out presumed general damages and punitive damages in states choosing to adopt a lower standard of liability such as negligence. But apparently in defamation actions against the media tried pursuant to the New York Times Co. standard, presumed and punitive damages might still be awarded.

This modification of the common law system of damages is clearly designed to protect the media from massive judgments based on the jury's imagination, its ideas of punishment and deterrence and its prejudices. An example of such a judgment is the $725,000 punitive damages originally awarded by the jury in Gertz against the defendant publisher of an unpopular right wing periodical.

Whether this modification provides sufficient protection to the media to discourage self censorship and undue timidity in their handling of news and information remains to be seen. Actual injury may still encompass such things as impairment of reputation, personal humiliation and mental and emotional distress, none of which may be reduced to precise monetary figures. Therefore, once the plaintiff proves the existence of these injuries, the jury, of necessity, must be given some latitude in fixing their value.

5. The Fact-Opinion Dichotomy

One other major modification of the common law was effected in Gertz to the benefit of the media. By way of dictum Mr. Justice Powell stated that "[u]nder the First Amendment there is no such thing as a false idea. However pernicious an opinion may seem, we depend for its correction not on the conscience of judges and juries but on the competition of other ideas." 418 U.S. at 339–40, 94 S.Ct. at 3007, 41 L.Ed.2d at 805. This dictum was restated and reaffirmed in the more recent case of Bose Corporation v. Consumers Union, 466 U.S.

485 at 504, 104 S.Ct. 1949 at 1961, 80 L.Ed.2d 502 at 518 (1984).

Thus as media lawyer David E. Kendall noted at a twentieth anniversary celebration of the decision in New York Times v. Sullivan, "We know one thing plainly, and that is that whatever opinion is, there is total immunity for it under the First Amendment; it can never give rise to an action for defamation." 2 ABA Communications Lawyer p. 5 (No. 3, Summer 1984); see Restatement of Torts 2d § 566. The basic reason for this is, of course, that opinion cannot be shown to be *factually* incorrect. But Justice Powell made clear in his dictum that in distinction with opinion, false statements of fact may be demonstrated to be such and are not protected when made with fault.

The difficulty is in distinguishing between fact and opinion and the dictum in Gertz provides little help with this problem. And it is a difficult problem because words often have different things in different contexts. Moreover, understanding of the meaning of words is subjective to both the publisher and the audience.

One who has grappled with the fact-opinion dictionary and has attempted to provide some guidelines in making the necessary distinction is Judge Starr of the United States Court of Appeals for the District of Columbia Circuit. He isolated four factors in determining whether statements made in a syndicated newspaper column were actionable. These are: (1) the common usage or meaning of the specific language of the complained of statements themselves; ② verifiability, i.e., the capability of objectively characterizing the statements as true or false; ③ the full context of the statements—here the entire syndicated column; and ④ the broader context or setting in which the statements appear—here a syndicated newspaper column generally appearing on editorial or "op ed" pages. Ollman v. Evans, 750 F.2d 970 (D.C. Cir. 1984), cert. denied 471 U.S. 1127, 105 S.Ct. 2662, 86 L.Ed.2d 278 (1985). Judge Starr's analysis was followed with some modification by the United States Court of Appeals for the Eighth Circuit sitting en banc in Janklow v. Newsweek, Inc., 788 F.2d 1300 (8th Cir.) cert. denied ___ U.S. ___, 107 S.Ct. 272, 93 L.Ed.2d 249 (1986) and viewed favorably by the New York Court of Appeals in Steinhilber v. Alphonse, 68 N.Y.2d 283, 508 N.Y.S.2d 901, 501 N.E.2d 550 (1986).

Whether the approach to the opinion-fact dichotomy taken by these two circuits will be adopted by the Supreme Court is not presently clear. But Judge Starr's approach does focus on several factors which are difficult to ignore.

6. The Public Figure—Private Person Distinction

a. Narrowing of the Public Figure Classification

In righting the perceived imbalance in constitutional protection between expression and reputation it was important for the Gertz majority to reduce the range of applicability of New York Times Co. This could be accomplished by defining narrowly who was a public figure and thus who was governed for purpose of defamation actions by the stringent New York Times Co. standards.

Gertz, of course, created the dichotomy between public figures and private persons and set out the basic tests for determining a public figure: (1) the general fame or notoriety of the plaintiff in the community; or (2) the plaintiff's thrusting himself or herself voluntarily into the middle of the specific public controversy involved in the suit. A third category of public figure has been added by the United States Court of Appeals for the District of Columbia, that of a limited public figure who becomes such involuntarily when events conspire to place him or her in the limelight, as an air traffic controller who is on duty when a plane crashes. See Dameron v. Washington Magazine, Inc., 779 F.2d 736, 740–743 (D.C. Cir. 1985), cert. denied ___ U.S. ___, 106 S.Ct. 2247, 90 L.Ed.2d 693 (1986).

But it was left to the progeny of Gertz to establish the truly restrictive nature of the public figure category. In Time Inc. v. Firestone, 424 U.S. 448, 96 S.Ct. 958, 47 L.Ed.2d 154 (1976), Mrs. Firestone brought suit for separate maintenance and her husband counterclaimed for complete divorce on grounds of extreme cruelty and adultery. Mrs. Firestone was a socially prominent hostess in Palm Beach, Florida and her husband was an heir to the Firestone tire empire. After a lengthy and spicy public trial the judge granted the husband's request for a complete divorce but without clearly setting out the ground or grounds therefor and granted Mrs. Firestone $3000 per month alimony. Time Magazine published the following item in its "Milestones" section: "Divorced by Russell A. Firestone, Jr., 41, heir to the tire fortune: Mary Alice Sullivan Firestone, 32 . . . on grounds of extreme cruelty and adultery . . . ." After her request for a printed retraction was rejected, Mrs. Firestone sued for libel in Palm Beach. The material in Time's Milestones section was defamatory and untrue because an adulterous wife could not, under Florida law, receive alimony and, of course, the Florida trial court had made a substantial award of alimony to her.

helpful analysis of the law ✱

Time however claimed that Mrs. Firestone was a public figure by reason of her celebrity in Palm Beach Society and the public nature of the trial and divorce, not to mention her impromptu press conferences on the courthouse stairs and her hiring of a press agent. Thus according to Time, she was required to show that the magazine was guilty of publishing a known falsehood or recklessly disregarding the truth.

In rejecting Time's contention the Supreme Court said that local social prominence is not enough to categorize a plaintiff as a public figure. More importantly, involvement in a public trial does not necessarily make one a public figure. Marriage dissolution is not the sort of "public controversy" referred to in Gertz. It is essentially a private matter which the state requires to be resolved in a public forum. The Court did not even mention Mrs. Firestone's open air press conferences or her hiring of a press agent designed to get out to the public her side of the divorce story.

Firestone considerably narrows the public figure category, given Mrs. Firestone's notoriety. The category was further narrowed by two cases decided by the Supreme Court on the same day in its 1978–1979 term.

In Wolston v. Reader's Digest Association, Inc., 443 U.S. 157, 99 S.Ct. 2701, 61 L.Ed.2d 450 (1979) defendant published a book about Soviet intelligence agents in the United States and listed Wolston as one of them. Sixteen years earlier Wolston had been subpoenaed to testify before a federal grand jury investigating the activity of Soviet agents in this country. Because of claimed poor health he did not comply with the subpoena and he was cited for contempt. His trial on the contempt charge was attended with great publicity but following the conclusion of the criminal proceedings at which he was sentenced to a one-year suspended jail term, Wolston sank back into anonymity.

Wolston denied any connection to the Soviet intelligence apparatus and sued the Reader's Digest Association for libel. The trial court granted the Association summary judgment on the basis that petitioner was a public figure and that the papers supporting and opposing summary judgment did not show knowing untruthfulness or reckless disregard for the truth on the part of the defendant. The United States Court of Appeals affirmed the summary judgment.

The Supreme Court reversed, ruling that Wolston was not a public figure. According to the Court, Wolston's failure to answer the subpoena was not of itself a voluntary thrusting of himself into the middle of the public controversy regarding Soviet espionage even though such failure was sure to generate publicity. Only if the failure had been designed as a protest against the investigation and to influence public opinion would Wolston have become a limited public figure in relationship to the Soviet spy controversy.

This holding restricts limited issue public figures to those who draw attention to themselves in order to advocate a particular view on a public matter and to affect public opinion. Thus, as in Firestone, mere involvement in a matter of public interest is not enough.

This same restrictive view of limited-issue public figures led the Court to reject the Association's other contention that any person who engages in criminal conduct automatically becomes a public figure regarding his trial and conviction. As in the Firestone case, one involved in a public trial (here a criminal one) does not necessarily become a public figure.

In the companion case of Hutchinson v. Proxmire, 443 U.S. 111, 99 S.Ct. 2675, 61 L.Ed.2d

411 (1979), Senator William Proxmire awarded his uncoveted "Golden Fleece of the Month" awards to NASA and the Office of Naval Research for spending almost a half-million dollars to fund Dr. Hutchinson's research on the aggressiveness of animals, particularly monkeys, for the purpose of finding ways to reduce aggressiveness in humans thrown together in close quarters for extended periods of time. In his speech making the award as well as in a related news release Proxmire described Hutchinson's research as transparently worthless and called for an end to his making "a monkey out of the American taxpayer" and putting the "bite" on the taxpayer's resources. Dr. Hutchinson sued the Senator and his administrative assistant for libel. As in Wolston, summary judgment was granted by the trial court because the plaintiff was a public figure. Public figure status was conferred on him, according to the trial court, because of his long involvement with publicly funded research, solicitation of such funds, local press coverage of his research and the public interest in the expenditure of public funds for such research. Applying the New York Times Co. standard the trial court could find no issue of malice in the pretrial papers. The United States Court of Appeals affirmed the summary judgment.

On the "public figure" issue the Supreme Court reversed rejecting the view that the plaintiff's successful application for federal funds, local newspaper reports regarding the grants and his research and his technical publications made him a limited-issue public figure. In so ruling the Court made these points:

1. Dr. Hutchinson's media celebrity or notoriety occurred only as a consequence of the defamatory Proxmire award; clearly those charged with defamation cannot create their own defense by themselves making the victim a public figure;

2. Merely receiving or benefitting from publicly funded research grants does not make one a public figure;

3. The access to the media required by Gertz is a regular and continuing one and not merely that made available to rebut a specific defamatory attack.

As to this last point, the Court appears to have shrunk the public figure category significantly because, as originally conceived in Gertz, the purpose of the media-access test for public figure status appeared to be the availability of self-defense to the victim of defamation, with a consequent lesser need for judicial remedy in the form of money damages. Here, Hutchinson had been given media access to defend himself. Consider how many (or few) persons in this country have regular and continuing access to the mass media.

In summary, the public figure category has been narrowed by the Gertz progeny in these important respects:

public figure limitations (?)

1. Simply appearing in the newspapers in connection with some newsworthy story or stories does not make one a public figure;

2. Social, professional or business prominence does not by itself make one a public figure;

3. Forced involvement in a public trial, either civil or criminal, does not by itself make one a public figure;

4. Those charged with defamation cannot by their own conduct in making their victims notorious thereby create their own defense;

5. Merely applying for, receiving or benefiting from public research grants does not make one a public figure;

6. In order to meet the Gertz test of thrusting oneself into the forefront of a public issue or controversy, the issue or controversy must be a real dispute, the outcome of which affects the general public or some segment of it in an appreciable way and one's conduct must be calculated or clearly be expected to invite public comment respecting that issue or controversy, e.g., the value and conduct of a federal investigation into KGB activity in the United States during the McCarthy era.

7. In order to meet the Gertz test of access to the media the access must be regular and continuing.

All in all, following the Firestone, Wolston and Proxmire decisions, the category of public figures for purposes of New York Times v. Sullivan protection is much smaller than could have been imagined when Gertz was decided. For an extended discussion of the public figure-private person dichotomy see Note, 30 Cath.U.L.Rev. 307 (1981).

b. The Effect of Time Passage on Public Figure Status

Wolston v. Reader's Digest Association was marked by an interesting concurring opinion by Justice Blackmun in which he assumed for purposes of argument that Wolston had become a public figure in 1958. But, Blackmun argued, by Wolston's return to anonymity and the passage of time until the offending book was published some sixteen years later, he no longer had "significantly greater access to the channels of communication" to defend himself and had no longer knowingly chosen to run the risk of public scrutiny. Consequently, he had lost his public figure status. Justice Blackmun recognized that such analysis implies that a person may be a public figure for purposes of contemporaneous reporting of his activities but not a public figure for purposes of historical commentary on the same activities and events.

Because Justice Blackmun's approach provides less protection for the historical commentator than it does for the contemporaneous journalist, it has been rejected by at least one lower court. See Street v. National Broadcasting Co., 645 F.2d 1227 (6th Cir. 1981); and compare Brewer v. Memphis

Publishing Co., Inc., 626 F.2d 1238 (5th Cir. 1980). Despite these lower court decisions the popular or scholarly historical commentator should be wary for the Supreme Court majority did not reject Justice Blackmun's analysis as a corollary means of narrowing the media's constitutional privilege. Thus, special care should be taken to achieve factual accuracy in the preparation of the "where are they now"—type features concerning formerly famous or notorious people.

7. The Broad Meaning of Gertz

The case of Gertz v. Robert Welch, Inc. sets, of course, the boundaries of the constitutional privilege established in New York Times Co. v. Sullivan. From here on the privilege of the media negligently to make false and defamatory communications may be limited by the states when it is determined that the complaining party is not a public person. But beyond this, Gertz puts an end, at least temporarily, to the expansion of the absolutist interpretation of the First Amendment which gives primacy to the societal interests in free expression.

As a result the media will have to be more concerned about what they communicate relative to the "unknowns" of our society and will have to review and strengthen verification procedures to avoid the charge of negligence in news gathering, interpretation and dissemination. The other side of the new coin minted in Gertz is the greater recognition of the individual's personal worth and dignity.

8. Specific Problems for the Media Created by Gertz

The media may find it difficult to come to terms with the system made possible by Gertz. Aside from the pervasive specter of self censorship raised by it, Gertz presents a number of very specific problems.

Distinguishing between public persons and private ones may not be easy for the media, particularly under the pressure of deadlines. Even the United States District Court and the United States Court of Appeals were at odds over the status of Gertz, an author and prominent attorney long active in community and professional affairs. The Supreme Court's guidelines here are, at best, difficult to apply. They present two standards for the characterization of a public figure: (1) general fame or notoriety of the plaintiff in the community, which makes the protection of the constitutional privilege general; or (2) the plaintiff's thrusting himself or herself voluntarily into the vortex of the specific public issue involved, in which event the media's protection is limited to communications concerning that issue. The Supreme Court stressed the fact in Gertz that the plaintiff had not achieved any general fame in the community—the jurors had never heard of him. Moreover, the Court did not think that simply because he was counsel in the civil litigation in question that he had "thrust himself into the vortex." But can a newspaper, for instance, make these fine judgments in advance of publication?

Another determination which the media may be required to make in advance of publication, depending on the standard of liability embodied in the relevant state law, is the reasonableness of its publishing procedures in every given case. But even if the particular publisher satisfies itself that its procedures are reasonable (non-negligent), the jury will have the last word on this question. Factors to be considered in making an assessment of reasonableness of publication include the apparent risk of defamation as perceived by a reasonable person in the publisher's position and the gravity of the injury to the victim if the risk is realized. These factors have to be balanced against the reasons for the publication, the deadline pressures on the publisher, the means actually used in verifying and interpreting the information, the alternative means of verification and interpretation available to the publisher which were not utilized, and, of course, the costs involved in using such alternative means. Since some of these factors which the jury must consider are qualitative and subjective, prudent communicators will be very cautious in what and how they publish and will be left to hope that juries will overcome any prejudices they may have against the media. One thing does seem clear even after Gertz. The head in the sand approach to verification taken by the defendant in St. Amant

v. Thompson, supra, a public official case, will almost certainly be deemed negligent or even grossly negligent by juries in private person cases.

Because of the great uncertainties involved in determining the reasonableness of the publisher's conduct prior to trial, the media can also expect less favorable treatment on motions for summary judgment against private plaintiffs. Unless the publisher's conduct can be held by the trial judge to be reasonable beyond question, a trial will have to be conducted to permit the jury to decide this issue. Thus, more protracted litigation can be expected with increasing pressure on media defendants to settle even nuisance claims.

Finally, the problem of large damage awards discussed previously will remain a very real concern of the media and may add to the pressure for out of court settlements that can only weaken the financial structure of media organizations.

9. Questions Raised by Gertz

Gertz raised important questions about the existence and operation of common law defenses. Who now has the burden of establishing the truth or falsity of the alleged defamatory communications?

After a number of years of uncertainty, this question was answered in Philadelphia Newspapers, Inc. v. Hepps, 475 U.S. 767, 106 S.Ct. 1558, 89 L.Ed.2d 783 (1986). There, the Supreme Court ruled, in a case involving a series of newspaper articles linking a private figure to organized crime and his use of those links to influence a state government's decisions, that the *plaintiff* had the burden of establishing the falsity of the articles. The Court made this choice on the ground that the Constitution requires the protection of true speech, and to insure such protection the common law presumption must be rejected when damages are sought against a media defendant for speech of public concern. This decision represents an obvious extension of the idea presented in New York Times v. Sullivan, supra, that the First Amendment is designed to encourage robust debate on matters of public interest and provides "breathing space" by allowing for non-malicious misstatements of fact.

The Court also noted that placing the burden of proof on plaintiffs to establish falsity does not involve undue hardship because plaintiffs already have the burden of establishing fault on the part of the defendant and juries are more likely to find defendants in libel cases at fault if convinced that the statements complained of are also false.

Publication of truthful information no matter how damaging is inconsistent with concepts of negligence and gross negligence.

The dictum in Gertz that under the First Amendment there is no such thing as a false idea or opinion raises questions as to the continued need of fair comment as a defense. That common law defense is, after all, designed to protect comment and opinion so long as they are based on correct facts. If the defense has vanished, the media has lost little or nothing, for now comment, opinion and ideas (as distinguished from supporting fact) are constitutionally protected from defamation actions. Nevertheless, the fair comment defense continues to be recognized in some state trial and appellate courts and has been upheld in at least a dozen appeals in the past decade.

Finally, the question remains as to what the states have done following Gertz. They had at least three fault standards of liability to choose from (see p. 89, supra). A few jurisdictions have indicated a preference for the New York Times Co. standard. See Walker v. Colorado Springs Sun, Inc., 538 P.2d 450 (Colo.1975); AAFCO Heating and Air Conditioning Co. v. Northwest Publications, Inc., 321 N.E.2d 580 (Ind.App.1974); Sisler v. Gannett Co., Inc., 104 N.J. 256, 516 A.2d 1083 (1986). In none of these cases, however, was the adoption of that standard of fault unanimous and subsequently the highest courts of most other states considering the question have opted for a simple negligence test. See e.g., Phillips v. Evening Star Newspaper Co., 424 A.2d 78, 87, 94 n. 10 (D.C.1980) (all state holdings on this issue collected); Triangle Publications, Inc. v. Chumley, 253 Ga. 179, 317 S.E.2d 534 (1984). But New York has chosen to impose liability for defamation only if the defendant "acted in a grossly irresponsible manner without due consideration for the standards of information gathering and dissemination ordinarily followed by responsible parties," (Robart v. Post-Standard, 52 N.Y.2d 843, 845, 418 N.E.2d 664, 437 N.Y.S.2d 71 (1981), an intermediate standard between that of New York Times Co. and ordinary negligence.

10. The Reaffirmation of New York Times, a Generation Later

Approximately a quarter of a century has elapsed since the truly landmark decision of New York Times Company v. Sullivan. It is not surprising that during this period criticism of the decision has arisen and a desire has been expressed by some to turn back the clock to the common law way of handling media libel cases. Perhaps the most thoughtful assault on the constitutional privilege developed in New York Times and refined in Gertz is that of Mr. Justice White. In his concurring opinion in Dun & Bradstreet, Inc. v. Greenmoss Builders, Inc., 472 U.S. 749, 105 S.Ct. 2939, 2948– 54, 86 L.Ed.2d 593, 606–612 (1985) Justice White said, "The New York Times rule . . . countenances two evils: first, the stream of information about public officials and public affairs is polluted and often remains polluted by false information; and second, the reputation and professional life of the defeated plaintiff may be destroyed by falsehoods that might have been avoided with a reasonable effort to investigate the facts. . . . Gertz is subject to similar observations. . . . I am unreconciled to the Gertz holding and believe that it should be overruled." 472 U.S. at 765–74, 105 S.Ct. at 2951–53, 86 L.Ed.2d at 609–12.

Nevertheless, in the preceding term, the Supreme Court in Bose Corporation v. Consumers Union, 466 U.S. 485, 104 S.Ct. 1949, 80 L.Ed.2d 502 (1984), by a vote of 6 to 3, gave a strong endorsement to the constitutional principles enunciated in New York Times Co. and its progeny a generation before, suggesting their long-term wisdom. And even with the changes in the makeup of the Court initiated by the retirement of Chief Justice Burger, there still appears at this writing to be a majority of justices committed to defending those principles.

The central issue in Bose was a procedural one involving the scope of a federal appellate court's review of a trial court's determination of actual malice on the part of a consumer magazine publisher. The publisher made an erroneous and derogatory statement about the quality of the sound delivered by the public figure plaintiff's newly designed stereo speaker system. The magazine reported that the sound of musical instruments heard through the speakers tended to wander "about the room" rather than "along the wall" between the speakers. But in the course of holding that a federal appellate court could make an independent determination of the mixed fact and constitutional law issue of actual malice, the Court plainly reaffirmed the constitutional privilege of New York Times Co. and said, "The statement in this case represents the sort of inaccuracy that is commonplace in the forum of robust debate to which the *New York Times* rule applies." 466 U.S. at 513, 104 S.Ct. at 1966, 80 L.Ed.2d at 525.

11. Attempts to "Get Around" New York Times

Because of the large burden placed upon public officials and public figures in libel cases, some enterprising plaintiffs' counsel have tried to avoid the "actual malice" standard and other requirements of defamation law by changing the designation of their claims. In Falwell v. Flynt, 797 F.2d 1270 (4th Cir. 1986), cert. granted ___ U.S. ___, 107 S.Ct. 1601, 94 L.Ed.2d 788 (1987), the Reverend Jerry Falwell sued "Hustler" Magazine publisher Larry Flynt for intentional infliction of emotional distress as well as libel because of a parody of an advertising campaign in which celebrities talk about their "first time," referring, of course, to their first encounter with Campari Liqueur. In Hustler's ad parody, Falwell, in a fictitious interview, allegedly details an incestuous "first time" with his mother in an outhouse. Mother and son are portrayed in the vilest of terms. At the bottom of the "ad" is a disclaimer which states "ad parody—not to be taken seriously."

The jury ruled for Flynt on Falwell's libel claim, finding that no reasonable person would believe that the parody was describing actual facts about the minister. But on the intentional emotional distress claim, the jury returned a substantial verdict for him.

On appeal, the Fourth Circuit affirmed the trial court decision for Falwell, holding that so long as the common law action for emotional distress required a standard of proof somewhat *analogous* to the actual malice standard of modern libel law, such cause of action was consistent with the First Amendment and could be maintained by a public figure against a member of the media.

There was a strong dissent from the full court's decision not to grant a rehearing en banc by Judge J. Harvie Wilkinson. See 805 F.2d 484 (4th Cir. 1986). Judge Wilkinson raised serious questions concerning the constitutionality of shielding public figures in the rough and tumble of politics from non-libelous attacks, even those designed to inflict great emotional distress. He stated flatly that "[O]ne simply cannot subject a parody of a political figure to a cause of action for emotional distress."

Nevertheless, William Peter Blatty, the author of "The Exorcist," also brought an action against a media defendant, The New York Times Company, of a nature similar to the one brought by the Reverend Falwell. Blatty's complaint against the Times was that the newspaper had failed to list his new novel "Legion" on its weekly list of best selling books despite the fact that it met all the criteria for such listing. He labeled one of his several causes of action as "intentional interference with prospective economic advantage." But ultimately the California Supreme Court viewed the claim as one for injurious falsehood and re-

quired Blatty to meet the identification requirement of libel law that a complained of communication be "of and concerning" the plaintiff and, of
course, Blatty could not do this. Blatty v. New
York Times Co., 42 Cal.3d 1033, 232 Cal.Rptr. 542,
728 P.2d 1177 (1986).

According to the Califonia court, unless causes of
action based on injurious false statements meet all
the criteria of modern libel actions they will run
afoul of the First Amendment. Blatty had cited
Falwell v. Flynt, supra, to counter this conclusion
since that case permitted substitution of an analogous standard for that of "actual malice" required
in libel cases by New York Times Co. v. Sullivan.
The California Supreme Court responded by saying
that Falwell was wrongly decided and would not be
followed.

Given the rather transparent efforts of plaintiffs'
attorneys to circumvent First Amendment standards by utilizing tort labels other than libel, the
well-reasoned dissent by Judge Wilkinson in
Falwell, the outright rejection of the approach by
the California Supreme Court in Blatty and the
recent strong reaffirmation of New York Times v.
Sullivan in Bose Corp. v. Consumers Union, 466
U.S. 485, 104 S.Ct. 1949, 80 L.Ed.2d 502 (1984) and
Philadelphia Newspapers, Inc. v. Hepps, 475 U.S.
767, 106 S.Ct. 1558, 89 L.Ed.2d 783 (1986), it is very
likely that the push to designate torts other than
libel based on injurious falsehood will ultimately
prove unsuccessful.

12. Miscellaneous Constitutional Privileges Claimed by Journalists in Defamation Cases

a. Nondisclosure of the Editorial Decision Making Process

In Herbert v. Lando, 441 U.S. 153, 99 S.Ct. 1635, 60 L.Ed.2d 115 (1979), a CBS news producer involved in the production and broadcast of "Sixty Minutes" claimed a First Amendment right not to divulge his state of mind in the preparation of a segment about Army Col. Anthony Herbert and his conduct during the Vietnam War. Col. Herbert, who did not contest his status as a public figure, claimed that the material in the segment was defamatory and was put together in a knowingly untruthful way or with reckless disregard of the truth. He attempted to establish this necessary element of malice in the course of a pretrial deposition of CBS News producer Lando. The United States District Court rejected Lando's claim of privilege and ordered him to answer Herbert's questions, but a divided United States Court of Appeals reversed.

The United States Supreme Court reversed the court of appeals and ruled that no First Amendment privilege existed to protect newspersons from testifying as to the editorial process when such testimony is material to the proof of a critical element of the plaintiff's action, here defendant's malice, i.e., knowing untruthfulness or reckless disregard of the truth.

Lando must answer the ques as to his state of mind during prep of the segment

In public figure cases, the plaintiff's inquiry into the editorial process may therefore include:

  1. the reporter's or editor's conclusions during research and investigation regarding people or leads to be pursued or not pursued;

  2. the reporter's or editor's conclusions about facts imparted by interviewees and his or her state of mind with respect to the veracity of the persons interviewed;

  3. the basis for the reporter's or editor's conclusions as to the veracity of persons or information.

  4. conversations with journalistic colleagues and others concerning the manner in which a story should be approached, handled and published, particularly discussions as to the inclusion and exclusion of material;

  5. the reporter's or editor's intentions as manifested by his decisions to include or exclude particular material.

While it is now clear after the Herbert case that no privilege exists under the First Amendment for newspersons to refuse to reveal the information listed above, at least one state reporter "shield" law has been construed as protecting newspersons from testifying as to editorial processes on the ground that forced revelations in this area would have a chilling effect on the free exchange of ideas between journalistic colleagues. Maressa v. New Jersey Monthly, 89 N.J. 176, 445 A.2d 376 (1982).

b. Neutral Reportage

An official of the National Audubon Society gave a reporter for the New York Times a list of five scientists whom the Society believed were being paid by the chemical industry to lie about the impact of DDT on the bird population. The story concerning the bird count with the names of the five scientists was subsequently published by the Times and three of the named scientists filed libel actions against the Society, Society officials and the Times.

In reversing the jury award and judgment against the Times, the United States Court of Appeals for the Second Circuit held that the First Amendment protects the accurate and disinterested reporting of charges by a responsible and prominent person or organization, regardless of the reporter's private views regarding their accuracy. Such protection of journalists from tort liability for defamation was characterized by the Second Circuit as "neutral reportage." Edwards v. National Audubon Society, 556 F.2d 113 (2d Cir. 1977), cert. denied 434 U.S. 1002, 98 S.Ct. 647, 54 L.Ed.2d 498. See also Medico v. Time, Inc., 643 F.2d 134, 145 (3d Cir. 1981), cert. denied 454 U.S. 836, 102 S.Ct. 139, 70 L.Ed.2d 116 (1981). In a subsequent case the Second Circuit made clear that the repetition of defamatory charges in a piece of advocacy journalism espousing and concurring in such charges did not constitute neutral reportage and was not con-

stitutionally pr̲o̲t̲e̲c̲t̲e̲d̲. Cianci v. New York Times
Publishing Co., 639 F.2d 54 (2d Cir. 1980).

Ultimate recognition of such a First Amendment
privilege by the Supreme Court is highly doubtful
because, at least in part, it flies in the face of St.
Amant v. Thompson, 390 U.S. 727, 88 S.Ct. 1323,
20 L.Ed.2d 262 (1968), which would deny First
Amendment protection under New York Times v.
Sullivan to those who would publish defamatory
material while entertaining serious doubts as to
the truth of the publication. See Dickey v. CBS,
Inc., 583 F.2d 1221 (3d Cir. 1978) rejecting the
neutral reportage privilege for this reason.

It seems unlikely that the Supreme Court would
deny the constitutional privilege recognized in
New York Times Co. to one who published a damaging charge he or she strongly suspected to be
untrue but then substitute another constitutional
privilege to protect one who, with reckless disregard for the truth, publishes the charge simply
because it came from a reputable and prominent
source. And if the publisher does not suspect the
story is untrue, he or she will be protected under
the New York Times Co. privilege if the target of
the charges is a public figure in relation to the
controversy, without regard to "neutral reportage."

Newspersons, therefore, may find the neutral
reportage privilege to be a very weak reed to rely
on when publishing questionable charges made by
even responsible sources.

CHAPTER III

PRIVACY AND THE MASS MEDIA

A. INTRODUCTION

The invasion of personal privacy by government, private organizations and the mass media has reached monumental proportions in the last decades of the twentieth century. This invasion is almost inevitable given our crowded society and the development of sophisticated electronic devices such as directional microphones, powerful miniature listening devices, telephoto lenses and the all-pervasive computer with its power to store and retrieve the minutiae of our lives. The problem is exacerbated by the power of the mass media to disseminate widely information about individuals, including their physical images.

The difficulty that confronts the law is to control this invasion without, at the same time, crippling a free society's ability to obtain the information necessary for its proper operation. Thus far, the common law has not been very effective in harmonizing the competing private and societal interests. Perhaps this is because the competing interests are so fundamental yet so difficult of definition. It has been said that the right to be let alone and to withdraw from the "madding crowd" is the essence

116

of individualism and that privacy is the first interest to go in a totalitarian state. Nevertheless, the
individual lives in a society which may, from time
to time, have curiosity about him or her. And the
mass media may become the instrument for satis-
fying that curiosity. As difficult as the task is, it is
for the law to determine when public interest concerning an individual fulfills a legitimate need of a
democratic society and when it does not.

B. COMMON LAW DEVELOPMENT

1. History

As common law torts go, invasion of privacy is of
relatively recent vintage. Its development is trace-
able to an article in the Harvard Law Review for
December 15, 1890 by Samuel D. Warren and his
then law partner Louis D. Brandeis. In it they
argued that accepted tort doctrine confirmed the
existence of a right to privacy, the violation of
which was actionable. 4 Harv.L.Rev. 193 (1890).
The article was apparently precipitated by the
Boston newspapers' coverage of Warren's private
social affairs. It should be remembered that this
was the era of vicious circulation battles and sensational and often fraudulent press coverage to win
readership—the age of "yellow journalism."

The article created great interest in the legal
profession but the first test of the theory was
unsuccessful. In Roberson v. Rochester Folding
Box Co., 171 N.Y. 538, 64 N.E. 442 (1902) a flour
mill ordered a woman's portrait lithographed on its

boxes without her consent. The woman, who did not relish being referred to as the "Flour of the Family" brought suit for damages for invasion of privacy. In a four-to-three ruling, the New York Court of Appeals held, contrary to Warren and Brandeis' contention, no right of privacy existed at common law. If interests in privacy were to be protected, the legislatures would have to do it. The New York legislature did just that the following year by enacting a civil rights statute making it both a crime and a tort to appropriate the name or likeness of any person for "trade purposes" without that person's consent.

The first judicial acceptance of the existence of a right to privacy came in Pavesich v. New England Life Insurance Co., 122 Ga. 190, 50 S.E. 68, 69 L.R.A. 101 (1905), a case very much like Roberson in which a newspaper advertisement for an insurance company contained a photograph of the plaintiff and attributed to him certain words encouraging the purchase of the company's life insurance. He had not consented to such depiction and sued the company. Contrary to the New York court the Georgia Supreme Court found a right of privacy in the common law and reversed the trial court's order dismissing Pavesich's complaint.

2. The Common Law Today

As of 1986 a common law right of privacy of some dimension was recognized in 46 states and the District of Columbia according to a study done by the Reporters Committee for Freedom of the Press. Four states, Nebraska, Rhode Island, Virginia and Wisconsin recognize the right only by statute. The right that is accorded varies to some extent in definition and scope from jurisdiction to jurisdiction, reflecting the immaturity of the tort and its imperfect development to date or conflicting legislative interests.

The imperfect development extends to the lack of any articulated theory of liability. While the tort in several of its forms is suggestive of an intentional civil wrong, it is possible that some aspects of it permit strict liability. The uncertainty as to the theory of liability may arise from the fact that the tort has four distinct branches:

(a) appropriation of another's name or likeness;

(b) unreasonable intrusion upon another's seclusion;

(c) publicity which unreasonably places another in a false light before the public; and

(d) unreasonable publicity given to another's private life.

See Cox Broadcasting Corp. v. Cohn, 420 U.S. 469, 493–94, 95 S.Ct. 1029, 1045–1046, 43 L.Ed.2d 328, 348–49 (1975); Restatement of Torts 2d 652A– 652E; W. Prosser and W. Keeton, Handbook of the Law of Torts, 851–866 (5th ed. 1984).

a. Appropriation

We have already come across this aspect of the right of privacy in relation to the Roberson and Pavesich cases and the New York statute. What is protected here is the individual's concern for the uses to which his or her name, personality and image are put. The law gives the individual the option to prevent others from trading on his or her name or likeness or to permit such trading for a price. In this respect the tort appears to protect something akin to a property right in one's own personality and image—a right of publicity.

The media are rarely sued for appropriation type invasions. It has long been settled that while the media normally disseminate news about individuals in the hope, overall, of obtaining a profit for their operations from circulation and advertising, this is not such appropriation as would justify the award of damages.

When such suits are brought they are usually in connection with a medium's self promotion in which a news or feature story involving the plaintiff is republished to evidence the medium's self-proclaimed excellence in informing the public. For instance, in Booth v. Curtis Publishing Co., 15 App.Div.2d 343, 223 N.Y.S.2d 737 (1962), affirmed 11 N.Y.2d 907, 228 N.Y.S.2d 468, 182 N.E.2d 812, the actress Shirley Booth, whose photograph had appeared by consent in Holiday Magazine in connection with an article about a prominent resort in Jamaica where she had been a guest, sued the magazine's publisher when it reproduced her photograph in full-page promotional advertisements for the magazine published in two other periodicals. Both advertisements presented the striking photograph of Miss Booth in a large straw hat and up to her neck in water as a sample of the contents of Holiday. Beneath the photograph were the words "Shirley Booth and chapeau, from a recent issue of Holiday." But even here, the court refused to award damages under the New York privacy statute because such advertising was only "incidental" to the sale and dissemination of news. The decision turned on the court's construction of the statute and it is uncertain that a similar case would have the same resolution in jurisdictions recognizing a common law right of privacy. Prudence therefore dictates that when a medium advertises itself by use of antecedent news and feature stories and photographs it obtain the permission for republication from the individuals involved.

b. Intrusion

(1) Common Law

This tort consists of the unconsented to violation of one's legally protected physical sphere of privacy. The intrusion may or may not also constitute the tort of trespass. Often the intrusion itself is not physical but consists of eavesdropping with telephoto lenses or electronic listening devices in areas private to the aggrieved individual such as his or her home or office. When the individual is in a public zone, however, he or she may be photographed or otherwise recorded without fear of legal action so long as the recordation is reasonable.

This particular aspect of invasion of privacy is different in nature from the other three in that no publication regarding the victim need be involved. This distinction is important when through an intrusion a news medium learns of matters of public interest and publishes them. In that situation, while the publication itself may be privileged on the basis of newsworthiness (see pp. 136–137 infra), the intrusion that made the story possible is not.

An excellent and fortunately rare example of media intrusion is Dietemann v. Time, Inc., 449 F.2d 245 (9th Cir. 1971). There, a male and female employee of Life Magazine went to the home of Dietemann, a plumber who practiced healing with clay, minerals and herbs. Through misrepresentations of fact they gained entry to the plaintiff's home. Once inside, the female employee complained to Dietemann of a lump in her breast. While examining the breast, with an assortment of gadgets, Dietemann was secretly photographed by Life's male employee using a hidden camera. In addition, the conversation between the woman and Dietemann was transmitted by a radio transmitter hidden in the woman's purse to a tape recorder in a parked car occupied by another Life employee and officials from the local district attorney's office and the California Department of Health. The whole affair was a cooperative venture of Life and the public officals to aid in the crackdown on quackery in Southern California and to allow the magazine to write about it. Life published its story and pictures following Dietemann's plea of nolo contendere to criminal misdemeanor charges.

Dietemann thereafter sued for invasion of privacy and won a trial court judgment for $1,000. In contending on appeal that the judgment should be reversed, Time, Inc. took the position that the First Amendment immunized it from liability for its intrusion because its employees were using the secret devices to gather news. In answer Judge Hufstedler pointed out that the First Amendment has never been construed to accord newspersons immunity from the consequences of torts or crimes committed in the process of newsgathering. In affirming the judgment for Dietemann, Judge Hufstedler clearly distinguished between the intrusion and the subsequent publication of the story and photographs. A privilege might exist for the publication but it does not extend to the antecedent intrusion.

Dietemann is a troubling case not so much because of its denial of any privilege to intrude in the course of bona fide newsgathering but because it raises questions as to the extent to which newsgatherers, especially investigative reporters may go before they are liable for intrusion. As media lawyer Floyd Abrams has said, "It is one thing to

say that as a general matter one's home is sacro-
sanct from invasion by outsiders and that journalists are as responsible as the rest of us for illegal or
improper eavesdropping . . . .

"It is quite another to conclude that when a person
passes himself off as a doctor and uses his home as
his office, journalists may not act as prospective
patients and record the illegal activities that occur
there." F. Abrams, "The Press, Privacy and the
Constitution," N. Y. Times Magazine, Aug. 21,
1977, p. 68.

There is great uncertainty as to the line between
legality and intrusion regarding admission to private property. But as a result of recent cases we
do know that:

(1) outright misrepresentation by newsgatherers to gain initial entry to private or even
public property is a very risky business and
should not be resorted to except in extremis;

(2) unauthorized entry by newsgatherers onto
private or public property constitutes intrusion
as to individuals present and trespass as to the
property, and that goes for private places of
public accommodation as well;

(3) permission of relevant public officials provides the necessary license to gather news in
public buildings;

(4) permission by police or fire officials to
newsgatherers to accompany the officials onto
private property while they conduct official busi-

ness in the absence of the owner will insulate newsgatherers against tort liability in Florida and very probably elsewhere (see Florida Publishing Co. v. Fletcher, 340 So.2d 914 (Fla.1976), cert. denied, 431 U.S. 930, 97 S.Ct. 2634, 53 L.Ed. 2d 245 (1977).

While Dietemann and other recent cases make clear the danger of intrusive behavior by representatives of the media, they are limited to situations in which media representatives are directly involved. In situations in which the media simply publicize the fruits of another's intrusion the courts have usually rejected the idea of liability on the part of the media. For instance in Pearson v. Dodd, 133 U.S.App.D.C. 279, 410 F.2d 701 (1969) employees of Senator Dodd rifled his files, made copies of some allegedly incriminating documents and turned the copies over to defendant Jack Anderson, who was aware of the manner in which they were obtained, and who subsequently published excerpts from them. The United States Court of Appeals held that the defendants had not themselves been guilty of any intrusion. See also Liberty Lobby, Inc. v. Pearson, 129 U.S.App.D.C. 74, 390 F.2d 489 (1968).

The position taken in the Dodd case makes considerable sense. If the media were required to consider the means by which news is obtained by independent sources out of fear for tort liability, the newsgathering process would be severely hampered. But it should be kept in mind that if media representatives actually encourage or aid and abet others in acts of intrusion, it is reasonably certain that they and their corporate employers will be held liable for such conduct under ordinary principles of tort law.

While outright intrusion by the media into the privacy of individuals is rare, an analogous problem is becoming increasingly frequent. Property owners may refuse to cooperate with newspersons, particularly television crews, seeking news on their premises. This raises the question whether media representatives have the right under the First Amendment to go without authorization upon private property or otherwise to utilize such property in the interest of obtaining news. The issue often comes up in connection with private property which is open to the public for business purposes. For example, a large new hotel in an eastern metropolitan area recently experienced a fire in which one of the hotel employees lost her life. A local television station sent a camera crew over to the hotel to film the after effects of the fire. The hotel management refused to permit the camera crew to enter the premises. The station news director told the crew to get into the hotel by subterfuge if necessary in order to get the story. The camera crew, sensing a serious legal problem, refused to follow orders and came away without the desired film.

The basic position of media executives in this kind of situation is that their representatives ought to be able to enter privately owned places of public accommodation along with the rest of the public and that if they are not allowed to enter, the flow of news will be constricted in violation of the First Amendment.

These arguments are doubtful for reasons suggested in the analogous case of Lloyd Corp., Ltd. v. Tanner, 407 U.S. 551, 92 S.Ct. 2219, 33 L.Ed.2d 131 (1972), involving the distribution of handbills protesting the draft and the Vietnam War in a privately owned mall-type shopping complex. First, the public's license to enter a private business establishment is limited to engaging in activities directly related to that business and does not normally extend to the pursuit of unrelated business, e.g., newsgathering or propagandizing customers. See Le Mistral, Inc. v. Columbia Broadcasting System, 61 A.D.2d 491, 402 N.Y.S.2d 815 (1978), in which the defendant was held liable for trespass when its employees in search of a story concerning health code violations entered a restaurant with camera rolling and bright lights blazing without permission. And cf. Hudgens v. N.L.R.B., 424 U.S. 507, 96 S.Ct. 1029, 47 L.Ed.2d 196 (1976), permitting a shopping mall owner to bar on his premises union picketing of a particular store involved in a labor contract dispute. Second, it is generally difficult to find state action when the ordinary property owner bars media representatives from using his or her property. The purpose of the First and Fourteenth Amendments is to protect freedom of expression from governmental encroachment only. Finally, even accepting the applicability of the First Amendment, the media's position assumes that First Amendment rights are always superior to common law property rights and statutory criminal trespass provisions. But given the current disposition of the Supreme Court and the revitalization of the balancing approach to the First Amendment this assumption is not necessarily correct.

(2) Federal Legislation

In recent years, the Congress has become increasingly concerned with governmental and private intrusions upon individual privacy. In the waning moments of the 99th Congress, the House and Senate finally enacted the "Electronic Communications Privacy Act of 1986," P.L. 99–508, 18 U.S.C.A. §§ 2510–21, which, in many cases, prohibits under criminal penalty (1) the intentional interception or attempted interception of wire, oral, or electronic communications; (2) the intentional use or attempted use of electronic, mechanical, or other device to intercept any oral communication in certain enumerated instances; (3) the intentional disclosure or attempted disclosure to others of the contents of wire, oral or electronic communication, by those knowing or having reason to know that the information was obtained through the interception of a wire, oral or electronic communication; and (4) the intentional use or attempted use of the contents of any wire, oral or electronic communication, by those knowing or having reason to know that the information was obtained through the interception of a wire, oral or electronic communication.

Civil actions are authorized for persons whose wire, oral or electronic communication are intercepted, disclosed, or intentionally used in violation of the act, and the United States Attorney General is authorized to initiate civil actions in the United States District Court to enjoin felony violations.

Law enforcement personnel and other government officers authorized to engage in electronic surveillance or, as in the case of employees of the Federal Communications Commission, to monitor electronic communications, are generally exempted from the provisions of the legislation when acting within their proper authority.

The same legislation also makes unlawful many acts of intentional unauthorized accessing of information storage facilities through which electronic communications services are provided, resulting in the obtaining or altering of information contained therein or the preventing of authorized access to the information while in electronic storage.

By this legislation, Congress has recognized the need to protect privacy of communication in our high technology-computer age.

The other important federal legislation in this field is the "Privacy Act of 1974," 5 U.S.C.A.

§ 552a. Because the purpose of this legislation is to curb abuses by the federal government in the handling and dissemination of information about individuals, it is discussed in the chapter on newsgathering and access to information by the media. See Chapter VII, pp. 261–265, infra.

c. "False Light"

(1) Nature and Limitations

Creating a false image for an individual or placing him or her in a false light through publication may be actionable as an invasion of privacy whether or not such falsity involves defamation. One form of this invasion is to ascribe to individuals political or other views which they do not in fact hold or falsely to attribute to them authorship of certain writings or remarks. Another dangerous practice is to use an individual's photograph out of context. For example, in Leverton v. Curtis Publishing Co., 192 F.2d 974 (3d Cir. 1951), a photograph of the plaintiff, a child who had been struck down on a public street by a careless motorist, was properly published in a local newspaper because of its newsworthiness. But when the same news photograph was published several months later in the Saturday Evening Post to illustrate an article entitled "They Ask to Be Killed" dealing with childhood carelessness, the defendant publisher was found liable for placing the child in the false light of being a careless pedestrian.

Still another dangerous enterprise is the intentional fictionalization of activities or events involving actual identifiable persons. One book publisher discovered to its sorrow the cost of such venture
when it published a fictionalized biography of the
great baseball pitcher Warren Spahn. The book
dramatized and fictionalized such matters as
Spahn's relationship to his father, his war record,
his courtship with his wife and even his thoughts
while on the pitching mound. The author even
invented long dialogues between Spahn and those
with whom he associated. While the New York
trial court in Spahn v. Julian Messner, Inc., 43
Misc.2d 219, 250 N.Y.S.2d 529 (1964) cast its decision for Spahn in terms of the New York privacy
statute, i.e., appropriation of Spahn's image and
personality by the defendant for commercial advantage, the decree to enjoin further publication
and distribution of the book and to award substantial damages was ultimately upheld by the New
York Court of Appeals on a theory consistent with
that underlying the United States Supreme Court's
first decision in the area of invasion of privacy by
the media—Time, Inc. v. Hill, 385 U.S. 374, 87
S.Ct. 534, 17 L.Ed.2d 456 (1967).

The importance of the element of intention in
false light cases was underlined by the Supreme
Court in the Hill case. There, the complaining
parties, James J. Hill and his wife and five children, had become the involuntary subjects of a
front page news story after being held hostage by

three escaped convicts in their home for 19 hours in the late summer of 1952. The family was released unharmed and Hill stressed to newspersons at the time that the convicts had treated the family courteously and had neither molested anyone nor acted violently. After the incident Hill discouraged all media efforts to keep the family in the public spotlight. Less than a year later Joseph Hayes' novel, "The Desperate Hours," was published depicting the experience of a family of four held hostage by three escaped convicts in the family's home. But, unlike the Hill family's experience, the fictional family suffered violence at the hands of the convicts; the father and son were beaten and the daughter subjected to verbal sexual insult.

At this point a lawsuit by Hill against Hayes and his publisher for invasion of privacy would have been doubtful because of the difficulty of identifying the fictional family of four with the Hill family of seven. That difficulty was removed when, in conjunction with the production of a play based upon the book, Life magazine published an article indicating that the play "The Desperate Hours," actually mirrored the Hill family's experience. The article was accompanied by staged photographs taken in the house in which the Hill family had been held captive. The photographs dramatized supposed incidents during the family's ordeal.

Though there was no doubt that the Life article and photographs had placed Hill and his family in a false light, a closely divided Supreme Court reversed a lower court judgment awarding compensatory damages to Hill because the trial court's instructions to the jury failed to require that the plaintiff establish that the defendant either knew the facts creating the false light were untrue or that it acted in reckless disregard of the truth. Innocent mistake or negligence in creating the false light were held to be improper bases for liability under the First and Fourteenth Amendments. This ruling is obviously parallel to that in New York Times Co. v. Sullivan, 376 U.S. 254, 84 S.Ct. 710, 11 L.Ed.2d 686 (1964), discussed supra, at pp. 78–79.

Thus, only intentional or reckless falsification by the media is presently actionable in the false light area. Although successful actions will be less frequent as a result of the Hill case, there is little doubt that this branch of the tort still lives. Certainly, a knowing use of a photograph out of context as in Leverton would be actionable as would a fabricated biography like that in the Spahn case. Indeed, the Supreme Court has upheld a properly instructed jury's award of damages in a false light case, Cantrell v. Forest City Publishing Co., 419 U.S. 245, 95 S.Ct. 465, 42 L.Ed.2d 419 (1974).

(2) Relationship to Defamation

While not every false light case involves untruths that injure reputation, e.g., the Hill case, every act of defamation will, while injuring reputation, also place the victim in a false light in the public's mind. Indeed, many actions for defamation are accompanied by actions for invasion of privacy. This raises the intriguing question whether the defamation action might not eventually fall into disuse because of the comparatively greater ease in establishing false light. The defamatory character of false communication need not be shown and many technical requirements of defamation actions may be bypassed. But unless and until defamation actions fade away, both invasion of privacy and defamation should be pleaded in appropriate cases.

d. Public Disclosure of Private Facts

(1) Nature and Limitations

Of the four common law branches of the invasion of privacy tort the most troublesome is the unreasonable publication of private facts of an embarrassing and objectionable nature. It is not always easy for reporters and editors to determine when publicity is unreasonable or even when facts must be viewed as private. There is the further problem of determining when private facts will be viewed by a reasonable person of ordinary sensibilities as offensive and objectionable, thus making public disclosure actionable. Then, too, in contrast to false light, truth will not shield the disclosing medium since the gravamen of the tort is the publication of private *facts* which the law deems worthy of protection.

Illustrative of this type of case is Sidis v. F–R Publishing Corp., 113 F.2d 806 (2d Cir. 1940). William James Sidis was a child prodigy in the field of mathematics and graduated from Harvard College at the age of sixteen amid considerable public attention. A shy and retiring person, Sidis attempted to live down his fame and succeeded quite well until the New Yorker magazine for August 14, 1937, published a brief biographical sketch of Sidis under the title "Where Are They Now?" The sketch recounted Sidis' unusual background, traced his attempts to conceal his identity through the years, described his menial employment far from the field of mathematics and detailed certain bizarre conduct such as his collecting old street car transfers. The facts stated in the article were not alleged to be untrue. Rather, Sidis sued for the destruction of the obscurity he had so laboriously constructed for himself. His suit was unsuccessful because, among other things, the facts disclosed were held not of such nature as to be offensive and objectionable to persons of ordinary sensibilities.

The Sidis case is fairly typical of the result reached in cases brought in this area of invasion of privacy. While such cases are troublesome, only a handful of plaintiffs have met with success in the years since publication of Warren and Brandeis' article. The reason for this is the recognition by the courts of a very broad defense peculiar to this branch of the tort.

(2) The Newsworthiness Privilege

By this common law defense the media are protected in publishing truthful matters of public interest. By and large, the courts have deferred to the media in determining what is of public interest. The motto of the judiciary here might be, "If they publish it, it must be a matter of public interest." This approach has two major virtues, according to Professors Don R. Pember and Dwight L. Teeter, Jr. First, it provides a wide range of freedom of expression and second, it is easy to administer because the judge does not have to act as a social censor, determining what is of public interest and what is not. Pember and Teeter, "Privacy and the Press Since Time, Inc. v. Hill," 50 Wash.L.Rev. 57, 77 (1974).

Given such deference, the media would be protected in the exercise of news judgment in publishing almost anything true about individuals which has any colorable claim to the public's interest, including the repetition, for instance, of years-old sensational stories about ex-convicts and other formerly unsavory characters. Certainly the content of public records, which, almost by definition, involve matters of public interest, may be publicized under this privilege. There are limits to judicial tolerance, however, such as the publication without consent of a photograph showing the plaintiff emerging from a fun house with her dress blown above her waist by a jet of air (Daily Times Demo-

crat v. Graham, 276 Ala. 380, 162 So.2d 474 (1964))
or publication of the intimate details of a hospital-
ized woman's exotic and embarrassing disease together with a picture of her in her hospital bed
taken without consent (Barber v. Time, Inc., 348
Mo. 1199, 159 S.W.2d 291 (1942)). But normal
judicial deference to media news judgment explains the general lack of success of plaintiffs in
this area.

The major exception here is California whose
courts refuse to defer to the media on the issue of
newsworthiness and, since Melvin v. Reid, 112 Cal.
App. 285, 297 P. 91 (1931), have balanced the social
value in publicity against the interests of the individual in maintaining privacy. This balancing is
not unlike that engaged in by the Supreme Court
in the area of defamation. In Melvin a prostitute
charged with murder and subsequently acquitted
in a sensational trial had abandoned her former
life, married and assumed a place of respectability
in society. Seven years after the trial a motion
picture entitled "The Red Kimono" was produced
and distributed, truthfully depicting the unsavory
facts of the woman's earlier life and using her true
maiden name. Mrs. Melvin sued for invasion of
privacy. The California court ruled that while
presentation of the events of the plaintiff's past
was permissible since they were matters of public
record, the producer had no right to identify the
plaintiff with these events because she had abandoned her former ways and had rehabilitated her-

self. To like effect is Briscoe v. Reader's Digest Association, 4 Cal.3d 529, 93 Cal.Rptr. 866, 483 P.2d 34 (1971) (exposure of a rehabilitated man's crime of truck hijacking eleven years after its commission).

Obviously relevant to such judicial balancing is the social value of the information published, the lapse of time between the matter in question and its publication, the manner and context in which it is publicized and the effect on the individual of the unwanted publicity. The latter factor seems to have weighed heavily in the Melvin and Briscoe cases because of the judicial fear that publicity might seriously affect efforts at rehabilitation.

Eventually, the time lapse factor may be the one that has the most impact on the availability of the newsworthiness privilege. Journalists often publish accounts of past events embarrassing to the participants in "where are they now" and other type feature stories or columns. While the original stories may be defended as being newsworthy because of their contemporaneousness, doubt has been expressed about the availability of the privilege when the stories have lost their immediacy. This doubt is increased by Justice Blackmun's concurring opinion in Wolston v. Reader's Digest Association, Inc., 443 U.S. 157, 99 S.Ct. 2701, 61 L.Ed.2d 450 (1979), discussed in greater detail at pp. 100–101, supra. There, Blackmun presented a legal theory in a defamation case that may have relevance to the time lapse factor. He argued that the substantial passage of time can change a former limited issue public figure into a private one. If that is so then a parallel case can be made for the erosion of the newsworthiness privilege in a given case with the passage of time and the consequently greater protection for the individual newsmaker's right of privacy as the embarrassing news event fades into the past.

Even if authorities who take the position that the press is generally protected against liability when it publishes accounts of past news events are correct (see, e.g., Pember, The Burgeoning Scope of "Access Privacy" and the Portent for a Free Press, 64 Iowa L.Rev. 1155, 1185–1186 (1979)), such republication is a fertile ground for litigation and the expenditure by the media of considerable time, energy and money.

Until First Amendment protection is accorded the media in cases like Sidis, Barber, Melvin and the time lapse cases, journalists should approach the intimate and embarrassing facts of an individual's past or even present life with caution and exercise discretion in publishing such material. In this area good taste is the watchword.

e. Common Characteristics of the Branches

While it is useful to an understanding of the tort of invasion of privacy to recognize the existence of its four branches, it must also be recognized that these branches often overlap each other or are bound up together. For instance, the same act of appropriating a woman's name and photograph for an advertisement endorsing a particular brand of whiskey may also place her in a false light as a serious drinker of alcoholic beverages. And an act of intrusion such as in the Dietemann case may be followed by publication of private information.

Moreover, the similarities between the branches probably outweigh the differences. The tort is a personal one in all of its manifestations and normally dies with the complaining party. The only apparent qualification is a deceased person's image or persona becoming so desirable for commercial exploitation that a transferable property right in the image may be held to have been created as in the case of the actor Bela Lugosi's image as Count Dracula or the Marx Brothers' show business persona. But even here there is a split of authority. The majority view is that such interest is descendible if it was exploited during the celebrity's lifetime. See M. Simensky and T. Selz, Descendibility of the Right of Publicity, 1 ABA Entertainment and Sports Lawyer p. 1 (No. 4, Spring 1983). What is "exploitation" qualifying celebrity persona for descendibility is a difficult question of fact that must be decided on a case-by-case basis.

Whatever the invasion the damages recoverable to the plaintiff are the same: (1) general damages; (2) special damages, though in contrast to slander or libel per quod they are not required; and (3) punitive damages, upon a showing of malice in the form of ill will, spite or improper motive.

Finally, there are certain defenses common to all four branches. The most obvious is consent. If the plaintiff can be found to have consented to the alleged invasion, the defendant's conduct is not actionable. Rarely in these cases will the plaintiff's alleged consent be express and unequivocal. With this defense the question for the trier of fact is normally whether the plaintiff's words or deeds implied consent to the defendant's appropriation, intrusion, false characterization or publication of private information.

The other common defense is that of privilege. It is generally accepted that the privileges recognized in the law of defamation are included in the law of privacy. If the circumstances would protect the publication of false and defamatory material, then the publication of truthful material is also protected.

C. THE CONSTITUTION AND PRIVACY

1. Applicability of First Amendment Theory to Appropriation and Intrusion Cases

It is now clear after the Supreme Court's decision in Zacchini v. Scripps-Howard Broadcasting Co., 433 U.S. 562, 97 S.Ct. 2849, 53 L.Ed.2d 965 (1977) that no First Amendment protection is afforded newsgathering organizations which appropriate the name, image, persona or unique presence of an individual, thus invading the individual's so-called right of publicity. Zacchini performed a "human cannonball" act in which he was shot into a safety net 200 feet away. Over his objection his act, presented at a local county fair, was videotaped by a reporter for the defendant's television station and was shown on a news program later the same day. Zacchini sued the broadcasting company for unlawful appropriation of his professional property.

While Zacchini was unsuccessful in the trial court, the United States Supreme Court ultimately upheld Zacchini's right to seek damages against the defendant. The Court held that the defendant's conduct invaded both Zacchini's right to earn a living as an entertainer and society's interest in encouraging creative activity. The First and Fourteenth Amendments were not designed to protect conduct of a newsgatherer which interferes with an individual's right to earn money by publicizing himself.

The rationale of the Court in refusing First Amendment protection to the newsgatherer who violates an individual's right of publicity is that news and information will not be denied the public in this type of situation because the individual will make it available to the public but for a price which he or she has a legally protected right to exact.

As for intrusion, since it involves no publication in and of itself, the First Amendment is not directly implicated. And as Judge Hufstedler said in Dietemann v. Time, Inc., 449 F.2d 245, 249 (9th Cir. 1971), "The First Amendment is not a license to trespass, to steal, or to intrude by electronic means into the precincts of another's home or office" simply because such means are used by media representatives in the course of newsgathering.

2. Applicability of First Amendment Theory to False Light Cases

In marked contrast to the appropriation and intrusion branches, the Constitution does place limits on the reach of the false light tort because of its potential to interfere with publication and restrict the flow of news and information to the public. The analogy with defamation impelled a bare majority of the Supreme Court in Time, Inc. v. Hill, 385 U.S. 374, 87 S.Ct. 534, 17 L.Ed.2d 456 (1967) to limit recovery in false light cases to those situations in which the falsity was known to the defendant or the communication was made by him or her in reckless disregard for the truth. The concern of the majority was to provide a margin for error for the media in gathering and reporting the news.

While the Hill case was narrowly decided after oral arguments in two successive terms of the Court, its basic First Amendment thrust was confirmed by a broad majority of the Court in Cantrell v. Forest City Publishing Co., 419 U.S. 245, 95 S.Ct. 465, 42 L.Ed.2d 419 (1974). Yet the Court in Cantrell did raise, without deciding, the question whether, parallel to Gertz v. Robert Welch, Inc., 418 U.S. 323, 94 S.Ct. 2997, 41 L.Ed.2d 789 (1974), a state might constitutionally limit Hill by applying a more relaxed standard of liability, i.e., negligence, for the communication of false light type statements injurious to private persons. The very act of questioning the scope of the ruling in Hill suggests that the Court may be disposed to limit the protection afforded the media in this area in much the same way it did with the protection originally afforded in the New York Times Co.- Rosenbloom line of defamation cases (see Chapter II, supra).

Without waiting for the Supreme Court to clarify its position, at least one state court, the West Virginia Supreme Court, has held that it is free to set negligence as the standard in false light cases involving private persons. Crump v. Beckley Newspapers, 320 S.E.2d 70 (W.Va.1984). See also Wood v. Hustler Magazine, Inc., 736 F.2d 1084 (5th Cir. 1984) (applying a negligence standard under supposed Texas law), cert. denied 469 U.S. 1107, 105 S.Ct. 783, 83 L.Ed.2d 777 (1985).

Because of the essential element of falsity involved in the Hill and Cantrell cases the constitutional doctrine formulated therein seems clearly confined to false light theory and should have little impact on the evolving constitutional law relevant to invasion of privacy involving publication of private matters. But for a contrasting view see Nimmer, "The Right to Speak from *Times* to *Time:* First Amendment Theory Applied to Libel and Misapplied to Privacy," 56 Cal.L.Rev. 935 (1968).

3. Applicability of First Amendment Theory to Public Disclosure of Private Facts

The applicability of First Amendment protection to the invasion of privacy tort seems most compelling in the case of communications involving truthful matters of a private and embarrassing or harmful nature. Without broad constitutional protection here the media can be required under existing tort law to respond in damages for truthfully informing the public about certain matters which individual plaintiffs consider private. As with false light the potential threat of damages could have a chilling effect on the enterprise of the media in gathering and disseminating news about individuals.

The issue here is whether the First and Fourteenth Amendments mandate the recognition of truth as an absolute defense in invasion of privacy cases. This broad issue was raised though not decided in Cox Broadcasting Corp. v. Cohn, 420 U.S. 469, 95 S.Ct. 1029, 43 L.Ed.2d 328 (1975). There, a reporter for an Atlanta television station learned the name of a 17-year-old gang rape victim during the course of the proceedings against the rapists by examining the indictments, which had been made available by the clerk of the court. Later the same day the reporter broadcast a news report concerning the court proceedings and named the deceased victim of the crime. Shortly after the broadcast the father of the victim brought a civil action for damages against the reporter and his company, relying on a Georgia statute which prohibited the media from communicating the name or identity of any female who is raped and made such communication a misdemeanor. The trial court rejected the broadcasters' claim that their report was constitutionally privileged and entered summary judgment for the plaintiff father, who claimed his own privacy had been invaded by the broadcast.

The Georgia Supreme Court initially held that the statute did not create a civil cause of action but that the plaintiff had stated a cause of action under the common law of invasion of privacy. Holding also that summary judgment was improper the Georgia court remanded the case for trial. Consistent with this latter holding the court ruled that the First and Fourteenth Amendments did not require that truth be a complete defense in every invasion of privacy action. On motion for rehearing the broadcasters argued that they were privileged to publish the victim's name because it was a matter of public interest. In countering this argument the court upheld the statutory prohibition as a legitimate limitation on the right of freedom of expression contained in the First Amendment.

On appeal to the United States Supreme Court the defendant broadcasters sought a broad holding that the press may not be made criminally or civilly liable for publishing information that is absolutely accurate, however damaging or embarrassing it may be to individual sensibilities. While

gaining a reversal the broadcasters lost their bid
for a sweeping privilege for the media when the
Court refused to go beyond ruling that both the
common law and the First and Fourteenth Amendments protected mass dissemination of truthful
matters contained in public records open to public
inspection, including indictments and other judicial papers.

The effect of the Supreme Court's narrow decision in Cox Broadcasting Corp. is to leave uncertain the constitutionality of the Georgia statute
and similar statutes in Florida, South Carolina and
Wisconsin insofar as they make punishable the
identification of rape victims when such identification is not a matter of public record. Similarly,
the common law rules permitting recovery of damages for the publication of truthful but embarrassing or harmful private information are left in
doubt.

Obviously, the issue whether the Constitution
mandates truth to be a complete defense in these
cases will have to be faced by the Supreme Court
eventually. At that time the Court could defer to
the media and hold that whatever is accurately
published about anyone is constitutionally privileged. Such approach is akin to the Black-Douglas
absolutist view of the First Amendment. Or the
Court might adopt Professor Meiklejohn's approach and ask if the particular truthful communication is important to the process of self-government. If the answer were "yes" then First

Amendment protection would be afforded. If the answer were "no," the states would be free to recognize a cause of action and permit the award of damages. Under this approach there will always be a degree of uncertainty prior to litigation concerning the legality of truthful communications.

Even greater uncertainty for the media would be engendered by the Court balancing competing interests on an ad hoc basis. Under this approach the communication of truthful but embarrassing matters of public interest could result in judgments against the media if it were found that the competing interest in individual privacy in particular cases outweighed the media's interest in free expression. Who could say in advance of litigation whether the media's interest in communicating the details of a rape, including the victim's identification, would outweigh her interest in avoiding further pain and embarrassment through public disclosure?

Such balancing was engaged in by the United States Court of Appeals for the Ninth Circuit. In Virgil v. Time, Inc., 527 F.2d 1122 (9th Cir. 1975), cert. denied 425 U.S. 998, 96 S.Ct. 2215, 48 L.Ed.2d 823 (1976), the plaintiff had been interviewed by a reporter for an article on body surfers practicing their sport at a California beach reputed to be the most dangerous site for body surfing in the world. When the plaintiff learned that the article to be published in Sports Illustrated would involve his lifestyle as well as his sport, he expressly revoked his consent to being mentioned in the article. The magazine published the article anyway and the publisher sought summary judgment when the surfer sued, in part on the ground that the facts detailed about him were true. In upholding the trial court's denial of summary judgment, the Ninth Circuit rejected the idea that truth is always a complete defense when private facts about an individual are published. Only if those facts are newsworthy and not merely the subject of the public's idle curiosity would the defense obtain. While recognizing that its decision posed serious judgmental problems for the news media, the Court said, "Where competing values are involved . . . unless one competitor is to be sacrificed outright . . . [the press] must accept that risks are inherent and the problem lies in attempting to minimize them to the extent that the conflict permits." 527 F.2d at 1129–1130.

Given the balancing approach taken by the Supreme Court in recent years, the availability of very respectable direct authority for a balancing approach found in the California cases, beginning with Melvin v. Reid, supra, and the decision of the Ninth Circuit, we would conclude that such approach is the one most likely to be embraced by the High Court should the issue present itself in the foreseeable future.

CHAPTER IV

RESTRAINT OF OBSCENE EXPRESSION

A. GENERAL THEORY

1. The Definitional Problem

Western societies generally seem to have a preoccupation with suppression of explicit public discussion or depiction of sexual matters. And English speaking societies are no exception. Censorship and confiscation of sexually obscene materials and even prison sentences may be the lot of the professional or amateur pornographer. There are those in positions of authority who would characterize all public expression concerning sex as obscene and suppress or punish it, but the prevailing view in this country is to the contrary and clearly not all sexual expression is condemned.

This view has within it the seeds of confusion because it requires a definition of what is obscene. And because obscenity, like beauty, is in the mind of the beholder, a precise definition seems beyond the reach of the law. Even the 1986 report of the United States Attorney General's commission on pornography fails to define it. It may be that the only honest test for obscenity is the one authored by the late Supreme Court Justice Stewart, "I know it when I see it."   Jacobellis v. Ohio, 378 U.S. 184, 197, 84 S.Ct. 1676, 1683, 12 L.Ed.2d 793, 804 (1964).   Because the First Amendment requires more than instinctual reaction to suppress and punish obscene expression, the Supreme Court has spent the last twenty or more years attempting to separate the chaff of obscenity from the wheat of protected sexual expression.

2. Background

Attempts at suppressing the dissemination of obscenity were sporadic in both England and the United States until shortly after the end of the American Civil War.   At that time the English judiciary crystallized a standard for suppression which was by and large accepted in the United States.   Contemporaneously, the Congress enacted certain statutes advocated by the notorious bluenose Anthony Comstock prohibiting, with criminal penalties, the importation or mailing of materials characterized as obscene (now 18 United States Code, Sections 1461–1463).   Many of the states followed suit with their own criminal obscenity statutes.

The standard set down in the English case of Regina v. Hicklin, L.R. 3 Q.B. 360 (1868) was a very broad one: suspect material was to be judged by the effect of isolated passages upon persons particularly susceptible to prurient appeal or lustful thoughts.   The combination of the Comstock laws and the Hicklin test provided much work for the censors and the prosecutors. Occasionally, lower federal courts inveighed against the Hicklin test but it remained influential well into the twentieth century.

3. Modern Doctrinal Development

Until 1957 the Supreme Court, while assuming the constitutionality of attempts to suppress obscene expression in Near v. Minnesota, 283 U.S. 697, 716, 51 S.Ct. 625, 631, 75 L.Ed. 1357, 1367 (1931), had never definitively held that obscenity was beyond the pale of First and Fourteenth Amendment protection. In that year in Roth v. United States, 354 U.S. 476, 77 S.Ct. 1304, 1 L.Ed. 2d 1498 (1957) the Court so ruled, over the strong dissent of Justices Black and Douglas. The Court then considered the appropriate standard for separating protected expression from unprotected obscene expression. In affirming the conviction of Roth for sending obscene matter through the mails, the Court rejected the Hicklin standard because its concern for isolated passages and particularly susceptible individuals would result in the condemnation of much material legitimately and seriously dealing with sexual matters that ought to be protected by the First and Fourteenth Amendments. In its place the Court adopted the test whether to the *average* person, applying contemporary community standards, the dominant theme of the material taken as a *whole* appealed to prurient interest.

While this test or definition of obscenity is clearly narrower than Hicklin and has had some liberating influence regarding serious expression concerning sex, it still permits censorship and criminal punishment for mere incitation to impure sexual thoughts not shown to be related to overt antisocial conduct. In the years since the decision in Roth, shifting majorities and pluralities of the Court have had difficulty and shown dissatisfaction with the test laid down there because of the uncertainty in (1) gauging the psychic effect of specific material on mythical "average" persons; (2) measuring the dominance of particular obscene themes in large unified works such as books or motion pictures or collections of materials such as in magazines; (3) determining the relevant community to be referred to in judging the suspect material, i.e., local, state or national; and (4) protecting against the danger of condemnation of serious expression.

New tests were formulated and coupled with the Roth standard in an effort to meet these problems until in the celebrated "Fanny Hill" case, A Book Named "John Cleland's Memoirs of a Woman of Pleasure" v. Attorney General of Commonwealth of Massachusetts, 383 U.S. 413, 86 S.Ct. 975, 16 L.Ed.2d 1 (1966), a plurality of the Court announced a basic three-fold formulation to isolate obscenity: (1) a restatement of the Roth standard; (2) a test that the material be patently offensive because it affronts contemporary community standards relating to the description or representation of sexual matters; and (3) a test that the material be utterly without redeeming social value. Because the tests were stated in the conjunctive a censor or prosecutor was required to establish that the expression in question met all three. This would be extremely difficult to do.

The question inevitably arises in a free society whether almost unrestricted publication, distribution and exhibition of obscenity is too high a price to pay for the protection of serious expression concerning sex. This is a political question as well as a legal one and a large portion of the electorate appeared to answer the question in the affirmative in the election of 1968 when they elected as President Richard M. Nixon, a man who had publicly pledged to clean up the spreading pornography traffic. But his pledge could only be redeemed by changing the direction of the Supreme Court and this in turn would require new faces on the Court.

4. The Last Word on Obscenity (at Least for the Moment)

By 1973, Nixon had made four appointments to the Supreme Court and in that year the Court signaled a change in attitude toward attempts to suppress obscenity. In Miller v. California, 413 U.S. 15, 93 S.Ct. 2607, 37 L.Ed.2d 419 (1973) and Paris Adult Theatre I v. Slaton, 413 U.S. 49, 93 S.Ct. 2628, 37 L.Ed.2d 446 (1973) a five-person majority made up of the Nixon appointees, Chief Justice Burger, and Justices Blackmun, Powell and

Rehnquist together with Justice White, a Kennedy appointee, laid down new and tougher legal standards for dealing with the problem of obscenity and made clear that even "consenting adults" might not be exposed to "hard core" pornography. The following term the same five-person majority elaborated on these rulings in the important case of Jenkins v. Georgia, 418 U.S. 153, 94 S.Ct. 2750, 41 L.Ed.2d 642 (1974). For a fuller understanding of the Court's new position these three decisions are considered together.

In Miller, the petitioner had been convicted of mailing unsolicited sexually explicit material to persons in Orange County, California in violation of a California statute that approximately incorporated the tests for obscenity formulated in the Fanny Hill decision. The trial judge gave these tests to the jury and instructed them to evaluate the materials in light of the contemporary community standards of the state of California. The new Supreme Court majority affirmed Miller's conviction and did the following:

1. reaffirmed the holding in Roth that obscenity is not protected by the First and Fourteenth Amendments;

2. rejected important aspects of the tests set out in Fanny Hill, especially the "utterly without redeeming social value" standard and substituted its own conjunctive three-fold test to guide the trier of fact (normally the jury):

(a) whether the average person, applying contemporary community standards, would find the material taken as a whole, appeals to prurient interest (a restatement of the Roth test);

(b) whether the work depicts or describes, in a patently offensive way, sexual conduct specifically defined by the applicable state law; and

(c) whether the work, taken as a whole, lacks serious literary, artistic, political or scientific value;

3. indicated that only "hard core" pornography might be condemned under these tests and included in that classification for the guidance of legislative draftspersons patently offensive representations or descriptions of ultimate sexual acts, normal or perverted, actual or simulated and patently offensive representations or descriptions of masturbation, excretory functions and lewd exhibition of the genitals; and

4. held that hard core pornography is to be determined by reference to local or state community standards and not national standards.

In the companion case of Paris Adult Theatre, decided the same day, the Court upheld the right of states to enjoin the exhibition of motion pictures which are hardcore pornography under the Miller standards even when the exhibitor makes every effort to limit the audience to consenting adults.

In so ruling, the majority recognized that the states, and, by necessary extension, the United States, have a legitimate interest in shielding from the obscene not only the young and the unwilling but the consenting adult as well. This legitimate interest encompasses the elevation of the quality of life and the environment in the community, the tone of commerce in the cities and, arguably, the public safety itself. In this connection the majority refused to extend the individual constitutional right of privacy in personal heterosexual intimacies of the home (see Griswold v. Connecticut, 381 U.S. 479, 85 S.Ct. 1678, 14 L.Ed.2d 510 (1965)) to the viewing of pornography in a place of public adult accommodation. By this refusal, the Court avoided the necessity of balancing the state's recognized interest in preventing the exhibition of pornographic films against any individual privacy interest in viewing them.

In Miller, the Chief Justice said all he could, given the limitations of the English language, to prevent local suppression of serious expressions concerning sex. This did not inhibit the State of Georgia from convicting Billy Jenkins, the manager of a movie theater in Albany, Georgia for exhibiting the film "Carnal Knowledge," produced by a recognized group of serious movie makers, including director Mike Nichols and actor Jack Nicholson. Jenkins' conviction was affirmed by a divided Georgia Supreme Court which concluded that the

judgment accorded with the standards laid down in
Miller.

The Supreme Court, in holding "Carnal Knowledge" not obscene and reversing the conviction,
was forced to confront the paradox of differing
community standards delimiting the protection afforded by a national constitution. The Court first
made clear its commitment to local community
standards though indicating its willingness to accept statewide community standards if the states
should decide to use them instead.

The Court then turned to the state's contention
that under Miller, the obscenity of the film was a
question for the jury and that the jury having
resolved the question against Jenkins under the
evidence and pursuant to local community standards, the conviction should be affirmed. In other
words, the state was arguing that appellate review
of the constitutionality of the conviction was precluded so long as the jury was properly instructed
pursuant to the three-fold test laid down in Miller.
Here the Court simply held that the scope of protection afforded by the First and Fourteenth
Amendments was ultimately for it to decide and
substituted its own judgment regarding the nature
of the film for that of the local jury.

But the paradox remained troublesome and in
Pope v. Illinois, ___ U.S. ___, 107 S.Ct. 1918, 95
L.Ed.2d 439 (1987), the Court acknowledged that
one aspect of an obscenity prosecution under the
three-fold test of Miller v. California could not be

made the subject of local community standards but had to be governed by an objective national standard if the First Amendment were to be complied with. There, over objection of defendants charged with selling obscene magazines in violation of Illinois law, the state trial courts instructed the respective juries that in determining whether the magazines, taken as a whole, lacked serious literary, artistic, political or scientific value (the third prong of Miller), they were to judge the materials by the standard of "ordinary adults in the whole state." The defendants were convicted and their convictions were upheld on appeal.

On certiorari, the United States Supreme Court vacated the convictions and remanded the cases for further proceedings, ruling that while the first two prongs of Miller should be decided with reference to contemporary community standards, the third or "value" prong is to be judged by whether a reasonable person would or would not find such value in the materials, taken as a whole. The Court reasoned that "just as the ideas a work represents need not obtain majority approval to merit protection, neither, insofar as the First Amendment is concerned, does the value of the work vary from community to community based on the degree of local acceptance it has won." ___ U.S. at ___, 107 S.Ct. at 1921, 95 L.Ed.2d at 445. The jury instructions therefore violated the First and Fourteenth Amendments.

In retrospect, it appears that the Court, in a very indirect way, was suggesting in Jenkins v. Georgia the solution to the national standard-community standard paradox which it finally articulated clearly in Pope.

5. Effects of Miller, Paris Adult Theatre and Jenkins

The Miller, Paris Adult Theatre and Jenkins decisions have had considerable effect on the administration of state and federal obscenity statutes and free expression. The most important effect is to encourage prosecutors and censors to renew the fight against obscenity. In the Atlanta, Georgia area, for instance, one zealous prosecutor managed to close down all of the "adult" movie houses.

The very fact that convictions were affirmed in two of the three cases should hearten the anti-obscenity forces. Moreover, the Court in Paris Adult Theatre relaxed the evidentiary burden on the public officials charged with suppressing obscene expression. The material is now allowed to speak for itself and expert testimony as to its obscene nature is not required. In addition, proof that the material is utterly devoid of redeeming social value is no longer necessary. Now the prosecutor need only show that it is patently offensive and lacks serious literary, artistic, political or scientific value.

Conversely, the burden on the defendant to rebut the claim of obscenity is increased because evidence that the material in question is acceptable by national standards is relevant only to the "value" prong of the three-fold Miller test. As to the first two aspects of the test, the defendant must make out his or her case with expert testimony that it is acceptable locally or, as in Miller, state-wide. The sanctioning of local standards also encourages the anti-obscenity forces to shop for the most unsophisticated and intolerant localities within which to seek criminal or civil suppression of material. Of course, the Supreme Court, as it demonstrated in Jenkins and Pope, stands ready to correct the worst abuses arising out of the application of local standards. But not all abuses are likely to be corrected.

Another effect is to narrow the theoretical boundaries of unprotected expression set by the majority in Roth. After Roth, even serious material could be condemned if, taken as a whole, it appealed to the prurient interest of the average person. After Miller, this is theoretically impossible because one of the three tests laid down there requires the prosecutor or censor to establish that the material taken as a whole lacks serious literary, artistic, political or scientific value. Of course, more practically, the Court has now made it easier than it once was to prove lack of serious value.

The other test in Miller which could have the effect of narrowing the area of unprotected expression is that of patent offensiveness. The Court equates this to hard core pornography and gives some reasonably explicit examples of what it means by hard core expression. If the state legislatures and the Congress were to amend existing general obscenity statutes in conformity with Miller by including concrete statements of sexual conduct which could not be publicly expressed, the target area for the anti-obscenity forces ought to be constricted.

The Paris Adult Theatre decision has the effect of limiting the area of the consenting adult's constitutional right of privacy to view pornographic material to one's own home. It seems clear that the majority did this to insure the primacy of the state's interest in maintaining and elevating the quality and tone of life and environment particularly in the large urban centers where commercial pornography often flourishes.

Finally, the Court's encouragement of local efforts at suppression will almost surely result in the disruption of the national distribution of sexual films, books, magazines and other materials. Rather than risk confiscation or prosecution in localities like Albany, Georgia, film makers and publishers may pass up these markets and distribute their wares only in more sophisticated urban population centers, if that is economically feasible. If it is not, the film maker or publisher's work may not see the light of day.

6. Difficulties With the New Approach

The Court's new approach perpetuates certain myths regarding obscenity control. The majority assert that beyond "knowing it when they see it," they can define obscenity with sufficient precision to give fair advance warning as to what is forbidden. But clearly the "serious value" test is highly subjective and in the final analysis only a majority of five justices can say, after the fact of publication, what is serious expression and what is not. And even the patent offensiveness-hard core pornography test will allow for subjectivity unless the legislatures are willing to define in obscene detail the sexual conduct to be suppressed. So far there has been no great trend in that direction.

The other major myth fostered by the Court is that obscenity can be constitutionally controlled at the local level using local standards. But as the Court was forced to admit in Jenkins and Pope, First and Fourteenth Amendment rights and protections are uniform and do not vary depending on the nature of the jurisdiction in which the attempt is made to suppress allegedly obscene expression. Try as it might, the Supreme Court, under the present approach, cannot escape the need to impose national standards to measure national rights and protections and, in the end, to act as a national censorship board.

7. Supplemental Obscenity Standards

Certain other standards have been developed by the Supreme Court to permit suppression and punishment of expression which does not meet the basic obscenity test directed to the average adult laid down in Miller and earlier in Roth and Fanny Hill. These supplemental tests are designed to prevent pandering of borderline material as the real thing, to suppress expression directed to the prurient interest of sexually deviant adults and to shield minors from "adult" materials such as "girlie" magazines and from exploitation and abuse in the production of sexually explicit material.

In Ginzburg v. United States, 383 U.S. 463, 86 S.Ct. 942, 16 L.Ed.2d 31 (1966), the defendant publisher of a purported sexual autobiography, a hardcover sex magazine and a sex newsletter, was convicted of sending obscene matter through the mail. His conviction for violation of Title 18, Section 1461 of the United States Code was affirmed at least in part because of his open advertising representations and other suggestions that the materials would appeal to the recipient's prurient interest. A majority of the Court ruled that where the purveyor's sole emphasis is on the sexually provocative aspects of his or her publications, that fact may be decisive in determining whether the material is obscene. Otherwise stated, in a close case, one who panders material as obscene will be taken at his or her word.

Since audiences vary as to age and sexual preferences, the Court has also held that the standards for suppression may also vary as to these audiences. In Mishkin v. State of New York, 383 U.S. 502, 86 S.Ct. 958, 16 L.Ed.2d 56 (1966), the Court rejected the argument of a publisher and seller of sex books for sadists, masochists, fetishists and homosexuals that his materials were not obscene because they would not appeal to the prurient interest of average persons but rather would disgust and sicken them. The Court held that where material is designed for and primarily disseminated to a clearly defined deviant group, the prurient appeal test of Roth is satisfied if the dominant theme of the material taken as a whole appeals to the prurient interest in sex of members of that group. And in Ginsberg v. State of New York, 390 U.S. 629, 88 S.Ct. 1274, 20 L.Ed.2d 195 (1968) the defendant, an operator of a stationery store and luncheonette, was convicted of violating a New York penal statute which prohibited the knowing sale to minors under the age of 17 of any picture which depicts nudity. Ginsberg sold two "girlie" magazines to a sixteen-year-old male. While conceding that the magazines were not obscene for adults, the Court affirmed the conviction because of its belief that obscenity varies with the age of the audience and that the state has the constitutional power more greatly to restrict minors in their access to sex materials. And finally in New York v. Ferber, 458 U.S. 747, 102 S.Ct. 3348, 73 L.Ed.2d 1113 (1982), the so-called "Kiddie porn" case, the court held that states may, consistent with the First Amendment, utilize more relaxed standards than those in Miller v. California, supra, to obtain criminal convictions in order to protect minors from exploitation and abuse in the production of sexual materials.

To combat the rising tide of sexual exploitation and abuse of minors exemplified by cases such as Ferber, Congress enacted the "Protection of Children Against Sexual Exploitation Act of 1977," P.L. 95–225, 18 U.S.C. §§ 2251–2253. This legislation imposes severe fines and penalties upon those convicted of encouraging or coercing minors to engage in sexually explicit conduct for still and motion picture cameras of any kind.

8. Feminist Proposals for Statutory Civil Actions to Counter Pornographic Depictions of Women

In recent years feminists have become concerned that pornography may serve as a "catalyst" to incite real-life violence against women. Social scientists have also gathered evidence that pornography has either incited or legitimized actual violence against women. There is also a growing body of laboratory and field research supporting the theory that pornography instigates or legitimizes actual violence against women. Citing such studies, the Attorney General's Commission on Pornography: Final Report, July 1986 (U.S. GPO 0–158–315) concluded that "the available evidence strongly supports the hypothesis that substantial exposure to sexually violent materials . . . bears a causal relationship to antisocial acts of sexual violence and, for some subgroups, possibly to unlawful acts of sexual violence" (p. 326). The Commission cites research suggesting that male subjects are more likely to accept "the legitimacy of sexual violence against women" when women are portrayed as enjoying rape or other abuse, a theme which pervades pornography.

One of the Commission's formal recommendations was that "[l]egislatures should conduct hearings and consider legislation recognizing a civil remedy for harm attributable to pornography." This recommendation was a direct reflection of a model anti-pornography ordinance drafted by feminists Andrea Dworykin and Catherine MacKinnon, citing pornography as a violation of women's civil rights. The legislation has been introduced in several city councils including Los Angeles, Minneapolis, Indianapolis and Cambridge, Massachusetts, but has not become law thus far. The legislation identified pornography as a form of discrimination on the basis of sex and defined it as "graphic sexually explicit subordination of women," meaning, for example, women "presented as sexual objects enjoying rape, pain or humiliation, being penetrated by objects or animals, . . . or in scenarios of degradation or torture in a context that makes these conditions sexual" (Indianapolis-Marion County, Ind., Ordinance 35, ch. 16 (1984)). Civil claims for damages are created for 1) coercion into pornography, 2) forcing pornography on a person, 3) assault incited by specific pornography, and 4) trafficking in pornography, i.e. production, sale, exhibition or distribution (Indianapolis-Marion County, Ind., Ordinance 35, S16–3(g)(4)–(7), (1984)). The Commission supported this because "the civil rights approach, although controversial, is the only legal tool suggested . . . which is specifically designed to provide direct relief to the victims of the injuries so exhaustively documented in our hearings throughout the country" (Report p. 749). The legislation was actually enacted in Minneapolis and Indianapolis. In Minneapolis the Mayor vetoed the ordinance. In Indianapolis its constitutionality was challenged in American Booksellers Association v. Hudnut, 771 F.2d 323 (7th Cir. 1985). The Seventh Circuit accepted the premise of the legislation, agreeing that "depictions of [female] subordination tend to perpetuate [it]" and that the "subordinate status of women in turn leads to affront and lower pay at work, insult and injury at home, battery and rape on the streets" (771 F.2d at 329), but upheld the district court decision overturning the ordinance because it was "vague and overbroad" and established "a prior restraint of speech" (771 F.2d at 326). The appeals court pointed out that the definition "graphic sexually explicit subordination of women . . ." did not refer to prurient interests, to offensiveness, or to the standards of the community required by Miller v. California, 413 U.S. 15, 93 S.Ct. 2607, 37 L.Ed.2d 419 (1973). The U.S. Supreme Court summarily affirmed the Seventh Circuit decision in Hudnut v. American Booksellers Association, Inc., 475 U.S. 1132, 106 S.Ct. 1172, 89 L.Ed.2d 291 (1986). Thus proponents of the anti-pornography ordinances will have to find a definition of pornography that courts will view as "constitutional" or accept defeat of their cause.

B.   IMPORTANT SPECIAL AREAS OF RESTRAINT OF SEXUAL EXPRESSION

1. Motion Pictures

A medium of expression which has felt the hand of the censor acutely over the years is the motion picture. Movies have been and are still being censored locally for obscenity prior to exhibition and more often are simply seized in police raids. Some of the leading prior restraint cases have involved motion pictures and a distinct area of obscenity law has been carved out.

a. *Background and Modern Doctrine*

Until 1952 the motion picture was not considered a medium of expression protected by the Constitution and the censors were free to control film exhibition in any way they saw fit. In that year the Supreme Court in Joseph Burstyn, Inc. v. Wilson, 343 U.S. 495, 72 S.Ct. 777, 96 L.Ed. 1098 (1952) rejected earlier doctrine and held that expression by means of motion picture film is protected by the First and Fourteenth Amendments even though it be assumed that motion pictures have a greater impact on the mind than other modes of expression. Thereafter, attempts at censorship for obscenity have generally been measured by prevailing constitutional standards. But since obscenity can be constitutionally suppressed under Roth and Miller, prior licensing and confiscation of films as well as subsequent punishment for their exhibition are permissible under certain circumstances and a general constitutional attack on a local ordinance or state statute requiring submission of motion pictures for prior censorship will fail. See Times Film Corp. v. City of Chicago, 365 U.S. 43, 81 S.Ct. 391, 5 L.Ed.2d 403 (1961).

One indirect approach to controlling "adult" motion pictures and thereby avoiding the constitutional standards of Roth and Miller and necessary procedural safeguards that accompany those standards is the control of land use in order to concentrate adult movie houses in so-called "combat zones" or, conversely, to prevent concentrations, which have the tendency to destroy commercial and residential neighborhoods. Either way, nonproliferation of such establishments is the goal. This indirect approach relying on time, place and manner limitations on the exhibition of "adult" films was approved by the Supreme Court in Young v. American Mini Theatres, Inc., 427 U.S. 50, 96 S.Ct. 2440, 49 L.Ed.2d 310 (1976) and City of Renton v. Playtime Theatres, Inc., 475 U.S. 41, 106 S.Ct. 925, 89 L.Ed.2d 29 (1986) because neither complete suppression of adult movies nor criminal sanctions were involved.

b. Procedural Safeguards for Film

After the Times Film Corp. case, supra, it was clear that there could be constitutional as well as unconstitutional prior restraint on motion pictures, and the Supreme Court began to evolve the rules under which the censors might operate. Freedman v. Maryland, 380 U.S. 51, 85 S.Ct. 734, 13 L.Ed.2d 649 (1965) involved a challenge by a film exhibitor to a state statute authorizing certain procedures of the now defunct Maryland Board of Censors, including a lengthy appeal process. The Supreme Court struck down the statute as unduly restrictive of protected expression and set out certain procedural safeguards for regulating the censor's business. Prior restraint statutes and ordinances are now required to:

(a)   place the burden of proving that the film in question meets constitutional standards for obscenity (i.e., Roth and Miller) on the censor;

(b)   provide that the censor will, within a specified very brief period, either issue a license for exhibition or go into court to seek to restrain exhibition and;

(c)   assure a prompt final judicial decision in order to minimize the deterrent effect of an interim refusal to license.

In addition, prior restraint legislation whether it involves outright censorship or merely mandatory film classification for the protection of minors, as in Interstate Circuit, Inc. v. City of Dallas, 390 U.S. 676, 88 S.Ct. 1298, 20 L.Ed.2d 225 (1968), must be narrowly drawn, detailed, and precise as to the standards to be employed by the classifier. Anything less will inhibit protected expression and run afoul of the First and Fourteenth Amendments.

Similarly, procedural safeguards have been established for the seizure of films by law enforcement officials. A judicial warrant issued consistent with Fourth and Fourteenth Amendment standards must be obtained before any seizure. The fact that First Amendment interests may be affected by such search warrants does not require a higher probable cause standard for issuing the warrants. New York v. P. J. Video, Inc., 475 U.S. 868, 106 S.Ct. 1610, 89 L.Ed.2d 871 (1986). Failure to obtain such warrant will result in the suppression of the film as evidence of obscenity law violations at subsequent judicial proceedings. Roaden v. Kentucky, 413 U.S. 496, 93 S.Ct. 2796, 37 L.Ed. 2d 757 (1973); Lee Art Theatre, Inc. v. Virginia, 392 U.S. 636, 88 S.Ct. 2103, 20 L.Ed.2d 1313 (1968). And it is not sufficient justification for the issuance of the warrant that the prospective seizing officer made conclusory assertions of the film's obscene nature. Rather, the magistrate must concern himself or herself deeply with the question of the film's probable nature before issuing the warrant. Ibid. But an adversary proceeding at this stage is not required. Heller v. New York, 413 U.S. 483, 93 S.Ct. 2789, 37 L.Ed.2d 745 (1973). The seizure of a copy of the film pursuant to a constitutionally valid warrant must be for the limited purpose of preserving it as evidence in a subsequent adversary proceeding and must not prevent continued exhibition of the film until a prompt determination of its nature is made in that proceeding. If there is only one copy at hand, the film seized must be made available to the exhibitor for copying so that he or she may continue its exhibition. Ibid.

These procedural safeguards may not be avoided by legislation providing for indirect prior restraints such as statutes (1) which permit enjoining the operation of adult movie houses as public nuisances because of past exhibition of obscene films; (2) which prohibit the unapproved future exhibition of motion pictures that have not yet been found to be obscene; and (3) which require the judiciary to place its imprimatur on such future exhibitions before the films may be shown to the public without penalty. See Vance v. Universal Amusement Co., 445 U.S. 308, 100 S.Ct. 1156, 63 L.Ed.2d 413 (1980).

While the focus here has been on the constitutional limitations on prior restraint of motion pictures because this is where most of the legal battles have been fought, parallel safeguards have been developed to protect other modes of expression from overzealous censors. See, e.g., Kingsley Books, Inc. v. Brown, 354 U.S. 436, 77 S.Ct. 1325, 1 L.Ed.2d 1469 (1957) (booklets); Marcus v. Search Warrant, 367 U.S. 717, 81 S.Ct. 1708, 6 L.Ed.2d 1127 (1961) (books and magazines). But cf. New York v. P.J. Video, Inc., 475 U.S. 868, 106 S.Ct. 1610, 89 L.Ed.2d 871 (1986).

2. Mail and Customs Censorship

Until recent times the United States Post Office Department carried on a largely futile campaign of administrative censorship of the mails in addition to referring certain cases to the Justice Department for criminal prosecution. Unsuccessful administrative devices have included removal of material from the mail, revocation of the publishers' second class mailing privilege and refusal to deliver mail to alleged commercial pornographers.

Recently a more indirect approach to the problem of obscenity in the mail has proved both workable and less threatening to First Amendment interests. Pursuant to present section 3008 of title 39 of the United States Code, individual addressees who have received "pandering advertisements" which offer for sale matter which the addressee believes to be erotically arousing or sexually provocative may request the Postmaster General to issue an order directing the sender and his or her agents to refrain from further mailings to the named addressee. If after notice and hearing it should be determined by the Postmaster General that the order has been violated, the Postmaster General may request the Attorney General to seek a federal court order directing compliance with the Postmaster's order. Violation of the court order will, of course, subject the sender to sanctions for contempt of court. The constitutionality of this statute was upheld in Rowan v. United States Post

Office Department, 397 U.S. 728, 90 S.Ct. 1484, 25 L.Ed.2d 736 (1970).

Customs censorship through seizure and confiscation of incoming materials has had a long history and continues to the present within obscenity standards laid down in Roth and Miller, supra, and pursuant to procedural safeguards required by Freedman v. Maryland, supra.

C. SUBSEQUENT CRIMINAL SANCTIONS

The threat of criminal prosecution can have a restraining influence on sexual expression almost as profound as prior censorship. While criminal prosecutions for obscene expression are in general outline much like other criminal prosecutions and the rights accorded defendants are the same, certain special aspects of criminal obscenity proceedings are particularly significant to the eventual outcome.

Before one can be convicted of violating any criminal statute, the statute must give reasonable notice of the conduct that is prohibited. This has presented substantial difficulties for the drafters of criminal obscenity legislation in the past because of the definitional problem; convictions have sometimes been reversed because the statute alleged to have been violated was held "void for vagueness." See, e.g., Winters v. New York, 333 U.S. 507, 68 S.Ct. 665, 92 L.Ed. 840 (1948); cf. Interstate Circuit, Inc. v. City of Dallas, 390 U.S. 676, 88 S.Ct.

1298, 20 L.Ed.2d 225 (1968). This drafting problem may be alleviated by legislatures utilizing the definition of unprotected obscenity set forth in Miller.

As noted earlier in connection with the discussion of the effects of the recent trilogy of obscenity cases, *where* an obscenity prosecution is brought is of the greatest importance because of the Supreme Court's sanctioning of the application of local standards. Because a prosecution for violation of the Comstock Law may be brought in any district from, through or into which the mail in question is carried, federal prosecutors will usually have an advantageous choice as to venue. Reed Enterprises v. Clark, 278 F.Supp. 372 (D.D.C.1967), affirmed 390 U.S. 457, 88 S.Ct. 1196, 20 L.Ed.2d 28 (1968). Similar options as to venue between counties are often available to state prosecutors. And thus a defendant in an obscenity prosecution may be tried far from his or her residence or base of operations.

The burden of proof is always upon the state or federal government and the standard is the same as in all criminal cases: guilt beyond a reasonable doubt. The burden has been eased somewhat by the Supreme Court's holding in Paris Adult Theatre that the material complained of "speaks for itself" and thus expert testimony as to its obscene nature is no longer required.

An important element of the prosecutor's burden is scienter or guilty knowledge. It may be difficult in certain cases to establish beyond a reasonable doubt that a book seller, magazine dealer or movie exhibitor knew of the obscene nature and contents of the material he or she was purveying. But neither the states nor the federal government may constitutionally eliminate this mental element in their criminal obscenity statutes. Smith v. California, 361 U.S. 147, 80 S.Ct. 215, 4 L.Ed.2d 205 (1959).

The chief defense in most obscenity prosecutions is that the material is protected expression under the prevailing Supreme Court tests. The defense will normally call expert witnesses to testify that the material has serious literary, artistic, political or scientific value and perhaps local psychologists or psychiatrists to testify that the material does not appeal to the prurient interest of the average person in the particular locality. Defense counsel may attempt to establish "tolerant" community standards through expert testimony and the introduction of comparable materials freely available in the local area. This latter defense is meeting with only mixed success before the courts.

CHAPTER V

RESTRAINT OF THE PRESS FOR PURPOSES OF NATIONAL SECURITY

A. THE CONFLICT

Since the founding of the Republic the federal and state governments have laid claim to the right to keep secrets on the ground that disclosures of certain matters would be harmful to the public interest. Obvious examples are troop deployments and diplomatic judgments concerning foreign governments. The working assumption of government officials is that the people would not want to know about sensitive matters if such knowledge would be harmful to their best interest.

While this assumption may have validity, official judgments as to precisely what knowledge would be harmful to the public interest are coming under increasing challenge. The common theme of the advocates of a freer flow of information is "the people's right to know" or "freedom of information."

The conflict has grown sharper with the growth of governmental activity since the New Deal and the increasing distrust of "big government" engendered in part by an unpopular war in Indochina and the Watergate scandal. Representative of the heightened conflict is the willingness of the media, particularly a once deferential press, to publish material which the government wishes to keep secret and a readiness on the part of governmental officials to retaliate against the media and to seek injunctions against publication of those secrets.

B. LEGAL BACKGROUND

There is no question but that the federal government has an inherent right to keep certain matters secret, especially information relating to national security and diplomatic affairs and that it may invoke executive privilege and establish a classification system to prevent disclosure. See United States v. Nixon, 418 U.S. 683, 703–713, 94 S.Ct. 3090, 3105–3110, 41 L.Ed.2d 1039, 1061–1067 (1974) (the Nixon Tapes case); United States v. Reynolds, 345 U.S. 1, 73 S.Ct. 528, 97 L.Ed.2d 727 (1953). Furthermore, there is little doubt that those individuals privy to secret government information or those who come across it accidentally might be enjoined from disclosing what they have learned or, in certain cases, be criminally punished for actually making disclosures to others. And in the process of protecting government secrets the executive's judgment concerning the need for secrecy for the specific material involved will not be reviewed by the judiciary because of the separation of powers doctrine.

The problem becomes considerably more complex, however, when disclosure is made or threatened by the media. In this situation, of course, First Amendment considerations first raised in Near v. Minnesota, 283 U.S. 697, 51 S.Ct. 625, 75 L.Ed. 1357 (1931) intervene. While in *Near* prior restraint of the press was generally disapproved as violative of the First and Fourteenth Amendments, the Supreme Court did recognize that such restraint might be permissible in extraordinary situations including the threatened publication of military secrets in time of war. This left the door open for the federal government forty years later to attempt to stop the presses from printing the so-called "Pentagon Papers."

C. NEW YORK TIMES CO. v. UNITED STATES

Disillusioned with the war in Vietnam he had once supported, Daniel Ellsberg, a former Department of Defense official, arranged for the photocopying, without authorization, of a "top secret" multi-volume Department of Defense study of American involvement in the war between 1945 and 1967 entitled "History of U.S. Decision Making Process on Vietnam Policy" and a one-volume "Command and Control Study of the Tonkin Gulf Incident" and made them available to selected newspapers throughout the United States. On June 12, 13 and 14, 1971 the New York Times became the first paper to publish summaries and portions of the text of the two studies popularly known as "The Pentagon Papers." The United

States Justice Department sought and obtained a temporary restraining order from the United States District Court to prevent the Times from continuing publication of the classified material. This restraining order remained in effect until the Supreme Court decided the case, thereby preventing further publication of the material for 15 days. At approximately the same time the Washington Post began publishing excerpts from the two studies and the government likewise sought to restrain the Post and for a short time succeeded. But the temporary restraining order binding the Post expired prior to the Supreme Court's resolution of the case and the anomalous situation was then presented of the Post being free to publish while the New York Times was not.

The issue presented to the Supreme Court in the historic case of New York Times Co. v. United States, 403 U.S. 713, 91 S.Ct. 2140, 29 L.Ed.2d 822 (1971) was very simply whether publication by the press of secret matters relating to the history and past conduct of an ongoing war could be enjoined consistent with the First Amendment. The Court by its judgment freed the Times to continue publication along with the Post. But its per curiam opinion is not, as some at first suggested, a ringing endorsement of a free press. The Court stated, " 'Any system of prior restraints of expression comes to this Court bearing a heavy presumption against its constitutional validity.' . . . The Government 'thus carries a heavy burden of showing justification for the imposition of such a restraint.' . . . The District Court for the Southern District of New York in the New York Times case and the District Court for the District of Columbia and the Court of Appeals for the District of Columbia Circuit in the Washington Post case held that the Government had not met that burden. We agree." 403 U.S. at 714, 91 S.Ct. at 2141, 29 L.Ed.2d at 824–825.

The Court thus implied that if the government had sufficient proof of some serious effect on the war effort or national security, the government could enjoin the media from publishing truthful matters of public interest. What saved the press from being permanently gagged by court order for the first time in our history was the government's inability to prove to the Court's satisfaction that publication of the Papers would clearly result in direct, immediate and irreparable damage to the nation or its people.

In addition to the (per curiam) opinion, the Pentagon Papers case is marked by six concurring and three dissenting opinions. A close analysis of these opinions must be considered generally discouraging to those favoring a free press. A majority of the Court did not rule that such prior restraint was unconstitutional—only that the government had not met the heavy burden of proving that such restraint was necessary in this particular case.

Thus, what appeared at first blush to be a great victory for the press was, at best, a pyrrhic one. The Court gave notice that there are limits to the media's right to publish and the people's right to learn government secrets relating to national security. As a result of this case, the media may have become more wary of publishing classified material obtained without authorization. At best, the Pentagon Papers case encourages self-censorship by the news media. At worst, it forms the predicate for successful government censorship and prosecutions in the future.

Indeed, in the three reported cases following the Pentagon Papers case, the government was successful in enjoining disclosure of certain CIA secrets in a book by a former agency official (United States v. Marchetti, 466 F.2d 1309 (4th Cir.1972), cert. denied 409 U.S. 1063, 93 S.Ct. 553, 34 L.Ed.2d 516 (1972); Alfred A. Knopf, Inc. v. Colby, 509 F.2d 1362 (4th Cir.1975)) and information on the workings of the hydrogen bomb contained in a magazine article (United States v. Progressive, Inc., 467 F.Supp. 990 (W.D.Wisc.1979)).

United States v. Marchetti began when former CIA agent Victor Marchetti submitted to Esquire magazine and six other publishers an article in which he reported some of his experiences as a CIA agent. Marchetti had spent 14 years with the CIA, rising to the position of special assistant to the executive director, but left because he had become disillusioned with the CIA's covert actions to destabilize governments considered unfriendly to the U.S. The government charged that Marchetti's article contained classified information concerning intelligence sources, methods and operations. The government won a broad injunction from the U.S. District Court for the Eastern District of Virginia to enjoin publication of the article. On appeal, Marchetti argued that the injunction should be barred by the Supreme Court decision in the Pentagon Papers case because the government had failed to meet the heavy burden against prior restraint of expression. But the court of appeals rejected Marchetti's argument and held that the secrecy agreement Marchetti had signed when he was first hired by the CIA in 1955 should be enforced. The agreement required Marchetti (and all CIA agents) to submit material to the CIA for approval before it was published. If the material was classified and published without prior review, the CIA could enjoin disclosure. Given this agreement, the court of appeals for the Fourth Circuit affirmed the district court's injunction, except to rule that the CIA could delete only classified information. Marchetti was the first writer in the United States to be subjected to such a censorship order.

Marchetti and a co-author John Marks, a former State Department employee, who had also signed an agreement not to disclose classified information learned during his employment, later wrote a book, "The CIA and the Cult of Intelligence," which they submitted to the CIA for prepublication review. The CIA demanded that they delete 339 passages, comprising 15 to 20 percent of the entire manuscript. Heavy deletions were made in chapters concerning the Bay of Pigs operation against Fidel Castro, the Vietnam War and the CIA's attempt to prevent Salvador Allende's election as president of Chile. With their publisher Alfred A. Knopf, Inc. the authors sued. By the time of the trial, the CIA had reduced the number of deletions from 339 to 168. The U.S. District Court for the Eastern District of Virginia permitted publication of all but 26 of the 168 passages, at which point all parties appealed.

The court of appeals ruled that if the government could prove that each item deleted disclosed classified information, then it could require deletion of those items solely on that basis. Alfred A. Knopf, Inc. v. Colby, 509 F.2d 1362 (4th Cir.), cert. denied 421 U.S. 992, 95 S.Ct. 1999, 44 L.Ed.2d 482 (1975). Furthermore, the court said that Marchetti and Marks effectively relinquished their First Amendment rights regarding disclosure of classified information when they signed the secrecy agreements. The First Amendment is no bar to an injunction forbidding such disclosure when the classified information was obtained during employment with the CIA. The court of appeals remanded the case to the district court, ruling that the authors could disclose only information which they had obtained after leaving the CIA and State Department. Ultimately the CIA permitted 25 of the 26 missing passages to be printed in whole or in part, leaving one to wonder why they had been deleted in the first place.

Four years after Knopf v. Colby, the Justice Department obtained an injunction to prohibit The Progressive magazine from publishing an article by free-lancer Howard Morland entitled "The H–Bomb Secret: How We Got It, Why We're Telling It." United States v. The Progressive, Inc., 467 F.Supp. 990 (W.D.Wisc.1979). The U.S. District Court for the Western District of Wisconsin issued a preliminary injunction against publication after concluding that some of the information would probably violate the Atomic Energy Act of 1954. The Justice Department contended that the Morland article contained "Restricted Data," defined by the Atomic Energy Act of 1954 as "all data concerning the design, manufacture or utilization of atomic weapons." 42 U.S.C.A. § 2104(y). This law specifically forbids anyone possessing "restricted data" about nuclear weaponry from disseminating it in a way that might be utilized "to injure the U.S." or "secure an advantage to any foreign nation." 42 U.S.C.A. § 2274. It also authorizes the attorney general to request a court order to enjoin communication of such restricted data. 42 U.S.C.A. § 2280.

The injunction was appealed, but three days after the court of appeals heard oral arguments and before it had made a decision, a small Wisconsin newspaper, the Madison Press Connection, published a letter, written by a California computer programmer, which contained essentially the same information as The Progressive article. When the Press Connection learned that the government had just won a temporary restraining order preventing another newspaper, the Daily Californian, a student newspaper at the University of California, Berkeley, from printing the letter, it rushed the letter into print.

When the Press Connection published the letter, the court of appeals dismissed the case against The Progressive. 610 F.2d 819 (7th Cir.1979). Many journalists expressed relief because numerous legal scholars had speculated that the injunction against The Progressive would have been sustained by the Supreme Court.

D.   OTHER INHIBITIONS ON PUBLICATION

1.   Withholding Passports

Aside from direct injunctive restraints on the release of national security information attempted in the New York Times Co., Marchetti, Colby and Progressive cases, the federal government has successfully employed other techniques to discourage disclosure of sensitive diplomatic, military and intelligence information.

The denial or revocation of a passport because of expression which the Government perceives as potentially damaging to national security or foreign policy is one technique for inhibiting the release of undesired information or comment. This technique was upheld by the Supreme Court in Haig v. Agee, 453 U.S. 280, 101 S.Ct. 2766, 69 L.Ed.2d 640 (1981). Haig involved former CIA agent Philip Agee's attempt to expose existing CIA agents in foreign countries and have them driven out by anti-CIA groups in those countries.

2. Legislative Prohibitions

Perhaps in response to Haig v. Agee, the Reagan Administration persuaded Congress in 1982 to make it a federal crime for anyone to publish anything they have reason to know will disclose the identity of United States intelligence agents, even if their source is public or unclassified information. Intelligence Identities Protection Act, P.L. 97–200, 50 U.S.C.A. §§ 421–426. A survey of news stories written before the act was passed in 1982 turned up more than 80 major books and news articles, the authors of which could arguably have been indicted under the law. (A representative sample would include The New York Times' investigation of ex-CIA agents Wilson and Terpil; revelations that former CIA agents were involved in the Watergate break-in; accounts of illegal domestic spying by the CIA; and disclosures that a CIA employee tried to infiltrate the House and Senate intelligence committees in 1980 at the direction of the KGB. Jay Peterzell, "The Government Shuts Up," Columbia Journalism Review, pp. 31–37 (July-August 1982).

3.   Contractual Prohibitions

In Snepp v. United States, 444 U.S. 507, 100 S.Ct. 763, 62 L.Ed.2d 704 (1980) the government, relying on its claimed contractual rights, got the courts to seize the profits from a book published without CIA prepublication review, causing financial disaster for the author.   Frank Snepp, a former CIA agent, published a book, "Decent Interval," about certain CIA activities in South Vietnam without submitting it for prepublication review as expressly required by his employment agreement with the CIA.   Even though the CIA conceded that "Decent Interval," did not reveal one item of classified information, the Government brought suit to enforce the agreement by, among other things, capturing all profits that Snepp might earn from publishing the book in violation of the agreement. The district court entered a judgment for the Government, giving it the relief it sought but the United States Court of Appeals refused to approve the turning over of the profits from the book to the Government.   The Supreme Court summarily and without benefit of briefs or oral argument on the subject, upheld the Government's right to capture all profits from the publication—over $125,000. Thus, the financial burden placed on Snepp to pay off the Government was substantial and should give pause to other government employees considering writing about sensitive official matters.

Perhaps the most chilling aspect of the Marchetti, Colby and Snepp cases is the subordination of First Amendment interests to "boilerplate" contract clauses in CIA employment agreements. In Snepp, the Supreme Court majority relegated First Amendment considerations to a footnote in rigorously enforcing the CIA employment contract against Snepp.

The Snepp opinion also contained broad language that could be interpreted to permit the same prepublication review procedure to be applied to the thousands of non-CIA employees who also have access to classified information. The Government had not sought that degree of power in the Snepp case, and it is not clear that the Court intended that result. But, citing the Snepp decision, in 1983 President Ronald Reagan issued National Security Decision Directive 84, "Safeguarding National Security Information." 9 Med.L.Rptr. 1759, July 5, 1983. This directive required thousands of federal employees to submit to lie detector tests if asked; an employee who refused to take such a test could be subject to "adverse consequences." Previously federal employees, except for those in the CIA and certain sections of the Justice and Defense Departments and the National Security Agency—had the right to refuse to submit to such tests without their refusal being held against them or included in their personnel files. The directive also required any federal employee with access to classified information to submit for prepublication review any manuscripts containing intelligence information. It would cover about 128,000 employees who would be bound by the contract for the rest of their lives.

In response to the President's directive, Congress attached a rider to a State Department appropriations bill ordering the administration to delay enforcement of the directive on prepublication review till 1984. The President signed the bill and agreed not to enforce the directive. But despite this promise, the General Accounting Office (GAO) reported in 1984 that aspects of the directive had been in effect since 1982. The GAO found that 156,000 employees of the Defense Department had signed the secrecy agreements and that there had been a sharp increase in the number of articles and books being reviewed by the Reagan administration. See FOI Digest, p. 1 (May-June 1984). Furthermore, thousands of government officials are being required to acknowledge in writing that they face criminal and civil penalties for unauthorized disclosures for the rest of their lives. See Washington Post, p. A16, May 7, 1986.

4. News Blackouts

The Reagan Administration exercised an even more controversial form of prior censorship when it ordered an unprecedented 48-hour news blackout of the invasion of Grenada by American troops in 1983. About 400 journalists were denied transportation to Grenada, and the military stopped and threatened to shoot a few reporters who tried to reach Grenada by boat from nearby islands. Pentagon officials argued that they had banned journalists for 48 hours because they needed absolute secrecy to launch the invasion, and they were also concerned for the journalists' safety. The press scoffed at both reasons. Journalists had accompanied American military forces in every war since at least the Mexican-American War of 1848. Although reporters did accede to censorship in both world wars and the Korean War, they had always been allowed on the scene to cover the fighting. Journalists even accompanied Allied forces when they invaded Europe in 1944 on D–Day, one of the most secret military operations of all time. There was little censorship, however, during the Vietnam War, and many in the military had apparently developed an intense distrust of the press, blaming the press in part for the United States having lost the war in Vietnam.

Following severe criticism of the administration and the military for its exclusion of the press from the early aspects of the Grenada operation, Defense Secretary Caspar Weinberger asked retired army Major General Winant Sidle to form a panel on press-military relations. The Sidle panel recommended that a small pool of reporters should accompany the military on all future missions, secret or not, and should share the information obtained with others in the press. The pool, formed in 1984, was activated for the U.S. bombing of certain targets in Libya in 1986. Eight reporters and photographers boarded a U.S. aircraft carrier in the Mediterranean and got first-hand reports of the bombing from the pilots and others.

Under guidelines issued by the Pentagon and approved by the American Newspaper Publishers Association and the American Society of Newspaper Editors, only Pentagon-accredited journalists may report on military operations and they may report only "releasable information," with releasable information defined by the Pentagon. Accreditation is lost if the groundrules are violated. The releasable information list does not include estimates of enemy strength (the issue in Westmoreland v. CBS, Inc.) and the "information not releasable" list prohibits such things as "cancelled operations," as in the Carter Administration's failed Iranian hostage rescue mission.

5. Criminal Prosecutions and Threats Thereof

In addition to barring reporters from Grenada initially, the Reagan Administration began a campaign to stem unauthorized leaks of sensitive government information. In 1985 the Justice Department successfully prosecuted former naval intelligence analyst Samuel Morison for furnishing three secret U.S. spy satellite photos to a British magazine. Morison was sentenced to two years for espionage and theft. He was the first person ever convicted of the crime of leaking national security information to the press, and was found guilty under an interpretation of the law that could subject news organizations, as well as their sources, to criminal prosecution. United States v. Morison, 604 F.Supp. 655 (D.Md.1985).

The interpretation under which Morison was convicted may have paved the way for threats of prosecution of members of the press by the late CIA Director William Casey against NBC News, The Washington Post, The New York Times, Time, Newsweek and The Washington Times for alleged violation of the 1950 "COMINT" (Communications Intelligence) statute that prohibits publishing classified information about codes, ciphers or "communication intelligence activities of the United States. . . ." It also forbids "the divulging of any information" gleaned from code-breaking activities in order "to prevent the indication to a foreign nation that we may have broken their code system." 18 U.S.C.A. § 798 (1953). The stories that triggered the CIA Director's threats of prosecution dealt with our interception of messages between Tripoli and the Libyan People's Bureau in East Berlin, and the government's prosecution of Ronald Pelton, a former intelligence specialist with the National Security Agency who later received a life sentence for selling secrets to the Soviets. When Time Magazine's attorney asked the CIA which of its articles had violated the law, the CIA refused to identify the article. Washington Post, p. A3, May 8, 1986.

The CIA Director also tried to persuade Department of Justice officials to obtain an injunction to restrain The Washington Post from publishing an article describing the technology used by American submarines in intercepting Soviet communications before this information-gathering technique was compromised by Pelton. But the Justice Department turned down Casey's request, citing New York Times Co. v. United States, supra. Casey then threatened the Washington Post with prosecution under the COMINT statute, which had never before been used against a news organization. The Post finally published a less informative version of the story, deleting three paragraphs describing the interception device. See Washington Post, p. A38, May 21, 1986.

E. KEEPING OUT THREATENING PERSONS AND MATERIALS FROM ABROAD

The Reagan Administration has also intensified use of the Immigration and Naturalization Act provision known as the McCarran-Walter Act (S 212(a), 8 U.S.C.A. § 1182). It was adopted over President Harry Truman's veto in 1952, and provides that foreigners may be denied visas to visit the U.S. if a consular officer or the Attorney General "has reason to believe" the prospective visitor seeks "to engage in activities which would be prejudicial to the public interest," or who "advocate the economic, international . . . doctrines of world communism. . . ." (§ 212(a)(28)(D).

The Supreme Court upheld the Attorney General's right to deny a visa in Kleindienst v. Mandel, 408 U.S. 753, 92 S.Ct. 2576, 33 L.Ed.2d 683 (1972). In that case, Ernest Mandel, a journalist and writer of a two-volume work, Marxist Economic Theory, was invited to speak at a Stanford University conference on Technology and the Third World in 1969. He had been in the United States in 1962 and 1968, but the Immigration and Naturalization Service denied his 1969 visa application on the grounds that his 1968 activities in the U.S. went beyond the stated purposes of his trip, although these activities were merely that he spoke at more universities than his visa application indicated. Furthermore, no one had given Mandel prior notice that he was required to adhere to a stated itinerary in 1968. Mandel and eight university professors challenged the decision, arguing that the Immigration and Naturalization Act § 212(a)(28) denied them equal protection by permitting entry of "rightists" but not "leftists." The district court observed that although Mandel had no personal right to enter the United States, U.S. citizens did have a First Amendment right to hear him explain his views, and it held that the Attorney General could not deny Mandel a visa.

On appeal, the U.S. Supreme Court acknowledged the idea that the First Amendment protects the public's right to hear differing viewpoints. But the Court concluded that it would not address or decide the First Amendment issue. It held instead that the Attorney General "had validly exercised plenary power delegated to the Executive and the courts would not look behind his decision or weigh it against the First Amendment interests of those seeking entry of [Mandel] to personally communicate with him or engage in academic exchange." 408 U.S. at 810, 92 S.Ct. at 2576, 33 L.Ed.2d at 683.

In 1986, Colombian journalist Patricia Lara met the same fate as Ernest Mandel. She was detained for five days in New York and then expelled. She had come to the United States with a valid visa to attend a Columbia University awards ceremony, but the State Department detained her at a maximum-security federal prison, said that her visa had been issued in error, revoked it, and then deported her to Colombia without giving her specific reasons for her deportation. After she left, Elliot Abrams, assistant secretary of state for inter-American affairs, claimed that Lara was a liaison with Cuba and a member of M19, a leftist Colombian guerilla movement. She denied the charge, and the Colombian foreign minister said he had no evidence that she was a member of M19 or an agent of the Cuban government. Immigration authorities have invoked the McCarran-Walter act against other foreign journalists as well. The News Media and the Law, Winter 1987, pp. 4–5.

The Reagan Administration has also given an expansive reading to the 1938 Foreign Agents Registration Act (FARA), 22 U.S.C.A. § 611, which requires that any film that is political propaganda and is produced in a foreign country must be so labeled. In 1982 the Department of Justice sought to require three films produced by the National Film Board of Canada to be labeled as propaganda. Two of the films were about acid rain, and the third film, "If You Love This Planet," won an Academy Award. The Justice Department summarized the message of the film as: "Unless we shake off our indifference and work to prevent nuclear war, we stand a slim chance of surviving the twentieth century." The Justice Department ordered the Film Board of Canada to include a message with the films that the U.S. government did not necessarily approve of its content and that they contained "political propaganda." The Film Board was also required under law to provide the Justice Department with the names of individuals and organizations who ordered the film. In Washington, D.C. and California respectively, the American Civil Liberties Union (ACLU) and California State Senator Barry Keene, who had planned to sponsor showings of these films to support his views, filed separate suits against the Justice Department in 1983, claiming FARA was unconstitutional. The ACLU argued that labeling the films as propaganda might prejudice potential viewers and might even deter people from viewing films at all, because the label "denigrates the films' messages." Furthermore, the ACLU argued that requiring a listing of the names of the exhibitors might injure exhibitors' reputations since they would be stigmatized as exhibitors of "un-Ameri-

can" or "unpatriotic materials." But the United
States District Court for the District of Columbia
dismissed the ACLU's suit, ruling that the term
"political propaganda" does not necessarily carry
negative connotations.   Block v. Smith, 583
F.Supp. 1288 (D.D.C.1984). The court of appeals
reversed in part, holding that Block, the distributor of the Canadian films, had proven "concrete
harm," but nevertheless affirmed the district court
ruling that the "propaganda" label was acceptable,
and that Block would have to report the names of
those who ordered the films. Block v. Meese, 793
F.2d 1303 (D.C.Cir.1986).   Meanwhile, Senator
Keene, objecting to being labeled a disseminator of
political propaganda, advanced similar arguments,
and the United States District Court in San Ber-
nardino, California enjoined application of FARA
to the three Canadian films, Keene v. Smith, 569
F.Supp. 1513 (E.D.Cal.1983), and this was affirmed
at the appellate level.   Keene v. Meese, 619
F.Supp. 1111 (E.D.Cal.1985).   But the United
States Supreme Court held that the label of "political propaganda" is used in a "neutral and even-
handed manner," is not intended as censorship,
and "has no pejorative connotation." Writing for
a 5 to 3 majority, Justice John Paul Stevens conceded: "There is a risk that a partially informed
audience might believe that a film that must be
registered with the Department of Justice is suspect. But there is no evidence that this suspicion
. . . has had the effect of government censor-

ship." Meese v. Keene, 481 U.S. ___, 107 S.Ct. 1862, 95 L.Ed.2d 415 (1987).

American-made documentary films destined for foreign audiences have also not escaped scrutiny. Under an agreement adopted by a United Nations conference in 1948, filmmakers pay no American export or foreign-import duties if the United States Information Agency (USIA) certifies that they are intended to "instruct or inform" rather than to propagandize. The USIA decided, for example, that ABC's acclaimed 1979 documentary about toxic waste, "The Killing Ground," should not be certified as being instructional or informational, thus forcing ABC to pay export and import duties. The documentary won two Emmys, first prize at the Monte Carlo Film Festival and was nominated for an Academy Award. But the Environmental Protection Agency (EPA) concluded in 1982 that the film was "mainly of historical interest" because the U.S. "has made great progress in managing hazardous wastes." The EPA feared that the film "would mislead a foreign audience into believing that the American public needed arousing to the dangers of hazardous wastes [when] this is no longer the case." F. Abrams, "The New Effort to Control Information," The New York Times Magazine, p. 24, Sept. 25, 1983.

The Iran-Contra Affair that rocked the Reagan Administration in its twilight years is a fertile ground for new attempts by the federal government to suppress the gathering and dissemination of news and information because of national security considerations. However, no concrete attempts to restrict the press because of this political and foreign policy disaster had surfaced at the time of this writing.

CHAPTER VI

THE FREE PRESS—FAIR TRIAL CONFLICT

A. THE PROBLEM

1. Introduction

The Sixth Amendment guarantees that in criminal prosecutions the accused shall be entitled to a speedy and public trial "by an impartial jury." A necessary implication of this constitutional mandate is that jurors must not be influenced in their determination of the guilt or innocence of the accused by forces outside the courtroom or by information or material not admitted into evidence at the trial.

But news stories concerning a criminal case published before or during trial, particularly those containing information adverse to the accused not presented to the jury at trial such as a past criminal record or some incriminating statement or confession may influence individual jurors and destroy their impartiality. Because accused persons are entitled only to "impartial" juries and not favorably biased ones, the constitutional requirement binding on the states through the Fourteenth Amendment may also be violated by publicity adverse to the prosecution.

In addition, the Fifth Amendment guarantees to every person, including criminal accused, that they will not be deprived of life, liberty or property without due process of law. Due process may be affected by the media and their representatives by both the generation of pressures on the trial judge through editorial content and by disruption of the repose of the courtroom, making fair procedure and calm deliberation difficult if not impossible.

The problem for the courts in attempting to safeguard an accused's Fifth and Sixth Amendment rights arises out of the potentially conflicting guaranty of the First Amendment that the Congress shall make no law abridging freedom of the press. This guaranty is interpreted to include court orders. Therefore, orders designed to assure fair and impartial trials and which directly or indirectly restrict the newsgathering and news disseminating functions of the press may run afoul of the First Amendment. Some restrictive orders, particularly those that bar newspersons from the courtroom, may also violate the "public trial" requirement of the Sixth Amendment itself.

While most of the potential conflicts between fair trial and free press might be avoided by the exercise of restraint and common sense by the media, judiciary, trial participants and law enforcement officials, these qualities are sometimes in short supply in relation to criminal cases of great public interest. Then the conflict becomes real and troublesome. One example will suffice to illustrate the extreme bounds of the problem.

2. A Case Study: Sheppard v. Maxwell

The classic case of excessive and abusive pretrial and trial publicity and improper courtroom behavior by the media is Sheppard v. Maxwell, 384 U.S. 333, 86 S.Ct. 1507, 16 L.Ed.2d 600 (1966). Correlatively, it is a classic case of abdication of responsibility by a member of the judiciary to safeguard the rights of an accused.

Dr. Samuel Sheppard's pregnant wife, Marilyn, was brutally bludgeoned to death in an upstairs bedroom of her home in a suburb of Cleveland. Dr. Sheppard's story was to the effect that at the time of the murder he was asleep on a couch in the living room. He heard his wife cry out and he rushed upstairs where, in the dim light from the hall, he saw a "form" standing near his wife's bed. As he struggled with the "form" he was struck on the back of the neck and fell to the floor unconscious. When he regained consciousness he found his wife dead.

From the beginning the coroner and the police believed Sheppard guilty of murder and interrogated him at great length and without benefit of counsel. He was also pressed by the police to take an "infallible" lie detector test or an injection of "truth serum" or to confess. Sheppard resisted. The local newspapers, which took great interest in the case, played up Sheppard's refusal to subject himself to a lie detector test and the injections, as well as a so-called "protective ring" thrown up around him by his family.

Thereafter, an editorial writer opened fire with a front page charge that somebody was "getting away with murder." The editorial attributed the ineptness of the investigation to "friendship, relationships, hired lawyers, a husband who ought to have been subjected instantly to the same third-degree to which any other person under similar circumstances is subjected." The following day another front page editorial was headed: "Why No Inquest? Do It Now, Dr. Gerber." The coroner called the inquest the same day. It was staged in a school gymnasium, televised live to the people of the Cleveland area, covered by a swarm of reporters and photographers and ended after three days in a public brawl.

Throughout the period prior to Sheppard's arrest the newspapers emphasized facts that tended to incriminate Sheppard and highlighted discrepancies in his statements. Much of this "evidence" was never introduced at trial and the editorials became more insistent as to Sheppard's guilt. An editorial entitled "Why Don't Police Quiz Top Suspect" demanded that Sheppard be taken to police headquarters and another asked: "Why Isn't Sam Sheppard in Jail?" Immediately thereafter Sheppard was arrested and charged with murder. Then the publicity intensified. Cartoons, editorials, news stories and features, most unfavorable to

Sheppard, poured forth from the local presses and
radio and television stations. Headlines announced, among other things, "Sheppard 'Gay Set'
Is revealed by Houk [Sheppard's neighbor and
mayor of the town in which the murder took
place]," "Blood Is Found In Garage," "New Murder
Evidence Is Found, Police Claim," "Dr. Sam Faces
Quiz At Jail On Marilyn's Fear Of Him." The
publicity continued unabated until Sheppard's conviction in December 1954 and the press clippings
alone from the three Cleveland newspapers filled
five volumes of the record.

The conduct of the trial was equally depressing.
Before the case was set the names of the prospective jurors were published along with their addresses. Consequently, anonymous letters and
telephone calls concerning the prosecution were
received by all of the prospective jurors. Most of
the space in the small courtroom was set aside for
the use of the media, including a large area inside
the bar where traditionally only those directly
involved in the conduct of trials are permitted.
Representatives of the news media used all the
rooms on the courtroom floor, and private telephone lines and telegraphic equipment were in-
stalled in these rooms for their convenience. Live
newscasts were made from a temporary broadcasting facility set up on another floor of the courthouse. Everywhere around the courthouse and
nearly everywhere within, there were newsreel
and still photographers with all of their parapher-

nalia, intent on capturing all the participants on film as often as possible.

All of these arrangements with the representatives of the media were permitted to continue throughout the nine weeks of trial and the courtroom remained crowded to capacity with news personnel. The confusion caused by their movement in and out of the courtroom made it difficult for witnesses and counsel to be heard. Because of the close quarters and crowding it was almost impossible for Sheppard and his counsel to hold confidential discussions in the courtroom. Participants in the trial had to run a human gauntlet of media representatives just to get into and out of the courtroom. It was all reminiscent of the circus atmosphere that pervaded the Bruno Hauptmann trial for kidnapping and murder of the Lindbergh child some thirty years earlier. The trial judge, who was running for reelection, did nothing to stop it. He failed to sequester the jury during the presentation of evidence. Consequently, the jurors were exposed to the publicity generated during the trial. The Supreme Court in its opinion in the Sheppard case listed several instances of highly prejudicial publicity during that period. Repetition of only a few of them will suffice to suggest the environment in which the jurors decided Sheppard's fate.

On the second day of voir dire examination of the prospective jurors a debate was presented over WHK radio. The participants, newspaper report-

ers, accused Sheppard's counsel of throwing road-
blocks in the way of the prosecution and claimed
that Sheppard had admitted his guilt by hiring a
prominent criminal lawyer to defend him. When
defense counsel complained about the broadcast to
the judge, he refused to take any protective action.
During the trial, a Cleveland police officer gave
testimony that tended to contradict portions of
Sheppard's written statement made to the police.
Two days later, in a broadcast again over WHK,
Robert Considine, Hearst feature writer and radio
personality, likened Sheppard to a perjurer and
compared the episode to Alger Hiss' confrontation
with Whittaker Chambers. Defense counsel asked
the judge to question the jury to determine how
many had heard the broadcast and, again, the
judge refused and overruled a motion for a continuance based on the same incident. Later, a story
dealing with the defendant's temper appeared under an eight column headline reading "Sam Called
A 'Jekyll-Hyde' By Marilyn, Cousin To Testify."
No such testimony was ever produced at trial.
Similarly, two weeks later a police captain not at
the trial and never called as a witness denied
certain trial testimony given by Sheppard under
the headline " 'Bare-Faced Liar', Kerr says of
Sam."

Only after the case was submitted to the jurors
were they sequestered. However, after the guilty
verdict was returned, defense counsel discovered
that jurors had been allowed to make telephone

calls every day and no record was kept of the calls. The trial judge had failed to instruct the bailiffs to prevent such calls. Defense counsel moved for a new trial. The motion was overruled. Sheppard's initial state appeals were unsuccessful and review by the United States Supreme Court was denied. He served ten years in the Ohio penitentiary before obtaining a review of his conviction in the federal courts under a habeas corpus application. In those ten years the Supreme Court's attitude toward trial and pretrial publicity had been changing. In 1959 in Marshall v. United States, 360 U.S. 310, 79 S.Ct. 1171, 3 L.Ed.2d 1250, the Supreme Court, exercising its supervisory authority over the lower federal courts, reversed a conviction for unlawfully dispensing drugs because jurors had seen newspaper stories indicating that the defendant had two prior convictions, one of which was for practicing medicine without a license. The Court ordered a new trial despite assurances from the jurors that they would not be influenced by these stories. Then in Irvin v. Dowd, 366 U.S. 717, 81 S.Ct. 1639, 6 L.Ed.2d 751 (1961), the Supreme Court held for the first time that the exposure of jurors to massive and highly inflammatory pretrial publicity (including news stories that the accused had confessed to six murders) violated the accused's right to a fair trial guaranteed by the due process clause of the Fourteenth Amendment. Again, in Rideau v. Louisiana, 373 U.S. 723, 83 S.Ct. 1417, 10 L.Ed.2d 663 (1963), a conviction was reversed because of pretrial publicity undermining a fair trial, this time in the form of a televised "interview" of the accused by the local sheriff during which the accused admitted to bank robbery, kidnapping and murder. Finally, in Estes v. Texas, 381 U.S. 532, 85 S.Ct. 1628, 14 L.Ed.2d 543 (1965), a conviction for large scale fraud was reversed because pretrial and trial proceedings were televised and filmed. The Court held that such coverage denied to the accused a fair trial because of the psychological impact on and the distraction of the jurors, judge, witnesses and the accused himself.

In requiring a new trial in Sheppard's case, the Supreme Court signalled its determination to end free-wheeling media coverage of important criminal cases. Its decision intensified the conflict between the judiciary and the media. While noting that a responsible press is regarded as an indispensible handmaiden of fair and effective judicial administration, the Court in Sheppard recognized that in cases involving probable jury exposure to massive publicity relating to information not introduced in evidence at trial, jurors might be improperly influenced in their deliberations and decisions. The Court then ruled, relying on almost a decade of precedent, that in cases involving a high probability of prejudice to one or the other of the parties stemming from pretrial and trial publicity, such prejudice could be presumed to exist and actual evidence of the exposure to and the effect on individual jurors of such publicity need not be presented.   Sheppard's case was held to be one of those in which the presumption would apply.

The Court further stated that the trial judge compounded the problem of undue publicity in the case by acting pursuant to the erroneous belief that he lacked power to control it in any way.   The Supreme Court catalogued a number of approaches and tactics that the judge might have utilized to guarantee Sheppard a fair trial without imposing restrictions or sanctions *directly* against the press. These will be discussed shortly.

The idea that massive trial and pretrial publicity automatically results in the denial of a fair trial to one or the other of the parties is not unqualified. Otherwise the more notorious the crime the less the likelihood of obtaining a valid conviction in this age of mass communications.   It has often been suggested that had Lee Harvey Oswald lived he could not have been convicted for the assassination of President Kennedy because a fair trial would have been impossible anywhere.   But the judicial system will not allow itself to be paralyzed. If the presumed prejudice is clearly rebutted on voir dire examination of the prospective jurors and the atmosphere in the local community and the circumstances surrounding the trial do not betray inflamed community sentiment, there is no denial of a fair trial merely because of the publicity.   This is made clear in Murphy v. Florida, 421 U.S. 794, 95 S.Ct. 2031, 44 L.Ed.2d 589 (1975).   Because of the notoriety of the defendant, his case was heavily

covered by the local and national media and his
prior felony convictions were widely reported. But
the jurors chosen were emphatic that they would
not be influenced by the publicity and only 20 of
the 78 potential jurors questioned were excused as
indicating an opinion as to the defendant's guilt.
In contrast, in Irvin v. Dowd 268 of the 430 venire-
men were excused. In addition, unlike the Sheppard, Rideau and Estes cases, the conduct of the
trial and atmosphere in and around the courthouse
was proper. In such circumstances, the Supreme
Court held that the defendant had not been deprived of his constitutional rights to a fair trial.
The importance of the Murphy case lies in its
necessary implication that claims of prejudicial
publicity will be considered on a case-by-case basis,
with careful scrutiny by the courts of the circumstances surrounding the trials. Convictions will
not be reversed automatically because of the presence of substantial publicity.

Even so there is still a serious free press-fair
trial problem created by media coverage of criminal and other proceedings. The blame for the
existence of the problem can be widely apportioned
among prosecutors and defense counsel who violate
their code of professional responsibility by trying
their cases in the news media, law enforcement
officals seeking glory for their agencies, judges who
cannot resist the limelight, prominent uninvolved
parties such as Presidents of the United States who
pass judgment on accused in advance of trial and,

of course, media representatives who aid, abet and encourage these sources.

B. APPROACHES TO THE PROBLEM

1. Voluntary Cooperation Between Bench, Bar and Media

a. *Press Councils*

One non-legal mechanism designed to eliminate unfairness and impropriety in reporting generally is the press council. Its functions include hearing grievances brought by members of the public, including lawyer groups, concerning the media, passing judgment on those grievances and, in the process, laying down guidelines for fair reporting and proper behavior in the future. Two such councils had been set up in the United States, the National and Minnesota Press Councils. These private organizations were headed by distinguished jurists with membership divided between journalists and lay persons. Having no power to sanction the media or its representatives for unfairness in the coverage of criminal cases and other matters, the councils relied on friendly persuasion and the leverage inherent in publicizing their opinions. Experience with these councils has not been encouraging. The National Council ceased functioning, primarily because of opposition from the media. The Minnesota Council has become more an archive than a functioning mediation mechanism.

b. *Voluntary Guidelines for Criminal Trial Coverage*

A more widely accepted non-legal approach is voluntary adherence to general guidelines and policies for covering criminal proceedings drafted jointly by bench, bar and media representatives. Voluntary guidelines are in effect in more than half of the states and are strongly backed by organizations such at the American Bar Association, the American Society of Newspaper Editors and the American Newspaper Publishers Association.

An example of these guidelines is the California Joint Declaration of Principles and Policy, which begins with a declaration supporting both First Amendment principles and fair criminal proceedings. Concrete policies for news coverage then follow, including restraint by the media in characterizing slayings as "murders" until a formal charge is made and characterizing those brought in for questioning as "suspects." Restraint is also urged in reporting confessions. If confessions are reported they are to be called "statements" thus leaving to the jury the decision whether the accused really confessed. Generally, under the California guidelines prior criminal records should not be reported. Recognizing a major source of prejudicial publicity, the guidelines caution reporters not to let prosecutors, police or defense attorneys use the media as "a sounding board for public opinion or personal publicity."

Being voluntary and non-binding, the guidelines provide no sanctions for violation beyond adverse publicity and peer disapproval for the offending subscriber. Moreover, assuming good faith adherence to the enunciated principles and policies by the bar and media, an irreducible number of problems will still arise, and the danger exists that some judges may choose to treat the guidelines as mandatory upon the press and condition access to their courtrooms upon adherence to the guidelines. See, e.g., Federated Publications v. Swedberg, 96 Wash.2d 13, 633 P.2d 74 (1981), cert. denied, 456 U.S. 984, 102 S.Ct. 2257, 72 L.Ed.2d 862 (1982).

2. Resort to Judicial Procedural Devices

In his opinion for the Court in Sheppard, Mr. Justice Clark listed certain procedural devices available to judges to neutralize the possible prejudicial effect of publicity and behavior of media representatives without *direct* limitation on them. These include postponing the case until the danger of prejudice abates, transferring it to another county if the publicity has not saturated the entire state, sealing off or sequestering the jury as soon as it is empaneled to shield the jurors from trial publicity, sequestering the witnesses or at least admonishing them not to follow the proceedings in the media until they have testified, strictly controlling the courtroom and courthouse environment and, if all else fails, ordering a new trial. The last device is an extreme one not to the judiciary's liking. But the others may not, in given circumstances, be fully effective in insuring a fair trial. For instance, postponements and venue changes will have little effect if the publicity is dramatic and pervasive and sequestration does not shield the jurors from prejudicial publicity before they are selected.

3. Limiting Access of the Media to Information About Pending Legal Matters

a. The Suggestions in Sheppard

Justice Clark seemed to recognize the shortcomings of these devices for he also recognized the constitutionality of action to eliminate the need for new trials by restricting the sources of much potentially prejudicial publicity. Speaking for a majority of the Court, he would permit trial judges to issue restrictive orders prohibiting the prosecuting and defense attorneys, parties, witnesses and court and law enforcement officials from divulging prejudicial matters to the media such as statements made by the accused, the identity and probable testimony of witnesses and comments concerning the merits of the case. In addition, trial judges were encouraged to admonish reporters who wrote or broadcast prejudicial stories of the impropriety and danger of publishing matters not introduced at trial. But it is important to note that Justice Clark did not authorize direct restrictions on and sanctions against the media. He left that issue open for later consideration by the Court.

b.   *Other Institutional Reactions Favoring Restrictions on News Flow to the Media*

The Judicial Conference of the United States, the agency responsible for formulating policy for the federal courts made a report to the Chief Justice of the United States also in the late 1960's recommending that the United States District Courts firmly regulate both the physical courtroom environs and the release of information by members of their bars and by federal court personnel. The Judicial Conference also rejected the use of the contempt power to prevent unwanted publicity. The recommendations of the Judicial Conference have generally been adopted by the federal trial courts in the form of local rules governing the behavior of counsel and court personnel. See Judicial Conference Fair Trial—Free Press Guidelines, 6 Med.L.Rptr. 1897 (1980).

In 1965, the United States Department of Justice promulgated a Statement of Policy Concerning the Release of Information by Personnel of the Department of Justice Relating to Criminal Proceedings. The statement, more commonly known as the Katzenbach Rules, for the Attorney General who approved it, applied to the release of information from the time a person is arrested or charged with a crime until the proceeding terminated by trial or otherwise and condemned all release of information designed to influence the outcome of a defendant's trial. Authorized personnel were generally permitted to release only uncontrovertible factual information concerning a defendant's identity and age, residence and other basic background information, the criminal charge, the identity of the investigating and arresting agencies, the length of the investigation and the circumstances immediately surrounding the arrest.

The same personnel were urged to refrain from making available to the media observations about a defendant's character, statements, admissions, confessions or alibis, references to investigative procedures such as laboratory tests, statements about the identity, credibility or testimony of prospective witnesses, statements concerning evidence or legal argument in the case and photographs of the defendant unless a law enforcement function would be served thereby. Nor were members of the Justice Department to volunteer information about a defendant's prior criminal record or to encourage or assist the news media in photographing or televising a defendant in federal custody.

Certain strengthening amendments to the rules have been subsequently approved, including ones to control the release of information in civil and criminal cases in which the United States is a party. See 28 C.F.R. § 50.2 (1980).

While the Katzenbach Rules apply only to the Department of Justice, the ABA's Code of Professional Responsibility establishes standards for all attorneys. Consistent with the Reardon Report, new Code disciplinary rule DR 7–107 provides guidelines for prosecutors and defense counsel alike regarding the release of information concerning pending criminal cases roughly parallel to the Katzenbach Rules. Guidelines are also provided for professional disciplinary proceedings, juvenile justice proceedings, civil cases and administrative proceedings. In those states that have adopted DR 7–107 by statute or court rule attorneys may be disciplined for violating its precepts. While the ultimate sanction of disbarment has yet to be invoked for violation of DR 7–107, harsher disciplinary penalties can be expected in the future.

c. Exclusion of Camera Operators and Equipment from the Courtroom and Environs

For 45 years the American Bar Association had vigorously opposed cameras in the courtroom and for much of that time the ABA's position was followed by the nation's judges. ABA Canon of Judicial Conduct No. 3A(7) stated that a judge should prohibit the broadcasting, recording or photographing of proceedings in the courtroom. The only exceptions recognized were ceremonial proceedings or those recorded for educational purposes. Canon 3(7) was preceded by ABA Canon of Judicial Ethics No. 35 adopted in 1937. Canon 35 stated that broadcasting, televising or recording of active court proceedings detracted from the essential dignity of the proceedings, distracted the witnesses and attorneys, and created misconceptions in the public's mind. But though the thrust of old Canon 35 was endorsed by a plurality of the United States Supreme Court in Estes v. Texas, 381 U.S.

532, 85 S.Ct. 1628, 14 L.Ed.2d 543 (1965), the Court
subsequently held in Chandler v. Florida, 449 U.S.
560, 101 S.Ct. 802, 66 L.Ed.2d 740 (1981) that the
United States Constitution did not prohibit a state
from authorizing the use of cameras in the courtroom even in criminal cases in which the defendants object to the presence of electronic and still
photographic equipment to record such trials. The
Court said that an absolute constitutional ban on
broadcast and still photographic coverage of trials
could not be justified simply because there is a
danger that, in some cases, the ability of jurors to
decide the issue of guilt or innocence on an impartial basis may be impaired. Rather, the appropriate safeguard against such prejudice is the defendant's right to demonstrate that media coverage
compromised the ability of the jury in his or her
case to adjudicate fairly.

The Chandler opinion was written by Chief Justice Burger, perhaps the leading judicial authority
opposing cameras in courtrooms, particularly his
own. It is not surprising then that the opinion is
very narrow, saying no more than that the due
process clause of the Fourteenth Amendment does
not per se prohibit photographic coverage of judicial proceedings. Certainly the opinion does not
endorse the idea that cameras should be permitted
in courtrooms and the First Amendment does not
require them to be allowed. Westmoreland v. CBS,
Inc., 752 F.2d 16 (2d Cir.1984), cert. denied 472 U.S.
1017, 105 S.Ct. 3478, 87 L.Ed.2d 614 (1985).

Despite ABA Judicial Canon 3A(7) and the opinions of a plurality of justices in the Estes case, a survey taken shortly after Chandler indicated that 31 states had begun to permit cameras in some or all of their courts on a permanent or experimental basis and another five were thinking about it. This turnabout is quite extraordinary, since as late as 1976 only three states were permitting camera access. See News Media and the Law, p. 64 (Oct.– Nov. 1981).

As a result of this change of judicial attitude toward the use of cameras in the courtroom, the American Bar Association, bowing to the inevitable, revoked Canon 3A(7) in 1982 and in its place adopted a guideline stating that judges should be able to authorize unobtrusive camera use under carefully devised local court rules. Cameras are increasingly making their appearance in the courtroom, though not yet in the Federal Courts.

d. Sealing Arrest and Other Public Records

Another increasingly popular tactic of the judiciary in restricting access of the news media to information potentially affecting criminal prosecutions is the sealing of arrest and other public records, either pursuant to statute or under the inherent power of the court. The premier example of this latter approach is the trial of the Watergate defendants in which Judge Sirica sealed many of the documents and tapes in the case from public view. When officials of the Reporters Committee

for Freedom of the Press wrote the Judge a letter
requesting that the material be unsealed and made
available for inspection by the news media as representatives of the public the letter itself was ordered sealed.

But while secrecy in judicial proceedings is increasing, the press is beginning to attack the practice of sealing public records and removing them
from public inspection. In Miami Herald Publishing Co. v. Collazo, 329 So.2d 333 (Fla.App.1976), the
Miami Herald successfully challenged a trial court
order entered at the request of all parties to a
negligence action sealing the settlement agreement
between the parties to prevent the press and public
from learning its terms. In reversing the order
the Florida Court of Appeals said, "An informed
public depends on accurate and effective reporting
by the news media. . . . [T]he 'open court'
concept is an indispensable part of our system of
government and our way of life." 329 So.2d at 337.
And in an unreported case involving the federal
prosecution of the Governor of Maryland and certain associates for political corruption, a trial court
order sealing pretrial papers and proceedings was
modified on appeal within four days of the Washington Post's initial legal challenge so as to open
all previously and subsequently filed pretrial papers to public scrutiny. See Wash. Post, June 30,
1976, p. A34, col. 1; ibid. July 3, 1976, p. A1, col. 7.
It is clear from these and other recent cases that
affected representatives of the media are now

recognized as possessing legal standing to assert the public's right to be informed about judicial proceedings when individual judges (or statutes) would otherwise shield those proceedings. See Sheridan Newspapers, Inc. v. Sheridan, 660 P.2d 785 (Wyo.1983). The Supreme Court is placing increasing importance upon openness as a constitutionally protected value. "Closed proceedings, although not absolutely precluded, must be rare and only for cause shown that outweighs the value of openness." Press-Enterprise Co. v. Superior Court, 464 U.S. 501, 104 S.Ct. 819, 820, 78 L.Ed.2d 629, 633 (1984). The openness concept extends not only to the trial itself but to preliminary hearings as well. Press-Enterprise Co. v. Superior Court (II), 478 U.S. ___, 106 S.Ct. 2735, 92 L.Ed.2d 1 (1986).

e. *Closing the Courtroom*

Parallel to the sealing of public records is the exclusion of the public and the news media from the courtroom during trial and pretrial proceedings, usually in sensational criminal cases. This device, though once rarely if ever resorted to by American courts (see In re Oliver, 333 U.S. 257, 266, 68 S.Ct. 499, 504, 92 L.Ed. 682, 690 (1948)), became increasingly popular following the Supreme Court's imposition of strict limits on trial court's power to issue injunctive orders preventing publication of news concerning pending criminal trials in Nebraska Press Association v. Stuart, 427 U.S. 539, 96 S.Ct. 2791, 49 L.Ed.2d 683 (1976), discussed infra, pp. 228–231. The problems engendered by judicial resort to the court-closing device are considered in detail in Chapter VII at pp. 278–289, infra.

4. Prior Restraint of the News Media

The devices previously discussed are employed to prevent the news media from obtaining information about judicial proceedings which the judiciary believes would prejudice such proceedings. An even more difficult legal question than restricting access to news is posed by the judiciary restraining the media from publishing news that they have already obtained. The media's pejorative term for such judicial conduct is "gag order" and, indeed, the effect of judicial restrictive orders is prior restraint of the press.

a. Problems Engendered

Once the news media obtain information about pending judicial proceedings which, if published, might seriously affect their conduct and outcome, the courts must choose between previously discussed procedural devices designed to minimize or eliminate the impact of publication and the issuance of restrictive or "gag" orders directly against the news media. Increasingly during the late 1960's and the 1970's the trial courts chose to restrict publication. While all restrictive orders that were challenged on appeal were ultimately reversed, they created serious problems for the media and news personnel. Not the least of these problems arose when news personnel refused to obey even constitutionally invalid orders enjoining publication of the news. In United States v. Dickinson, 465 F.2d 496 (5th Cir. 1972), cert. denied 414 U.S. 979, 94 S.Ct. 270, 38 L.Ed.2d 223 (1973), two reporters assigned by their news service to cover a federal hearing challenging the legality of an allegedly baseless Louisiana murder conspiracy prosecution against a black civil rights worker were orally ordered by the presiding judge not to report the details of the evidence given in open court in the case. Notwithstanding the order, the two reporters wrote articles summarizing the testimony in detail. They were subsequently found guilty of criminal contempt and each was fined $300. On appeal of the contempt convictions the restrictive order was held to violate the First Amendment but the United States Court of Appeals further held that even constitutionally invalid injunctive orders must be obeyed until they are successfully challenged on appeal. This means that reporters, editors and publishers may properly be prosecuted for knowingly ignoring restrictive orders obviously violative of the First Amendment while such orders are ostensibly in effect. The principle enunciated in the Dickinson case that one must, under threat of criminal penalties, obey unconstitutional judicial orders until they are dissolved has generally been recognized in the state courts as well. See Annot., 12 A.L.R.2d 1059, 1107–16 (1950). But see State ex rel. Superior Court of Snohomish County v. Sperry, 79 Wn.2d 69, 483 P.2d 608 (1971) (crimi-

nal contempt convictions of two reporters for violation of patently unconstitutional restrictive order
vacated on appeal). See also Note, "Defiance of
Unlawful Authority," 83 Harv.L.Rev. 626, 633–638
(1970).

A very recent case suggests that the force of
Dickinson may be weakening. In In re Providence
Journal, 809 F.2d 63 (1st Cir.1986), modified and
reissued 820 F.2d 1354 (1987), cert. granted ___ U.S.
___, 108 S.Ct. 65, ___ L.Ed.2d ___ (1987) a newspa-
per was temporarily restrained by a United States
District Court from printing FOIA material obtained from the FBI concerning a deceased alleged
organized crime boss until a permanent injunction
action brought by the dead man's heirs could be
heard. The newspaper appealed the temporary injunction and, before the appellate court could decide
the appeal, published the material. Ironically, the
district court itself later removed the restraining
order. Nevertheless, the newspaper was found
guilty of contempt, fined $100,000 and the executive
editor sentenced to 200 hours of community service
in lieu of an 18-month jail sentence.

The First Circuit reversed the conviction, specifically distinguishing the Dickinson principle. The
court first held that a "transparently" invalid order could not lay the basis for a contempt conviction and, in the court's eyes, the temporary restraint was "transparently" invalid because there
was no possible basis upon which such a restraining order could validly be based. The boss'

"privacy" rights were not sufficient to lay the basis for a prior restraint and, even if they could, the district court had not demonstrated that less extreme measures were unavailable. The court distinguished Dickinson on two grounds: First, Dickinson was based upon the Sixth Amendment right to a fair trial, while Providence Journal involved merely an asserted right of privacy, a right which the court found not of equal magnitude. Second, the court noted that Dickinson was decided prior to the Supreme Court decision in Nebraska Press Association v. Stuart discussed below. Because Nebraska Press Association made even stronger the constitutional protection against prior restraint (requiring, inter alia, a consideration of other alternatives to a gag order), the First Circuit doubted whether Dickinson would have been decided the same way had it arisen after the Nebraska case.

But then the appeals court, in an en banc modification of its opinion, (820 F.2d 1354 (1987)) made clear that news organizations covered by what they believe to be transparently invalid restraining orders must exhibit good faith when they publish restrained material by seeking emergency relief from the appropriate appellate court first. If timely access to the appellate court is not available or if timely decision is not forthcoming, the publisher may then proceed to publish and challenge the constitutionality of the order in the subsequent contempt proceeding.

Dickinson and Providence Journal can, of course, be reconciled by noting that in Dickinson the prior restraint was not "transparently" invalid, while the Providence Journal restraint was held to be so. This is a rather dangerous distinction for the press depending, as it does, upon what a court might later determine to be the proper characterization. It is by no means self-evident that an asserted right of privacy can never be the basis for some type of prior restraint. All a news organization can do to reduce the risk of contempt sanctions is build a record of good faith action if it decides to publish.

b. Nebraska Press Association v. Stuart

Fortunately for the news media the indiscriminate issuance of restrictive orders directly binding their representatives was finally halted by the United States Supreme Court in Nebraska Press Association v. Stuart, 427 U.S. 539, 96 S.Ct. 2791, 49 L.Ed.2d 683 (1976). There the Court unanimously reversed restrictive orders of Nebraska courts barring newspersons from (1) reporting testimony and evidence presented in an open preliminary hearing concerning a ghastly multiple murder; (2) reporting the existence and nature of any confessions or admissions made by the accused to law enforcement officers or others; and (3) reporting any other facts "strongly implicative" of the accused. This was the first time the Court had considered the question of judicial restrictive orders aimed directly at the press. It took the oppor-

tunity to make clear that its distaste for prior
restraints on the press first expressed in Near v.
Minnesota, 283 U.S. 697, 51 S.Ct. 625, 75 L.Ed.
1357 (1931) had not abated.

Terming prior restraints on expression "the most
serious and the least tolerable infringement on
First Amendment rights" (427 U.S. at 559, 96 S.Ct.
at 2802, 49 L.Ed.2d at 697), the Court reaffirmed
the idea expressed in the "Pentagon Papers" case
(pp. 157–162, supra) that every form of prior restraint comes to the Court with a strong presumption of its unconstitutionality. But a majority of
the justices explicitly rejected the idea that the
First Amendment (at least at this time) absolutely
bars all prior restraints of the press when First
and Sixth Amendment interests are in competition. Instead the majority set out certain considerations to aid trial courts in determining whether in
a given and obviously rare case the proponents of a
judicial restrictive order might meet their heavy
burden of justifying prior restraint of the media on
Sixth Amendment grounds.

First, the courts must seriously examine the
alternatives to prior restraint of publication that
may be available to them such as change of venue
and postponement of the trial and make findings
supported by probative evidence that alternatives
short of prior restraint orders will not be effective.

Second, even where the courts believe that they
can establish the ineffectiveness of less drastic
alternatives, they must also assess the probable

effectiveness of prior restraint on publication as a
method of safeguarding the accused's right to a fair
trial. If, as a practical matter, a prior restraint
order will not safeguard the accused's rights it
should not be entered. In the Nebraska Press
Association case the facts (militated) against entry
of such orders. Among other things, the issuing
courts could not obtain jurisdiction over all news
media organizations and persons reporting on the
murder case and thus might not be able to enforce
their orders uniformly and effectively and, because
the murders took place in a small community of
850 persons, mouth-to-mouth rumors would satu-
rate the community anyway and might be more
prejudicial to a fair trial than reasonably accurate
news accounts.

Third, trial courts must consider whether proposed restrictive orders would prevent the reporting of events transpiring in open court. To the
extent they have this effect, such orders are constitutionally invalid.

Finally, the courts must consider carefully the
terms of such orders. The prohibitions on the
media must be precise and not overbroad. In the
Nebraska Press Association case one restriction on
the news media was that they not disseminate
information "strongly implicative of the accused as
the perpetrator of the slayings." This language
was held too vague and too broad to avoid abridgment of the First Amendment.

Regarding this last consideration, a restrictive order to be valid must be appropriately narrow and precise and yet must also be effective in safeguarding the accused's Sixth Amendment rights. Walking this constitutional tightrope will not be easy. It is safe to say that the matters which must be considered before a prior restraint order may be entered will severely curtail resort to such orders in the future. For this reason and because of the Supreme Court's unanimous reaffirmation of its attitude of hostility toward prior restraints, Nebraska Press Association v. Stuart was an important victory for the press.

5. Subsequent Criminal Punishment of the News Media

Subsequent criminal punishment of the news media may be just as dangerous to the media's ability to inform the public about judicial matters as prior restraints such as "gag orders." In Landmark Communications, Inc. v. Virginia, 435 U.S. 829, 98 S.Ct. 1535, 56 L.Ed.2d 1 (1978) the Supreme Court struck down as unduly restrictive of press freedom a Virginia statute making it a crime to divulge information regarding proceedings before a state judicial review commission hearing complaints alleging the disability or misconduct of sitting judges. In this case a newspaper corporation was convicted of violating the statute by accurately reporting on a pending commission inquiry and identifying the judge involved. The corporation was fined $500 plus costs.

In reversing the conviction the Court made it clear that subsequent punishment of the press for the publication of accurate information of interest to the public can be just as dangerous a violation of the First and Fourteenth Amendments as judicial and legislative attempts to prevent publication in the first instance. Compare the media contempt cases of Bridges v. California, 314 U.S. 252, 62 S.Ct. 190, 86 L.Ed. 192 (1941); Pennekamp v. Florida, 328 U.S. 331, 66 S.Ct. 1029, 90 L.Ed. 1295 (1946); Craig v. Harney, 331 U.S. 367, 67 S.Ct. 1249, 91 L.Ed. 1546 (1947); Wood v. Georgia, 370 U.S. 375, 82 S.Ct. 1364, 8 L.Ed.2d 569 (1962).

A case similar in effect to the Landmark decision is Smith v. Daily Mail Publishing Co., 443 U.S. 97, 99 S.Ct. 2667, 61 L.Ed.2d 399 (1979) in which a newspaper publishing corporation was indicted for violating a West Virginia statute which made it a crime for a *newspaper* to publish, without the written approval of the juvenile court, the name of any youth charged as a juvenile offender. The corporation then sought and received from the West Virginia Supreme Court of Appeals an order prohibiting prosecution under the indictment. The state high court's ruling that the statute on which the indictment was based violated the First and Fourteenth Amendments was upheld by the United States Supreme Court.

Both Landmark and Smith require a balancing of the media's interests in free dissemination of information against the state's interests in confidential judicial proceedings. In Landmark, the Supreme Court held that the state's interests in confidentiality of investigations of members of the judiciary simply did not outweigh First Amendment interests while in Smith the Court held that the state's interests were not weighty enough and further that whatever the weight of the state's interest in confidentiality of juvenile proceedings, it would not be furthered by a criminal statute which permitted media other than newspapers to disclose the names of alleged juvenile offenders.

C. THE FREE PRESS—FAIR TRIAL ISSUE TODAY: A SUMMARY

We now summarize what we believe to be the major aspects of the legal situation following Nebraska Press Association v. Stuart, supra:

1. Except in the most extreme cases, judicial orders directly restraining the dissemination of news by the media concerning judicial proceedings will be held invalid.

2. However, if timely access to an appellate court is available, presumptively invalid prior restraint orders must be obeyed by media personnel under penalty of criminal contempt until they are judicially dissolved. Thus, the possibility still exists that some judges may continue to issue unconstitutional restrictive orders against the media for the temporary advantage such action may gain.

3. News media personnel may not be excluded from open judicial proceedings and may not be restricted in the reporting of what transpires in open court.

4. Affected news media personnel and organizations have legal standing to challenge the closing of a criminal trial even when the accused chooses to waive his or her constitutional right to an open and public trial, and only in certain very narrow circumstances may the trial judge be allowed to exclude the public and the media. See Richmond Newspapers, Inc. v. Virginia, 448 U.S. 555, 100 S.Ct. 2814, 65 L.Ed.2d 973 (1980); Globe Newspaper Co. v. Supreme Court, 457 U.S. 596, 102 S.Ct. 2613, 73 L.Ed.2d 248 (1982).

5. Where statutes and state constitutional provisions permit, the courts may, consistent with the First, Sixth and Fourteenth Amendments of the United States Constitution, close pretrial proceedings to the public and the press. See Gannett Co., Inc. v. De Pasquale, 443 U.S. 368, 99 S.Ct. 2898, 61 L.Ed.2d 608 (1979).

6. An increasing practice of the courts in criminal cases is to seal pretrial and trial papers and transcripts and physical evidence such as the Nixon tapes. While affected members of the news media have legal standing to question individual "sealing" orders, in appropriate and narrowly circumscribed situations, such orders will be upheld. Overly broad "sealing" orders will be stricken as constitutionally infirm. See Press-

Enterprise Co. v. Superior Court, 464 U.S. 501, 104 S.Ct. 819, 78 L.Ed.2d 629 (1984); Press-Enterprise Co. v. Superior Court II, 478 U.S. ___, 106 S.Ct. 2735, 92 L.Ed.2d 1 (1986).

7. Restraining orders restricting those involved in criminal prosecutions such as witnesses and lawyers from extrajudicially communicating certain matters to the news media are constitutionally valid if the exigencies of a fair trial demand their entry (Sheppard v. Maxwell, 384 U.S. 333, 361–62, 86 S.Ct. 1507, 1521–22, 16 L.Ed. 2d 600, 619–20 (1966)) and the orders meet appropriate constitutional standards of precision and narrowness. See Chicago Council of Lawyers v. Bauer, 522 F.2d 242 (7th Cir. 1975), cert. denied, sub nom. Cunningham v. Chicago Council of Lawyers, 427 U.S. 912, 96 S.Ct. 3201, 49 L.Ed.2d 1204 (1976).

8. A newsperson who receives information proscribed by this type of restrictive order may be subpoenaed and compelled to disclose the source of such information under penalty of criminal contempt if he or she is not protected by a newspersons' shield statute. Such subpoena will be enforced in order to allow the issuing court to determine whether anyone bound by the order had violated it. See Farr v. Pitchess, 522 F.2d 464 (9th Cir. 1975), cert. denied 427 U.S. 912, 96 S.Ct. 3200, 49 L.Ed.2d 1203 (1976); Rosato v. Superior Court, 51 Cal.App.3d 190, 124 Cal.

Rptr. 427 (Dist.Ct.App.1975), cert. denied 427 U.S. 912, 96 S.Ct. 3200, 49 L.Ed.2d 1204 (1976).

9. State and federal statutes and court rules and state constitutional provisions which prevent resort to changes of venue, postponement of trial and other devices designed to avoid undue publicity and to insure fair trial may be held unconstitutional in specific applications.

10. Extensive publicity surrounding a criminal case without more does not result in a denial of a fair trial to the accused.

11. But news media misconduct in and around the courtroom and television and film coverage of pretrial and trial proceedings together with other extensive publicity may result in mistrial or reversal of convictions. Such misconduct is censurable and newspersons may be found guilty of criminal contempt for violation of reasonable regulations governing the physical conditions under which criminal trials are to proceed.

12. The broader power of the courts to hold members of the news media in criminal contempt for disseminating information outside the courtroom and its environs in the absence of the violation of any prior existing order restraining publication is in serious doubt since Bridges v. California, 314 U.S. 252, 62 S.Ct. 190, 86 L.Ed. 192 (1941) and its use seems unlikely to be revived, the ABA's Reardon Report to the contrary notwithstanding.

Two philosophical strands of thought can be discerned as underlying many of the above principles and rules. The first is the Blackstonian distinction between prior restraint of the press and subsequent press responsibility for what is published. The second is the increasing recognition by the Supreme Court that the First Amendment not only protects free dissemination of information but also requires "openness" and access to information in the first place. The court's language in Globe Newspaper Co. v. Superior Court, 457 U.S. 596, 102 S.Ct. 2613, 73 L.Ed.2d 248 (1982) and in the two Press-Enterprise Co. cases (464 U.S. 501, 104 S.Ct. 819, 78 L.Ed.2d 629 (1984); and 478 U.S. ___, 106 S.Ct. 2735, 92 L.Ed.2d 1 (1986)) have reaffirmed the proposition that openness is a constitutional imperative subject to defeasance only for the most compelling and narrowly circumscribed reasons.

CHAPTER VII

FREEDOM TO GATHER NEWS AND INFORMATION

A. INTRODUCTION

The freedom of expression guaranteed by the First Amendment would have little meaning if there were nothing to express. The First Amendment assumes that the citizenry will have access to information, particularly concerning their governance, as the grist for meaningful expression in a democratic society. As James Madison wrote, "A popular Government, without popular information, or the means of acquiring it, is but a Prologue to a Farce or a Tragedy; or, perhaps both. Knowledge will forever govern ignorance: And a people who mean to be their own Governors, must arm themselves with the power which knowledge gives." Letter to W.T. Barry, August 4, 1822, quoted in Environmental Protection Agency v. Mink, 410 U.S. 73, 110–111, 93 S.Ct. 827, 847, 35 L.Ed.2d 119, 145 (1973) (dissenting opinion of Douglas, J.).

Nevertheless, since the time of George Washington, the federal and state governments have claimed the right to withhold information about their activities and operations in the "public interest" and to restrict the access of individuals and the media to certain sources of information. But it is clear that not all governmental secrecy and restrictions on the gathering of information are justified. If nothing else the tragedies of Vietnam and Watergate have taught us that much.

A movement to reverse the trend toward secret government, led by the media, began to develop in the 1960s. And by the late 1970s it had resulted in some notable successes in the fight for open government, such as the federal Freedom of Information Act (FOIA) and federal and state open meetings legislation. However, a reaction has set in to the relatively easy access of the press and public to government information. One of the first orders of business of the Reagan Administration was the introduction of a comprehensive package of amendments to FOIA, which could only be described as constricting the flow of information from the government to the press and public.

It is clear, then, that ease of access to government data cannot be taken for granted but depends to a large extent on the good will and grace of the legislative and executive branches of government.

B. THE FEDERAL FREEDOM OF INFORMATION ACT (FOIA)

1. Provisions

In 1966 Congress passed the Freedom of Information Act (FOIA), 5 U.S.C.A. § 552, which requires federal executive and independent regulatory agencies to publish indexes in the Federal Register and make documents and records available to anyone who requests them if they are not specifically exempted from disclosure by the Act itself. The language of the Act is affirmative in requiring disclosure; nowhere does it require nondisclosure. Documents generated by Congress and the Office of the President are not subject to FOIA, but those of federal agencies are. An agency may, if it chooses, refuse to release information under a claim that the information is covered by one or more of the nine enumerated exemptions, but then it may be required to defend its refusal in federal court where the burden of justification is on the withholding agency, not on the person or organization seeking disclosure. With Congress' bestowal of jurisdiction upon the federal courts to hear complaints of alleged FOIA violations, agency officials are no longer the sole judges of what information should and should not be made available to the public.

The enumerated exemptions which may be invoked to avoid disclosure cover information:

(1)(a) specifically authorized under criteria established by an executive order to be kept secret in the interest of national defense or foreign policy and (b) are in fact properly classified pursuant to such executive order.

In Environmental Protection Agency v. Mink, 410 U.S. 73, 93 S.Ct. 827, 35 L.Ed.2d 119 (1973), the Supreme Court held in effect that the executive branch had some authority to determine under

Executive Order 10501 (setting up the present government classification system) what information was to be kept secret in the interest of national defense or foreign policy. The Court ruled that Exemption (1) as originally adopted in 1966 permitted no challenge whatsoever to the classification of a document. It would not allow a United States District Court to study in closed chambers classified documents concerning an underground nuclear test on Amchitka Island in order to isolate nonsecret portions and order their release. A classified stamp on a file meant that nothing in that file could be disclosed. The Mink case became the catalyst for Congress to amend FOIA in 1974 to give courts the power to inspect classified documents in closed chambers to determine whether they are properly classified, and order their release if they are not. P.L. 93–502, 88 Stat. 1561.

In 1982 President Reagan issued Executive Order 12,356, which calls for a review of classified material only at the time when it is classified, in contrast to President Carter who had ordered that classified material be reviewed every 20 or 30 years. Reagan's order created additional classification categories, and any information not given a pre-determined declassification date could be classified and exempt from disclosure forever. Under President Carter, an agency had to show that identifiable damage to national security would result in order to withhold information. Under the Reagan standard, the damage need not be identifiable and the agency need not balance its interest in withholding information against the public interest in disclosure. Exec. Order No. 12,356, 3 C.F.R. § 166 (1983).

(2) related solely to the internal personnel rules and practices of an agency.

The only real controversy regarding Exemption 2 is whether it applies to agency staff manuals. When a citizen sought access to a Bureau of Alcohol, Tobacco and Firearms staff manual titled "Surveillance of Premises, Vehicles and Persons," the Bureau released all but 20 pages, which it said described internal practices of the agency. Referring to the original debate in Congress which made it clear that Exemption 2 was designed to protect law enforcement investigatory manuals from disclosure, the United States Court of Appeals upheld the Bureau's decision to withhold the material. Crooker v. Bureau of Alcohol, Tobacco & Firearms, 670 F.2d 1051 (D.C.Cir.1981).

(3) Matters specifically exempted from disclosure by statute (other than [the Privacy Act]), provided that such statute (a) requires that the matters be withheld from the public in such a manner as to leave no discretion on the issue, or (b) establishes particular criteria for withholding or refers to particular types of matters to be withheld.

This exemption is designed to prevent disclosure of information required or permitted to be kept secret by numerous other federal laws. An example of a statute which would exempt information from disclosure is the National Security Act of 1947, which Congress amended in 1984, exempting entire systems of CIA files from search and review. Files dealing with conduct of foreign intelligence or counterintelligence, background investigations of informants, liaison agreements with other governments, and technical means of gathering information could be exempted. 50 U.S.C.A. § 403 (1982). The law provides for judicial review of whether the files are classified, but judicial review has not been effective because judges are reluctant to second-guess the executive branch on classification of national security materials.

The courts' willingness to give deference to Exemption 3 in the interests of national security is illustrated by the case of CIA v. Sims, 471 U.S. 159, 105 S.Ct. 1881, 85 L.Ed.2d 173 (1985). From 1953 to 1966, the CIA financed a research project code-named MKULTRA in which 185 researchers at over 80 universities received funding to study the effects of mind-altering substances on people. Several MKULTRA subprojects involved experiments in which researchers surreptitiously administered dangerous drugs such as LSD to unwitting human subjects. At least two people died as a result of MKULTRA experiments, and others may have suffered impaired health. In 1963 the CIA's inspector general investigated the project and reported that people were being used as guinea pigs without their knowledge. CIA files on MKULTRA were declassified in 1970. The Public Citizen Health

Research Group and a private attorney filed a FOIA request, asking for the names of universities and individuals who had conducted the experiments. The CIA refused to disclose names of the researchers and 21 of the institutions involved, saying that they had been promised confidentiality. The CIA argued that their names were exempt from disclosure under the National Security Act of 1947 which states that "the Director of Central Intelligence shall be responsible for protecting intelligence sources . . . from unauthorized disclosure." The Supreme Court agreed with the CIA that Exemption 3 of FOIA, providing that an agency need not disclose matters specifically exempted from disclosure by statute, was applicable, and the CIA could withhold the information. The Court added that the CIA Director's decisions, because he "must of course be familiar with the whole picture, as judges are not, are worthy of great deference given the magnitude of the national security interests and potential risks at stake." CIA v. Sims, 471 U.S. at 179, 105 S.Ct. at 1893, 85 L.Ed.2d at 190 (1985). The Court has thus given the CIA an indeterminate degree of latitude in making disclosure decisions within the context of intelligence-gathering. The Court's "great deference" standard may encourage the CIA to assert national security justification in an effort to hide improvident behavior. In effect, CIA v. Sims expands permissible Exemption 3 nondisclosure in a manner that may virtually exempt the CIA from FOIA coverage. L. Good and D. Williams, "Developments under the

Freedom of Information Act—1985," 1986 Duke L.J. 384, at 433.

(4) in the nature of trade secrets and commercial or financial information obtained from a person and privileged or confidential.

The so-called "reverse FOIA case," Chrysler Corp. v. Brown, 441 U.S. 281, 99 S.Ct. 1705, 60 L.Ed.2d 208 (1979) gives an expansive interpretation to FOIA to permit federal agencies to release certain classes of information required to be submitted to these agencies by private businesses, including their trade secrets and confidential statistical data. In so ruling the Court repeated the idea that FOIA is exclusively a disclosure statute and that the exemptions in it, particularly the one dealing with trade secrets, permit agencies to withhold records but do not require them to do so. This ruling has created problems for the government in collecting privately held confidential business information; it has resulted in calls from the business community for amendment of the Act to require agencies to withhold certain records in order to prevent harm to businesses which make disclosures of information to the government.

In 1982 two agencies did release information that hurt some companies. The EPA mistakenly disclosed the formula for one of Monsanto's most profitable products, a herbicide, to one of its major competitors in response to the latter's FOIA request. Washington Post, Sept. 18, 1982, p. A1. The Food and Drug Administration (FDA) released "the ingredients and molecular structure of a new drug about to be marketed by a major pharmaceutical company" to that company's competitor. 4 Gov.Disclosure Rep.Bull. No. 2, Prgrph. 2.2 (Feb. 8, 1983). These two incidents contributed to corporations' long-standing fears that the commercially sensitive data that they are compelled to disclose would inadvertently be made available to competitors through FOIA.

Possibly in response to these incidents and Chrysler v. Brown, Congress passed the National Cooperative Research Act of 1984, P.L. 98–462, 15 U.S.C.A. § 4305(d), which limits antitrust liability for companies embarking on joint research projects if they notify the Federal Trade Commission (FTC) and the Attorney General about their joint projects. The Research Act qualifies as an Exemption 3 statute of the FOIA by mandating nondisclosure by the FTC. Because it permits no agency discretion regarding disclosure, the Research Act limits the effect of the pro-disclosure interpretation in Chrysler v. Brown.

(5) in the nature of inter-agency or intra-agency memoranda or letters which would not be available by law to a party other than an agency in litigation with the agency.

This exemption is designed to protect working papers, studies and reports prepared within an agency or circulated among government personnel as the basis of an agency's final decision. Communications between an agency and its legal counsel are also shielded from disclosure.

This exemption is also called the executive privilege exemption. Executive privilege is a common law privilege which presidents beginning with George Washington have invoked to keep records and documents of the executive branch and the administrative agencies secret. In United States v. Nixon, 418 U.S. 683, 94 S.Ct. 3090, 41 L.Ed.2d 1039 (1974), Richard Nixon argued that his White House tapes were protected by executive privilege when the special prosecutor subpoenaed them. But the Supreme Court ruled that the president has an absolute executive privilege only when the material in question consists of military or diplomatic secrets. Because the White House tapes did not contain such secrets, there was only a limited privilege, and Nixon was ordered to surrender the tapes.

Another dispute over Exemption 5 occurred in Badhwar v. United States Department of the Air Force, 615 F.Supp. 698 (D.D.C.1985); 629 F.Supp. 478 (D.D.C.1986). In this case, two of Jack Anderson's reporters sought military air accident investigation reports for a comprehensive story on the military's aviation safety program. The Air Force said that the "benefit to the general public would not be the primary result when compared to the private interests of the requester," and invoked Exemption 5 in withholding statements made by a witness to military air accidents. In this case, the

Air Force quoted the witness in a safety board report which contained intra-agency recommendations. The question then was whether documents or statements given to an agency by persons independent of that agency are deemed transformed to "intra-agency memorandums" when they are included in internal agency reports. The court upheld the Air Force's decision to withhold the statements, thus raising a substantial question as to the scope of an "inter-agency or intra-agency memorandum."

(6) in the nature of personnel and medical files and similar files the disclosure of which would constitute a clearly unwarranted invasion of personal privacy.

An example of litigation involving Exemption 6 occurred when NBC legal correspondent Carl Stern requested information about three FBI officials who had been censured for their involvement in the FBI's domestic surveillance operations (COINTELPRO) in the 1970s. Stern obtained copies of the letters of censure, but the names were deleted. The U.S. Court of Appeals for the District of Columbia Circuit ordered the FBI to release the names, rejecting the FBI's claim of invasion of privacy and ruling that such privileges do not exist "when relatively high-placed officials entrusted with the performance of important public business actually jeopardize an agency's integrity by covering up a government wrong doing." Stern v. FBI, 737 F.2d 84 (D.C.Cir.1984).

In another case, Arieff v. United States Department of the Navy, 712 F.2d 1462 (D.C.Cir.1983), a journalist sought lists of the names and amounts of prescription drugs supplied by the Navy-operated Office of the Attending Physician to the U.S. Congress. The United States District Court had refused to compel disclosure, finding that, although the records did not contain personal details of any individual's medical condition, the journalist could combine the list of drugs with other information to discover much about the personal health of the members of Congress. But the United States Court of Appeals reversed, holding that the Navy had established only a "mere possibility" that among 600 possible recipients, one individual's medical condition would be disclosed. Furthermore, the drugs are given free to Congresspersons, and the public has an interest in knowing whether name-brand versus generic drugs are prescribed, for example.

(7) in the nature of investigatory records compiled for law enforcement purposes, but only to the extent that the production of such records would (a) interfere with enforcement proceedings, (b) deprive a person of a right to a fair trial or an impartial adjudication, (c) constitute an unwarranted invasion of personal privacy, (d) disclose the identity of a confidential source and, in the case of records compiled by a criminal law enforcement authority in the course of criminal investigation, or by an agency conducting a law-

ful national security intelligence investigation, confidential information furnished only by the confidential source, (e) disclose investigative techniques and procedures, or (f) endanger the life or physical safety of law enforcement personnel.

Congress tightened disclosure under this exemption in 1986. Under the 1986 amendments, informant files are no longer disclosable under FOIA. In addition, the FBI need no longer confirm or deny the existence of documents in counter-intelligence and terrorism files if the files are classified. P.L. 99–570, amending 5 U.S.C.A. § 552. The FBI had argued that those who were targets of its investigations were being tipped off by utilizing the FOIA to determine whether files had been compiled on them.

In addition to these disclosure-restricting amendments, there has been litigation over the definition of a "confidential source," (Exemption 7(d)). In Kuzma v. I.R.S., 775 F.2d 66, 69–70 (2d Cir.1985), the Second Circuit held that even agency personnel may be considered confidential sources if they receive assurances of confidentiality. The United States Court of Appeals for the Seventh Circuit has also ruled that a person may be considered a "confidential source" if he or she provides unsolicited information to an agency in circumstances in which there is an implicit, though not explicit, assumption of confidentiality. Brant Construction Co. v. EPA, 778 F.2d 1258, 1264–65 (7th Cir.1985).

The court held in Brant that if (1) the communication in all likelihood would not have been made if confidentiality had not been assured (implicit confidentiality), and (2) the information was treated confidentially by the agency, then the agency had the right to withhold the information.

(8) contained in or related to examination, operating or condition reports prepared by, on behalf of, or for the use of any agency responsible for the regulation or supervision of financial institutions.

This exemption is designed to prevent disclosure of sensitive financial reports or audits that if made public could undermine public confidence in banks and other financial institutions. It is seldom litigated.

(9) in the nature of geological and geophysical information and data, including maps, concerning wells.

This exemption protects the valuable proprietary information of oil companies and mining companies from disclosure.

2. Operation of the Original Act

a. *In the Courts*

Results of litigation under the original FOIA were mixed. While the courts placed the burden on the agencies to justify withholding information and exercised the injunctive jurisdiction to force disclosure when deemed appropriate, they also construed certain of the exemptions broadly.

In FAA Administrator v. Robertson, 422 U.S. 255, 95 S.Ct. 2140, 45 L.Ed.2d 164 (1975), the Court construed exemption (3) as referring to statutes broadly granting discretionary authority to agency officials to withhold unspecified information if in the "public interest" to do so. The Center for the Study of Responsive Law, an organization associated with Ralph Nader, had sought the release of the FAA's Systems Worthiness Analysis Program Reports (SWAP) concerning the operation and maintenance performance of the commercial airlines. The airlines voluntarily provide SWAP information to the FAA, and the industry's trade association, the Air Transport Association, objected to the release of the reports claiming that publication would adversely affect the airlines and make them less cooperative in the future with consequent adverse effect on air safety. The FAA Administrator denied the Center's request under Section 1104 of the Federal Aviation Act of 1958, which provides in relevant part that whenever an objection to release of information such as that of the ATA is made, "the Board or Administrator shall order such information withheld from public disclosure when, in their judgment, a disclosure of such information would adversely affect the interests of such person [objecting] and is not required in the interest of the public."

The Center successfully argued in the district court and the court of appeals that exemption (3) refers only to statutes which specifically designate particular classes of documents which might be withheld by the agencies and the SWAP reports were not so designated in Section 1104. The Supreme Court could find no such narrow limitation to exemption (3) either in its wording or legislative history and held that the FOIA permitted the Administrator to withhold information so long as he or she exercised discretion consistent with the general dictates of Section 1104. The Robertson decision had great potential for limiting the flow of information from the agencies to the public because there are nearly 100 statutes or parts of statutes which restrict public access to the records of executive and independent regulatory agencies in more or less general terms. But the Congress nullified the Supreme Court's construction in the new "Government in the Sunshine Act," P.L. 94–409, 90 Stat. 1241 (1976) and has essentially adopted the Nader group's position. See 5 U.S.C.A. § 552b(c)(3). This aspect of the legislation is discussed in Consumer Product Safety Commission v. GTE Sylvania, Inc., 447 U.S. 102, 121–22, n. 18, 100 S.Ct. 2051, 2063, n. 18, 64 L.Ed.2d 766, 780, n. 18 (1980).

b. *At the Administrative Level*

While litigation or the threat of it is very important to the operation of FOIA, the proof of the legislation is in its day-to-day administration by the agencies themselves. Litigation is costly and time consuming. Information is needed by the media quickly and at reasonable cost. At the administrative level, too, the results have been mixed. Some agencies such as the Department of Justice (excluding the FBI) and the Department of Defense have promulgated fair and reasonable regulations for the expeditious release of information and are generally following them. Some agencies have not been as conscientious. Charges for searches and copying have too often been exorbitant and extensive delays in releasing information have been frequent. Nevertheless, vast amounts of information have been made routinely available to the public and the media which prior to the Act would have been kept from view.

3. The 1974 Amendments

After experience with the operation of FOIA over several years, Congress amended it in 1974 to increase and expedite governmental disclosure. The amendments are both substantive and procedural. One substantive amendment defines a federal agency to encompass any executive or military department, including the Executive Office of the President itself, government corporations, and any independent regulatory agency. This amendment was needed because in the past some administrative units had tried to avoid responding to FOIA requests by claiming they were not "agencies."

As mentioned above, another substantive amendment was designed to override the decision in Environmental Protection Agency v. Mink, supra; it gives federal trial courts explicit authority to inspect in closed chambers any classified material involving national defense and foreign policy. If the material is not properly classifiable and can be reasonably released to a reporter or the public, the judge can order that it be disclosed.

The procedural amendments are designed to speed the release of information and reduce the costs to those who request it. The amendments require the agencies to establish uniform fee schedules and limit fees to reasonable charges for document searches and duplication. Agencies must respond to FOIA requests within 10 working days, for example, and are given 20 working days to process an appeal of a denial of a request. If the agency fails to comply with the time limits, the requester is given immediate access to the appropriate U.S. District Court for a hearing with the agency.

4. New Problems: What Are "Agency Records" and What Is an "Agency?"

Despite Congress' efforts in its 1974 amendments to increase the effectiveness of FOIA, problems persist. Surprisingly, the FOIA does not define "agency record." Because federal courts review denial of FOIA requests upon a showing that an agency has "improperly withheld agency records," this omission creates a problem when one agency is holding documents generated by another agency. It is unclear whether such documents are properly considered agency records of the agency in possession of them.

A related problem was considered in Kissinger v. Reporters Committee for Freedom of the Press, 445 U.S. 136, 100 S.Ct. 960, 63 L.Ed.2d 267 (1980), the Supreme Court ruled that the United States District Court had no jurisdiction to order the Library of Congress to return to the State Department certain telephone records made by Henry Kissinger while Secretary of State and later transferred by him to the Library in apparent violation of the Federal Records Act. Reading the agency "withholding" requirement quite narrowly, the Supreme Court ruled that an agency does not withhold agency records from a requester when it does not physically possess or control them. That being so the refusal of an agency to turn over records no longer in its possession does not violate the FOIA.

This decision creates a rather large loophole in the Act and a potential for agency abuse as Justice Stevens points out in his dissent. "It . . . creates an incentive for outgoing agency officials to remove potentially embarrassing documents from their files in order to frustrate future FOIA requests." 445 U.S. at 161, 100 S.Ct. at 974, 63 L.Ed. 2d at 288. Justice Stevens might have added that it also encourages venal federal agency officials to move records out of the agencies that generated them even while they remain in office.

Another problem with the Act came to light in the companion case of Forsham v. Harris, 445 U.S. 169, 100 S.Ct. 977, 63 L.Ed.2d 293 (1980) in which the Court ruled that documents produced by a private medical research group under a federal grant from and with supervision by an agency of the then Department of Health, Education and Welfare but with custody of the documents remaining with the private research group were not "agency records" accessible under FOIA. Thus, it is possible for federal agencies to avoid the reach of the Act by contracting with private organizations for controversial studies and reports so long as physical custody of the documents generated remains with the private contractor.

Not only has there been litigation over what constitutes an "agency record;" there has also been litigation over the definition of an "agency." In Rushforth v. Council of Economic Advisers, 762 F.2d 1038, 1043 (D.C.Cir.1985), the United States Court of Appeals held that the President's Council of Economic Advisers (CEA) was not an "agency" because its "sole function" is to advise the president. It has no regulatory power and cannot fund projects; thus, its records are not subject to FOIA. Those critical of this ruling point out that the information which the CEA gathers and analyzes forms the predicate for decision-making by the Executive Branch. By excluding such information from FOIA, the "sole function" test shields data, its interpretations and policy recommendations from evaluation by press and public, according to the critics of CEA secrecy.

5. Attempts to Use (or Abuse) FOIA in Discovery

Some critics of the FOIA charge that it is being abused by private litigants and their lawyers who use it to circumvent ordinary pretrial discovery procedural rules. This was the issue in United States v. Weber Aircraft Corp., 465 U.S. 792, 104 S.Ct. 1488, 79 L.Ed.2d 814 (1984), in which the FOIA plaintiffs were defendants in a damages action arising from the crash of an Air Force plane. During pretrial discovery, they sought to discover all of the Air Force investigative reports pertaining to the accident. But the Air Force refused to release confidential parts of its safety investigation. The U.S. Supreme Court ruled that confidential statements do not have to be disclosed under FOIA Exemption 5. A contrary ruling, the Court observed, would "create an anomaly in that the FOIA could be used to supplement civil discovery," a position that the Court has consistently rejected because of its belief that Congress did not intend to create a situation in which litigants could use the FOIA to gain information not discoverable under the Federal Rules of Civil Procedure.

6. Assessment of FOIA

There is other criticism regarding the uses to which FOIA is put. Some have claimed that journalists under-utilize it because they are more interested in breaking news than painstaking stories about government that can be documented with the aid of FOIA. Others attack the FOIA as permitting too much government information to be released under it. But, pressed repeatedly for examples of how FOIA has hurt government or hindered CIA or FBI activities, officials simply cannot give substantive examples. See B. Sanford, "The Information-less Age," Special Libraries, October 1983, p. 320.

Journalists and lawyers reject these charges. One reporter told a congressional committee: "For every one or two formal requests under the act . . . there are 12 or 14 we didn't have to make. The act is there, and the bureaucrats are aware of it." Journalists also point to their routine use of the FOIA to expose government waste and abuse and corporations' unsafe products and practices. For example, journalists have recently used the FOIA to expose the following abuses:

—disclosures about nuclear bomb testing and danger of the radiation to Utah residents

—the litany of FBI and CIA excesses during the 1960s and 1970s, such as illegal spying on Americans

—organized crime's infiltration of the coal industry

—Navy admirals with $14,000 sofas and $41,000 carpets on their destroyers

—the Pentagon permitting military contractors to charge the Department of Defense for the
costs incurred in lobbying Congress for appropriations for their weapons systems.   See New
Statesman, Jan. 10, 1986, pp. 12–13.

In short, despite its problems and limitations,
FOIA provides the American people and the media
which serve them with a significant instrument for
holding their government accountable.   To date,
much information has been released pursuant to
its provisions, and it has been estimated that plaintiffs have been successful in 60 to 70 percent of the
court cases.   The 1974 amendments have improved
on this record.   Already the new timetables seem
to be having the desired effect.   From discussions
with agency counsel it appears that some of the
agencies even defer important projects in order to
provide the personnel needed to expedite FOIA
requests.   And the Act's new limitation on agency
charges, together with the efforts of private organizations such as the Washington-based Freedom of
Information Clearinghouse and the Reporters Committee for Freedom of the Press to educate the
public and media representatives concerning the
Act, has encouraged increased utilization.   Equally
important large amounts of information are obtained by the media without formal request because of the mere existence of the Act.   For a more
detailed assessment of the original FOIA and the
amended version see Clark, "Holding Government

Accountable: The Amended Freedom of Information Act," 84 Yale L.J. 741 (1975).

C. LEGISLATION LIMITING ACCESS IN THE NAME OF PERSONAL PRIVACY

In contrast to the movement toward disclosure embodied in FOIA, more and more legislation is being passed to prevent public scrutiny of government-assembled information about individuals. In 1974, Congress passed the Privacy Act, 5 U.S.C.A. § 552a, to curb abuses by the federal government in its handling of personal information about individual citizens. The idea behind the federal statute has spread to the states and by 1980, some 16 states had enacted some kind of privacy act. See I Prentice-Hall Government Disclosure Service, p. 30,001 (1980). Seventeen states have legislation providing for expungement of nonconviction arrest records. See Biweekly Comparison of Key Statutes, National Law Journal, February 11, 1980, pp. 12–14. Because of privacy claims, the press has less access to government records, especially arrest records.

Though the intent of these statutes to protect individual citizens is laudatory, journalists must recognize that the more the government restricts access to information it collects, the less the press can fulfill its historic function of overseeing government operations on behalf of society.

For example, under the federal FOIA, all government documents must be disclosed upon request unless one of the nine exemptions is invoked. Before the Privacy Act was passed, an agency could waive exemptions at its discretion and release the information anyway. In contrast, the Privacy Act requires the Federal Government not to disclose certain information it has about individual citizens unless there is an exemption permitting its release. 5 U.S.C.A. § 552a(b). One of these exemptions permits release of such information when it is required to be disclosed under FOIA. The apparent implication here of the Privacy Act as it intersects with FOIA is that a government agency may no longer release personal information about individuals to others if such information is subject to one of the nine FOIA exemptions, as for instance, the personnel and medical files exemption (5 U.S. C.A. § 552(b)(6).

In Greentree v. United States Customs Service, 674 F.2d 74 (D.C.Cir.1982), Frank Greentree was convicted on federal drug charges, but filed a civil suit to block state prosecution for the same offenses. Greentree filed both a FOIA request and a Privacy Act request to get information contained in the Investigations Record System, which is exempt from the access provisions of the Privacy Act. Because the information Greentree wanted was exempt from disclosure under the Privacy Act, the government argued that it was also exempt from disclosure under Exemption 3 of FOIA. But the court ruled, "We must conclude that [there is] a congressional mandate that the Privacy Act not be used as a barrier to FOIA access." Congress could not have intended that a section of the Privacy Act could serve as a withholding statute under FOIA Exemption 3, the court added.

A more recent case illustrating the potential conflict between the FOIA and the Privacy Act is that of Cochran v. United States, 770 F.2d 949 (11th Cir.1985). In Cochran, the Army issued a press release indicating that Major General James Cochran had been fined and reprimanded for misuse of government resources. Cochran sued for damages, arguing that the disclosure of this information violated the Privacy Act. He claimed that the press release was not "required" under the FOIA because the disclosure constituted a "clearly unwarranted invasion of privacy," covered by Exemption 6. But the court disagreed, ruling that the press release was a "textbook example" of the type of information that the FOIA directs agencies to disclose. In weighing the privacy interests of the plaintiff against the public interest in disclosure, the court held that "to forestall future abuses, the public has an interest in any deterrent effect disclosure might provide." 770 F.2d at 956. Significantly for the media, the court added, "The legislative history of the [Privacy] Act does not evidence any intent to prevent the disclosure by the government to the press of current, newsworthy information of importance and interest to a large number of people." 770 F.2d at 958.

More generally, federal and state privacy statutes impose penalties on government agencies which improperly release information, but do not penalize the agencies when information which should be released is not. It is likely, then, that government personnel responsible for release of information will err in favor of nondisclosure when there is any question about whether it should be released or not. For a thorough discussion of the relation of the Federal Privacy Act to the Freedom of Information Act and the problems created by that relationship, see 2 J. O'Reilly, Federal Information Disclosure § 20.13 (Sheppard's 1977).

A potential conflict parallel to that of the FOIA–Privacy Act is embodied in the 1985 "Computer Crime Act," P.L. 98–473, 18 U.S.C.A. § 1030 (1984), amended P.L. 99–473 (1986), which prohibits unauthorized accessing and disclosure of data in government-operated computers. Senator Charles Mathias and others have voiced concern that the Computer Crime Act may apply even if the FOIA mandates disclosure of the information (131 Cong. Rec. S2728–29, Mar. 7, 1985). As in the case of the Privacy Act, employees who face possible prosecution and imprisonment under the Computer Crime Act for a mistake in releasing information under FOIA will likely resolve any doubt in favor of nondisclosure.

After various conflicting lower court decisions, Congress tried partially to resolve the conflict between FOIA and the Privacy Act (5 U.S.C.A.

§ 552a(q)(1) with a 1984 amendment to the National Security Act of 1947 (50 U.S.C.A. § 431) which declared that the Privacy Act is not an Exemption 3 statute. If the Privacy Act had been declared an Exemption 3 statute, it would have protected all information within its scope from disclosure under FOIA; entire systems of records could have been withheld. The Privacy Act clearly states that "no agency shall disclose any record . . . unless disclosure of the record would be required [under FOIA]."

D. OPEN MEETINGS—OPEN RECORDS LEGISLATION

1. The Federal Government in the "Sunshine"

Parallel to the Federal Freedom of Information Act are federal and state "government in the sunshine" statutes which require federal, state and local governmental units to conduct their business in the open. In 1976 Congress passed the Government in the Sunshine Act, the federal open meetings law. P.L. No. 94–409, 5 U.S.C.A. § 552b. This statute affects about 50 federal boards, commissions and agencies which are required to conduct their business meetings in public. The law also prohibits informal communication between officials of an agency and representatives of companies with whom the agency does business unless this communication is recorded as part of the public record.

Agencies may not automatically hold budget deliberations behind closed doors: "The Sunshine Act contains no express exemption for budget deliberations as a whole. Specific items discussed at budget meetings might, however, be exempt and might justify closing portions of a commission meeting on an individual and particularized basis." Common Cause v. Nuclear Regulatory Commission, 674 F.2d 921 (D.C.Cir.1982). In each case the agency must defend its closure by demonstrating that the discussion would fall under one of ten exemptions. The first nine of these parallel the FOIA exemptions. The tenth exemption deals with situations in which an agency is involved in arbitration or adjudication of a case. The tenth exemption was used to block access to a Nuclear Regulatory Commission meeting, for example, when it was considering reopening the Three Mile Island nuclear power plant. According to the United States Court of Appeals of the District of Columbia Circuit, this meeting could be closed to the press and public because it would probably focus on the final adjudication of the federal government's actions involving the nuclear reactor. Philadelphia Newspapers, Inc. v. Nuclear Regulatory Commission, 727 F.2d 1195 (D.C.Cir.1984).

Notice of public meetings must be given one week in advance, and the agencies are required to keep careful records of what occurs at closed meetings. All agencies subject to the law are required to draft regulations applying to their meetings and publish these in the Federal Register.

The Sunshine Act provides that an improperly closed meeting can be enjoined by a court, and that the court can issue an injunction against all future agency closings which violate Sunshine procedures. This might be called the "one mistake rule," because future improper closings could evoke a contempt sanction from a federal court against the agency which lost the earlier dispute. "Government in the Sunshine," Freedom of Information Center Report No. 366, January 1977, pp. 4–5.

There has been relatively little litigation under the Government in the Sunshine Act. In one case, a federal court held that the Act did not prevent the Atomic Safety and Licensing Board from meeting in secret to write a report on the nuclear steam supply system to be used in a proposed power plant. Hunt v. Nuclear Regulatory Commission, 468 F.Supp. 817 (N.D.Okl.1979), affirmed 611 F.2d 332 (10th Cir.1979), cert. denied 445 U.S. 906, 100 S.Ct. 1084, 63 L.Ed.2d 322 (1980). In another case involving licensing of a nuclear power plant, the court held that the Sunshine Act did not protect demonstrators who chained themselves to the door of a meeting room to prevent a secret meeting. United States v. Rankin, 616 F.2d 1168 (10th Cir. 1980).

2. State Open Meetings Laws

Statutes similar to the federal Government in the Sunshine Act are now in force in a large majority of states, but vary considerably, and journalists and lawyers must acquaint themselves with the provisions in their particular jurisdiction if the legislation is to be effectively utilized. Space limitations do not permit a state-by-state analysis here, but the general outline of the legislation and the basic legal issues may be considered in relation to one state's law.

a. Basic Provisions

One of the more influential "sunshine" statutes is that of Florida, where a ten-year debate in the Florida legislature created interest in "sunshine" legislation among other states. In addition, members of the Florida congressional delegation, apparently convinced of the utility and effectiveness of Florida's statute, were instrumental in persuading Congress to enact the federal Government in the Sunshine Act.

The Florida statute provides that

(1) Meetings of state, county and municipal agencies are open to the public, and no resolutions, rules or regulations are binding unless they are made at an open public meeting.

(2) Minutes of the meetings of any boards or commissions of state agencies are open to public inspection, and the circuit courts can enforce this by issuing an injunction to any agency

which does not make its minutes open to the public.

(3) If anyone serving in a state, county or municipal agency violates the two provisions above by attending a meeting not held in accordance with these provisions, he or she is guilty of a misdemeanor of the second degree, punishable as provided in § 775.082, § 775.083 or § 775.084. Fla.Stat.Ann § 286.011 (1975).

(1) Coverage

While the Florida statute covers all meetings of nearly all state and local executive and administrative units, statutes in other states are not as broad. Some states limit their "sunshine" legislation to the final stages in the decision-making process such as meetings at which final votes are taken. The spirit of open government may be easily avoided by agencies making the real decisions behind closed doors and then ratifying their decisions in the "sunshine."

(2) Exemptions

The "sunshine" statutes of most states provide specific exemptions from the public meeting requirement to ameliorate unwarranted disclosure. These exemptions are generally similar to those in the federal Sunshine Act.

(3) Public Notice of Meetings

It is axiomatic that unless the public and the media have notice of meeting times and locations, the requirement of open meetings is virtually worthless. Yet Florida and a number of the other "sunshine" states have no provision in their statutes requiring governmental units to set regular times and places for their meetings and to prohibit special or emergency meetings without some advance notice to the public generally or at least to the local media. Because it is the special or emergency meeting which often generates newsworthy actions, the media and the public need special notice legislation covering at least the same governmental units as are covered by the "sunshine" acts themselves. In this connection, California's notice requirement for special meetings and North Dakota's notice requirements for emergency and special meetings furnish useful models. Section 54956 of the California Government Code requires notice in writing to local newspapers and radio and television stations of special meetings of covered agencies at least 24 hours before the time of the meeting as specified in the notice, provided the media have previously requested receipt of such notices from the agencies. The one exception to this notice requirement is in the case of an emergency situation involving matters requiring prompt action by a legislative body because of the disruption or threatened disruption of public facilities. Section 54956.5.

North Dakota's open meetings legislation provides that the official calling an emergency or special meeting of a public body covered by the act must notify representatives of the news media who have requested to be notified of such meetings at the same time as the members of the public body are notified. North Dakota Cent.Code § 44–04–20 (Cum.Supp.1981).

(4) Enforcement and Sanctions

In addition to an adequate notice provision, an open meetings statute must have enforcement provisions and sanctions for violations if it is to be effective. In contrast with the federal Sunshine Act which permits litigation against a federal agency but does not punish individuals for violations, some states decree fines and/or jail terms for violators. In Florida, willful violation of the statute is a misdemeanor punishable by fine, imprisonment or both. Moreover, if a meeting is not made open to the public, any actions taken are nullified.

Most of the other states recognize the need for enforcement in their legislation, and provide for minor criminal prosecutions, civil actions for injunctive relief, or both. In 1986, public officials in Oklahoma and Detroit, Michigan were jailed for refusing to comply with open meetings laws and refusing to release public documents to reporters, respectively. A few states, like Florida, provide for nullification of final agency actions, but most states shy away from this extreme enforcement device. In some states, violators of sunshine laws may be removed from office.

b. Assessment

Of course, conducting government business in a fishbowl may interfere with free and frank discussion of the merits of proposed actions at least in the preliminary stages. Government officials, like nearly everyone else, are loathe to go out on limbs in public. There is bound to be some loss of input when nearly every move of the government employee or official is subject to public scrutiny. This loss of input can adversely affect the final product of government. Thus, the public will have to decide whether open government is worth the price.

But if the public does want open government, it must be noted that at present, the "government in the sunshine" statutes have not lived up to their billing. One study showed that nearly half of the federal agencies affected by the Sunshine Act were not opening a majority of their meetings. FOI Digest, March/April 1981, pp. 4–5. Journalists in Washington, D.C. report that compliance with the Government in the Sunshine Act is generally not good. Too often journalists are bullied or misled by uninformed or untruthful public employees who insist that they are not permitted by law to allow reporters to attend government meetings. Knowledge of the law, constant pressure and litigation against government agencies and officials who refuse to comply may be the only way for journalists to make the Government in the Sunshine Act live up to its promise.

An example of that promise occurred in a 1985 case in which a Utah federal trial court ruled that both press and public had a First Amendment right to attend a fact-finding hearing held by the Mine Safety and Health Administration (MSHA). The hearing dealt with the causes of a mine fire that killed 27 people.   MSHA chose to close the hearing, relying on a federal statute which held that an open hearing was not required, but the court said: "It is doubtful that there are any governmental interests compelling enough to warrant complete closure of the MSHA hearings." Society of Professional Journalists v. Secretary of Labor, 616 F.Supp. 569 (D.Utah 1985).

E. MEDIA ACCESS TO GOVERNMENTALLY RESTRICTED PLACES AND INSTITUTIONS

A field in which the freedom to gather news and information has not expanded in recent years is that of access to governmentally restricted institutions such as military bases and penitentiaries and geographic areas such as unfriendly foreign countries.   While the Supreme Court recognized in the abstract in Branzburg v. Hayes, 408 U.S. 665, 681, 92 S.Ct. 2646, 2656, 33 L.Ed.2d 626, 639 (1972), that "without some protection for seeking out the news, freedom of the press could be eviscerated," the Court in that very case appears to have restricted

First Amendment protection for newsgathering to those areas accessible to the general public.

Such an approach to access assures that the media will not be discriminated against in the gathering of information. But no guarantee is given that public access and, hence, media access to sources of information will not be further curtailed by a security conscious government.

Initially it was thought that because Branzburg involved a claim of indirect restriction on newsgathering (see pp. 296–299 infra for a discussion of the case), the limitation on protection for newsgathering might not be applicable to direct governmental restrictions on media access. This has not proven to be the case. In Pell v. Procunier, 417 U.S. 817, 94 S.Ct. 2800, 41 L.Ed.2d 495 (1974) and Saxbe v. Washington Post Co., 417 U.S. 843, 94 S.Ct. 2811, 41 L.Ed.2d 514 (1974) the California Department of Corrections and the Federal Bureau of Prisons had by regulation barred representatives of the media from interviewing specifically designated penitentiary inmates. The rationale for such restriction is that only a relatively small number of inmates are of interest to the media and those inmates who are conspicuously publicized tend to become the source of substantial disciplinary problems that can affect large portions of the prison population. Certain individual journalists and the Washington Post attacked the state and federal regulations as violative of the First Amendment's protection of newsgathering activities.

In the face of a detailed evidentiary record in the Washington Post case supporting the press' need for interviews with designated prisoners and a powerful dissent by Mr. Justice Powell, the Court decided by 5–4 votes that both the California and federal regulations totally banning designated interviews were constitutionally valid. Relying on Branzburg, the Court held that newspersons have no constitutional right of access to prisons or their inmates beyond that afforded the general public. Since the public is given no general access to the prisons or their inmates, the regulations did not abridge the First Amendment. As if to underline the limited constitutional protection afforded the newsgathering function, the Court said, "The proposition 'that the Constitution imposes upon government the affirmative duty to make available to journalists sources of information not available to members of the public generally . . . finds no support in the words of the Constitution or in any decision of this Court.'" 417 U.S. at 850, 94 S.Ct. at 2815, 41 L.Ed.2d at 520. This view of the Constitution was reaffirmed by the High Court in Houchins v. KQED, Inc., 438 U.S. 1, 98 S.Ct. 2588, 57 L.Ed.2d 553 (1978).

The principle that journalists are not accorded special access to news sources by the First Amendment is a broad one and would seemingly apply to any situation in which the state or federal government limits public access reasonably and in a nondiscriminatory way. A common situation is the setting up of police lines to seal off a geographic area in the interest of public safety. By definition police lines are designed to keep the public out of even public areas for limited periods of time and if there exists a reasonable basis for the lines it would seem to follow that the media could also be excluded. In practice, accredited journalists are often permitted by police authorities to cross the lines. If such permission is given, however, it must be extended on a nondiscriminatory basis to all journalists with proper credentials and the credentials must be issued in a fair and nondiscriminatory manner.

An analogous situation was considered by the Supreme Court in Zemel v. Rusk, 381 U.S. 1, 85 S.Ct. 1271, 14 L.Ed.2d 179 (1965). There, a private citizen contended that he had a First Amendment right to visit the then off-limits nation of Cuba to inform himself of the conditions on that island. In rejecting Zemel's contention the Court upheld Department of State passport regulations which, in effect, set up exclusionary lines around an entire country. While media representatives were not involved in the Zemel case and, in fact might, by Department of State regulation, be given special authorization to travel to Cuba and other restricted foreign areas to report the news (see 22 C.F.R. § 51.73(b)(1) (1981)), they could be prohibited from travelling to large areas of the world pursuant to the rulings in Pell and Washington Post Co. if such prohibition ostensibly serves some reasonable governmental purpose.

The danger to international newsgathering by American journalists posed by Zemel is further emphasized by Haig v. Agee, 453 U.S. 280, 101 S.Ct. 2766, 69 L.Ed.2d 640 (1981) in which the Supreme Court upheld the authority of the Secretary of State to revoke passports for conduct and expression which he considers damaging to national security or foreign policy. Presumably this could include newsgathering which the Secretary views as harmful or embarrassing to the country's interests.

Instead of rejecting the special societal interest in the newsgathering function, Justice Powell, in dissent in the Washington Post Co. case, would have recognized it in the context of Pell and Washington Post Co. and would have imposed upon the Government the same heavy burden of justification for denial of access of the press as for prior restraint of publication required in New York Times Co. v. United States, 403 U.S. 713, 91 S.Ct. 2140, 29 L.Ed.2d 822 (1971) (the "Pentagon Papers" case). Of course, the Justice recognized that his approach raises problems avoided by the majority. Prison agencies would have to make individual judgments regarding requests for inmate interviews and would have to define who or what is included in the term "press" for purposes of protecting the societal interest. But these problems, he asserted, are not insuperable.

While the prevailing judicial view refuses to mandate constitutional protection for the media in their newsgathering function beyond that afforded the general public, special consideration may still be accorded the media by legislative or administrative grace. We have already cited the examples of credentialed newspersons being permitted to cross police lines and the Department of State regulation giving professional journalists special authorization for travel to restricted foreign areas if the purpose of the travel is to make information available to the public concerning these areas. Others could be mentioned. But, of course, what is given at the government's discretion may also be withdrawn at its discretion.

F. MEDIA ACCESS TO COURTS AND JUDICIAL RECORDS

1. Access to Trial Proceedings

Another major source of concern about media access to governmentally generated information has recently developed, this time in relation to the courthouse. While it had long been our history that the doors of American courtrooms were open to the public and press (see Justice Black's opinion In re Oliver, 333 U.S. 257, 266, 68 S.Ct. 499, 504, 92 L.Ed.2d 682, 690 (1948)), a trend toward closing the courtroom developed in the 1970s as a judicial response to the threat to fair trials allegedly posed by publicity surrounding those trials. By the end of that decade the Reporters Committee for Freedom of Press had documented several dozen cases in which pretrial and trial proceedings across the country had been closed to the public and press by judicial order. This movement to deny access of the media to judicial information and news reached its zenith with the decision in Gannett Co. v. De Pasquale, 443 U.S. 368, 99 S.Ct. 2898, 61 L.Ed.2d 608 (1979). There, the two defendants in a murder case asked the judge to close a pretrial hearing in the case on the ground that the unabated publicity in Gannett's local Rochester, New York newspapers was jeopardizing their ability to receive a fair trial. The prosecuting attorney did not oppose the motion and a Gannett reporter present in the courtroom did not object at the time the closure motion was made and granted. The next day, however, the reporter wrote a letter to the trial judge asserting a "right to cover this hearing." When her request was rejected, Gannett formally moved the court to set aside the closure order. This motion was subsequently denied. On appeal the Appellate Division of the New York Supreme Court vacated the trial court's order but, in turn, the New York Court of Appeals reinstated the closure order.

In affirming the judgment of the New York Court of Appeals upholding the closing of the pretrial hearing, the United States Supreme Court rejected, in a five-to-four decision, Gannett's contentions that the Sixth and First Amendments, which are applicable to the states through the

Fourteenth Amendment, conferred upon the press a right of access to the pretrial proceedings in the case. Regarding the Sixth Amendment claim of access, the majority held that members of the public and press have no enforceable right independent of the parties to the litigation to demand a public trial. Rather, the public trial guarantee of the Sixth Amendment was created for the benefit of the defendant, and he or she may waive that protection.

Alternatively, the majority argued that even assuming that the Sixth Amendment could be understood as embodying the right of the public and press to attend criminal *trials,* it did not apply to *pretrial* proceedings.

Turning to Gannett's First Amendment claim to access, the majority, speaking through Justice Stewart, held that if such a right of access to criminal trials existed, Gannett's assumed right of access was not violated in this case. Justice Stewart asserted that such assumed First Amendment right would not be absolute but would have to be balanced against the defendant's right to a fair trial and that this balancing had been fairly done by the trial judge and he had determined that the balance should be struck in favor of closure of the courtroom in this case.

Moreover, any denial of First Amendment access in the case was temporary, for as soon as the danger of prejudicial publicity had dissipated, a transcript of the suppression hearing was made available to the press and public. Thus, no First Amendment right of Gannett to attend the criminal trial was violated.

The four dissenters warned that secret judicial proceedings would be a menace to liberty. Judges, police and prosecutors should be subjected to scrutiny at every stage of the criminal justice system to prevent potential abuse. More than 80 percent of federal criminal prosecutions never reach a full trial. Serious plea bargaining often takes place, perhaps because a prosecutor realizes that the case is not as strong as desired. Therefore, the prosecutor allows the defendant to plead guilty to a lesser charge or to the original charge with a promise of a light sentence. When such plea-bargaining takes place, there are no public proceedings after the pretrial hearing, which then is the last point for the public to learn what happens to the defendant. An example of abuse which can occur during plea-bargaining in a closed pretrial hearing occurred in Chico, California in 1979. When three white hunters were unable to find deer to shoot, they went looking for "dark meat," as they put it. They maliciously shot and killed a deaf and mentally retarded black man. The judge closed the preliminary hearings. He allowed the three hunters to plead guilty in return for lesser sentences and placed a gag order on the press for a year. Detroit Free Press, Feb. 24, 1980, pp. 1B, 4B. The local media assumed that the black man's death was a random hunting accident, and did not learn that

the murder was premeditated and racially motivated. Thus, they did not bother to challenge the gag
order.

Such abuses of plea-bargaining during closed pretrial hearings were a source of concern to the four
dissenters in the Gannett decision. Perhaps because of the broad manner in which the majority
opinion was written and the seemingly inconsistent
opinions by some of the justices who had formed
the majority, considerable confusion arose as to
whether the decision covered actual trials as well
as pretrial proceedings and whether there was or
was not a First Amendment right of access.

Fortuitously, a case was already in the judicial
system of the State of Virginia which squarely
raised these questions and would quickly give the
Supreme Court an opportunity to clarify what it
had decided in Gannett. In Richmond Newspapers, Inc. v. Virginia, 448 U.S. 555, 100 S.Ct. 2814,
65 L.Ed.2d 973 (1980), a murder trial was closed to
the public and the press on the motion of the
defendant, who had already gone through three
previous mistrials of the same case. The reason
given for the motion was that the defense did not
want information being shuffled back and forth
during recesses as to what particular witnesses had
testified to. Neither the prosecutor nor the reporters covering the trial for the Richmond newspapers
objected to the closure at the time the trial judge
granted the motion. But later that same day, the
Richmond Newspapers and their reporters sought

a hearing on their motion to vacate the closure order. A hearing was held the next day at which time constitutional objections were raised by Richmond Newspapers and the reporters. The court denied the motion to vacate and ordered the trial to proceed "with the press and public excluded." The media corporation and its employees then appealed to the Virginia Supreme Court which denied the petition for appeal. The United States Supreme Court then granted a petition for certiorari to review the case.

The Court, in reversing the judgment of the Virginia Supreme Court, noted at the outset of its opinion that the Richmond Newspapers case involved exclusion from a trial and not from a pretrial proceeding. The Court then went on to hold that while the Sixth Amendment provided the press with no right of access to trials, the First Amendment, as applied to the states through the Fourteenth Amendment, did. Chief Justice Burger speaking for the Court said, "We hold that the right to attend criminal trials is implicit in the guarantees of the First Amendment; without the freedom to attend such trials, which people have exercised for centuries, important aspects of freedom of speech and 'of the press could be eviscerated.'" 448 U.S. at 580, 100 S.Ct. at 2829, 65 L.Ed. 2d at 991–92 (1980).

But Chief Justice Burger made clear that the First Amendment right of access to trials was not absolute. If the trial court could find, as the

Virginia trial court did not, that there was a specific overriding interest in closing a trial, then an occasional courtroom closure might pass constitutional muster.

However, he did not state the precise constitutional standards that litigants would have to meet to obtain such closures or whether different standards might be applied to the closing of pretrial proceedings permitted by Gannett. Pretrial proceedings pose greater risks of generating publicity prejudicial to a fair trial because prospective jurors may be influenced by the news stories arising out of such proceedings before they are even chosen, and the judicial devices to prevent potential prejudice in such cases are limited.

However, there has been a clear trend toward upholding access to courtrooms for press and public in nearly all situations since the Richmond Newspapers decision. In Globe Newspaper Co. v. Superior Court, 457 U.S. 596, 102 S.Ct. 2613, 73 L.Ed.2d 248 (1982), the state of Massachusetts closed a rape trial involving minor victims because of a state law requiring that trials be closed without exception when juvenile victims of a sexual assault testified. The Supreme Court struck down the statute, holding that it violated the First Amendment right of access to court proceedings. Even the compelling interest of the state to protect minor victims of sex crimes from further trauma and embarrassment was held insufficient to justify indiscriminate exclusion of the press and public

from those portions of criminal trials during which
the victims testify.

The qualified right of access to attend criminal
trials outlined in Richmond and upheld in Globe
was extended to civil trials by the United States
Court of Appeals for the Third Circuit in Publicker
Industries, Inc. v. Cohen, 733 F.2d 1059 (3d Cir.
1984). But because the Supreme Court did not
clearly resolve the question of access to pretrial
hearings in Gannett Co. v. De Pasquale, supra,
some confusion remained in the lower courts during the five years following Gannett concerning the
openness of these often significant civil proceedings.

2. Access to Pretrial Proceedings

Then in 1984 the Supreme Court issued the first
of three decisions that helped resolve the issue.
The first of these cases began when the Press-
Enterprise in Riverside, California protested the
exclusion of reporters from nearly six weeks of jury
questioning (voir dire) at the trial of Albert Green-
wood Brown, who was later convicted and sentenced to death for the rape and murder of a 13
year-old girl. In a unanimous opinion, the Supreme Court ruled that voir dire proceedings
should be open to press and public unless those
wishing to close the proceedings could demonstrate
that 1) there is an overriding interest that would
be prejudiced by open proceedings, 2) the closure is
no broader than necessary to protect that interest,

3) reasonable alternatives to closure have been considered, and 4) the trial court made findings adequate to support closure. Press-Enterprise Co. v. Superior Court, 464 U.S. 501, 104 S.Ct. 819, 78 L.Ed.2d 629 (1984).

In the second case signalling a trend toward increased access to pretrial proceedings, Waller v. Georgia, 467 U.S. 39, 104 S.Ct. 2210, 81 L.Ed.2d 31 (1984), the state of Georgia tried to close the pretrial hearing in one case so that they might use the same wiretap evidence against other people not yet charged. But Waller, the defendant, wanted the hearing to be open. The Supreme Court upheld his position, ruling that hearings are presumptively open and cannot be closed against the defendant's wishes unless there are compelling reasons to do so. The Court held that the defendant's Sixth Amendment right to a public trial extends to pretrial hearings except where the party seeking to close the hearing meets the four-part test outlined above in Press-Enterprise. Writing for a unanimous Court, Justice Powell repeated the concern raised in Gannett Co. v. De Pasquale, supra, that pretrial hearings are often as important as the trial itself and may in fact be the only trial if defendants plea-bargain; thus, the arguments used to justify access to criminal trials apply equally to pretrial hearings. Powell also noted that one of the reasons often advanced for closing judicial proceedings, i.e. to avoid biasing the jury by pretrial publicity, is probably absent when the defendant wants the proceedings to be open.

Finally, in Press-Enterprise Co. v. Superior Court (II), 478 U.S. ___, 106 S.Ct. 2735, 92 L.Ed.2d 1 (1986), the same newspaper that had won access to the voir dire two years before won a Supreme Court ruling that the public and media have a qualified First Amendment right to attend pretrial proceedings in criminal cases. The case began when a California court closed a pretrial hearing at the request of a nurse accused of murdering 12 elderly patients at a nursing home by injecting them with lethal doses of the heart drug lidocaine. The Press-Enterprise protested the closure, and ultimately the Supreme Court ruled that a pretrial hearing may be closed only if 1) there is a substantial probability that the defendant's right to a fair trial will be prejudiced by publicity, and 2) a judge cannot find reasonable alternatives to closure to protect the defendant's fair trial rights. Mere risk of prejudice does not automatically justify refusing public access to pretrial hearings. If the judge finds a "substantial probability" of prejudice, he or she may order closure only in the narrowest manner which will be effective. For instance, if three hours of testimony during a four-day pretrial hearing might cause prejudice, the hearing may be closed only during those three hours. The Supreme Court has thus made it extremely difficult for those wishing to close pretrial hearings. Although the Court's opinion is directed to pretrial hearings in California, the question arises whether the 7–2 decision tacitly overrules the Court's earlier decision in Gannett Co. v. De Pasquale that criminal pretrial hearings may be closed to press and public. On the other hand, the majority opinion relies heavily on historical analysis, arguing that if pretrial hearings have generally been open in the past, there is a presumptive First Amendment right of access. However, the Court avoided a blanket ruling that pretrial proceedings must be open to the public and press.

3. Access to Evidence Introduced in Judicial Proceedings

Although the press and public previously have had some difficulty in gaining access to some pretrial hearings and occasionally even to trials, it is a general rule that evidence introduced in a civil or criminal case is open to public scrutiny. Journalists may describe or photograph it. Is the law different if such evidence is on a video or audiotape? Can radio and TV stations broadcast such tapes?

Lower courts are divided on this issue, partly because of a Supreme Court decision which held that whether or not broadcasters should be allowed to air Richard Nixon's Watergate tapes would be "left to the sound discretion of the trial court, a discretion to be exercised in light of the relevant facts and circumstances of the particular case." Nixon v. Warner Communications, 435 U.S. 589, 98 S.Ct. 1306, 55 L.Ed.2d 570 (1978).

Exercising its own discretion, the United States Court of Appeals for the Third Circuit has ruled that there is a strong presumption favoring access to video and audiotapes, and this presumption is not outweighed by speculations about any effect that broadcasting the tapes might have on related court proceedings. United States v. Martin, 746 F.2d 964 (3d Cir.1984). See also Washington v. Coe, 101 Wn.2d 364, 679 P.2d 353 (1984) and Valley Broadcasting v. United States District Court, 798 F.2d 1289 (9th Cir.1986).

In contrast, the U.S. Court of Appeals for the Fifth Circuit refused broadcasters access to audiotapes made during an FBI sting operation on the grounds that broadcasting the tapes might interfere with a defendant's right to a fair trial. Belo Broadcasting Corp. v. Clark, 654 F.2d 423 (5th Cir. 1981). Other courts have followed this precedent. See, e.g., United States v. Beckham, 789 F.2d 401 (6th Cir.1986).

As long as the Supreme Court is content to let lower courts use their discretion in these cases, there will be different rules in different jurisdictions. But if there is a trend, it is toward giving the mass media access to video and audiotapes introduced as evidence during a trial, provided that broadcasting these tapes will not interfere with the fair trial of another defendant against whom the same tapes might be used as evidence.

CHAPTER VIII

NEWSPERSONS' PRIVILEGE, SUBPOENAS, CONTEMPT CITATIONS AND SEARCHES AND SEIZURES

A. SUBPOENAS VS. CLAIMS OF PRIVILEGE

1. The Contemporary Problem

Until relatively recently the subpoenaing of newspersons by various branches and agencies of federal, state and local governments to testify as to their sources and other information did not pose much of a problem for the media. Until the 1950's, there were only a handful of cases involving attempts by government to force disclosure from unwilling members of the press. And as late as the advent of the Nixon Administration the problem was not one of major concern.

But then a number of social and political forces combined to embolden prosecutors, judges, legislators and other government officials to seek unpublished information of interest to them in the hands and heads of newspersons. Mutual distrust and even enmity between public officials and reporters began to grow, particularly in the large urban areas, fueled at least in part by the Vietnam war, a troubled economy, widespread graft and corruption at all levels of government, leaks of secret government information, doubtful media coverage of government and its personnel and what some might characterize as anti-establishmentarianism by some elements of the media. Then too, stories about the drug and sex subcultures and violence-prone anti-government organizations became of greater interest to the press. As a result, reporters were made privy to information concerning law violations that prosecutors wanted and could not obtain through traditional means. In addition, "law and order" concerns began to grip the land in the wake of an ever-increasing crime rate and public posturing by President Nixon and other members of his administration. The 1970s engendered a widespread attitude among government officials that if reporters had unpublished information concerning crimes and anti-establishment conduct, they had the same legal duty as anyone else to disclose it.

This attitude has persisted into the 1980s, and poses special problems for newspersons. First, the ethics of their profession require that they not divulge information obtained in confidence. Second, any disclosure or appearance of disclosure of sources or other information obtained in confidence will mark reporters as "unreliable" in the view of those from whom they are obtaining information and will have an inhibiting effect on their ability to gather and disseminate news. Third, reporters think of themselves as "professionals" like lawyers or doctors. This gives them a basis for claiming protection from disclosure of their non-published work product. News media personnel thus insist that the law must accord them a privilege not to testify or produce materials under compulsion of subpoena when their testimony would run counter to their ethical obligations or have an adverse effect on their ability to gather the news. But the National Labor Relations Board has ruled that journalists are not "professionals" within "the statutory definition of that term because they are not . . . in a field that requires all of its members to have knowledge of an advanced type customarily acquired by a prolonged course of specialized intellectual instruction." The Express-News Corporation and San Antonio Typographical Union # 172 a/w International Typographical Union, AFL–CIO. Case 23–RC–4219, 223 NLRB No. 97 at 628 (1976).

Not having professional status may be an advantage to journalists with regard to making them eligible for collective bargaining, but it is a disadvantage in that courts do not accord them an absolute privilege against being compelled to testify, in contrast, for example, with physicians and attorneys. Whether the courts consider them professionals or not, in many cases today, newspersons are refusing to obey subpoenas and choosing to face jail for contempt when the claimed privilege is denied.

There is now a serious and growing confrontation between those who would gather the news and those who would use these newsgatherers to provide information for governmental purposes. What makes the problem especially difficult is that both sides to the dispute may say, with some justification, that by their actions they are serving the public interest.

2. Legal Background

a. *Common Law Privilege*

The common law, while recognizing testimonial privileges for the attorney-client, doctor-patient and marital relationships, has never accorded a like privilege to the newsperson-news source relationship or any other aspect of the newsgathering process. A strong policy argument can be made that a newsperson's privilege is at least as necessary to the public welfare as the recognized privileges are because of its societal benefit in encouraging a freer flow of news and information to the public. But the law has accepted the strong opposing policy that the public, in the words of the master of the law of evidence, Dean Wigmore, "has a right to every man's evidence." The more testimonial privileges that are recognized, the less evidence will be available to those who must attempt to reconstruct the truth in a judicial proceeding or establish public policy in the halls of a legislature or in an executive office. Not surprisingly, then, the common law courts have consistently refused to expand the number of recognized privileges in order to cover newspersons.

b. Newspersons Shield Statutes

An alternative to persuading the courts to fashion a newsperson's privilege is to convince legislatures to enact statutes embodying such privilege. The first so-called newspersons' shield law was enacted in Maryland in 1898 to protect the confidentiality of news sources. It remained unique for more than three decades before New Jersey adopted a similar statute. Thereafter, lobbying campaigns by the newspaper industry have resulted in the enactment of shield statutes of one type or another in approximately one half the states. These acts are analyzed below at pp. 310–314.

Though such legislation is now widespread, the statutes at best provide uncertain protection for the newsperson because they are subject to interpretation and application by the state courts which have generally been hostile to their aim. They are, with few exceptions, narrowly construed and sharply limited as to the protection they afford.

The first federal shield statute was proposed in 1929 but though bills have been introduced in Congress with increasing frequency since then, no federal statute extending a testimonial privilege to newspersons has been enacted. Perhaps this is because no consensus has ever developed within the media as to either the necessity for such legislation or its proper scope. See pp. 299–310.

c. Claims of Privilege Under the First Amendment

A comparatively recent claim of newspersons to immunity from testimonial compulsion is based on the Constitution. The argument is that compelling reporters to testify in judicial and other proceedings will have a detrimental effect on their access to sensitive and confidential news sources and consequently restrict the flow of news to the public in violation of the First Amendment.

The argument was first made in Garland v. Torre, 259 F.2d 545 (2d Cir.1958), cert. denied 358 U.S. 910, 79 S.Ct. 237, 3 L.Ed.2d 231 (1958). Judy Garland had brought an action against the Columbia Broadcasting System alleging, inter alia, that the network had authorized and induced the publication of false and defamatory statements about her. Some of the allegedly defamatory statements appeared in a radio-TV column in the New York Herald Tribune written by Marie Torre and were attributed by her to an unnamed CBS executive. When Garland's attorney deposed Torre she refused to disclose the name of the executive, asserting that to do so would violate a journalistic confidence. Court proceedings were initiated to compel her to disclose the name. Again Torre refused to make disclosure. She was held in criminal contempt and sentenced to ten days imprisonment. On appeal she raised the constitutional issue. In affirming her conviction Judge (later Mr. Justice) Stewart, while recognizing that compulsory disclosure of a journalist's confidential sources might

entail an abridgment of press freedom, held that
such abridgment had to be balanced against the
obvious need in the judicial process for testimonial
compulsion. And where, as here, the need for the
testimony sought went to the heart of the plaintiff's claim, the Constitution conferred no right on
Torre to refuse to answer.

In his opinion for the Second Circuit Judge Stewart pointed out that the judicial process was not
being used to force wholesale disclosure of a news
source or to discover the identity of a source of
doubtful relevance or materiality. He thereby implied that there might be situations in which the
First Amendment would provide the newsperson
with a qualified privilege not to testify under compulsion of legal process.

On the other hand some state court decisions
after Garland and prior to 1972 held that the First
Amendment provided no testimonial privilege of
any kind. See In re Taylor, 412 Pa. 32, 193 A.2d
181 (1963); State v. Buchanan, 250 Or. 244, 436
P.2d 729 (1968), cert. denied 392 U.S. 905, 88 S.Ct.
2055, 20 L.Ed.2d 1363 (1968). Thus, the existence
of even a limited First Amendment testimonial
privilege for the newsgatherer was in doubt and
the issue could only be decided by the Supreme
Court.

3. The Branzburg-Pappas-Caldwell Trilogy

The issue was finally presented to the Supreme
Court in three different contexts in Branzburg v.

Hayes, In re Pappas and United States v. Caldwell
and eventually decided in one consolidated opinion
at 408 U.S. 665, 92 S.Ct. 2646, 33 L.Ed.2d 626
(1972). In addition to the impact on newsgathering from its dictum that "the First Amendment
does not guarantee the press a constitutional right
of special access to information not available to the
public generally," 408 U.S. at 684, 92 S.Ct. at 2658,
33 L.Ed.2d at 641 discussed at pp. 188–193, supra,
the majority opinion in this trilogy of cases denied
to newsgatherers a testimonial privilege to refuse
to appear before grand juries and testify as to
possible criminal activities they may have wit-
nessed in the course of their professional responsibilities and the identity of those who engaged in
such activities.

a. What the Supreme Court Decided

What the Court decided in the trilogy of
newsperson privilege cases is not entirely clear
because of the failure of Justice White, the author
of the majority opinion, to relate his lengthy reasoning to the three cases at hand and to make
distinctions between them and because of the presence of what appears to be a conflicting concurring
opinion of Justice Powell, a member of the five-
person majority.

It is clear that the majority recognized no basis
for a newsperson to refuse to appear and answer
some questions when summoned by a grand jury.
And it is also clear that the majority held that

members of the news media may be compelled to provide information concerning their witnessing of criminal activity. It also seems to follow from these holdings that the appearance and testimony of newspersons would be compelled in criminal and civil trials. If immunity against compelled testimony is denied in a closed and freewheeling grand jury proceeding, it would be difficult to justify its extension to open public trials controlled by strict evidentiary rules. The Court thus clearly rejected the idea that the First Amendment confers an absolute privilege upon newspersons not to appear and testify in judicial proceedings.

Less clear is whether the majority ruled that not even a qualified privilege may be claimed by the newsperson. Justice White's opinion rejected the idea of the existence of such a privilege and gave two reasons: 1) a court test would be required to determine whether it were available in specific cases, and 2) the difficulty of defining what a "reporter" is. But a careful reading of the other justices' opinions in Branzburg suggests that Justice White's rejection of the qualified privilege does not have the force it might at first appear to have. Whereas Justice White appeared to be using definitional balancing (weighing the need for a reporter's privilege against the problem of defining "reporter,") Justice Powell argued for ad hoc balancing: Powell would recognize the privilege depending on the situation, but only after the newsperson appeared before a grand jury and refused to answer specific questions on First Amendment grounds. In any event, Justice White's rejection of the qualified privilege does not have the force one would expect.

In contrast to Justice Powell, dissenters Stewart, Brennan and Marshall would have required ad hoc balancing *before* the reporter was required to appear before a grand jury. Under their approach the government, in a proceeding to quash the subpoena, would have to: (1) show that there is probable cause to believe that the newsperson has information that is clearly relevant to a specific probable violation of law; (2) demonstrate that the information sought cannot be obtained by alternative means less destructive of First Amendment rights; and (3) demonstrate a compelling and overriding interest in the information. 408 U.S. at 743, 92 S.Ct. at 2681, 33 L.Ed.2d at 676. In the years following Branzburg, many federal and state courts have applied Justice Stewart's three-part test in deciding whether to compel journalists to testify or not. The strength and clarity of the dissenters' three-part test may explain the continued interest of these courts in determining the scope of a qualified constitutional privilege for newspersons.

b. The Legal Situation After Branzburg

(1) In Detail

Most lower federal and state courts are limiting the application of Branzburg in civil cases and in certain aspects of criminal proceedings. In the

leading civil case of Baker v. F & F Investment,
470 F.2d 778 (2d Cir.1972), cert. denied 411 U.S.
966, 93 S.Ct. 2147, 36 L.Ed.2d 686 (1973), plaintiffs,
alleging racial discrimination in the sale of houses
to blacks in Chicago, sued certain local real estate
organizations and sought prior to trial to depose
Alfred Balk, a writer and editor, as to the true
identity of the fictitiously named "Norris Vitchek,"
a real estate agent and the main source for Balk's
article published in the Saturday Evening Post on
"blockbusting" in Chicago. Balk and his publisher
had previously promised Vitchek that they would
not reveal his true identity. Consequently Balk,
while highly sympathetic to the plaintiffs' cause,
refused to provide Vitchek's true identity, claiming
First Amendment protection. The plaintiffs
sought an order from the United States District
Court directing Balk to provide the information.
The order was denied and the Second Circuit handed down a decision after Branzburg affirming that
denial. Recognizing that the compelling of disclosure of newspersons' confidential sources has a
"chilling effect" on the flow of news to the public,
the court of appeals balanced the competing interests along the lines suggested by Justice Stewart in
his dissent in Branzburg, thereby recognizing the
existence of a qualified constitutional privilege in
civil cases. See Silkwood v. Kerr-McGee Corp., 563
F.2d 433 (10th Cir.1977) (documentary film-maker
treated as a reporter when making film about
mysterious death of Karen Silkwood after she
found she had been contaminated by plutonium

radiation at processing plant run by Kerr-McGee);
Loadholtz v. Fields, 389 F.Supp. 1299 (M.D.Fla.
1975) (disclosure of unpublished background mater-
ials sought and refused); Democratic National
Committee v. McCord, 356 F.Supp. 1394
(D.D.C.1973) (disclosure of unpublished background
materials sought and refused); Apicella v. McNeil
Laboratories, Inc., 66 F.R.D. 78 (E.D.N.Y.1975) (disclosure of identity of anonymous author sought
and refused). Los Angeles Memorial Coliseum v.
National Football League, 89 F.R.D. 489 (C.D.Cal.
1981). But see Dow Jones and Co., Inc. v. Superior
Court, 364 Mass. 317, 303 N.E.2d 847 (1973);
Caldero v. Tribune Publishing Co., 98 Idaho 288,
562 P.2d 791 (1977) (reporter refused to reveal
name of source of libelous story; court inferred
that no source existed); Matter of Farber, 78 N.J.
259, 394 A.2d 330 (1978), cert. denied 439 U.S. 997,
99 S.Ct. 598, 58 L.Ed.2d 670 (1978) (reporter found
to be in criminal contempt for refusing to give up
his notes).

Of course, the balance may, on occasion, be
struck in favor of compelling the newsperson to
reveal confidential sources and to provide unpublished background materials and work product.
See Winegard v. Oxberger, 258 N.W.2d 847 (Iowa
1977), cert. denied 436 U.S. 905, 98 S.Ct. 2234, 56
L.Ed.2d 402 (1978). With the exception of Matter
of Farber, which was a criminal case, the cases
cited above involved only the claim of the reporter's privilege at the pretrial discovery or motion

stage in civil proceedings. At that stage the relevance and materiality of the journalist's information may not be as clear, and the person suing the reporter will probably not have thoroughly explored alternative sources for the same information.

It is not yet clear whether the newsperson will be protected as regularly and to the same degree at the *trial* of a civil case when a litigant seeks confidential information from a journalist which will likely make or break his or her case. In such situation the interests of the individual litigant and the public in fair and peaceable settlement of private disputes comes into direct confrontation with the First Amendment interest of the public in the free flow of news.

In addition, the cited cases did not involve journalists as defendants. Availability of the qualified privilege can be affected by this factor. The courts are not likely to be very sympathetic to a reporter defendant sued for libel or invasion of privacy who asserts the qualified privilege to prevent an allegedly wronged plaintiff from proving his or her case. In this context Garland v. Torre, 259 F.2d 545 (2d Cir.1958), cert. denied 358 U.S. 910, 79 S.Ct. 237, 3 L.Ed.2d 231 (1958) discussed earlier, states the applicable principle: the balance is to be struck in favor of disclosure if the information sought goes to "the heart of the plaintiff's claim."

This principle has taken on increased importance with the advent of the New York Times v.

Sullivan line of defamation cases requiring the plaintiff, if a public official or public figure, to establish knowing falsity or reckless disregard for the truth on the part of the defendant. This may be impossible to prove unless the plaintiff can see the defendant's notes and background materials and examine his or her sources for the defamatory message. The Supreme Court expressed such a concern in Herbert v. Lando, 441 U.S. 153, 99 S.Ct. 1635, 60 L.Ed.2d 115 (1979), discussed in detail in Chapter II, supra. In that case, Lando, an editor-producer for CBS' "Sixty Minutes," was sued by Army Col. Anthony Herbert, an admitted public figure. Lando claimed a privilege under the First Amendment not to divulge his thought processes or state of mind he possessed when he was editing and producing the program segment complained of. The Supreme Court, in rejecting the claimed privilege ruled that to give Lando the privilege would make it far more difficult for Herbert to establish actual malice as required by New York Times Co. v. Sullivan. It would appear then that if a newsperson has evidence relevant to the actual malice issue in a libel suit brought by a public figure, and if the evidence cannot be otherwise obtained and goes to the "heart of the case," the courts will not grant a qualified privilege. Ironically, despite Herbert's victory in the Supreme Court battle over the reporter's privilege, the court ultimately granted summary judgment for Lando, finding that Herbert did not have enough evidence for the case to go to a jury. 781 F.2d 298 (2d Cir.1986).

The one caveat to the Garland principle is that if it is immediately clear to the trial judge that the plaintiff has little hope of success even if the journalist testifies, such testimony need not be compelled. An example of this is Cervantes v. Time, Inc., 464 F.2d 986 (8th Cir.1972), cert. denied 409 U.S. 1125, 93 S.Ct. 939, 35 L.Ed.2d 257 (1973), in which St. Louis mayor Alfonso Cervantes sued Life magazine for suggesting that he had underworld connections. Cervantes said he could not prove malice without knowing the names of the FBI sources of Life reporter Denny Walsh. But Cervantes objected to only four paragraphs of an 87–paragraph, extremely well-documented story, and the court noted that so far "as the vast amount of the other material is concerned, its truth is either admitted or not explicitly denied." 464 F.2d at 991. The court thus ruled that it was virtually impossible for Cervantes to prove malice in this case. Because Cervantes did not make a prima facie case showing that the Life article was false, the court refused to require Life reporter Denny Walsh to disclose his sources during pretrial discovery.

Turning from civil to criminal proceedings, the lower federal and state courts are generally following the narrow holding of Branzburg and are denying the privilege when newspersons assert it before grand juries to protect (1) the identity of sources who may have engaged in criminal activity and (2) reporters' unpublished notes, information and background materials which might lead to the discovery of the criminals. See Lewis v. United States, 501 F.2d 418 (9th Cir.1974), cert. denied 420 U.S. 913, 95 S.Ct. 1106, 43 L.Ed.2d 386 (1975) (claim of privilege by radio station manager to withhold original document of Weather Underground and tape recording of Symbionese Liberation Army from federal grand jury rejected). Because the grand jury has evolved by and large into a prosecutorial device, prosecutors have been quite successful both before and after Branzburg in having claims of constitutional privilege rejected during the preliminary stages of criminal investigations.

On the other hand, the cases since Branzburg indicate that reporters are more successful in claiming the privilege when it is the criminal defendant rather than the prosecutor who is seeking disclosure of the reporter's sources. In United States v. Burke, 700 F.2d 70 (2d Cir.1983), cert. denied 464 U.S. 816, 104 S.Ct. 72, 78 L.Ed.2d 85 for example, Sports Illustrated reporter Douglas Looney interviewed a reputed underworld figure who was the prosecution's chief witness in connection with a basketball point-shaving scheme at Boston College. The defendant asked the court to subpoena Looney's notes and drafts for the story, but the United States Court of Appeals quashed the subpoena.

Another example of a criminal defendant failing to compel a reporter to disclose his source is State

v. Rinaldo, 102 Wn.2d 749, 689 P.2d 392 (1984) in which reporter Gary Larson wrote six articles for the Everett Herald about cult activities at Eden Farms, partly owned and operated by Theodore Rinaldo, who was charged with statutory rape, assault, coercion and intimidating a witness. Larson promised his sources he would keep their identities confidential, but Rinaldo tried to force Larson to reveal the names of those who had given him the information for the articles. The Washington Supreme Court quashed the subpoena, thus extending the qualified common law privilege, formerly recognized only in civil cases, to criminal cases. See Note, "Qualified Common Law Privilege for News Reporters in Criminal Cases" 60 Washington L.Rev. 535–541 (1985).

Reporters cannot successfully claim the privilege in every case involving a criminal defendant, however, especially if disclosure of an informer's identity is relevant to the defense of an accused. In Matter of Farber, 78 N.J. 259, 394 A.2d 330 (1978), the court rejected New York Times reporter Myron Farber's claim of privilege not to disclose sources and documents he used in his articles leading to prosecution of Dr. Mario Jascalevich for poisoning five patients. And in Kansas v. Sandstrom, 224 Kan. 573, 581 P.2d 812 (1978), in which a woman was charged with killing her husband, reporter Joe Pennington testified at the trial that a confidential source had told him that one of the state's witnesses had threatened to kill the husband shortly be-

fore the murder. Pennington said the informant
had heard about the threat from someone who had
attended a party at which the state's witness made
the threat, but Pennington refused to identify the
informant, claiming a privilege. Noting that after
Branzburg, courts had generally tried to balance
the need of the defendant for a fair trial against
the reporter's need for confidentiality, the Kansas
Supreme Court ruled that the constitutional privilege did not apply in this case because the informant's identify was critical to the defense and there
was no other way to get the information.

(2) In Summary

While generalization in the field of reportorial
privilege is risky, the following principles and rules
are suggested in summary:

(1) There is no absolute First Amendment
newspersons' privilege.

(2) The recognition by the courts of a qualified
newspersons' privilege depends to a great extent
on the legal context in which the claim of privilege is made.

(3) The courts will not honor the claim of
privilege made before grand juries and trial
courts when it would protect sources and others
who have been seen by the reporter engaging in
the suspected criminal activity under investigation.

(4) The courts will not honor such claim made before grand juries when the reporter is asked to produce physical evidence in his or her possession of suspected criminal activity under investigation such as tape recordings and documents.

(5) The courts will not honor such claim at a criminal trial or collateral hearing when the information or evidence is sought by the prosecutor and it is relevant and material to his or her case.

(6) The courts will honor such claim at a criminal trial or collateral hearing when the confidential information or evidence is sought by the accused and it is not critical to his or her defense.

(7) The courts will generally honor such claim in civil pretrial proceedings and trials unless the information or evidence sought by the litigant goes to the heart of his or her case and there is no alternative source for that information.

(8) When the newsperson is a defendant in civil litigation (usually defamation or invasion of privacy actions), the courts are more likely to find that the information or material sought to be protected under the privilege goes to the heart of the plaintiff's case and cannot be obtained from alternative sources.

(9) When the newsperson is a plaintiff in civil litigation and claims the qualified privilege to prevent the defendant from obtaining informa-

tion relevant to his or her defense, the claim of privilege will be denied. See Anderson v. Nixon, 444 F.Supp. 1195 (D.D.C.1978).

(10) If the newsperson's claim to a qualified privilege in the particular context is not accepted, he or she will have to choose between revealing confidential information or material and accepting the consequences of disobedience of a lawful court order.

c. The Practical Effect of Branzburg on Newsgatherers

Despite the limitation placed on the scope of Branzburg by Justice Powell's concurring opinion and the well meaning efforts of lower federal and state courts to carve out a qualified privilege particularly in civil cases, the holding in Branzburg has had a serious effect on newsgatherers. The majority's rejection of an absolute privilege has left the newsperson to guess whether and to what extent the courts will protect promises of confidentiality that journalists make to their sources. At the time assurances of secrecy are given to sources a reporter will often be unable to determine in what legal context he or she will be asked to breach such confidences. Thus, even assuming the rules of the game to be clearly established after Branzburg, the reporter cannot always be sure which rule or rules will be applicable when his or her testimony is sought to be compelled.

This uncertainty must necessarily lead to greater caution on the part of the newsperson in making commitments to protect sources in return for information of interest to the public. Where such commitments are made they are leading to increased confrontation between the press and the judiciary. Hardly an issue of The News Media and the Law published by the Reporters Committee for Freedom of the Press goes by without the detailing of numerous cases involving contempt citations against reporters who have refused to testify pursuant to subpoena. This abrasive confrontation between two of the most important institutions in our free society has prompted renewed interest in legislative approaches to the problem of the newspersons' privilege.

B. NEWSPERSONS' SHIELD LAWS

In Branzburg Justice White wrote that Congress and the state legislatures were free to write laws extending to journalists a privilege against being forced to testify so long as such "shield" legislation did not run afoul of the First Amendment. Since Branzburg, a number of states have added shield statutes and numerous bills have been introduced in Congress to provide some kind of protection for newsgatherers.

1. State Shield Laws

a. Statutory Analysis

At the time this is written 26 states have enacted some form of shield legislation, and one state—California—has adopted a constitutional provision protecting newspersons. Although they vary somewhat in their language and provisions, these statutes usually address the following essential issues: (1) who should be protected against testimonial compulsion (reporters only or others communicating to the public and those aiding and abetting in such communication)?; (2) which kinds of media should be covered (newspapers only or radio, television, motion pictures)?; (3) what information should be protected (the identity of confidential sources or other unpublished matter as well)?; (4) at what types of government proceedings and at what stages in these proceedings is the privilege against testimonial compulsion available (judicial proceedings alone or legislative, executive and administrative proceedings)?; (5) whether there are any exceptions or conditions to the availability of the privilege (e.g., the need for regular publication and general circulation, thereby excepting many nonestablishment publications)?; and (6) whether the privilege may be waived by the protected individual (e.g., by disclosing the identity of a source to third persons)? In analyzing one's local shield legislation, these are the issues that determine the availability and scope of the privilege afforded.

State shield statutes are divided into three main groups, according to a study of the Freedom of Information Center of the University of Missouri School of Journalism. The first group of statutes provides for the unqualified protection of reporters against having to divulge the source of information obtained in the course of their employment, but most statutes in this group only refer to sources and do not expressly cover the reporter's work product or unpublished information and materials. Given the propensity of the courts to construe shield statutes narrowly, it is not safe for reporters to assume that these matters are also protected by such statutes. The second group of shield laws provides a privilege against disclosure of the source of information actually published or broadcast. While absolute in their terms, statutes in this group are very weak in protecting sources because neither the source nor the reporter can be certain at the time the information is given that the information will actually be published or broadcast. Moreover, like the statutes in the first group, these statutes do not protect the information itself. The third group includes statutes which are conditional in their grant of privilege to newspersons or which provide a basis for the waiver of the privilege. The statutes in this category are also narrow in scope, protecting only sources and often only sources connected with the print media. More important, even when a privilege in this category appears to cover a particular reporter's situation, there is no certainty that the courts will uphold it when the reporter actually invokes it.

Journalists are no doubt better off with narrowly-written shield laws than with none at all. There are fewer subpoenas issued for reporters to testify before grand juries than there were in the 1970s, and there are a few cases in which a shield law has actually protected a reporter. See, for example, Beach v. Shanley, 62 N.Y.2d 241, 476 N.Y.Supp.2d 765, 465 N.E.2d 304 (1984), in which the New York Court of Appeals ruled that New York's shield law provided an absolute privilege to a reporter, preventing disclosure of the name of a confidential source to a grand jury. In another case, In re Grand Jury Matter, Gronowicz, 764 F.2d 983 (3d Cir.1985), a United States Court of Appeals ruled that Antoni Gronowicz did not have to appear before a grand jury in a criminal fraud investigation because the government had not shown a compelling interest in gaining disclosure of the notes for Gronowicz' book "God's Broker," supposedly a biography of Pope John Paul II, but a book of doubtful origin. Beach v. Shanley and In re Gronowicz are the exceptions. In nearly all other cases, reporters have been compelled to appear before grand juries, including those in California, where the shield law is written into the state constitution.

Thus, the availability of qualified protection from the shield laws is not great. Still worse from the reporter's point of view is the attitude of the courts toward these statutes.

b. Judicial Treatment

The common law tradition of hostility toward the creation of privileges not to testify in judicial, legislative and administrative proceedings has been carried over to the interpretation of newspersons' shield statutes. The courts construe these statutes very narrowly and refuse to extend their protection beyond the literal words of the acts. Even where the literal wording of a statute would seemingly provide protection for the newsperson, courts have been known to construe it otherwise. Thus, while the Kentucky statute speaks in terms of protecting a newsperson against being compelled to disclose "the source of any information procured or obtained by him," the Kentucky Supreme Court has construed the word "source" to exclude those who permit the newsperson to observe their criminal activities. Branzburg v. Pound, 461 S.W.2d 345 (Ky.1971), affirmed sub nom. Branzburg v. Hayes, 408 U.S. 665, 92 S.Ct. 2646, 33 L.Ed.2d 626 (1972).

Apart from limiting the scope and efficacy of shield statutes through narrow and distorted construction of their meaning, a generally hostile judiciary has also begun to question the very constitutionality of such legislation. The most damaging constitutional ruling so far has come from the New Jersey Supreme Court. In the highly publicized shield law-privilege-contempt case of New York Times reporter Myron Farber, the New Jersey court ruled that the state's shield legislation violated the state constitutional provision that in all criminal prosecutions, the accused shall have the right "to have compulsory process for obtaining witnesses in his favor." The court interpreted this provision as affording defendants in criminal prosecutions the right to compel the attendance of witnesses, including newspersons, at trial, and to compel the surrender of documents which the defendant believes he needs in preparing a defense. Privileges against being compelled to testify found in modern shield legislation were thus held by the court to violate the state's constitution when they were invoked by newspersons to prevent criminal defendants from obtaining testimony or documents relevant to their defense. Matter of Farber, 78 N.J. 259, 394 A.2d 330, cert. denied sub nom. New York Times Co. v. New Jersey, 439 U.S. 997, 99 S.Ct. 598 L.Ed.2d 670 (1978).

The Farber decision is potentially very harmful to legislative attempts to protect newspersons' sources and confidential information because the New Jersey compulsory process clause is identical to that found in the Sixth Amendment to the United States Constitution. Some observers feared that if the Supreme Court ever interpreted the Sixth Amendment in the same way the New Jersey Supreme Court interpreted the state's constitutional provision in Farber, statutory shield privileges would be rendered ineffective everywhere when invoked to prevent criminal defendants from obtaining testimony or other evidence. This is because the Supreme Court has previously ruled that the compulsory process clause of the Sixth Amendment is applicable to the states through the Fourteenth Amendment.

But in response to the court's assault on New Jersey's shield law in Farber, the state legislature amended its shield law (N.J.S.A. 2A:84A-21) in 1980 to require a criminal defendant's attorney to prove at a special hearing that information sought by subpoena is (1) relevant to the defense and (2) that it cannot be obtained elsewhere. If the court upholds the subpoena, the information would be given to the judge for in camera inspection to determine if it is admissible as evidence.

New Jersey's 1980 shield law did in fact withstand a Sixth Amendment challenge in State of New Jersey v. Boiardo, 82 N.J. 446, 414 A.2d 14 (1980). In this case, four defendants on trial for murder, loan sharking, extortion and armed robbery tried to subpoena a letter sent to reporter Robin Goldstein by Patrick Pizuto, a prospective prosecution witness, claiming that the letter would impeach Pizuto's credibility. The trial court ordered Goldstein to produce the letter for in camera inspection, but she appealed, and the New Jersey Supreme Court quashed the subpoena. It did so partly because one of the defendants claimed to have tapes of telephone conversations with Pizuto which contained the same information which was in the letter, and the trial court had not tried to use these tapes or other "less intrusive" means to obtain the same information. The court added that the amended shield law required that "a defendant seeking information in a newsperson's possession must prove that, on balance, the value of the particular information to a fair trial outweighs the importance to a free press of shielding that information from disclosure." 414 A.2d at 16.

In addition to affording journalists greater protection in criminal cases, the New Jersey shield law has been held to provide "an absolute privilege not to disclose notes, memoranda, rough drafts, editorial comments, sources and other information sought by plaintiffs" in defamation cases. See Resorts International, Inc. v. NJM Associates, 89 N.J. 212, 445 A.2d 395 (1982) and Maressa v. New Jersey Monthly, 89 N.J. 176, 445 A.2d 376 (1982). In these cases the New Jersey Supreme Court has been one of the few courts to read the protections to newspersons afforded by a state shield law broadly.

The moral of all this is that a legitimate newsgatherer cannot rely with confidence even upon the plain language of his or her jurisdiction's shield law, but must also be aware of the case law construing such statutes. Even then, journalists should assume that in sensitive cases the courts will not uphold their claims to the statutory privilege and they should act as cautiously as possible consistent with "getting the story."

2. Administrative Protection for the Newsperson: Department of Justice Guidelines

Though no federal shield legislation has ever been enacted, the Department of Justice has adopted a set of guidelines that define when and how a U.S. attorney can obtain a subpoena against a working reporter. 28 C.F.R. § 50.10. In striking a balance between free dissemination of information and effective law enforcement, the following matters must be considered by Department of Justice personnel: (1) there should be reasonable belief based on non-media information that a crime has occurred: (2) there should be reasonable ground to believe that the information sought is essential to a successful investigation—particularly with reference to directly establishing guilt or innocence; (3) the government should have unsuccessfully attempted to obtain the information from alternative non-media sources; (4) except under exigent circumstances subpoenas should be limited to verification of published information; (5) even the appearance of harassment of media personnel should be avoided if at all possible; (6) subpoenas should, wherever possible, be directed at material information regarding a limited subject matter, should cover a reasonably limited period of time, and should avoid requiring production of a large volume of the newsperson's unpublished material.

In 1980 the guidelines were extended to afford similar protection in civil actions and to telephone toll records of journalists.

While the guidelines reflect the Department's sensitivity to the problem of compelling testimony from newspersons, they provide only minimal and uncertain protection because they are limited in scope to federal criminal prosecutions and are construed by government officials whose main concern must, of necessity, be for effective law enforcement. Moreover, the protection afforded is by administrative grace and that protection can be modified or withdrawn by the Department of Justice almost at will.

C. CONTEMPT FOR UNPRIVILEGED REFUSAL TO TESTIFY

1. The Real Importance of the Privilege

The existence of a privilege in a particular case of a refusal to testify or produce material is important in shielding a newsperson from the sanctions associated with the contempt power of courts and legislatures. Without a privilege to refuse to comply with a judicial or legislative subpoena, the newsperson will almost surely be held in contempt if the information sought is deemed relevant and material to the work of the governmental unit seeking the information. Depending on the type of contempt involved, the sanctions may include determinate and indeterminate jail sentences, crimi-

nal fines and civil payments to parties injured by
the contemptuous conduct.

2. Types of Contempt

Traditionally, contemptuous conduct is categorized in two ways. First, there is the distinction
drawn between direct and indirect contempt. This
distinction is based primarily on whether the disapproved conduct occurred within the presence of
the court or legislature or outside such presence.
It is essentially a question of location and the
significance of the place of the contempt lies in the
procedural disposition. If, for instance, a reporter
at a trial were to refuse without privilege to testify,
this refusal would constitute contempt in the presence of the court and could be dealt with by the
court summarily. The reporter could be held in
contempt immediately and punishment within constitutional limits could be imposed without further
proceeding.

If, on the other hand, the refusal to testify occurred in a grand jury proceeding, this would ordinarily be taken to be a contempt outside the presence of the involved court, and, before a sanction
could be imposed by the court, the reporter would
be entitled to some notice as to what was complained of together with a hearing on the matter
before the appropriate judge.

The other major distinction is between civil and
criminal contempt. This dichotomy is based on the
purpose for which the sanction is imposed. If the

sanction is designed, for example, to force the contemnor to testify, the sanction is viewed as coercive and nonpunitive and hence civil in nature. If the sanction is imposed to uphold the dignity and authority of the court and its orders without concern for coercion, it is deemed punitive in nature and thus the contempt is considered criminal.

The significance of the dichotomy is two-fold. First, in a civil contempt the period of incarceration must, of necessity, be indeterminate. Since the sanction is coercive the contemnor may purge himself or herself of contempt at any time by agreeing to comply with the court's order, thereby effecting his or her release from custody. If the civil contemnor does not choose to purge himself or herself, release from custody theoretically comes only when the information sought is no longer of value as when a grand jury term or trial proceeding has actually ended or the information is obtained from an alternative source. In contrast, a sentence of imprisonment for criminal contempt is of determinate duration and though the contemnor may have a change of heart and wish to obey the court's order once the jailhouse doors close, he or she will have to serve the sentence imposed. Such was the case of Marie Torre who refused to divulge the identity of the CBS executive who had allegedly libeled Judy Garland. The trial judge could have treated the refusal as a civil contempt and ordered her to jail until she talked. Instead he ordered Torre imprisoned for a definite period to protect the authority of his orders. See Garland v. Torre, 259 F.2d 545 (2d Cir.1958), cert. denied 358 U.S. 910, 79 S.Ct. 237, 3 L.Ed.2d 231 (1958).

Second, if the contempt is treated as criminal and does not occur in the presence of the court, procedural safeguards peculiarly associated with a criminal prosecution such as proof beyond reasonable doubt are applicable to the contempt proceeding. Within the criminal contempt category a further dichotomy exists between serious and petty contempts. If the contempt is serious, as defined by the length of the prison sentence which might be or actually is imposed, the alleged contemnor is entitled to a jury trial under the United States Constitution. See Bloom v. Illinois, 391 U.S. 194, 88 S.Ct. 1477, 20 L.Ed.2d 522 (1968); Muniz v. Hoffman, 422 U.S. 454, 475, 95 S.Ct. 2178, 2190, 45 L.Ed.2d 319, 334 (1975). The point of division between the serious contempt proceeding which requires a jury trial and the petty contempt proceeding which does not is a prison sentence in excess of six months. See Cheff v. Schnackenberg, 384 U.S. 373, 86 S.Ct. 1523, 16 L.Ed.2d 629 (1966); Muniz v. Hoffman, supra. Whether the imposition of a fine only against news organizations and personnel as punishment for criminal contempt would be considered serious and entitle them to jury trial is an open question. See Muniz v. Hoffman, supra.

3. The Impact of Contempt on Newspersons

The number of contempt citations issued against newspersons for refusal to testify before or otherwise cooperate with government units has increased dramatically in the last decade. But while the number of newspersons actually languishing in jails around the country is not yet great, the potential for such a situation is. The courts know that the imposition of fines or civil payments is not likely to intimidate or chasten the reporter who, for principle, refuses to cooperate in a grand jury or judicial proceeding.

Only imprisonment is at all likely to have the desired effect. And thus the newsperson who digs in his or her heels must be ready to accept incarceration of either determinate or indeterminate duration. About the only comforting note from the newsperson's perspective is that if the contempt is treated as criminal the likelihood of a sentence in excess of six months is remote because of the burden on the judicial system of granting the newsperson a jury trial.

4. Alternatives to Contempt Citations and Jailing of Newspersons

Courts are learning that even imprisonment for contempt is rarely effective in achieving the goal of disclosure by newspersons of confidential information. The courts are slowly changing tactics and choosing alternatives to contempt in an effort to enforce their disclosure orders. One tactic utilized

in libel actions against newspapers and their reporters when the reporters refuse to divulge the
identity of sources for their stories is for the courts
to presume that such sources do not in fact exist.
Such presumption aids the public figure plaintiff in
establishing actual malice as required by New
York Times Co. v. Sullivan and aids the private
figure plaintiff in making the showing of negligence on the part of the defendant as required by
most jurisdictions following Gertz v. Robert Welch,
Inc. See Downing v. Monitor Publishing Co., 120
N.H. 383, 415 A.2d 683 (1980); De Roburt v. Gannett Co., 507 F.Supp. 880 (D.Haw.1981).

Another device to force compliance by reporters
with judicial disclosure orders employed by at least
one state trial court is to strike the newspaper
defendant's pleadings and to enter a default judgment for the plaintiff in its libel action. Because
this device raises a serious question about the
deprivation of due process, courts must be very
careful to employ it only when the information
sought is absolutely essential to the plaintiff's case
and cannot be obtained by less drastic means. For
example, when the Twin Falls, Idaho Times-News
refused to disclose confidential information, the
trial judge ruled it in default and awarded $1.9
million to the plaintiff. The Idaho Supreme Court
reversed this ruling, noting that the plaintiff's inability to discover the reporter's sources had not
been shown to obstruct the plaintiff's ability to
prove the story false. Ultimately the plaintiff

dropped the libel action altogether. Sierra Life Insurance Co. v. Magic Valley Newspapers, Inc., 101 Idaho 795, 623 P.2d 103 (1980).

More recently, Jerry Plotkin, one of the Americans held hostage during 1980–81 in Iran, filed a $60 million lawsuit against the Los Angeles Daily News and two of its reporters, Adam Dawson and Arnie Friedman, when they published an article headlined: "Plotkin May Be Questioned in Drug Probe." When the two reporters refused to disclose their sources, Judge Sara Radin entered a default judgment against the defendants. The Daily News then ordered Dawson and Friedman to disclose their sources (sparking a storm of criticism from other journalists). The reporters refused, hiring separate attorneys to defend them. The default order was later vacated, but Judge Radin said that if no sources were named within 20 days, it would be "established as a matter of law" that no sources existed. One of the reporters finally identified two sources, both of whom were Drug Enforcement Administration agents. "News Notes," Med.L.Rptr. (Jan. 17, 1984).

In similar cases where reporters refuse to reveal the name of a source in libel proceedings, some courts have declared that such a refusal may allow an inference that no source exists. This is tantamount to saying the story was fabricated, making it much easier for the plaintiff to prove malice or reckless disregard for the truth. Courts have used this tactic in Caldero v. Tribune Publishing Co., 98

Idaho 288, 562 P.2d 791 (1977); Greenberg v. CBS Inc., 69 A.D.2d 693, 419 N.Y.S.2d 988 (1979); and Downing v. Monitor Publishing Co., 120 N.H. 383, 415 A.2d 683 (1980).

D. THE EFFECT ON NEWSGATHERING OF SEARCHES AND SEIZURES IN THE NEWSROOM

1. Zurcher v. Stanford Daily

Searches and seizures in the newsrooms of the nation by law enforcement officers pursuant to properly issued search warrants have been rare in American history. Normally, prosecutors seeking evidence of crimes which they believe can be found in the desks or files of a newsroom have simply subpoenaed someone associated with the news operation to bring the evidence, if any, to court. This procedure avoids the disruption of a search of the newsroom, avoids the chilling effect on the gathering of sensitive news and information and gives the subpoenaed party an opportunity to move to quash the subpoena.

But in Zurcher v. Stanford Daily, 436 U.S. 547, 98 S.Ct. 1970, 56 L.Ed.2d 525 (1978), a local district attorney obtained a search warrant issued on a judge's finding of probable cause to believe that the Stanford Daily, a student newspaper, possessed photographs and negatives revealing the identity of demonstrators who assaulted and injured police officers who were attempting to quell a riot at the Stanford University Hospital. A search of the paper's newsroom was undertaken pursuant to the warrant but no incriminating evidence was found. Thereafter, the paper and certain staff members sought a judicial declaration that the search had deprived them of their constitutional rights and an injunction against further searches. The United States District Court denied the injunction but granted the declaratory relief sought. The United States Court of Appeals affirmed the judgment of the District Court.

In the Supreme Court, the Stanford Daily argued that such searches of newspaper offices for evidence of crimes committed by others seriously threatened the ability of the press to gather, analyze and disseminate news, thereby violating the First Amendment. More specifically the newspaper argued that (1) searches are physically disruptive to orderly publication; (2) confidential sources of information will dry up and access to various news events will be denied because of fear that press files will be readily available to law enforcement authorities; (3) reporters will be dissuaded from recording and preserving their recollections for verification and future use; (4) the processing of news and its dissemination will be chilled by the prospect that searches will disclose internal editorial deliberations; and (5) the press will resort to self-censorship to conceal its possession of information of potential interest to the police.

While Justice Stewart in dissent generally agreed with the newspaper's contentions, a majori-

ty of the Court led by Justice White held that
searches and seizures in newsrooms pursuant to
warrant did not violate First Amendment guarantees because the drafters of the Constitution had
not, under the Fourth Amendment, forbidden
search warrants directed to the press, did not require special showings that subpoenas would be
impractical before warrants could be issued to
search the premises of the press, and did not insist
that if a press organization was named in a search
warrant, the police would first have to show the
organization's complicity in the alleged offense being investigated.

Justice White argued in support of his conclusion
that if law enforcement officers and the courts
properly administer search warrants, the precondi-
tions for their issuance—probable cause, specificity
with respect to the place to be searched and the
things to be seized, and overall reasonableness in
searches and seizures—should afford sufficient protection against infringement of First Amendment
interests. Further, Justice White doubted, in the
face of numerous press organization affidavits to
the contrary, that confidential sources would dry
up or that the press would suppress news because
of fears of warranted searches.

2. Federal Legislation in the Wake of Zurcher

Less than three years after the decision in
Zurcher, a Congress less sanguine about the dangers posed by searches and seizures in newsrooms

enacted P.L. 96–449, the Privacy Protection Act of 1980, 42 U.S.C.A. 2000aa–1 et seq. This act substantially restricts the situations in which a newsroom search and seizure may legally occur. Title I of the statute divides evidence subject to possible seizure into two categories (1) work product materials possessed by newspaper persons, authors or broadcasters and (2) all other documentary materials possessed by these same classes of persons. The Privacy Protection Act makes it unlawful for federal and state government officers or employees to search for or seize materials in the first category except in two cases: (1) where the person holding such materials has committed the crime, *unless* the "criminal activity" is merely the possession of the material or the information it contains; and (2) where there is reason to believe that the immediate seizure of such materials is necessary to prevent the death of, or serious bodily injury to, a human being.

The Act also makes it unlawful for federal and state government officers or employees to search for or seize materials in the second category with four exceptions. The first two exceptions are exactly the same as the exceptions for the first category of material. The two additional exceptions permitting lawful searches and seizures of second category material are first that there is reason to believe that the giving of notice pursuant to a subpoena of the material would result in its destruction, alteration or concealment; and second that such materials have not been produced in response to court order and all appellate court remedies have been exhausted or that "there is reason to believe that the delay . . . occasioned by further proceedings relating to the subpoena would threaten the interests of justice." As to the quoted portion of the last exception, the person possessing the sought after material is afforded an opportunity under the Act to oppose the issuance of the search warrant.

CHAPTER IX

REGULATION OF COMMERCIAL SPEECH

A. CONSTITUTIONAL HISTORY

First Amendment protection for commercial speech—particularly commercial advertising—has had a checkered history in the Supreme Court. First the Court refused to recognize any such protection. Then, after recognizing some protection utilizing the language of ad hoc balancing, the Court appeared to move toward absolutist protection of such speech qualified only by time, place and manner considerations. Now the Court, for the present at least, has settled upon a seemingly well-defined balancing approach that nevertheless leaves the Court great latitude in its specific application.

The chronology begins with Valentine v. Chrestensen, 316 U.S. 52, 62 S.Ct. 920, 86 L.Ed. 1262 (1942), in which the Court unanimously sustained an ordinance which banned the distribution of commercial handbill advertising. After being prohibited by local authorities from distributing a handbill announcing the exhibition of a submarine, the promoter had printed on the reverse side of the handbill a protest against an official refusal to allow him to use city wharfage facilities for such

331

exhibition. The court found this supposed political protest to be a mere subterfuge to evade the ordinance and suggested that "purely commercial advertising" was not protected by the First Amendment. In short, the government could constitutionally regulate product or service advertising without abridging the First Amendment.

This distinction between types of expression has been a controversial one. In Cammarano v. United States, 358 U.S. 498, 514, 79 S.Ct. 524, 534, 3 L.Ed.2d 462, 472 (1959), Justice Douglas said that the Chrestensen opinion was "casual, almost offhand" and "has not survived reflection." But thereafter the Court reiterated the distinction between purely commercial advertising and all other expression in New York Times v. Sullivan, 376 U.S. 254, 84 S.Ct. 710, 11 L.Ed.2d 686 (1964).

This was the state of commercial speech until Bigelow v. Virginia, 421 U.S. 809, 95 S.Ct. 2222, 44 L.Ed.2d 600 (1975). Jeffrey C. Bigelow was the managing editor of the Virginia Weekly, a newspaper published in Charlottesville, Virginia. The Weekly ran a referral service for an abortion clinic in New York City. Bigelow was convicted for violating a Virginia statute which made it a misdemeanor for any person by advertisement to encourage or promote the procuring of abortions. His conviction was reversed by the Supreme Court which held that merely because an advertisement is labeled commercial speech does not mean that it is stripped of all First Amendment safeguards, as had been implied in Valentine v. Chrestensen. Such speech retains some degree of constitutional protection which must be weighed against the state's interest in regulating the particular advertisement. Justice Blackmun, writing for the Court, then found some value in the abortion referral ad as a vehicle for conveying information of potential interest to Virginia Weekly readers. According to Justice Blackmun, the ad did more than fulfill Bigelow's profit motive. His interest coincided with the constitutional interests of certain of his audience who might need the service offered, or who were concerned about New York's laws or who were seeking abortion law reform in Virginia. Justice Blackmun noted that the availability of legal abortion in New York was information of value to the public and that, as previously decided, the right to early term abortion itself involved a woman's constitutional right to privacy. See Roe v. Wade, 410 U.S. 113, 93 S.Ct. 705, 35 L.Ed.2d 147 (1973) and Doe v. Bolton, 410 U.S. 179, 93 S.Ct. 739, 35 L.Ed.2d 201 (1973).

On the other side of the balance, Virginia contended that abortion referral agencies breed practices such as fee splitting that tend to decrease the quality of medical care and that advertising these agencies will encourage women to seek abortions from those interested only in financial gain and not in providing professional medical service. Virginia, however, made no claim that this advertisement would in any way affect the quality of medi-

cal care within its own boundaries, and the Court
reasoned that the state was actually asserting an
interest in regulating what Virginians hear or read
about another state's services. This interest, in
the Court's view, was entitled to little, if any,
weight. Consequently, the state's interest was not
sufficient to permit it to punish Bigelow for running the ad and his conviction was reversed.

Bigelow seemed to say that if First Amendment
protection was to be accorded to commercial
speech, it would be on an ad hoc balancing basis.
But in Virginia State Board of Pharmacy v. Virginia Citizens Consumer Council, Inc., 425 U.S. 748, 96
S.Ct. 1817, 48 L.Ed.2d 346 (1976), the Court appeared to adopt an absolutist approach to the protection of commercial speech in a case where the
state statutorily prohibited pharmacists from advertising the prices of prescription drugs which
they offered for sale—advertising which, unlike
that in Bigelow, is *purely* commercial in nature.

In striking down the Virginia statute, Justice
Blackmun, speaking for the Court, appeared to
reject the balancing process when he said, "There
is no claim . . . that the prohibition on prescription drug price advertising is a mere time,
place, and manner restriction. We have often approved restrictions of that kind provided that they
are justified without reference to the content of the
regulated speech, that they serve a significant governmental interest, and that in so doing they leave
open ample alternative channels for communica-

tion of the information . . . . Whatever may
be the proper bounds of time, place, and manner
restrictions on commercial speech, they are plainly
exceeded by this Virginia statute, which singles out
speech of a particular content and seeks to prevent
its dissemination completely." 425 U.S. at 771, 96
S.Ct. at 1830, 48 L.Ed.2d at 363–64. To similar
effect are Linmark Associates, Inc. v. Township of
Willingboro, 431 U.S. 85, 97 S.Ct. 1614, 52 L.Ed.2d
155 (1977) (local ordinance forbidding display of
"for sale" signs in front of houses struck down);
Carey v. Population Services International, 431
U.S. 678, 700–702, 97 S.Ct. 2010, 2024, 52 L.Ed.2d
675, 694–95 (1977) (statute prohibiting advertisement of contraceptives struck down).

B. THE FOUR–PART COMMERCIAL SPEECH ANALYSIS OF CENTRAL HUDSON

Following Bigelow, Virginia Pharmacy Board,
Linmark and Carey, the issue was no longer
whether purely commercial speech is protected expression but rather what First Amendment philosophy and analysis would govern the extension of
such protection. That question appeared to be
answered in Central Hudson Gas and Electric
Corp. v. Public Service Commission, 447 U.S. 557,
100 S.Ct. 2343, 65 L.Ed.2d 341 (1980).

There, a regulation promulgated by the New
York Public Service Commission banned electric
utilities in the state from engaging in advertising

which promoted the increased use of electricity. In striking down the regulation as violative of the First and Fourteenth Amendments, a bare majority of the Court enunciated a four-part test for determining the availability of constitutional protection for commercial speech. The test emphasizes the balancing of state interests in the regulation of commercial speech against individual free speech interests.

In short, the four-part test includes first a determination whether the expression is at all protected by the First Amendment. Commercial speech which involves or advertises unlawful activity or is false or misleading is *not* protected. For examples of this idea see Pittsburgh Press Co. v. Pittsburgh Commission on Human Relations, 413 U.S. 376, 93 S.Ct. 2553, 37 L.Ed.2d 669 (1973) (ordinance prohibiting newspapers from carrying help wanted ads categorized by gender upheld); Princess Sea Industries, Inc. v. Nevada, 635 P.2d 281 (Nev.1981), cert. denied 456 U.S. 926, 102 S.Ct. 1972, 72 L.Ed.2d 441 (1982) (statute prohibiting advertising of prostitution service in Nevada counties in which such service is illegal upheld); Friedman v. Rogers, 440 U.S. 1, 99 S.Ct. 887, 59 L.Ed.2d 100 (1979) (statute prohibiting practice of optometry under a trade name upheld because ill-defined association of trade name with price and quality could be manipulated by user of trade name to mislead the public).

If the commercial speech does not involve illegality and is neither false or misleading, then the second part of the analysis comes into play. The test here is whether the asserted governmental interest in regulation or prohibition of certain commercial speech is substantial. If the state's interest is substantial, then regulation or complete prohibition of the particular commercial expression may be permitted, depending on the results of the third and fourth parts of the test.

The third part asks whether the state's regulation directly advances the asserted governmental interest. Such regulation will not be upheld unless it is actually effective in advancing the state's interest directly. Indirect or speculative advancement of the state's interest will not suffice.

The final part of the test and the one the New York Public Service Commission failed in the Central Hudson case is whether the state's regulation is only as broad as is necessary to serve the state's substantial governmental interest. In Central Hudson, the Court's five-member majority was not persuaded that the Commission's complete suppression of promotional advertising by New York electric utilities was necessary to further the State's interest in energy conservation. The majority pointed out that the Commission had made no showing that a more limited restriction on the content of promotional advertising would have been inadequate to serve the state's interests.

The second and third parts of the Court's four-part test clearly call into play the ad hoc balancing of First Amendment interests against conflicting legitimate state interests while the fourth part attempts to limit the degree of conflict and the extent of intrusion into the First Amendment area posed by the second and third parts.

In his concurring opinion Justice Blackmun pointed out the contradictions of the four-part balancing test with the more absolutist approach taken earlier in Virginia Pharmacy, Linmark and Carey. He noted that such test would permit a complete ban on utilities advertising, for instance, the advantages of air conditioning, assuming that a more limited restriction on such advertising would not effectively deter members of the public from cooling their homes.

Because the Central Hudson four-part test leaves each justice great latitude to insert personal views on the degree of protection to which specific commercial speech is entitled, subsequent decisions have not followed a clear direction or rationale. For example, in Metromedia, Inc. v. San Diego, 453 U.S. 490, 101 S.Ct. 2882, 69 L.Ed.2d 800 (1981), the Court struck down a city ordinance banning almost all off-site billboards. The decision featured five separate opinions, causing Justice Rehnquist to term it "a virtual Tower of Babel."

Three years later, in City Council v. Taxpayers for Vincent, 466 U.S. 789, 104 S.Ct. 2118, 80 L.Ed.2d 772 (1984), the Court was faced with another sign ordinance, this time a ban on posting signs on public property. By a 6–3 vote, the ordinance, was found directly to advance the city's interest in limiting "visual clutter and blight." "By banning these signs, the City did no more than eliminate the exact source of evil it sought to remedy."

Although limiting visual clutter and blight is a sufficient government interest to justify restricting commercial speech, protecting people from offensive material is not. In Bolger v. Youngs Drug Products Corp., 463 U.S. 60, 103 S.Ct. 2875, 77 L.Ed.2d 469 (1983), the Court unanimously struck down a postal regulation prohibiting the mailing of unsolicited advertisements for contraceptives. In addition to the offensiveness assertion, the government argued that the regulation was necessary to help parents control "the manner in which their children became informed about sensitive and important subjects such as birth control." The regulation there was deemed more extensive than necessary to accomplish the latter goal.

The seeming inconsistency of some of these cases illustrates the true ad hoc nature of the Central Hudson four-part test. The weight given the asserted state interest appears to depend more on the personal views of the justices and less on the degree of evidence offered by the government. A majority of the Court seems willing to defer to the legislative or administrative body's judgment, except where a justice personally disagrees with that judgment.

That view was again evident in Posadas de Puerto Rico Associates v. Tourism Company of Puerto Rico, 478 U.S. ___, 106 S.Ct. 2968, 92 L.Ed.2d 266 (1986). By a 5–4 vote the Court upheld a Puerto Rico statute prohibiting advertising of casino gambling directed at residents of Puerto Rico, while permitting similar advertising aimed at tourists.

Justice Rehnquist, writing for the majority, found that the speech in question met the first part of the four-part test because the advertising concerned a lawful activity and was not inherently false or misleading. He then accepted the government's contention that the substantial government interest served by the regulation was the reduction of casino gambling by the residents of Puerto Rico as well as the claim that casino gambling leads to increases in corruption, prostitution, local crime and organized crime. The application of the advertising ban solely to casino gambling was also seen as reasonable because other forms of gambling such as cockfighting, horse racing, and the lottery might be "traditionally part of the Puerto Rican's roots."

The government's assertion that the advertising ban directly advanced that interest was also accepted without much scrutiny. Justice Rehnquist observed that the Puerto Rico legislature believed that banning advertising would reduce demand and that in his opinion such a belief was reasonable.

Finally, the ban, in Justice Rehnquist's view, was no more extensive than necessary. He rejected an argument that counterspeech, speech aimed at reducing casino gambling, was a less First Amendment intrusive way to accomplish the same ends. Whether counterspeech would be effective in accomplishing the same end was a decision for the legislature not the Court.

One of the more disturbing aspects of Justice Rehnquist's opinion is its extreme deference to the legislature. Essentially he seems to be saying that as long as the government's assertions are plausible they will be accepted even though there is no direct evidence to support the assertions. Justice Brennan, in his dissent, argued that, at least where the government's asserted purpose was to influence citizen behavior, a stricter standard was needed. He would have required the government to show that casino gambling had serious harmful effects, that banning advertising would reduce the demand for casino gambling and that neither counterspeech nor strict regulation of casino gambling itself would accomplish the same end. He found no showing that the government had evidence for any of these assertions.

C. ATTEMPTS TO BAN ADVERTISING OF LEGAL PRODUCTS

In Posadas the Court finally addressed another important commercial speech question. Can the government consistent with the First Amendment ever ban advertising for a legal product? The question has received increased attention in the past few years with the proposals by SMART (Stop Marketing Alcohol on Radio and Television) to ban broadcast advertising for beer and wine and the American Medical Association to ban all advertising for tobacco products. The latter proposal has been incorporated in proposed federal legislation.

In response to arguments that it was unconstitutional to ban advertising of a legal product, Justice Rehnquist stated that whenever the state has the authority to ban an activity it has the right to take the less intrusive step of banning advertising for that activity. He thought it would be "strange" to hold the state can ban an activity outright, but not reduce demand for that activity by banning advertising. He also cited with approval several lower court cases upholding advertising bans on legal activities or products. See Dunagin v. Oxford, Mississippi, 718 F.2d 738 (5th Cir.1983), cert. denied 467 U.S. 1259, 104 S.Ct. 3553, 82 L.Ed.2d 855 (1984) (Mississippi ban on alcoholic beverage advertising held constitutional under the Central Hudson test.); Capital Broadcasting Co. v. Mitchell, 333 F.Supp. 582 (D.D.C.1971) (Federal ban on cigarette advertising on electronic media found constitutional).

Justice Brennan strongly disagreed. He argued that the advertising ban was not less intrusive than a prohibition of the actual activity. "The 'constitutional doctrine' which bans Puerto Rico

from banning advertisements concerning lawful casino gambling is not so strange a restraint—it is
called the First Amendment."

Opponents of advertising bans have argued that
because Posadas involved a Puerto Rico statute,
the unique history and status of Puerto Rico provides a basis for limiting Posadas to the facts of
that case. Nevertheless, Posadas clearly was a
blow to industries such as liquor and tobacco that
are currently threatened with advertising bans.
The Court's approving references to Capitol Broadcasting and Dunagin are especially disturbing for
those industries.

D. THE SPECIAL PROBLEM OF PROFESSIONAL ADVERTISING

Advertising by professionals had been generally
frowned upon in the twentieth century and individual members of a number of the learned professions such as law and medicine were prohibited by
the states at the behest of professional organizations such as the ABA and the AMA from advertising their services, ostensibly because such advertising was unseemly and unprofessional but more
realistically because such bans reduced economic
competition within the professions.

1. Advertising by Lawyers: A Case Study

After the Supreme Court's decisions in Bigelow
and Virginia Pharmacy Board according First
Amendment protection to commercial speech, it

was inevitable that bans on professional advertising would come under attack. As might be expected the first legal challenges came from members of the legal profession.

As the legal profession began to change and develop new forms of delivery systems for legal services such as legal clinics for the less affluent in society, advertising became an important tool in achieving volume business to sustain lower fee schedules. But the use of such a tool was in direct conflict with established law.

In Bates v. State Bar of Arizona, 433 U.S. 350, 97 S.Ct. 2691, 53 L.Ed.2d 810 (1977), two Phoenix legal clinic attorneys, in seeking business from persons of modest income in need of legal services, placed an ad in the Arizona Republic, a daily general circulation newspaper saying "Do You Need a Lawyer? Legal Services at Very Reasonable Fees" and listing the services available, the charges for such services and the name of the clinic, the address and the telephone number. The ad clearly violated the American Bar Association Disciplinary Rule 2–101(B), embodied in Rule 29(a) of the rules of Arizona Supreme Court. The president of the state bar immediately filed a complaint with the Arizona Supreme Court and ultimately that court censured the two attorneys.

By a 5–4 vote, the United States Supreme Court reversed that portion of the state court order which had upheld the total ban on advertising. In so ruling the majority emphasized the consuming public's First Amendment interest in receiving truthful information about available services and products. Justice Blackmun, writing for the majority, noted that the ABA itself had reported that the middle 70 percent of the population on the economic scale was not being reached or adequately served by the legal profession. According to Justice Blackmun, advertising could help solve that problem.

But in holding that lawyer advertising could not under the First Amendment be subjected to blanket suppression, Justice Blackmun made clear that such advertising was too risk-filled not to be regulated. Regulation would be permitted to insure truthful advertising by lawyers for the protection of the public. Reasonable restrictions on the time, place and manner of advertising would be permitted, as would the suppression of false and misleading information and even accurate advertising concerning illegal transactions. In addition, advertising via electronic broadcast media might warrant special consideration and control. Justice Blackmun expected that the organized bar would have "a special role to play in assuring that advertising by attorneys flows both freely and cleanly." 433 U.S. at 384, 97 S.Ct. at 2709, 53 L.Ed.2d at 836.

Emphasizing cleanliness over freedom, the American Bar Association responded to the Bates decision by promulgating two alternative substitutes for the now dead letter DR 2–101(B). "Plan A"—the preferred alternative—listed 25 categories of information that a lawyer could include in his or her advertising. Nothing more could be included. The less restrictive "Plan B" simply permitted advertising that did not run afoul of a small number of general guidelines designed to prevent fraud, deception or the misleading of the public.

Despite warnings from legal scholars that "Plan A" was too restrictive to pass constitutional muster, a majority of the states that considered the ABA's alternative proposals adopted "Plan A" or some variation of it.

Missouri was one of them. The Missouri Supreme Court's Rule 4 listed only ten categories of information that could be included in newspaper, periodical and telephone directory ads. When attorney R_____ M. J_____ placed ads in local newspapers and the St. Louis telephone directory containing material not included in Rule 4 such as the fact that he was licensed in Illinois and had been admitted to practice before the United States Supreme Court, the Advisory Committee of the Missouri Bar filed a complaint in the Missouri Supreme Court seeking the imposition of sanctions. Following a hearing the attorney was officially reprimanded by the Missouri Supreme Court and required to pay the costs of the action despite his contention that his advertising was protected speech.

On appeal the United States Supreme Court, reflecting the principles laid down in Central Hudson and Bates, voted unanimously to reverse the judgment of the Missouri court. First Amendment protection was accorded the lawyer's advertising because none of the information contained therein was shown to be misleading nor did the Missouri Supreme Court identify any substantial state interest in so sharply limiting lawyer advertising that would outweigh the lawyer's or the public's interest in such advertising. In the Matter of R_____ M. J_____, 455 U.S. 191, 102 S.Ct. 929, 71 L.Ed.2d 64 (1982). As a result of this decision the constitutionality of state bar advertising rules based upon restrictive "Proposal A" of the American Bar Association is now in doubt.

One of the special problems of professional advertising is that at some point it shades off into personal solicitation of business. The prohibition of these personal attempts by professionals to generate business has been upheld by the Supreme Court in the face of First Amendment claims because of the inherent dangers of fraud, undue influence, intimidation, overreaching and vexacious conduct. See Ohralik v. Ohio State Bar Association, 436 U.S. 447, 98 S.Ct. 1912, 56 L.Ed.2d 444 (1978).

In Zauderer v. Office of Disciplinary Counsel, 471 U.S. 626, 105 S.Ct. 2265, 85 L.Ed.2d 652 (1985), an attorney had been disciplined for running a newspaper advertisement stating that he was available to represent on a contingent fee basis women injured through use of the Dalkon Shield, an intra-uterine contraceptive device. The advertisement stated that there would be no legal fees unless there was some recovery. The advertisement was accompanied by a drawing of the Dalkon Shield. The Ohio Supreme Court held that the advertisement violated Ohio Disciplinary Rules prohibiting self-recommendation and banning the use of illustrations in lawyer advertising.

By a 5–3 vote the United States Supreme Court struck down the self-recommendation prohibition as overbroad because it applied even to nondeceptive advertising. The Court distinguished Ohralik as applying to face-to-face solicitation, which in its view posed a much greater threat of undue influence and intimidation. Using the same reasoning the Court also struck down the ban on all illustrations. The Court did, however, find one aspect of the lawyer's ad misleading in that he stated no legal fees would be charged without some recovery, but failed to mention that court costs could be charged. The Ohio court's finding that this violated a full disclosure requirement for contingency fee rates, was therefore upheld.

The major question left unanswered in this area is whether direct mail solicitation is protected. The state courts remain split on this question, although the trend appears to be to grant at least some protection to such activity. See Florida Bar v. Schreiber, 420 So.2d 599 (Fla.1982) (absolute prohibition on mail solicitation is unconstitutional); Adams v. Attorney Registration and Disciplinary Commission of the Supreme Court of Illinois,

617 F.Supp. 449 (N.D.Ill.1985) (preliminary injunction against enforcement of prohibition of direct mail advertising to targeted audiences granted). Compare Leoni v. State Bar of California, 39 Cal.3d 609, 217 Cal.Rptr. 423, 704 P.2d 183 (1985) (targeted mailings found deceptive); Matter of Allessi, 60 N.Y.2d 229, 469 N.Y.S.2d 577, 457 N.E.2d 682 (1983), cert. denied 465 U.S. 1102, 104 S.Ct. 1599, 80 L.Ed.2d 130 (1984) (ban on mail solicitation of real estate brokers to solicit business from their clients held constitutional).

The separation between protected commercial speech and prohibited solicitation appears to be at the point where the expression is so immediate and personal that danger exists that the potential client's privacy may be invaded or the potential client may not be able to exercise his or her free will in deciding whether to accept a particular professional's services.

2. The Effect of the Lawyer Advertising Cases on the Other Professions

The principles espoused in the lawyer advertising cases seem generally applicable to restraints on advertising imposed on the other professions. Responding to these cases, the American Dental Association, for instance, has entered into a consent decree with the Federal Trade Commission agreeing not to engage in unfair competition by unduly restricting the advertising of its members. This agreement was contingent upon the success of the FTC's litigation with the American Medical Association to eliminate the AMA's restrictions on price advertising and advertising of the availability of individual and alternative medical services. The FTC prevailed in American Medical Association v. FTC, 638 F.2d 443 (2d Cir. 1980), affirmed per curiam by an equally divided Supreme Court, 455 U.S. 676, 102 S.Ct. 1744, 71 L.Ed.2d 546 (1982).

Overall, there has been a decided loosening of strictures on professionals advertising their services. This trend was given fresh impetus by the Supreme Court's affirmance of the FTC's victory over the AMA in the Second Circuit.

E. ACCESS OF THE PUBLIC TO THE PRIVATE ADVERTISING MEDIA

Thus far in this chapter the thrust of discussion has been the constitutional protection afforded to individual and corporate commercial speech. But it is important to remember that the First and Fourteenth Amendments are directed only to governmental action and do not compel private media interests to communicate commercial expression. Indeed, the Supreme Court has held that those Amendments do not require newspapers and broadcasters to accept paid editorial messages let alone purely commercial advertising. See CBS Inc. v. Democratic National Committee, 412 U.S. 94, 93 S.Ct. 2080, 36 L.Ed.2d 772 (1973); Miami Herald Publishing Co. v. Tornillo, 418 U.S. 241, 94 S.Ct. 2831, 41 L.Ed.2d 730 (1974).

Thus, while the Constitution limits governmental regulation of commercial speech, there is no guarantee that it will be heard if the speaker is dependent on private means of communications controlled by others. The exception occurs where the media outlet in question has monopoly power and refuses advertising for the purpose of furthering that monopoly. For example, in Home Placement Service, Inc. v. Providence Journal Co., 682 F.2d 274 (1st Cir.1982), cert. denied 460 U.S. 1028, 103 S.Ct. 1279, 75 L.Ed.2d 500 (1983) the Providence Journal refused to accept advertising for a rental referral service. Because the newspaper was the only daily newspaper in the city and Home Placement was a direct competitor for real estate advertising, the court held that the refusal to accept Home Placement's advertising violated § 1 and § 2 of the Sherman Act.

———

The fact that until very recently commercial speech generally was not accorded First Amendment protection and false and misleading speech specifically has never been constitutionally protected accounts, at least in part, for the rise of statutory and administrative controls on advertising at both the state and federal levels designed to protect the public from commercial loss. In the remaining sections of this chapter we consider the agencies that exercise these controls, the nature of the controls, available sanctions against commer-

cial wrongdoers and limitations on the imposition
of these sanctions.

F. STATE STATUTORY REGULATION

As manufacturing began to dominate the early
American agrarian economy and the frontier
pushed westward, the distances between the manu-
facturers and their markets constantly expanded,
making regional and national advertising increasingly necessary. Gradually the use of brand
names, trademarks, magazine advertising and even
advertising agencies grew to fulfill this need.
Along with this dramatic growth of advertising use
came flagrant advertising abuses. The patent
medicines were the epitome of this advertising era,
with elixirs such as Dr. J. W. Poland's White Pine
Compound, claiming to cure "sore throat, colds,
coughs, diphtheria, bronchitis, spitting of blood,
and pulmonary afflictions generally." Flamboyant
misleading copy writing, false testimonials, slo-
gans, jingles and trade characters quickly became
the rule in local and national advertising. Advertisers could, and did, promise anything and everything.

Common law and early state statutory remedies
proved inadequate to curb advertising abuses. See
E. Kintner, A Primer on the Law of Deceptive
Practices: A Guide for The Businessman 7–8, 405–
407. Today a majority of the states have added
legislation similar to the Federal Trade Commission Act, discussed below, to encourage criminal

prosecutions and to provide civil remedies for aggrieved consumers.

G. FEDERAL STATUTORY AND ADMINISTRATIVE REGULATION

1. The Federal Trade Commission

a. Nature and Jurisdiction

The original Federal Trade Commission Act was not directed toward false advertising but rather toward the prevention of monopolistic and unfair methods of competition in interstate commerce. Despite the absence of a clear congressional mandate in the advertising area, the early commissioners regulated deceptive ads by labeling them "unfair methods of competition." They took the position that exaggerated or misleading claims for an advertiser's product gave him or her an inequitable competitive advantage over those sellers who told the truth. This position was affirmed by the Supreme Court in Federal Trade Commission v. Winsted Hosiery Co., 258 U.S. 483, 42 S.Ct. 384, 66 L.Ed. 729 (1922). Justice Brandeis, speaking for the Supreme Court, upheld an FTC determination that when a manufacturer labels its underwear "Natural Wool" and "Natural Worsted" the product must be all wool, not merely 10 percent wool. The Court agreed that when misleading ads are marketed in competition with truthful ads, potential customers are unfairly diverted from the honest advertiser's products. By 1925 three quarters of the Federal Trade Commission's orders concerned false and misleading advertising.

All of the Federal Trade Commission's orders of this period were tied to the concept of unfair competition. The question remained whether the Commission could protect the public from false advertising directly, without having to demonstrate economic injury to a business competitor. Finally, in Federal Trade Commission v. Raladam Co., 283 U.S. 643, 51 S.Ct. 587, 75 L.Ed. 1324 (1931), the Supreme Court answered that question in the negative. In a unanimous decision the Court held that the Commission had no authority to ban purely false advertising, unless it could be shown to be an unfair method of competition. The Raladam decision prompted Congress in 1938 by the Wheeler-Lea Act to amend the Commission's enabling act to permit regulation of "unfair or deceptive acts or practices in commerce" that injure the consumer. Congress also provided for substantial civil fines for violations of Commission orders to "cease and desist" from proscribed advertising practices and for criminal penalties for and injunctions against the dissemination of false advertising pertaining to cosmetics, therapeutic devices and drugs.

b. Organization and Enforcement

The Federal Trade Commission is an independent regulatory agency with five commissioners appointed by the President for renewable seven-year terms. No more than three members can belong to the same political party. It has more than 1200 employees divided primarily among four bureaus. The one most concerned with advertising is the Bureau of Consumer Protection. Through this bureau the Commission may institute an investigation upon the receipt of even a single letter of complaint from a member of the public. Unfortunately, because of its large work-load and reduced budget, investigations often take a considerable length of time to start and complete, if begun at all.

If, as a result of the investigation, the Commission feels a formal hearing is necessary to determine the issues, it will draft a detailed complaint specifying the alleged false or deceptive practices and will hold a hearing. At the hearing an administrative law judge will make an initial decision after both sides present their respective positions. The judge's decision is final unless it is reviewed by the Commissioners. If the decision is unfavorable to the advertiser the Commission may issue a cease and desist order which, if violated, will subject the advertiser to an action in a federal district court for civil fine. The advertiser may seek review of the cease and desist order in the United States Court of Appeals.

Because of the delays inherent in such formal proceedings, the Commission has developed faster, less expensive methods of halting or preventing deceptive advertising. Indeed, the general policy has been to avoid litigation if possible by offering some form of settlement to offenders. This settlement can be effected through an "assurance of voluntary compliance" wherein the advertiser merely signs an affidavit that it will discontinue the practices involved. A second and more common approach is the use of the consent decree. Under this procedure the Commission drafts a proposed complaint together with a cease and desist order and attaches them to a notice of intent to commence formal proceedings. This package is sent to the alleged offender who must advise the Commission within 10 days if it is willing to forego a formal hearing and have the issues resolved by consent decree. Once a settlement is negotiated and accepted by the parties, it has the same effect as an order issued after a formal proceeding.

These settlement methods are made palatable to the businesses involved because they do not have to admit any violations of law. Another individualized approach, involving anticipatory regulation, is the advisory opinion. This is simply an informal nonbinding statement of advice from a responsible member of the Commission staff to assist the businessperson in determining in advance the legality of proposed conduct such as a future advertising campaign. The request must anticipate the act; the Commission will not give advice concerning current business practices.

The Commission also employs certain industry-wide approaches to illegal advertising and other business practices. One generalized method the

Commission utilizes to promulgate its views on advertising is the publication of practical manuals or "Guides." The Guides, in pamphlet form, are disseminated to both industry and public to inform them of the Commission's position on certain business practices such as bait and switch advertising, testimonial advertising and deceptive pricing. These Guides reflect the view of the Commission as to what might be considered illegal practices. Violation of a guideline is not itself a violation of law. Rather, where a guideline has not been followed, the Commission must plead and prove that the accused business violated a provision of the Federal Trade Commission Act itself. For litigation purposes, it is as if the Guide did not exist.

This is in marked contrast to cases involving violations of Commission Trade Regulation Rules which state the types of conduct that will be deemed unfair or deceptive by the Commission under the Federal Trade Commission Act. In these cases the Commission need only show that its Trade Regulation Rules have been violated. Thus, these Rules are treated as having the force of law and their violation may result in civil penalties of up to $10,000 for each offense.

c. *The Federal Trade Commission Improvement Act of 1974*

Another major grant of power to the Commission was effected by the Magnuson-Moss Act, 15 U.S. C.A. § 2301 (1975). The 1938 amendments to the Federal Trade Commission Act had placed deceptive advertising squarely within the Commission's jurisdiction, but the advertising was required to be "in commerce." In most other areas of federal regulation the quoted phrase, drawn from the Constitution, has been expanded by court decision to allow federal regulation of matters which merely "affected" interstate commerce. This liberal interpretation was denied to the Commission in Federal Trade Commission v. Bunte Brothers, 312 U.S. 349, 61 S.Ct. 580, 85 L.Ed. 881 (1941). The Bunte Brothers decision declared that only a congressional amendment could expand the scope of the Commission's powers to permit regulation of local business activity "affecting" interstate commerce. Thirty-three years later that amendment was made in the Magnuson-Moss Act. Accordingly, the Commission now has clear regulatory power over advertising reaching down to the local level and may, of course, control local advertising by Trade Regulation Rule, if necessary. In addition, as a result of a "rider" attached to the Trans-Alaskan Pipeline Act of 1973, violations of Commission rules outlawing certain trade practices can now be enjoined. See 15 U.S.C.A. § 53 (Cum.Supp.1976).

Industry claims that the FTC was abusing its powers by using the unfairness standard to regulate truthful, nondeceptive advertising led Congress in its 1980 FTC reauthorization bill to remove the FTC's authority to use that standard to initiate any new rulemakings. In subsequent years the House and Senate have been unable to agree on an FTC authorization bill, but each year have included the unfairness prohibition in the Continuing Resolutions providing operating funds for the FTC.

d. Constitutional Limitations on the Federal Trade Commission's Power to Impose Sanctions

Even before the Central Hudson case, supra, it was accepted constitutional doctrine that no protection was afforded false or deceptive advertising. Nevertheless, several United States Courts of Appeal have held that the First Amendment limits the *remedies* the Federal Trade Commission can fashion to protect the public against the risks created by such advertising. And thus it is not correct to assume that the FTC (and state agencies as well) are free to wield unlimited power against fraudulent or misleading advertising. These courts, while mindful that the First Amendment does not shield false or deceptive commercial speech from governmental control, insist that the Commission's exercise of that control be no greater than necessary to protect the public.

For example, in Beneficial Corp. v. FTC, 542 F.2d 611 (3d Cir. 1976), cert. denied, 430 U.S. 983, 97 S.Ct. 1679, 52 L.Ed.2d 377 (1977), the Commission ordered a combined loan and income tax preparation company to stop using the words "Instant Tax Refund Plan" or "Instant Tax Refund Loan" in its advertising because such terms mislead the public as to the nature of the transaction by which consumers received amounts of money from the company equivalent to their prospective tax refunds (actually loan transactions with a substantial interest charge). While not questioning the correctness of the Commission's findings that Beneficial's ads were misleading, the Court refused to approve the Commission's complete ban on the use of the delineated phrases. Rather, the court permitted advertising with the inclusion of those phrases provided they were sufficiently qualified so as not to mislead the audience. The Court said, "The Commission, like any governmental agency, must start from the premise that any prior restraint is suspect, and that a remedy, even for deceptive advertising, can go no further than is necessary for the elimination of the deception." 542 F.2d at 620.

Similar rulings modifying FTC remedial orders were made in National Commission on Egg Nutrition v. FTC, 570 F.2d 157 (7th Cir. 1977), cert. denied 439 U.S. 821, 99 S.Ct. 86, 58 L.Ed.2d 113 (1978) (FTC order requiring a trade association whose advertising on the risks of egg consumption was misleading to present arguments in its future advertising in opposition to its own position disapproved); Warner–Lambert Co. v. FTC, 562 F.2d 749 (D.C.Cir. 1977), cert. denied 435 U.S. 950, 98 S.Ct. 1575, 55 L.Ed.2d 800 (1978) (FTC order requiring corrective advertising to counteract previous false claims that a mouthwash prevented or moderated the common cold modified so as to delete the prefatory phrase "Contrary to prior advertising").

2. The Federal Communications Commission

The Federal Communications Commission licenses radio and television broadcasters to operate in the "public interest, convenience and necessity." This includes broadcast advertising, but historically the FCC has relied on self-regulation by the broadcasters to avoid the specter of government censorship forbidden by Section 326 of the Federal Communications Act of 1934. For a long time there was an absence of any clear boundary between the FCC's authority over advertising through commercial broadcasting facilities and the FTC's general authority over advertising. This issue was finally resolved by agreement between the two agencies. The FCC has responsibility for assuring that commercials are neither objectionably loud nor excessive in number and that a separation is maintained between advertising and programming, especially during children's programs. Misleading or deceptive advertising on radio or television is to be controlled by the FTC.

PART TWO

REGULATION OF THE ELECTRONIC MASS MEDIA

CHAPTER X

THE FEDERAL COMMUNICATIONS COMMISSION—WHAT IT DOES AND DOES NOT DO

One of the most important government agencies which affects the communication of information, and which has played an increasingly important role in shaping what we see and hear is the Federal Communications Commission. However, because its activities are often so technical, and because much of its work is phrased in language not susceptible to easy comprehension, there is much confusion in the public mind as to the precise role which the Commission plays in communications regulation. We will see that the Commission is more limited in its impact in certain areas, and more expansive in other areas than is generally believed by the public.

A. HISTORY OF THE FEDERAL COMMUNICATIONS COMMISSION

The existence of the Commission is, in effect, a typical American reaction to a practical and scientific problem. Government regulation of radio began in 1910 at a time when radio was perceived primarily as a safety device in maritime operations and as a potential advance in military technology. The government's primary concern was to assure itself of efficient use of this safety and defense technology, and its role was roughly analogous to that played by the police in registering automobiles. Persons desiring to use radio frequencies would register with the Department of Commerce and frequencies would be assigned to them. Pervasive regulation of the type we have come to accept as routine did not exist because there was no need.

Radio technology made quantum leaps during World War I and the commercial possibilities of radio began to be recognized by entrepreneurs. By the mid-1920's there were hundreds of radio stations operating for commercial use and frequencies were set aside by the Secretary of Commerce for commercial application. However, the powers of the Secretary to regulate such broadcasting were questionable, particularly the Secretary's power to require a radio applicant to broadcast on a particular frequency at a particular power. Two opinions, one by the courts (United States v. Zenith Radio Corp., 12 F.2d 614 (D.C.Ill.1926)) and one by the

Attorney General, (35 Ops.Atty.Gen. 126 (1926)), concluded that the legislation then in force did not permit the Secretary to limit applicants in the use of power and frequencies. The Secretary could only record the applications and grant frequencies, but he did not possess the expansive powers required to regularize radio operations.

These decisions threatened to throw the emerging radio industry into chaos and led to repeated requests by the industry itself for a government agency with greater power than had been possessed by the Secretary of Commerce—an agency which could assign applicants to specific frequencies, under specific engineering rules and with the power to enforce these rules through its licensing function. These efforts culminated in the Radio Act of 1927, which established the Federal Radio Commission and which transformed licensing from a ministerial act to a judgmental one, empowering the Commission to create and enforce standards for the broadcasters' privilege of using the public's airwaves.

The Federal Radio Commission created by the Radio Act of 1927 to supervise broadcasting was, pursuant to the Communications Act of 1934, merged into what is today the Federal Communications Commission. The 1934 Act, modeled largely after the Interstate Commerce Commission Act, and embodying much of the law that had already been made by the 1927 Radio Act, remains the organic legislation which controls American commercial and educational broadcasting. The Communications Act prescribes the basic task of the Federal Communications Commission to be that of "regulating interstate and foreign commerce in communication by wire and radio so as to make available, so far as possible, to all the people of the United States a rapid, efficient, Nationwide and world-wide wire and radio communication service with adequate facilities at reasonable charges for the purpose of the national defense, for the purpose of promoting safety of life and property through the use of wire and radio communication . . ." 47 U.S.C.A. § 151. The standard to which the Commission must conform in carrying out this responsibility is that of action "consistent with the public interest, convenience [and] necessity." 47 U.S.C.A. § 307. The courts have repeatedly emphasized that the standard is sufficiently broad to allow the Commission to act dynamically in areas of changing or emerging technology while, at the same time, sufficiently precise to prevent the Commission from acting in a wholly arbitrary, unreasonable or capricious manner.

B.   SCOPE OF THE COMMISSION'S POWER

It is important, at the outset, to recognize that the Commission's jurisdiction and power are strictly limited in scope to that which is granted by its enabling legislation, the Communications Act of

1934. It can only act in those areas in which it is specifically empowered to act.

This limitation has numerous practical implications. There are many areas which might be considered part of the "communications realm," but with which the Commission does not treat on a primary basis. Perhaps most important, and least known, is the fact that the Commission does *not* have jurisdiction and power over the entire radio spectrum space available to the United States under international treaty. In fact, the Commission has jurisdiction of only approximately one-half of this available radio space. Section 305 of the Communications Act exempts from the Commission's power or jurisdiction all "radio stations belonging to and operated by the United States." The United States government, through its various agencies, offices and departments (military and civilian), operates a host of radio services occupying approximately one-half of the total available frequency space. This allocation of spectrum space among the various governmental branches is made through a governmental coordinating group which is now housed in the National Telecommunications and Information Administration (NTIA), a division of the Department of Commerce. The Commission coordinates with this group but exercises no jurisdiction over the government's stations. It is only that part of the spectrum allocated to non-federal government use over which the FCC exercises jurisdiction. It is instructive to recall this fact when the concept of a "scarcity" of frequency space is discussed. At least in part, the scarcity of frequency space for commercial broadcasting is man-made and its dimensions are initially defined by the Executive Office of the White House. For a fuller discussion of the problem of radio frequency allocation between governmental and non-governmental uses, see Metzger and Burrus, "Radio Frequency Allocation in the Public Interest: Federal Government and Civilian Use," 4 Duquesne L.Rev. 1 (1966).

But even when dealing with those frequencies over which the FCC clearly possesses jurisdiction, there are large areas in which it is forbidden to or has chosen, as a matter of policy, not to exercise power. Thus, for example, the Commission is not empowered by the Act to enforce or decide antitrust issues as embodied in the Clayton and Sherman Antitrust Acts; it has been explicitly forbidden to do so by the courts. United States v. Radio Corp. of America, 358 U.S. 334, 79 S.Ct. 457, 3 L.Ed.2d 354 (1959). Although the Commission may, and sometimes must take into consideration, as part of its public interest standard, economic considerations involving such matters as competition, merger, market share, and the like, it is nevertheless free to ignore the policies favoring competition underlying the Sherman and Clayton Acts if to do so would be in the public interest, convenience and necessity. Federal Communications Commission v. RCA Communications, Inc., 346 U.S. 86, 73 S.Ct. 998, 97 L.Ed. 1470 (1953).

Similarly, the Commission does not determine whether a particular advertising message is "false and misleading." That question has been delegated by law to the Federal Trade Commission. Of course, the FCC would act where a licensee continues to broadcast an advertisement which has been finally adjudicated by the FTC to be false and misleading. But the Commission regularly refuses to make the initial determination as to the nature of the advertising. See FTC–FCC Liaison Agreement, Current Service, Pike and Fischer Radio Reg., p. 11:212 (hereafter cited as R.R.).

In addition, the FCC does not ordinarily become involved in civil or contractual litigation between broadcasters. It does not set advertising rates or oversee ordinary and usual business practices such as production charges, commission arrangements, and salaries of artists. It does not regulate rates which may be charged the public by pay television or cablevision system owners. It does not regulate closed circuit television or radio. It does not license networks. There are many other areas which might appear to fall within its power but which do not.

The reason is at once simple and complex. The American system of broadcasting is an attempt to introduce state regulation of the radio spectrum while, at the same time, allowing as much free market play as possible. The Commission sets the ground rules by which stations can be licensed. It will choose between applicants for conflicting licenses, set up a framework which attempts to insure some competition, and then allow the free market to determine, as well as possible, such matters as advertising costs, expenses, cost of equipment and, perhaps most important, choice of programming by broadcasters. The simplicity of the system breaks down at those points where free market considerations may not work well. A free marketplace may not automatically serve up programming for minority, ethnic or cultural groups. At a number of points (many of which are discussed later), the government has chosen to intervene; more recently (as the number of media types and outlets have grown) the government has "deregulated" some areas and given market forces more scope. Much of communications law cannot be understood unless it is recognized that the basic bias of our communications system is toward allowing, where possible, the free market to determine matters. See Report and Order, Deregulation of Radio, 46 Fed.Reg. 13888 (1981).

C. STRUCTURAL ORGANIZATION OF THE COMMISSION

Having been delegated broad powers to make rules and regulations as may be necessary to carry out the provisions of its enabling legislation, the Commission faces the task first of attempting to satisfy the differing demands for communications in a modern industrial economy. Although most familiar to the public in the role of a regulator of commercial and educational broadcasting, the Commission has the equally demanding responsibility of regulating non-broadcast use of communications facilities such as interstate common carrier systems, radio systems for industrial use such as truck-to-truck communications, taxi cab networks, communications between central plant and repairmen or servicemen, communications between hospital and doctor, marine and ship radio, aviation frequencies, citizen band radio, international "ham" communications, police and fire communications networks, computer to computer communications, and emerging new technologies such as cable television, pay television and satellite communications. In the case of common carriers, the FCC acts as a rate-making agency for interstate common carriage in a manner similar to state public utilities commissions.

The Commission itself is composed of five commissioners, appointed by the President with the advice and consent of the Senate. The President designates the chairman. Not more than three members of the Commission can be members of the same political party. Commissioners are appointed for a term of five years on a staggered basis. See 47 U.S.C.A. § 154(a).

To meet its responsibilities, the Commission has established a number of bureaus to carry out its functions. The most important of these bureaus and a description of the matters with which they deal are as follows:

1. *Mass Media.* This bureau handles all matters which we normally associate with commercial broadcasting, i.e., initial licensing of applicants, processing of applications for periodic renewal of licenses, inspection and supervision of stations to determine their compliance with technical and operational rules and regulations, and development of rules covering broadcasting. It also handles cable television matters and items associated with emerging television delivery technologies. We will emphasize the work of this bureau and its review by the courts in the pages that follow.

2. *Common Carrier Bureau.* This bureau regulates the interstate and foreign common carrier wire and radio system (telephone, telegraph, facsimile, telephoto and satellites), and acts not only as a licensing and regulatory agency, but also as a rate-making agency for interstate and foreign services. It also acts, in some respects, as a coordinating body for the various state public utilities commissions which regulate intrastate common carrier services.

3. *Private Radio Bureau.* This is the bureau which handles other types of radio uses not regulated by the other three. This bureau regulates such matters as industrial use, police and fire use, aviation and marine use, and citizens band radio.

D. ALLOCATION OF FREQUENCIES

The Commission handles the problem of allocation of frequencies between uses in a rather
straightforward manner. Certain frequencies are
specifically allocated to commercial "broadcasting
uses"; other frequencies are specifically allocated
to common carrier uses (i.e., telephone, telegraph
and other communications services for hire); other
frequencies are dedicated to uses such as industrial
communication, marine and ship radio, aviation
and medical services. These initial allocations are
quite important, for they establish the relative
"scarcity" of frequencies which, as we will see, is
the basic justification for governmental action in
the broadcasting realm.

E. JURIDICAL BASIS FOR COMMISSION REGULATION OF BROADCASTING

Government regulation of broadcasting is anomalous. We accept a depth and type of regulation
over broadcast facilities which we do not, as a
Constitutional matter, tolerate with respect to
print media. The most obvious example is governmental licensing of broadcast stations. The First
Amendment flatly forbids any such licensing requirement for newspapers, books or magazines.
See Near v. Minnesota, 283 U.S. 697, 51 S.Ct. 625,
75 L.Ed. 1357 (1931); New York Times Co. v.
United States, 403 U.S. 713, 91 S.Ct. 2140, 29 L.Ed.
2d 822 (1971). Yet the licensing of radio stations

has long been upheld. Federal Radio Commission
v. Nelson Brothers Bond and Mortgage Co., 289
U.S. 266, 53 S.Ct. 627, 77 L.Ed. 1166 (1933). Broadcasters operate under the constraints of the Fairness Doctrine, requiring them not only to air controversial issues of public importance, but to do so
in a manner allowing presentation of contrasting
views. See Red Lion Broadcasting Co. v. Federal
Communications Commission, 395 U.S. 367, 89
S.Ct. 1794, 23 L.Ed.2d 371 (1969). No such requirement could constitutionally be enforced against the
print media. Moreover, "indecent" (though not
obscene) material, which would be protected under
the First Amendment if seen in a movie or magazine, may nevertheless be prohibited from broadcast over the air. The Supreme Court has noted
that ". . . of all forms of communication, it is
broadcasting that has received the most limited
First Amendment protection." Federal Communications Commission v. Pacifica Foundation, 438
U.S. 726, 748, 98 S.Ct. 3026, 3040, 57 L.Ed.2d 1073,
1092 (1978).

Although the courts have justified these apparent contradictions on the ground that different
media present different First Amendment considerations, they do not often explain in any rigorous
analytical detail how the differences in media result in constitutional distinctions; and it is even
rarer for a court to test the breadth or scope of its
holding against the constitutional justification for
differences in regulation. For example, the United

States Supreme Court in Miami Herald Publishing Co. v. Tornillo, 418 U.S. 241, 94 S.Ct. 2831, 41 L.Ed. 2d 730 (1974), struck down a type of political "equal time" legislation imposed by the Florida legislature on Florida newspapers, without ever mentioning or attempting to distinguish the cases that allow precisely such regulation in the broadcast area.

The justification for broadcast regulation has been stated in terms of the "scarcity" of broadcast frequencies. The leading case discussing this point (National Broadcasting Co. v. United States, 319 U.S. 190, 213, 63 S.Ct. 997, 1008, 87 L.Ed. 1344, 1361 (1943)) set the formulation:

> The plight into which radio fell prior to 1927 was attributable to certain basic facts about radio as a means of communication—its facilities are limited; they are not available to all who may wish to use them; the radio spectrum simply is not large enough to accommodate everybody. There is a fixed natural limitation upon the number of stations that can operate without interfering with one another. Regulation of radio was therefore as vital to its development as traffic control was to the development of the automobile.

But numerical scarcity alone does not justify regulation of other media. As has often been pointed out, there are far more broadcasting stations than daily newspapers in the United States, and it is more difficult (from an economic point of

view) to start a newspaper than a radio station.
By numerical standards, newspapers are "scarcer".
The Commission itself, in discussing the scarcity
rationale has suggested that the advent of cable,
satellite and other new technologies demonstrate
that broadcasting is no longer a "scarce" resource.
See FCC Report: General Fairness Doctrine Obligations of Broadcast Licensees, 50 Fed.Reg. 35418
at 35421 (Aug. 30, 1985); 58 R.R.2d 1137.

It is not numerical scarcity, then, that justifies
the regulatory difference. Rather, broadcasting
imposes a duty upon the government which it does
not face in the print media—the duty of making
choices as between two or more potential broadcasters wishing to utilize the same broadcast space.
Two newspapers can, without governmental intervention, physically operate in the same community
at the same time; their survival would depend on
competitive market forces. In radio, however, if
there is but one frequency available for use in a
particular community, then, by the laws of physics,
two stations cannot physically operate on it, for to
do so would result in neither being heard. And
since it has been determined to be important to the
society at large that *someone* be heard, at base it is
the necessity for governmental choice which distinguishes broadcasting from other types of media,
and which requires governmental intervention in
order that the choice be made. So long as there
are more persons desiring to broadcast than there
are frequencies available to accommodate them, a

broadcast frequency is a "scarce" resource. Despite sharp criticism of the scarcity rationale from some quarters, the Supreme Court recently refused to reconsider it without some signal from Congress or the Commission that revision of the long-standing regulatory system is required. See League of Women Voters, supra, 468 U.S. at 376 n. 11, 104 S.Ct. at 3115 n. 11, 82 L.Ed.2d at 289 n. 11. The Commission attempted to give that signal in the 1985 Fairness Doctrine Report.

Theoretical problems remain, even with the "choice" rationale. The government is not always faced with the necessity of choice. There may be only one applicant for a particular open frequency. The Commission may be considering a proposed sale from A to B so that the only question before it is B's qualifications. The case may involve merely a protest by a citizens' group that a particular broadcaster is not operating "in the public interest" because it fails to give coverage to minority points of view or fails to hire minority or women employees. There is in these cases no requirement of choice between competing applicants. Yet even here the Commission can constitutionally, and indeed does, regulate.

Perhaps the best rationale for governmental regulation is that the legal basis for Commission action is an amalgam. There is a clear public need that some form of broadcasting exist. And to some extent broadcasting must be recognized as a public resource, perhaps analogous to an interstate traffic system, or a national park system, or a national environmental policy. Technical considerations make broadcast frequencies "scarce" resources and impose an obligation on the government to (a) make choices and (b) set standards to make certain that the "resource" is not wasted or misused. Because the Government grants broadcasters a limited monopoly in the sense that it will protect a broadcaster's right exclusively to use a frequency, the argument is that it is not inappropriate to extract a quid pro quo in the form of requiring that broadcasters operate in the "public interest." The government's traditional "police power" further allows it to impose certain limitations (as, for example, to protect children from "obscene or indecent" material). All governmental regulation of broadcasting can be traced to at least one of these considerations and, although they are not present at all times, together they represent the foundation of broadcast regulation.

This foundation will not support every form of governmental action. The First Amendment places limits even upon government regulation of "scarce" resources. See Columbia Broadcasting System, Inc. v. Democratic National Committee, 412 U.S. 94, 93 S.Ct. 2080, 36 L.Ed.2d 772 (1973). The Congress, for example, cannot forbid a station from editorializing in favor of a particular candidate or issue. Restrictions on broadcasting can be upheld only when the courts are satisfied that the restriction "is narrowly tailored to further a sub-

stantial governmental interest, ..." Federal
Communications Commission v. League of Women
Voters of California, 468 U.S. 364, 365, 104 S.Ct.
3106, 3109, 82 L.Ed.2d 278, 282 (1984). And procedural and substantive due process considerations
impose requirements on the Commission that
sometimes outweigh even considerations of administrative necessity. The tension between the necessity for governmental regulation and the common
recognition of the dangers posed by such regulation
forms the matrix in which broadcast law has developed.

F. NATURE OF THE BROADCAST RIGHT

Although there may have been other methods of
insuring the existence of a nationwide communications system, as, for example, by lottery or by
auctioning off frequencies to the highest bidder
and granting the winner a right in perpetuity
subject to defeasance for misconduct, Congress nevertheless chose to institute a licensing procedure
by which broadcasters are granted a limited privilege to broadcast over a particular frequency for a
fixed term. Congress stipulated that the grant of
the privilege gives the licensee no vested property
interest in the frequency or any guarantee that the
license will be renewed. 47 U.S.C.A. § 309(h).
Section 307(d) of the Communications Act limits
the license of a radio broadcasting station to a
maximum of seven years, with a requirement that

the broadcaster file for renewal of that license every seven years if it wishes to continue broadcasting. Television station licenses are granted for a period of five years, with provisions for renewal every five years (see Omnibus Budget Reconciliation Act of 1981, 95 Stat. 736–37). Licenses will be granted only if the "public convenience, interest, or necessity will be served thereby." Section 310(b) of the Act states that no license may be transferred to any person or entity, directly or indirectly, without the prior approval of the Commission, and Section 310(a) of the Act mandates that station licenses shall be granted only to citizens and cannot be held by aliens, foreign governments, or corporations of which any officer or director is an alien or of which more than one fifth of the stock is voted by aliens or representatives of foreign governments.

These restrictions have practical implications. Although, as will be seen, a licensee who has given "meritorious service" has a "legitimate renewal expectancy," nevertheless, there is no guarantee that its license will be renewed or, indeed, that there will even be an available frequency over which to operate at the expiration of the license term. Transcontinent Television Corp. v. Federal Communications Commission, 113 U.S.App.D.C. 384, 308 F.2d 339 (1962). Nor is the Commission required to grant a license for the full five or seven year term. It may, and occasionally does, grant a license for a shorter term if it believes that action

would be more appropriate or if it has doubts about
the qualifications of the licensee sufficient to desire
an opportunity to review its operation for an interval shorter than five or seven years. Moreover,
the license, pursuant to statute, carries obligations
which have been held to be constitutional. Thus,
for example, the licensee must make equal time
available for political candidates; it cannot broadcast material which is "obscene" or indecent; it
cannot broadcast lottery information (except for
state-run lotteries under certain conditions); and,
in general, it must "operate in the public interest."

On the other hand, the licensee possesses certain
constitutional and statutory protections which de-
rive not from any "right" in the license itself, but
rather from constitutional protections against arbitrary action of government. Thus, although a license can be revoked during its term, the Commission can only do so after giving notice to the
licensee and a full opportunity to be heard. 47
U.S.C.A. § 312(c). Moreover, the Commission carries the burden of proof in such a revocation proceeding whereas in the initial licensing phase and
in the renewal phase it is the applicant who must
carry the burden of persuading the Commission
that it is qualified. Similarly, the Commission
cannot act arbitrarily or capriciously and must
explain its decisions through written findings (Sag-
inaw Broadcasting Co. v. Federal Communications
Commission, 68 App.D.C. 282, 96 F.2d 554 (1938))
on a public record containing full explanation of its

rationale and actions. Greater Boston Television Corp. v. Federal Communications Commission, 143 U.S.App.D.C. 383, 444 F.2d 841 (1970). The Commission's decisions are appealable to the United States Court of Appeals and the court must be satisfied that the Commission has exercised its decision-making powers in accordance with constitution and statute.

G. COMMISSION FUNCTIONS IN BROADCASTING REGULATION

Analytically, the Commission exercises three different types of functions in the regulation of broadcasting: (1) licensing, which involves the choice of licensee either initially or at renewal time; (2) operational supervision, which involves oversight as to whether a licensee is meeting the conditions of its license; and (3) planning, by which the Commission attempts to integrate new and emerging technology into the broadcast regulatory scheme. These functions will be discussed in this and the following chapters.

H. LICENSING POLICIES OF THE COMMISSION

The Commission's primary statutory function is licensing. Section 301 of the Communications Act stipulates that no person shall use or operate any apparatus for radio transmission except by virtue of a license to operate granted by the Commission. Section 307(a) requires that licenses be granted to applicants only "if public convenience, interest, or necessity will be served thereby." Section 303 gives the Commission the power to classify different types of stations, to prescribe the nature of the service to be rendered by different types of stations, and to assign the bands of frequencies for each individual station. A license from the Commission is, in essence, an exclusive right to operate a station on a particular frequency at a prescribed power.

Before turning to the intricacies of the licensing process, it is instructive to consider the Commission's frequency allocations policy. The nature of that policy has a profound impact upon the type of communication system that the public possesses.

1. Frequency Allocation

The Commission has designated a portion of the spectrum for "broadcast" use, and has further subdivided the broadcast "band" into distinct portions. One set of frequencies is set aside for standard (or AM) broadcast stations, another group for frequency modulation (FM) stations, and a third for use by television stations. But the manner in which it chooses to assign specific frequencies within these groupings is not the same.

a. AM Allocation

The Commission immediately confronts a fact of physics: because of electrical interference considerations, the number of individual broadcast stations which can operate in a particular bandwidth varies inversely with their power. The higher the power, the smaller the number of stations which can be accommodated. The Commission could have chosen an allocations policy which would have led to a small number of very powerful stations, each being given the task of covering very large distances. This system was rejected on the ground, inter alia, that the nation should have a large rather than a small number of individual voices. Conversely, the Commission could have allowed a very large number of stations, giving each low power. The difficulty here was that the coverage area of such stations might be so small as to preclude financial viability. Instead, the Commission opted for a compromise. The present AM allocation policy allows three classes of stations;

(1) The so-called "clear channel" stations, approximately 25 in number, which operate at 50 kilowatts (the highest permissible power for any commercial AM station), and which cover a radius of approximately 80 to 90 miles during daytime hours and which (because of a scientific phenomenon) can be heard during the night at distances which sometimes reach 500 or 600 miles. These few "clear channel" stations are heavily protected from interference by other stations;

(2) Lower power, so-called "regional" stations which operate at a power usually of 5 or 10 kw and which cover a radius of approximately 25 or 30 miles (depending on the terrain); and

(3) So-called "local" stations which operate at a power no greater than 1 kw, cover an area of approximately 8 to 10 miles in radius, and many of which (because of interference considerations) are allowed to operate only during daytime hours. By far the majority of the approximately 4,600 standard broadcast stations in the United States are local stations which operate on a so-called "local" frequency.

See 47 C.F.R. §§ 73.21–73.29 and Regulations of the Commission for a full exposition of the AM broadcast allocations rules.

The second characteristic of the AM allocation system is that, unlike FM or TV, it operates on a "demand" basis. To illustrate, the Commission could have taken all of the available frequencies in the AM band and allocated specific frequencies to specific communities. Thus, New York City, for example, could have been allocated 5 clear channel stations, 6 regional stations and 13 local stations. Chicago could have been allocated a different number of specific classes of stations, Des Moines, Iowa yet a third, and so on throughout all communities in the United States. This type of specific allocation by city has the advantage of ensuring that significant cities have a certain number of broadcast stations, and it also has the virtue of reserving frequencies for future use in areas which are now relatively sparse in population, but which later might become more heavily populated.

Instead, in AM the Commission used an allocation policy which, in effect, allowed maximum scope for a "market type" of demand and which operated with a lesser degree of governmental planning involvement. The Commission first established engineering ground rules stipulating certain power requirements, and also stipulating the amount of allowable interference which a proposed station could cause or accept. Within these ground rules, applicants were entitled to apply for any of the various classes of stations in any community. It was believed (and proved to be the case) that the larger population centers, being able to support the larger number of stations, would attract the largest number of applicants. The Commission desired to put as few restrictions as possible on the number of applicants so that the benefit of radio communication could be realized throughout the country as quickly as applicants could design proposed facilities which would fit within the Commission's overall engineering guidelines.

The "demand" system still governs the allocation of AM stations, although the engineering ground rules have become so stringent that it is virtually impossible to design a new AM station which will fit within them. Moreover, as FM stations continue to multiply, their superior technical performance have made them the dominant radio medium, to the economic detriment of AM broadcasting. The number of AM stations has not significantly increased in the past decade, and (absent a radical policy change) is not likely to do so in the future.

b. Television Allocation

Although the technology of television was virtually fully developed by 1934, a number of factors (including WW II) delayed its entry into the marketplace until the late 1940's. By that time the Commission had considerable experience with the "demand" allocation system and had identified certain shortcomings in it, particularly the fact that it engendered a great deal of complicated, lengthy and difficult litigation. It tended to favor the more populated areas over the less populated, since every time a station is granted to a larger community, by necessity it might preclude use of that frequency in smaller communities which had not as yet stimulated entrepreneurs to view them as places for radio stations. The demand system was essentially an "unplanned" one whereby future growth might not adequately be considered.

The Commission therefore discarded the demand system in television and turned towards a simplified, more specific allocation policy which assigned specific frequencies to specific communities. Certain frequencies were reserved for non-commercial, educational (now termed "public") stations. There are no different *classes* of television stations. All television stations are either on VHF or UHF frequencies. They can all operate day and night, and all have the same maximum power limitations (though, for technical reasons, the power limitations of VHF stations as a group are somewhat different than those of UHF).

Each city only has available to it those specific frequencies which the Commission has chosen to assign. Those allocations are part of the Commission's rules, and any change in them requires a formal request for the Commission to institute a rule-making proceeding in accordance with the Administrative Procedure Act. Moreover, certain frequencies are reserved for use only by non-commercial stations, and some of these frequencies, even now, lie fallow, an example of the Commission allowing for future growth. Because there are no interference "ground rules" for television, there is much less engineering litigation in television cases, and there is no need for the Commission to compare in the hearing process (as it does in AM) the relative needs of communities for a particular frequency which is sought by competing applicants. The needs of the various communities have already been evaluated in the rule-making process by which the frequencies were assigned.

The exception to the above TV allocation scheme is low power television (LPTV) inaugurated in 1982. The LPTV service allows low power stations (maximum power of 100 watts VHF and 1000 watts UHF, encompassing a coverage area of approximately 10–15 miles) to operate on any available channel, on a secondary (i.e., non-interference) basis to regular full service stations. "Secondary basis" means that any low power station creating interference to a full service station must either eliminate the interference or cease operations. See Final Rule, LPTV General Docket No. 82–107, 47 Fed.Reg. 21468, May 18, 1982.

c. FM Allocation

FM allocation, though originally on a "demand" basis, is now handled in the same manner as television allocation. Specific frequencies are assigned to specific cities according to a table of allocations, which can be changed only through the institution of a formal rule-making proceeding. The only essential difference is that in FM there are essentially four classes of stations, higher powered ones (which can operate up to 100 kw) and lower powered ones (which are limited to 50 kw, 25 kw or 3 kw). There are also channels reserved strictly for educational use. The number of FM stations has been increasing at a rapid rate and the Commission in 1985 allocated hundreds more.

2. The Showing an Applicant Must Make— Basic Qualifications

Having found a frequency which can be used in accordance with the Commission's rules, what type of showing must be made by the applicant in order to convince the Commission that the public interest requires a grant of the license?

The Commission is not always faced with the necessity of choosing between particular applicants; there may be only one applicant for the particular frequency. But whether or not a choice is required, there are certain qualifications which *all* applicants must meet, some specifically required by the Communications Act itself, and others having been set by the Commission under its policy making authority to determine requirements in the public interest.

a. Citizenship

Section 310 of the Act mandates that a license may not be held by a non-citizen, a foreign government, a foreign corporation, or any corporation of which any officer or director is an alien or of which more than one fifth of the capital stock is owned by non-citizens. If the corporation is a holding company, no more than one-fourth of the capital stock can be owned by non-citizens. The above restrictions are mandatory. They cannot be waived by the Commission and can be changed only by Congress. Other provisions of Section 310 specifically allow licenses to be held by foreign pilots, ships and radio ham operators under certain circumstances.

b. Character

By statute (Section 308(b) of the Act), the Commission must evaluate the applicant to determine whether it possesses the requisite "character" qualifications. But neither the Act nor the Commission's rules spell out the requirements which constitute "good character" or those which will be deemed "bad character", leaving the matter to the

Commission's discretion. "Bad character" traits could be as extensive as human experience and considerations of "character" per se could involve the Commission in abstract value judgments which it would rather avoid. Thus, the Commission primarily concerns itself only with the type of bad character traits which would raise questions as to the honesty of the applicant, its potential performance as a broadcaster, or its proclivity towards obeying, or violating, Commission regulations. See Matter of Policy Regarding Character Qualifications in Broadcast Licensing, 102 F.C.C.2d 1179 (1986).

Honesty and candor are essential because the Commission could not function effectively if its licensees were dishonest. The Commission possesses neither the staff nor the budget to check independently every licensee representation. The information with which it deals is almost always information given to it by its licensees; it relies upon their veracity to do its work. Therefore, a licensee or an applicant who has been found to have knowingly misrepresented a fact to the Commission is in serious danger of having its license application denied, even if the misrepresentation is in an area of little significance. The significance of the misrepresentation is far less important than the fact that the misrepresentation occurred. Federal Communications Commission v. WOKO, Inc., 329 U.S. 223, 67 S.Ct. 213, 91 L.Ed. 204 (1946). A review of the cases where the Commission either denied an initial application or renewal of an existing license indicates that, by far, the greatest percentage of denials occurred where the Commission found knowing misrepresentation to have occurred.

Violations of criminal law also raise the risk of denial of an application on character grounds, although here the Commission has adopted a more flexible attitude. Felonious violation of criminal law involving moral turpitude (such as murder, robbery, rape, etc.) almost certainly would result in denial. But disqualification is not automatic. There have been instances of serious violations which have not resulted in outright denial such as, for example, a conviction for gun running to Israel in 1950, a felony. Las Vegas Television, Inc., 14 R.R. 1273 (1957). The Commission is likely to be forgiving if the crime occurred years ago and involved a law which had been routinely disregarded, for example, operating a speakeasy during Prohibition at a time and place where such operation was not uncommon. See WGCM Broadcasting Co., 3 R.R. 1138 (1947). In general, the Commission's policy is that criminal convictions not involving fraudulent conduct are not relevant unless it can be demonstrated that there is a substantial relationship between the criminal conviction and the applicant's proclivity to be truthful or comply with the Commission's rules and policies.

Somewhat related are violations of regulatory statutes of other government agencies. An applicant convicted of having repeatedly violated federal regulatory laws in his non-communications related business, has had his application denied on basic character grounds (Bulova and Henshel, 11 F.C.C. 137 (1946), affirmed sub nom. Mester v. United States, 70 F.Supp. 118 (E.D.N.Y.1947), 332 U.S. 749, 68 S.Ct. 70, 92 L.Ed. 336 (1947), because the nature of the violation showed a knowing disdain for governmental regulations. But an unintentional violation of the Food, Drug, and Cosmetic Act did not result in denial in another case. Brown Radio & Television Co., 5 R.R.2d 288 (1965). As a general rule, the Commission believes that non-FCC regulatory violations do not have sufficient relationship to the Commission's concerns to be relevant unless they involve a specific adjudication of misrepresentation to another government unit.

Nor are criminal violations of the Federal antitrust laws necessarily grounds for disqualification. A number of nationwide companies (among them General Electric and Westinghouse) were found to have violated the Sherman Act through price fixing in their non-communications related businesses. In considering whether to take away their broadcast licenses, the Commission found that the communications sections of these companies were separate from the other areas, were not handled by any of the persons involved in the price fixing, and were characterized by a history of meritorious programming and pioneering broadcast efforts. Weighing these factors (which, as noted above, it is not required to do in misrepresentation cases) led the Commission to renew the licenses. Westinghouse Broadcasting Co., Inc., 22 R.R. 1023 (1962); General Electric Co., 2 R.R.2d 1038 (1964).

But violations of the Sherman Act by a newspaper which engaged in predatory competitive tactics, and with no past broadcasting history against which to weigh them, could be grounds for refusal (see, e.g., Mansfield Journal Co. v. Federal Communication Commission, 86 U.S.App.D.C. 102, 180 F.2d 28 (1950)). The Commission will not, in any event, adjudicate controversies that are the subject of other court proceedings. In such cases the Commission will condition its actions upon the outcome of the adjudication in the courts. See, e.g., RKO General, Inc., 15 R.R.2d 943 (1969). The general rule is that where non-broadcast related antitrust or anticompetitive activity is involved, even adverse adjudications will not be considered relevant unless they suggest a proclivity toward fraud or unreliability. The factors which weigh most heavily in the analysis are the willfulness of the misconduct, the frequency of such behavior and its currency.

At one time, the Commission considered character not only as a basic qualifying condition but also as a factor to be weighed on a comparative basis. Even if the alleged misconduct was not sufficient to totally disqualify an applicant, nevertheless, it could be used as a standard to choose one competitor over another. This is no longer the case. The

Commission's present policy is that a character defect either disqualifies the applicant or is irrelevant. See Matter of Policy Regarding Character Qualifications in Broadcast Licensing, 102 F.C.C.2d at 1232.

c. *Financial Qualifications*

The Communications Act and the Commission's policies require that an applicant demonstrate its financial capability to construct and operate its proposed facility. The theory behind this requirement is that a "scarce" public resource should not be wasted in the hands of an operator that does not have the financial capability to run it. Thus, the Commission has established a minimum standard which applicants must meet. Applicants for new stations (AM, FM or television) must demonstrate financial capability to construct and operate the station for 90 days, even assuming that the station earns no revenue. Financial Qualifications, 43 R.R.2d 1101 (1978); 45 R.R.2d 925 (1979).

A similar policy applies to the purchase of a broadcast station. Purchasers must have sufficient capital to consummate the transaction and to meet expenses for a three-month period. See Financial Qualifications, 49 R.R.2d 1291 (1981). Significantly, applicants are not required to demonstrate their financial capabilities through balance sheets or other documents. They need merely state that they have the requisite financial wherewithal. Only if an adversary (or the Commission itself, through random sampling) raises prima facie questions concerning whether the statement is accurate will the applicant be required to furnish proof of financial capability.

Financial qualifications are *not* considered on a comparative basis. The fact that one applicant may have more finances available than a competing applicant will not result in a preference for the former, because to do so would reward wealth alone, a result which the Commission does not desire. Scripps-Howard Radio, Inc. v. Federal Communications Commission, 89 U.S.App.D.C. 13, 189 F.2d 677 (1951). Every applicant need only certify that it has sufficient capital to meet minimum qualifications. Once it has done so, additional financial capability per se is ignored.

d. Technical Showing

All applicants, of course, must demonstrate that they will meet all of the technical requirements set forth in the Commission's rules such as, for example, utilizing transmitting equipment that has been appropriately "type approved" by the Commission, proposing to operate within the height and power limitations for the various classes of stations, operating during the hours appropriate for the frequency sought and causing or receiving no more than the allowed amount of interference. This showing of technical qualifications, moreover, has extremely important procedural ramifications because although normally the Commission cannot deny an application without giving the applicant a hearing, the Commission may properly refuse even to consider an application if it fails to meet certain technical requirements. As a matter of practice, an application is not "filed" with the Commission; it is only "tendered" for filing and must first be "accepted" for filing even before the processing stage is reached. If an application, on its face, patently fails to meet certain technical minimum requirements, it will not even be "accepted" for filing, much less processed. For example, as noted above, in AM radio the Commission has established a set of engineering "ground rules" which every applicant must meet. In FM and television allocations, the Commission has allocated specific frequencies to specific cities. If an AM application fails to meet the ground rules, or if an FM or TV applicant specifies a frequency other than one already assigned to the particular community involved, the Commission will not accept these applications for filing. United States v. Storer Broadcasting Co., 351 U.S. 192, 76 S.Ct. 763, 100 L.Ed. 1081 (1956); Ranger v. Federal Communications Commission, 111 U.S.App.D.C. 44, 294 F.2d 240 (1961). Moreover, the Commission is becoming increasingly insistent upon applications being filed in a letter-perfect manner. Whereas, in the past, it was lenient in allowing perfecting amendments to cure facial defects, the Commission will no longer permit this. It has formally advised that, at least with respect to applications for newly designated FM frequencies and for low-power television stations, an application will not be accepted for filing unless it includes *all* required information. See Salzer v. FCC, 778 F.2d 869 (D.C.Cir.1985). Because many applications must be filed by a specific date or be forever barred, failure to file a letter-perfect application can be fatal.

But the courts have ruled that the Commission cannot refuse to accept an application failing to meet minimum technical requirements where the applicant makes a strong prima facie showing in the application that because of its particular situation, the requirements should not be applied. See Storer Broadcasting Co., supra. Thus, for example, where the Commission's rules did not permit AM applications for nighttime operation of local stations on "clear channels," an applicant which sought such operation argued that its application should be considered because it was a unique "good music" station which would directionalize its antenna to protect the clear channel station. The Commission's refusal even to accept the application for filing was reversed by the court of appeals on the grounds that the applicant had at least made a prima facie showing that the rule should be waived in its case, and the Commission was required to give the application "reflective consideration." WAIT Radio v. Federal Communications Commission, 135 U.S.App.D.C. 317, 418 F.2d 1153 (1969). But such a holding is unusual. Absent special circumstances, an application which does not meet fundamental technical standards need not be processed through the hearing phase.

e. Diversity of Media Ownership

One premise upon which the First Amendment is based is the existence of a flourishing market-place of ideas, with truth emerging not from governmental regulation but, rather, from the clash of many voices. Associated Press v. United States, 326 U.S. 1, 65 S.Ct. 1416, 89 L.Ed. 2013 (1945). Where no government regulation is constitutionally permitted, the economic marketplace determines the number of voices to be heard; the government's role is limited to ensuring (through appropriate antitrust involvement and legislation) that the economic model succeeds. Where, as in broadcasting, government regulation is allowed, and where inherently it creates market monopolies, the question arises as to in what manner the Commission should act to ensure hoped-for multiplicity and diversity.

The Commission has attempted to respond to the problem by enacting so-called "multiple ownership rules" which restrict persons or entities from acquiring excessive power through ownership of radio and television facilities. Congress (or the Commission) might, of course, have attempted to limit each applicant to only one radio facility, either AM, FM or television, so that no one could own more than one station anywhere in the United States; neither has chosen to do so. Conversely, the absence of any limitation posed the threat that radio economics might well follow the path of newspaper economics whereby a relatively small number of entities control a large number of daily newspapers throughout the country, and sometimes control all of the daily newspapers in a particular community. The Commission's multiple ownership rules attempt to strike a balance between these extremes, allowing multiple ownership of commercial media by a single entity in certain instances, and forbidding it in others. Non-commercial stations are exempt from the operation of these rules. The multiple ownership rules operate in much the same way as the engineering rules. If an applicant attempts to apply for more radio facilities than the rules allow, its application will not be accepted for filing, again excepting special circumstances requiring waiver.

There are basically three types of multiple ownership rules: (a) those forbidding multiple ownership of facilities in the same community or area; (b) those limiting ownership of broadcast facilities by single entities no matter where the facilities are located; and (c) those forbidding newspapers from owning television stations in the same community in which they publish. These rules operate as follows:

(1) Ownership in a single community. The Commission's present multiple ownership rules (47 C.F.R. § 73.3555) forbid a single entity from owning more than one station in the *same* ser-

vice in the same community, or even in nearby communities if their signals would overlap to a proscribed degree. Thus, no single entity could own two AM stations or two FM stations, or two television stations in the same community, the only exception being if the stations are non-commercial. The reasons are obvious. The Commission desires as much competition as possible, at least among stations in the same service area, and will act to stimulate that competition even to the extent of disallowing cross interests of any type, be they directorships, officerships, or ownership even of minority shareholdings.

But what about commercial ownership of stations in *different* services in the same community? Here the matter becomes more complex. It is not prohibited for a single entity to possess an AM and an FM station in the same community. It is prohibited, however, for a single owner to have both an AM and a VHF television station in the same community, or in nearby communities if their signals overlap to a proscribed degree, although the Commission has now proposed to relax this rule and allow AM–TV overlap. Moreover, it is forbidden for a single entity to own a VHF-TV and an FM station in the same community or in nearby communities if their contours improperly overlap. The question of UHF–TV overlap with either AM or FM is handled on a case-by-case basis. The rules also prohibit common ownership of a broadcast station and a cable television system that lies

within the station's local service area.   47 C.F.R.
§ 76.501 (1986).   The reader recognizes, of course,
that there exist today a number of instances where
a single entity owns an AM, FM and a VHF
television station in the same community in apparent violation of the rules.   The explanation is that
these combinations grew up prior to the passage of
the present multiple ownership rules, and were
"grandfathered" so that divestiture was not required.   These rules will not be waived for these
"grandfathered" stations in case of a future sale, so
that, in practical effect, combinations in contraven-
tion of the now existing multiple ownership rules
cannot be sold as a package, absent a waiver of the
rules.

(2) The second aspect of the multiple ownership rules is an absolute limit on the number of
commercial AM, FM or television stations which
a single entity can own, no matter where located.
A single entity can own no more than twelve
AM, twelve FM and twelve television stations
anywhere in the United States—a total of 36
stations.   These numbers can be increased from
12 to 14 for each of the three services if two of
the stations in each service are controlled by
minority groups, a relaxation of the rules aimed
at increasing ownership of broadcast stations by
members of recognized minorities.   There is one
further limitation.   No single group or entity
can directly or indirectly have an interest in
television stations which have an aggregate na-

tional audience exceeding 25% (or 30% if the stations are minority controlled). See 47 C.F.R. § 73.3555(d). In counting the number of permissible stations, the Commission will include in the total any station in which the same person is an officer, director or voting shareholder owning 5% or more of the station's outstanding shares. If the corporation, however, has one stockholder holding more than 50% of the voting stock of the company, then the Commission will not consider any other stockholders as "owners" for purposes of the rule. If the stockholder is a mutual fund or other type of purely investment vehicle, then it is considered only if it holds more than ten percent of the voting stock of the company or if its representatives are officers or directors of the company.

For example, if A is a director of six AM stations in different cities, a five-percent voting stockholder in five other AM stations in five other cities (none of which have a single dominant majority stockholder), and is an officer in a twelfth AM station in a twelfth city, none of these twelve licensees can apply for another AM station, no matter where located, because to do so would allow common ownership of a number of stations in excess of those allowed. This "cumulative effect" can cause quite complex problems which cannot be adequately covered in this work. The reader is referred to 47 C.F.R. § 73.3555 for a more detailed exposition. The key point to remember, however, is that there is an absolute limit to the number of commercial broadcast facilities that can be held under common ownership.

(3) Broadcasting/Newspaper Combinations. Until 1975, there was no prohibition against ownership of a broadcast station by a newspaper in the same community. Although the Commission acknowledged as early as 1944 that such ownership might lead, at least in certain circumstances, to a monopoly both in the economic and the informational senses, nevertheless, it was not persuaded that the feared results were inevitable nor that the problem could not be handled in ways other than outright prohibition. In 1975, though still finding no specific evidence of monopoly abuse, the Commission nevertheless concluded on policy grounds that the public interest would be best served, and the twin goals of economic competition and competition in the marketplace of ideas furthered, if future newspaper-broadcasting combinations were prohibited by rule. Therefore, it prohibited the ownership of either AM, FM, or TV stations by daily newspapers in communities over which the AM, FM or TV stations place a signal of a particular strength. See Second Report and Order, Docket No. 18110, 50 F.C.C.2d 1046 (1975). Existing combinations were almost all grandfathered with the proviso that they could not be sold as a unit to a third party. In 16 instances, the Commission actually ordered divestiture by newspaper-

broadcaster owners. See FCC v. National Citizens Committee for Broadcasting, et al., 436 U.S. 775, 98 S.Ct. 2096, 56 L.Ed.2d 697 (1978).

The Commission's trend during the past five years has been to relax the stringency of the multiple ownership rules so as to allow common control of a larger number of stations than previously was the case. The purpose here is to allow the economic marketplace greater sway in ownership decisions and to improve competition by allowing broadcast combinations to become stronger and, thus, be in a better position to compete with national networks. Nevertheless, the continued existence of the multiple ownership rules testifies to the concern that no one group should control broadcasting stations to an unwarranted degree. Diversity of ownership still remains a Commission goal.

The above discussion relates to the showing which must be made to meet basic qualifications, i.e., they represent multiple ownership standards which must be met even to have an application considered by the Commission. But the Commission also considers multiple ownership characteristics on a comparative basis. Thus, if applicant A for an FM license already holds an AM license for the same community, and applicant B holds no other broadcast interests, applicant B will, all other things being equal, be preferred. Applicant B may be preferred even if in another area of comparison, for example past broadcast experience, A would be found slightly superior. Industrial Business, 30 R.R.2d 1123 (1974). The fact that A's application complies with the multiple ownership rules allows A to be considered. It does not foreclose the issue if a choice must be made.

f. Community Ascertainment Studies

The Commission has evolved a policy requiring broadcasters to become familiar with the community to be served, and particularly familiar with the needs and problems of that community. Although the broadcaster has by statute (47 U.S.C.A. § 326) discretion to choose the programming it wishes to present, it nevertheless must do so in light of the particular problems and needs of its community if it is to operate "in the public interest."

Although the Commission had at one time erected a highly formularized ascertainment process which applied to all types of broadcasting stations, its relatively recent "deregulation" thrust has eliminated the need for formal and specific ascertainment procedures. The broadcaster now has discretion to utilize whatever ascertainment methodology seems appropriate; its obligation is "issue oriented" in that the broadcaster must provide programming relevant to the issues confronting its community. There are no specific procedures that must be followed. The broadcaster may exercise its responsibility to become familiar with local issues in the manner it deems best. The only paperwork required is a listing in the station's public file of programs that the broadcaster has presented to meet the pressing issues the broadcaster believes to be most significant. Persons dissatisfied with a station's performance have the burden of demonstrating, at renewal time, the manner in which the station has failed its programming obligations. For applicants, the manner of ascertainment of public issues is neither a basic nor a comparative criterion.

g. Programming

Contrary to a widely held misconception, the Commission never established, even in its pre-deregulatory period, official minimum norms or requirements for any programming category. There never has been a requirement that a station broadcast a specific minimum percentage of "public affairs" programs, or "news." Station licenses (usually FM) have been granted even though the applicant proposed no public affairs or news programming. Although frequently asked to set minimum norms, the Commission insistently refused to do so, primarily on First Amendment grounds. Section 326 of the Act forbids the Commission to act as a "censor." Setting up required minimums would, in the Commission's view, be tantamount to censorship. See Hubbard Broadcasting, Inc., 48 F.C.C.2d 517 (1974); Report and Order, 66 F.C.C.2d 419, 428–29 (1977); National Black Media Coalition v. FCC, 589 F.2d 578, 581 (D.C.Cir.1978).

Despite the absence of specific programming minimums, the Commission had evolved a series of unofficial "guidelines" which, prior to 1981, were used as application processing criteria. The industry was made aware of those program proposals which the Commission granted as a matter of routine (i.e. by staff action alone, without the necessity of action by the Commissioners), and those which were at least delayed in processing while the Commission requested additional information from the applicant to determine why it believed the particular proposal would serve "the public interest." The Commission's staff used a rule of thumb to separate the unquestionably acceptable from the troublesome, and that rule of thumb became the standard that most applicants for a new or renewed license in fact used. In practice, the "guideline" became a de facto quota.

As part of its "deregulation" effort, the Commission in 1981 abandoned use of the "programming guidelines" for radio stations (AM or FM) and in 1984 abandoned them for television stations as well. Programming for radio and television stations is now regulated essentially by the marketplace, subject to the right of listeners to attack a station's performance at renewal time. This policy is grounded upon a belief that there are a sufficient number of broadcast stations to insure a broad range of coverage which will cover minority as well as majority taste. See Deregulation of Radio, 46 Fed.Reg. 13888 (1981). The Commission ((to the consternation of the court of appeals—see Action for Children's Television v. Federal Commu-

nication Commission, 821 F.2d 741 (D.C.Cir.1987))
has even refused (on the "marketplace" theory) to
impose program guidelines on the amount or nature of children's programming to be presented,
although it noted that broadcasters have a duty to
provide some programming to satisfy the unique
needs of children. No programming information is
required from applicants for new stations or for
the transferrees of existing stations. Operating
stations must merely place in their files a quarter-
ly list of programs which they believe to have met
significant needs of the community.

Nor has the Commission ever enacted a formal
limitation on the amount or type of commercial
time that can be broadcast in a program hour.
Here also a rule of thumb had developed whereby
stations whose commercial proposals meet a particular norm would pass muster unquestioned, whereas those exceeding that norm must explain further.
These norms were originally derived from standards self-imposed by the National Association of
Broadcasters. The norms for radio were deleted in
1979 and in 1984 for television as part of the
deregulation effort. The self-imposed standards of
the NAB code were eliminated in 1982 as part of a
consent decree in an antitrust action.

Commercial television advertising during children's programs has been a source of Commission
concern. But, the Commission has refused, even
here, to adopt specific limitations on commercial
advertising, although repeatedly requested to do

so. The National Association of Broadcasters had imposed some commercial norms upon its members with respect to children's programs. See Action for Children's Television v. FCC, 564 F.2d 458, 464 (D.C.Cir.1977). These norms died with the abolition of the NAB code.

The deregulatory trend of the last decade has shifted the balance of programming discretion significantly in favor of the broadcaster. However, it has also made more difficult the determination of whether a broadcaster is operating "in the public interest." If the public interest becomes equated solely with broadcaster discretion, the standard loses effective meaning. At this writing, some Congressmen are proposing a new quid pro quo. Instead of granting licenses for limited terms, subject to renewal, it has been suggested that licenses be granted in perpetuity (subject to defeasance for misconduct) in return for the broadcaster's promise to present specified amounts of non-entertainment, public service and children's programming, and subject to limits upon the amount of commercial advertising to be presented. This proposal has drawn some industry support. Whether or not it will become the future broadcasting structure is not yet known.

h. Equal Employment Showing

Since 1969 the Commission has required all applicants to adopt and file an affirmative action equal opportunity program to ensure non-discrimination against minority groups such as Blacks, Chicanos, American Indians, Spanish surnamed and women. See 47 C.F.R. § 73.2080. In essence, this program obligates the applicant to take specific and affirmative action in recruiting, advancement, and training to ensure equality of opportunity. The program must be positive in terms of recruitment and training; merely refraining from overt discrimination is insufficient. The representations in the application then become the standard against which the applicant's performance is tested. Report and Order, 18 F.C.C.2d 240 (1969). Stringent reporting requirements may be imposed upon stations whose programs appear to be in less than full compliance with the Rules. Bob Jones University, Inc., 42 F.C.C.2d 522 (1973).

The Commission has not adopted a required system of quotas, goals and time tables with respect to hiring and advancement. There is no requirement, for example, that a station's minority employment be specifically consistent with the percentage of minority or female population in the particular community. There is no case in which the Commission has denied an application because of imbalance in the work force. But the court of appeals has indicated the possibility that a renewal application might be denied where the licensee indicates the percentage of minority or female employment to be "outside the zone of reasonableness" when compared with the demographics of the community as a whole. Stone v. Federal Communications Commission, 151 U.S.App.D.C. 145, 466 F.2d 316, rehearing denied 466 F.2d 331 (1972). It has also indicated that this "zone of reasonableness" is not a constant and may change over time—what is reasonable for a station merely beginning its affirmative action program might not be reasonable three years later. The Commission utilizes a series of "guidelines" in determining whether a station's employment profiles merit routine approval of their renewal applications. Under current guidelines, stations employing from five to ten employees must have a profile for ethnic and racial employment in lower paying jobs that reflects, in percentage terms, at least fifty percent of the racial and ethnic mix in the local employment market generally. In the top four job categories (i.e., officers and managers, professionals, technicians and sales persons), the personnel profile must reflect twenty-five percent or more of the local employment mix. Stations with more than ten employees must reach the fifty percent figure for overall employment and for the top four job categories as well. Stations with 50 or more employees receive a complete review of their equal employment programs regardless of their employment profile. The Commission continually monitors equal employment opportunity performance by requiring stations with five or more full-time employees to file yearly employment profiles. See FCC Public Notice, EEO Processing Guidelines, 45 Fed. Reg. 16335 (Feb. 13, 1980).

3. Processing the Application

Section 307 of the Act states that the Commission "shall grant to any applicant therefor" a license if the public convenience, interest or necessity will be served thereby. Sections 307(a) and 309(d)(2) of the Act allow the Commission to grant an application making the proper showing without evidentiary hearing, but Section 309(e) states that if (a) a substantial and material question of fact is presented or (b) the Commission "for any reason" is unable to make a finding that the grant would be in the public interest, then the application must be designated for "full hearing" with the "burden of proof" upon the applicant. The key with respect to factual disputes is that they must be material and substantial. Factual ambiguity that would not be significant even if resolved does not require hearing. See Stone v. Federal Communications Commission, 466 F.2d 316 (D.C.Cir.1972). The importance of the second condition is that the Commission may be required to hold a hearing even if there are no factual disputes, if there are policy or public interest questions that can only be resolved after public evidentiary hearing. See Citizens Committee to Save WEFM v. Federal Communications Commission, 506 F.2d 246 (D.C.Cir.1973); Citizens Committee to Preserve Voice of the Arts in Atlanta v. Federal Communications Commission, 436 F.2d 263 (D.C.Cir.1970). But instances of the latter type of hearing (i.e., where there are no substantial or material factual issues) are extremely rare.

4. Participation by Non-applicants in the Processing of Applications

The broadcast application process is not merely a duet between the Commission and the applicant. Other participants may have a significant role in the process, even if they are not themselves applicants. Generally, these non-applicant participants are either (1) other broadcast stations that may be affected by a grant of the application, or (2) representatives of the public who may be affected.

a. *Participation by Other Broadcast Stations*

There are essentially two reasons why another broadcast station might be allowed to intervene in the application process:

(a) because a grant would itself act as a "modification" of the intervening station's license, thus requiring a hearing by statute; or

(b) because the intervening station might be a party economically "adversely aggrieved or affected" by a grant, thus being accorded intervenor's status.

An example of the first is the grant of the application to station A would cause objectionable electrical interference (as defined in the FCC Rules) within the normally protected contours of station B. All AM stations have an area in which they are protected from interference by the Commission's engineering rules. The normally protected contours of station B as defined in the rules at the time of the grant to B become part of B's license. Because Section 316(a) of the Act forbids a "modification" of B's license without a "public hearing," B is entitled to protest the grant to A and to be accorded a hearing on its protest. It should be noted, however, that the "modification" would occur only if the grant becomes effective during B's seven-year license term.

Aside from a Section 316 modification, however, an existing station might also intervene in Commission proceedings if it can demonstrate that grant of a pending application would have an adverse economic effect on it. The Supreme Court has held that the regulatory system allows other broadcasters to act as "private attorneys general," bringing to the Commission's attention shortcomings in applications by other applicants. Naturally, such action would not be altruistic, but would be spurred by potential economic injury to the intervening station. Because such intervention might bring to the Commission's attention matters which it otherwise might miss, such intervention is allowed, so long as the prima facie fact of adverse economic impact is demonstrated. Importantly, however, the intervening station cannot urge economic injury to itself as a ground upon which to deny the pending application. The Commission is not required to shield stations from competition. The economic injury to the station only acts to allow it entry into the proceeding. Once in the proceeding, however, it must base its objection on public, not private, interest factors. See Federal Communications Commission v. Sanders Bros. Radio Station, 309 U.S. 470, 60 S.Ct. 693, 84 L.Ed. 869 (1940).

b. *Participation by the Public*

Until the landmark decision by the United States Court of Appeals for the District of Columbia in Office of Communications of the United Church of Christ v. Federal Communications Commission, 123 U.S.App.D.C. 328, 359 F.2d 994 (1966), the public played virtually no part in the licensing process. Standing to participate in that process was limited to persons who were "parties in interest," a classification limited by Commission practice and interpretation to other stations complaining of electrical interference or to those persons or stations claiming specific adverse economic injury. The interests of the listening public at large were to be represented by the Commission itself, which, by statute, was required to act only in the public interest.

United Church of Christ opened up the Commission's forum to public participation. Rejecting the notion that only economic injury or electrical interference conferred participatory rights and recognizing that the Commission may not always be able to reflect public sentiment as effectively as the persons actually affected, the court held that repre-

779 F.2d 702 (D.C. CIR 1985)

sentatives of the public could participate in the
licensing process upon a showing that a grant of
the application sought would have a particular
effect upon them.   Examples of such representatives might be a Black group in a southern community protesting a renewal grant to a licensee who,
in the past, had repeatedly manifested disregard of
the needs or interests of the Black members of that
community.   The Commission can, of course, properly protect the orderly character of its proceeding
by refusing to allow the public to participate en
masse, and by requiring that they do so through
representative groups.   The Court did not hold
that a citizen could gain entry merely by asserting
a bare general listenership interest without specific injury to himself or herself.   Indeed, unless
injury in fact occurs to a person or a member of an
organization which claims to speak in his or her
name, the courts will refuse to grant standing to
sue in court.   American Legal Foundation v. FCC,
808 F.2d 84 (D.C.Cir.1987).   But a representative
citizens group which can demonstrate a particular
injury which a member might suffer as a result of
the grant would have sufficient statutory "standing" to participate.

Since United Church of Christ, citizens' groups
have participated with respect to hundreds of applications.   Public interest law firms have been
organized specializing in the representation of minority group interests in application proceedings.
Women's groups have been effective in attacking

applicants as being unresponsive to women as listeners and employees. Ethnic groups have been allowed to participate on the grounds that particular applicants did not evidence sufficient awareness of their needs.

The form that such participation ordinarily takes is the filing of a "Petition to Deny" the application. If the Petition raises a substantial or material question of fact or a policy issue which the Commission cannot resolve on the basis of the information in the application alone, the application will be designated for hearing. The burden of proceeding with the evidence on the issue or issues raised in the Petition will be placed by the Commission upon the party best suited to do so. The ultimate burden of proof, however, remains with the broadcast applicant as to the grant of its application for license.

5. Comparative Qualifications—The Need for Choice

How does the Commission choose between competing applicants? This question arises in two different contexts. The first concerns applicants for a new frequency. The second concerns an existing station seeking renewal of its license and a challenge by new competitors who desire to take the license away. We will discuss each separately.

a. The Non-renewal Situation

The Commission must often choose between applicants for the same new frequency, and the choice may depend not only upon the nature of the applicants but also upon the nature of the facility sought.

This can best be illustrated as follows. In allocating the AM spectrum, the Commission did not follow the policy of allocating specific frequencies for use in specific cities. Thus, two applicants might file to use the same frequency in different communities and, under the Commission's engineering rules, the frequency could only be used in one of them. Thus, the choice was not only between applicants, but between communities. Should the Commission choose the best qualified applicant? Or should it award the station to the applicant who seeks to serve the community with the greatest need?

The answer can be found in Section 307(b) of the Communications Act which specifies that the Commission shall make such distribution of licenses "among the several States and communities as to provide a fair, efficient, and equitable distribution of radio service to each of the same." This statutory mandate, as interpreted by the Supreme Court (Federal Communications Commission v. Allentown Broadcasting Corp., 349 U.S. 358, 75 S.Ct. 855, 99 L.Ed. 1147 (1955)), requires the Commission to determine first which community has the greatest need for the frequency and to award the station to the applicant seeking to serve that community, without making any comparison between the nature of the applicants with respect to their background, history, multiple ownership characteristics, and other considerations. So long as the applicant for the community of greatest need possesses basic qualifications, its application will be granted without considering comparative qualifications.

This mandate requires that the Commission establish criteria for determining relative need as among different communities. Generally speaking, the criteria are as follows:

(a) every community of substantial size is entitled to its own local transmission facility and, if it does not have one, will be presumed to have a greater need than another community that already has one or more local stations;

(b) the Commission desires to maximize competition and, given a choice, will prefer competition to its absence. Thus, regardless of the size of the communities, the Commission will prefer to add a second station to a community in preference to adding a third or fourth to another community since, by so doing, it would create competition where none exists; and

(c) if the contesting communities already have multiple broadcast stations, the Commission will then look to the applicant that will make more effective use of the frequency; this usually means the applicant applying for the community with the larger population, but may also involve other complex engineering valuations.

These criteria have introduced certain problems of their own, particularly with respect to suburban communities. Applicants seeking to take advantage of the priority given to applicants for the *first* station in a particular community have applied for facilities in small suburban towns or communities which do not have their "own" station, but from which they could also cover a large metropolitan area, including the central city which already has a number of stations. Had the applicant applied for the central city, it would have lost its comparative advantage, although in fact the intent of the applicant really is to serve the larger community, using its designation of the suburban community merely as a method of obtaining a comparative preference.

The "suburban community" problem has been particularly vexing and led at one time to a policy where an applicant for a small community which places a strong signal over an adjacent larger community would be presumed to be applying for the larger community. This presumption is now no longer made. Whether or not an applicant for a suburb will be considered as one for the suburb or the central city is now handled on a case-by-case basis, depending upon the facts. The key point to remember, however, is the basic premise of the Communications Act: Congress has opted for a system of essentially community based stations rather than a centralized system with offices in various cities.

But sometimes the Commission simply cannot make the choice based upon a comparison of communities either because the communities demonstrate equal need or because the applicants seek to serve the same community. How then does the Commission choose between applicants? Until 1965, the criteria used to compare applicants were less than clear, and the relative weight accorded the criteria by the Commission was so inconsistently applied at times as to raise serious charges that the purported criteria were used merely to mask preconceived results. In 1965, to clarify and simplify the comparative process, the Commission set forth its present policy on comparative broadcast hearings. Policy Statement on Comparative Broadcast Hearings, 1 F.C.C.2d 393 (1965). Asserting its primary objectives to be (a) the "best practicable service" to the public and (b) a maximum diffusion of control of the media of mass communications, the Commission indicated the material comparative criteria to be:

(i) *Diversification of Control of Mass Communications.* This has become, in practice, the most important non-engineering criteria. All other things being equal (and even when all other things are not necessarily equal) the applicant who possesses no other broadcast interests will be preferred to the one who has other commercial media interests in the same area. Of course, the nature of the applicant's interests is itself important. The less the degree of interest in other stations or media, the less will be the significance of the multiple ownership factor. The Commission's policy is to consider the applicant's interests in existing media to the degree that they are larger, are in or are close to the community being applied for, are significant in terms of size and are significant with respect to other media in their respective locality. But there is no doubt that an applicant with significant holdings in other mass media is at a comparative disadvantage.

(ii) *Full-Time Participation in Station Operation by Owners and Local Residence of Applicants.* This factor is considered to be of "substantial" importance since the Commission believes that "it is inherently desirable that local responsibility and day-to-day performance be closely associated" and that "there is a likelihood of greater sensitivity to an area's changing needs" to the extent that the proprietors participate in day-to-day operation. 1 F.C.C.2d at 395. Thus, the applicant who proposes to participate actively in the station's operation will be preferred to one who will rely solely upon a hired staff. But the Commission is interested in *full-time* participation. To the extent that the owner proposes only part-time participation, the credit given drops sharply, and no credit will be given to participation of any person who will not devote "substantial amounts of time on a daily basis" in such positions as General Manager,

Station Manager, Program Director or Business Manager. Ibid.

It is in the context of the "participation" criterion that the 20–year battle over whether to accord preferences to minority groups and women has been fought. The 1965 Comparative Hearing Policy Statement did not discuss the question of whether minority groups and women should receive preferences in comparative hearings. The Commission never considered these as relevant criteria until the court of appeals decision in TV 9, Inc. v. FCC, 495 F.2d 929 (D.C.Cir.1973), cert. denied 419 U.S. 986, 95 S.Ct. 245, 42 L.Ed.2d 194 (1974) where the court decreed that the Commission could not ignore the question of minority group status but, rather, must take it into consideration as an "enhancement" feature in applying the "participation" criterion. If two applicants, for example, proposed that all of their owners would actively participate in station operations, but all of the owners of one applicant were black, whereas the owners of its opponent were white, it would be appropriate for the Commission to "enhance" the participation weight of the black applicant because it would be likely that the black applicant might be more sensitive to the needs of the black residents in the area. Subsequent to the TV 9 decision, the Commission on its own recognizance, applied a similar theory to women applicants and "enhanced" (i.e., gave added weight) to female ownership when comparing applicants who proposed that their owners would all work at the station. In closely contested cases, it became routine for the Commission to award the frequency to the black or female applicant because of these enhancement preferences.

In 1985, however, a panel of the same court of appeals (although not the same judges) that rendered the TV 9 decision nevertheless questioned the statutory basis for the female enhancement criteria, holding that the Commission had never demonstrated any factual predicate for the assertion that female ownership made an applicant more sensitive to the needs of its community. It remanded the case for a more detailed Commission investigation of the issue. Steele v. FCC, 770 F.2d 1192 (D.C.Cir.1985). While a petition for reconsideration en banc of Steele was pending, the Commission in a rather extraordinary action asked (and was granted) a remand of the case because the Commission now began to question whether in light of more recent Supreme Court holdings in the "affirmative action" field, preference based upon minority status or gender could pass constitutional muster. It has, therefore, begun an investigatory proceeding on the entire question of the constitutionality and propriety of granting such preferences. Notice of Inquiry, MM Docket No. 86–484, 1 FCC Rcd 1315 (1986). All cases in which the question may be dispositive are being held in abeyance until the matter is clarified. The implications, of course, of the Notice of Inquiry proceeding are far reaching.

(iii) *Proposed Program Service.*   Although seemingly anomalous, the Commission will not ordinarily use as a comparative criteria the proposed program services of competing applicants unless there are material and substantial differences between them of a magnitude such as is demonstrated by one applicant proposing an all foreign language station and another proposing a contemporary music format.   The reason derives from the Commission's experience which indicates that applicants generally propose similar program formats, and even if they differ somewhat, the "minor differences among applicants are apt to prove to be of no significance."   1 F.C.C.2d at 397.   Moreover, comparing program proposals might turn the application process into a type of "bidding" auction with applicants vying to outpromise each other and with little likelihood that their programming would, in fact, be significantly different from the bulk of the programming presented by other stations.   The Commission is also concerned with keeping hearing records free of immaterial clutter (1 F.C.C.2d at 394) in the form of fulsome expositions more suited to advertising agency prose.   The Commission is always concerned that forcing it to compare different program formats would cast it in the role of censor, and might involve subjective qualitative judgments of the type that the Commission would prefer not to make. Thus, as part of its recent "deregulation" effort, the Commission adopted a policy of ignoring changes in radio entertainment programs on the ground that there are a sufficient number of radio stations to allow that issue to be determined by the economic marketplace. This policy was affirmed by the Supreme Court in FCC v. WNCN Listeners Guild, 450 U.S. 582, 101 S.Ct. 1266, 67 L.Ed. 2d 521 (1981). The same reasoning has now been largely extended to television. See Report & Order, MM Docket No. 83–670, 98 F.C.C.2d 1076 (1984).

(iv) *Past Broadcast Record.* The Commission uses an applicant's past broadcast record as a significant comparative factor only if the past record is either "unusually good or unusually poor," since such factors give some indication of performance in the future. A past record which is "within the bounds of average performance will be disregarded." 1 F.C.C.2d at 398.

(v) *Efficient Use of the Frequency.* Where one or more competing applicants propose an operation that, for one or more engineering reasons, would be more efficient, this fact will be considered of significance in determining the preference.

(vi) *Other Factors.* The above framework does not exhaust the possibilities. Since the comparisons take place on a case-by-case basis, it would be impossible to list all situations which might arise. But it does indicate the nature of the pertinent criteria which the Commission generally considers. If an applicant desires consideration of another factor not specifically enumerated above, it must make a special request that the matter be considered. Unless the Commission specifically designates the requested issue for hearing, it will not be considered.

Obviously, in the real world, comparisons between applicants do not fall neatly into place. One applicant may deserve a preference on diversification grounds, whereas its opponent may show a superior past broadcast record. The precise manner in which the Commission weighs the various preferences can only be discerned by reviewing the many cases in which the preferences have been applied.

b. *The Renewal Situation*

What are the comparative factors when one of the applicants is not a newcomer, but instead, seeks a renewal of its license in competition with a newcomer which seeks to replace it? Will the Commission apply the same criteria as it does when the applicants are applying for a new facility, or will it give a preference to an applicant who has demonstrated its ability by actually running the station sought? This is a particularly vexing question because, on the one hand, giving preference to the existing licensee would tend to freeze out newcomers. On the other, ignoring past performance would be unfair to a licensee who has spent considerable sums in building up its station, which might not be recovered if its license were to be denied. Moreover, such a policy might introduce an element of instability in the broadcast industry which ultimately would not serve the public interest. But if credit is to be given for past performance, how much and in what way is it to be given?

The Commission first resolved this problem (Hearst Radio, Inc. (WBAL), 15 F.C.C. 1149 (1951)) by giving a decisive preference to the renewal applicant. The Commission reasoned that it was weighing a proven past record against a mere proposal, and feared a challenger might easily out-promise but not necessarily outperform an existing station. This policy, of course, virtually ruled out successful challenges at renewal time.

Although the Commission later became dissatisfied with the stringency of the Hearst policy, its attempts to change that policy (at one point to liberalize it and at another to tighten it) came to nought. See, e.g., Greater Boston Television Corp. v. Federal Communications Commission, 143 U.S. App.D.C. 383, 444 F.2d 841 (1970); Citizens Communications Center v. Federal Communications Commission, 145 U.S.App.D.C. 32, 447 F.2d 1201 (1971). The present posture of renewal comparisons is essentially that embodied in Hearst, with this gloss: an applicant can rely on what has come to be known as a "renewal expectancy." The Ad-

ministrative Law Judge will determine whether
the incumbent was providing "minimal" or "substantial" service. If "minimal," the incumbent
will not receive a comparative plus and, if the
challenger's proposal appears viable and likely to
be effectuated, the challenger would receive a programming plus. However, if the incumbent is
found to have rendered "substantial" service, its
renewal expectancy will be recognized and it will
be given a comparative preference of major, and
probably decisive, significance. See Deregulation
of Radio, 46 Fed.Reg. 13888, 13896 (1981); FCC v.
National Citizens Committee, 436 U.S. 775, 782,
805–07, 98 S.Ct. 2096, 56 L.Ed.2d 697, 706, 720–22
(1978). This may be true even where the challenger is entitled to a significant preference in the area
of ownership of mass media and would ordinarily
have been preferred if both applicants had sought
a new facility. See Central Florida Enterprises,
Inc. v. FCC, 683 F.2d 503 (D.C.Cir.1982). Here
again, only broad principles can be outlined. The
resolution of individual cases (and particularly
what will and will not be considered "substantial
service") must depend upon the facts of each case.

The tension underlying the comparative renewal
problem arises because of the inescapable conflict
between the desire for stability in the broadcast
industry, and the view that a broadcasting license
is a limited privilege which must be periodically
renewed. There is a significant public interest
component in stability because unless licensees can

be reasonably assured that their heavy investment will not be rendered valueless after five or seven years, they might not make a long-term investment in public service programming. Rather, they will operate the station solely to maximize short-term profit. Yet, there is also a public interest benefit in insuring licensee responsibility through the veiled threat of loss of license in the event the broadcaster fails to fulfill its public service obligations.

During most of the Commission's regulatory history, the balance was weighed in favor of the latter consideration. The hearing procedure (initially and at renewal time) lay at the heart of the comparative licensing process. Recent experience, however, particularly the extraordinarily lengthy and expensive proceedings characterizing license renewal challenges (and the potential for mischief in challengers filing only for the purpose of being "paid off") has made the Commission less enamored of the license challenge procedure as a prophylactic device. The Chief of the Mass Media Bureau has been most vociferous: "[E]very effort to rid the public of this offensive process called comparative renewal should be made. The public interest demands it." Final Report of the Mediator/Facilitator in the RKO Settlement Process, (unpublished report; available on request) (Feb. 3, 1987). Whether Congress will agree is yet to be seen.

6. The "Settlement Policy"

One of the early Congressional fears was that the comparative hearing process (whether for determining a new license or for challenging an existing one) could be abused by applicants who filed not for the purpose of obtaining a broadcast station but, rather, simply for the purpose of extracting a cash payment in return for dismissing its application. Congress attempted to meet this problem by prohibiting any applicant from receiving a cash settlement for dismissing its application over and above its actual expenses in prosecuting the application. Because an applicant could, therefore, not make a profit by prosecuting its application, the likelihood of filing solely for that purpose would be eliminated.

The problem with this policy was that comparative hearings literally took years, cost huge amounts of money, and introduced a lengthy period of uncertainty as to who would be the ultimate licensee, without much demonstrated public interest benefit. It also tended to increase the likelihood and length of conflict and litigation, in contrast to the law's usual policy, which is to encourage resolution of conflict through settlement. Therefore, in 1981 and 1982, Congress repealed its prohibition against applicants receiving more than their legitimately expended costs (see Public Law 97–259, 96 Stat. 1087, 1095; Public Law 97–35, 95 Stat. 357, 737–38) and directed the Commission to encourage rather than discourage settlements of hearing conflicts. This legislative policy was soon put into effect (see Bison City Television 49 Ltd. Partnership, 93 F.C.C.2d 4 (1983)) with the result that settlements in contested cases have now become the norm rather than the exception.

7. Random Selection as a Licensing Mechanism

Congress and the Commission have expressed dissatisfaction with the traditional comparative hearing process as a mechanism to choose between competing applicants. It has been estimated that the average delay caused by a comparative hearing is three years; some have taken as long as ten years. There is an enormous economic and social loss associated with the process. The frequency lies fallow during the hearing, thereby depriving the public of a needed service. There are high tangible costs to the applicants not only through out-of-pocket and legal and engineering fees, but also through unrealized profits. There are extensive costs to the Commission (and ultimately, of course, to taxpayers) in terms of engineering and legal manpower drains. See Notice of Inquiry, 45 Fed.Reg. 29335 (May 2, 1980).

Prior to 1982, the comparative hearing mechanism was mandated by statute. In 1981, Congress amended Section 309(i) of the Communications Act (47 U.S.C.A. § 309(i)) to allow the Commission the discretion to utilize a random selection (i.e., lottery) licensing mechanism, but only after the Commission first determined the basic qualifications of applicants. Congress further mandated that the Commission (if it wished to use a random selection method) must establish rules and procedures to ensure that members of groups or organizations "which are underrepresented in the ownership of telecommunications facilities will be granted significant preferences." (Omnibus Reconciliation Act of 1981, 95 Stat. 736–37).

After studying the possibilities of instituting such a mechanism, the Commission, in 1982, declined to adopt a random selection methodology, primarily because it believed that requiring the Commission to determine basic qualifications of all applicants prior to holding a lottery "would not produce the operating economies which Congress sought to provide" (Report and Order, February 25, 1982, General Docket No. 81–768, 47 Fed.Reg. 11886 (Mar. 19, 1982)). The Commission also identified some problems under the 1981 legislation:

1. The key to expeditious processing is the reduction in the number and rigidity of the criteria used to establish "basic qualifications." Paradoxically, however, the easier it becomes to meet these criteria, the more applicants will apply, thus increasing the Commission's processing burdens. Expedition may have to be purchased at the expense of foregoing close scrutiny of potential applicants. Is this in the public interest?

2. The statutory provisions requiring "significant preferences" to groups or organizations, or their members, that are "underrepresented" in the ownership of telecommunications facilities pose particularly vexing problems. There may be serious constitutional challenge to the statutory language as being overbroad and overinclusive, violating First Amendment and equal protection requirements. The preference provisions are subject to the attack that they establish a quota system without any finding of specific *past* Commission discrimination, and thus violate the Supreme Court's Bakke holding (Regents of the University of California v. Bakke, 438 U.S. 265, 98 S.Ct. 2733, 57 L.Ed.2d 750 (1978)).

Congress responded to certain (although not all) of these points by revising Section 309(i) of the Act in 1982, in a manner which gave the Commission more flexibility in establishing a lottery mechanism for licensee selection. The 1982 legislation, however, (Public Law 97–259, § 115) continues to require that the Commission, if it chooses to institute a lottery system, must grant "significant preferences" to applicants who would increase "diversification of ownership of mass media" and to any applicant "controlled by members of a minority group." No preferences however, are given to women.

Despite these difficulties, the Commission appears to favor a lottery system, and this may very well be the wave of the future in broadcast licensing. Lotteries are already being used to award low power television frequencies, cellular radio frequencies and multipoint distribution system frequencies. The lottery system is still not used to award full service broadcast stations.

CHAPTER XI

FCC CONTROL OF BROADCAST OPERATIONS

Although the Commission's primary function is and has been the licensing of broadcast stations, it has been involved from its inception, and increasingly in the past two decades, with the supervision of the manner in which stations are operated. Section 326 of the Act specifically forbids the Commission to "censor" material broadcast by a radio facility, and an overly broad reading of this restriction might make it appear that the Commission plays no part in the content of program material. Such is not the case; there are some areas in which, Section 326 notwithstanding, the Commission can and does control or influence program content. These areas include: (1) political broadcasting; (2) obscenity and lottery programming; (3) so-called network "prime time" programming; (4) "anti-payola" and "anti-plugola" statutes; (5) regulations requiring separation between network ownership and program production; and (6) nebulous regulation by "raised eyebrow" in such areas as "family viewing time," drug lyrics and sexually stimulating radio programming. Also included was programming under the so-called "Fairness Doctrine", when the Commission was still enforcing that doctrine.

436

A. POLITICAL BROADCASTING

From the inception of broadcast legislation, Congress has recognized the enormous potential of radio as a political tool. A major concern of the lawmakers is that a broadcasting facility might improperly influence an election by affording only one candidate access to its audience. To prevent this possibility, Congress enacted what is now Section 315 of the Communications Act which provides that "If any licensee shall permit any person who is a legally qualified candidate for any public office to use a broadcasting station, he shall afford equal opportunities to all other such candidates for that office in the use of such broadcasting station," (47 U.S.C.A. § 315) subject to certain specific exceptions. Although clearly a statute which regulates program content, it has survived attacks on its constitutionality. See, e.g. Branch v. Federal Communication Commission, 824 F.2d 37 (D.C.Cir. 1987). The section, as amended, also provides that the rates charged each candidate must be equal and that during election campaigns candidates must be given the "lowest unit charge" which is offered by the station to commercial advertisers for comparable time. The concept of equality extends not only to rates but also to station business practices. Thus, for example, a station cannot require one candidate to pay by certified check while another is allowed to pay by regular check in the normal course of business. Alpha Broadcasting Corp., 102 F.C.C.2d 18 (1984). Although rarely invoked, there are civil and criminal penalties for willful and knowing violations of the statute.

The political broadcasting statute is quite precise in its application and leaves virtually no room for broadcaster discretion except in the area of news coverage. It operates with a type of mathematical certainty not usually found in broadcasting regulation. Nevertheless, despite Congress' attempt at clarity, Section 315 law is often misunderstood because of its ad hoc application.

1. "Use"

Although it is generally thought that the "equal opportunities" provision of Section 315 applies to all election broadcasts, the provision is limited to those circumstances where the candidate himself or herself appears on (i.e. "uses") the program. Section 315 thus does not apply to a broadcast or advertisement on behalf of the candidate in which the candidate does not appear. This is a critical distinction. Unless the candidate appears, Section 315 simply does not apply.

The candidate's appearance is considered a "use" whenever (a) his or her identity can reasonably be presumed to be known to the audience and (b) when the appearance is of sufficient magnitude to be considered an integral part of the program. Thus, where a station staff person is also a candidate for a local office, his or her voice might be used, for example, as an unidentified voice in a radio station commercial. If the voice is not distinctive or well known enough to be immediately identifiable, the use of the voice would not be considered an "appearance." See, e.g., National Urban Coalition, 23 F.C.C.2d 123 (1970); Letter to WNEP–TV, 40 F.C.C. 431 (1965). If, however, the voice is so familiar as to be reasonably identified with the staff person-candidate, then the appearance would be a "use." Station WBAX, 17 F.C.C.2d 316 (1969). Similarly, a five-second introduction by a candidate to a one-half-hour program devoted to appearances by supporters of the candidate and on which a candidate appears at no other time, would not be so integral to the program as to make the entire one-half-hour program a "use" by the candidate entitling an opponent to one half hour of time. Whether the opponent would be entitled to a five-second appearance would be governed by the so-called "fleeting use" doctrine. The Commission has held that appearances of two and three seconds were too minimal to invoke the equal time doctrine. Time, Inc., 55 R.R.2d 581 (1984). The problem becomes much more complicated when the candidate appears for one minute on a five-minute program. In this latter case the Commission would probably consider the one-minute appearance to be of sufficient magnitude to entitle an opponent to equal time for the entire five-minute program.

The above discussion also illustrates another aspect of the "use" doctrine: a candidate's appearance will be considered a "use" even if the candidate is appearing for a completely unrelated purpose and never mentions his or her candidacy. Letter to United Community Campaigns of America, 40 F.C.C. 390 (1964). The classic example would be a station weatherperson or announcer who is also a candidate for local office. An appearance by either in their normal roles, in which they present the news or the weather, would, nevertheless (assuming they can be identified) be considered a "use" entitling their opponent to equal time, even if they never mention their candidacy. See Newscaster Candidacy, 40 F.C.C. 433 (1965); Station WBAX, 17 F.C.C.2d 316 (1969). When Ronald Reagan sought the Republican Presidential nomination in 1976, stations which presented his 20-year-old movies during the campaign incurred equal time obligations. Adrian Weiss Productions, 36 R.R.2d 292 (1976). The reason is that candidates' appearances would, if nothing else, be to their benefit merely because of the "identification factor" in politics, i.e. people are more likely to vote for persons whose names they can remember or identify.

2. Exemptions From Equal Time Requirement

The stringency of the "use" doctrine led Congress in 1959 to create certain specific exemptions to the "equal time" doctrine. Thus, the equal time doctrine is not applicable where the appearance by the candidate takes place on any:

(1) bona fide newscast,

(2) bona fide news interview,

(3) bona fide news documentary (if the appearance of the candidate is incidental to the presentation of the subject or subjects covered by the news documentary), or

(4) on-the-spot coverage of bona fide news events (including but not limited to political conventions and activities incidental thereto). 47 U.S.C.A. § 315(a).

The exemptions were enacted in 1959 so as to avoid the situation where an appearance by an incumbent at a routine affair such as a ribbon cutting ceremony or a greeting of visiting dignitaries on a newscast could trigger demands for equal time by all of his or her opponents. See Columbia Broadcasting System, Inc., 18 R.R. 238, recon. den. 26 F.C.C. 715 (1959). It was believed that applying the "use" doctrine in all its rigor would, in practice, force stations to ignore such events in their news programming even though, in the exercise of their editorial judgment, they would otherwise have presented such material because of its interest or importance.

The first three exemptions, i.e., newscasts, news interviews and news documentaries are rather straight-forward and have been further defined by extensive legislative history indicating their scope. Underlying them is the notion that such programs are essentially under the control of the station (and not the candidate) so that the candidate cannot misuse his or her appearance to gain an improper advantage. The inclusion of the concept "bona fide" in the exemption represents a restriction on the station. If the appearance on the news program is intended by the station to be aimed at favoring one candidate over another, the appearance would not be "bona fide" under the statute and thus would not be exempt.

The fourth exemption, however, "on-the-spot coverage of a bona fide news event" is less well defined in the legislative history and raises the question whether the definition of bona fide news event should be based upon the subjective determination of the broadcaster or upon an objective determination by the Commission. For example, two gubernatorial candidates have been invited by a local professional group to debate important issues. The debate is considered a "bona fide news event" by a local station which desires to carry it live as a matter of interest to its audience. Would the debate be an exempt program so that the station need not offer equal time to other candidates for the same office who are not invited to the debate? Similarly, if a station believed a presidential press conference to be a newsworthy item to be presented in its entirety, would the station's belief in the program's newsworthiness render it an exempt "bona fide news event"? The Commission first held in 1964 that the mere subjective judgment of the station was not alone dispositive and that the Commission would ultimately determine exemptions based on objective criteria such as whether the fact of candidacy was an integral part of the appearance or merely incidental thereto. Columbia Broadcasting System, Inc., 40 F.C.C. 395 (1964). The Commission later changed its mind. Now, at least with respect to debates and press conferences by candidates, it is the bona fide subjective judgment of the station which determines the exemption. If the station, in good faith, believes the debate or news conference to be newsworthy, it can cover these items without invoking the equal time rules for opposing candidates. Petitions of the Aspen Institute, 55 F.C.C.2d 697 (1975), affirmed Chisholm v. Federal Communications Commission, 538 F.2d 349 (D.C.Cir. 1976), cert. denied 429 U.S. 890, 97 S.Ct. 247, 50 L.Ed.2d 173. It can even sponsor the debate, so long as it does so without intending to benefit a particular candidate. Henry Geller, 95 F.C.C.2d 1236 (1983), affirmed without opinion League of Women Voters v. FCC, 731 F.2d 995 (D.C.Cir.1984). This interpretation, however, has been limited to debates, press conferences and, on occasion, to speeches by incumbent officials on issues affecting the electorate. Whether or not the same theory will in the future apply to other types of appearances by candidates is unclear.

The Commission has also expanded its interpretation of "on-the-spot" coverage. While "on-the-spot" coverage was originally interpreted to mean that the event had to be broadcast within 24 hours, the Commission subsequently relaxed this restriction and now holds that a delayed broadcast of "reasonably recent events" could be considered "on-the-spot" so long as the determination was made by the station in good faith. Henry Geller, 95 F.C.C.2d 1236 (1983).

It should be emphasized that the "equal time" doctrine is not the sole determinant of a candidate's ability to obtain air time. Even if a particular program would be considered "exempt" from the equal time requirements of Section 315, or the broadcast is not a "use" invoking equal time requirements, nevertheless there are other doctrines which could be used to gain access to the media. These include the "reasonable access" doctrine of Section 312 of the Act, and the "personal attack rule" discussed below.

3. Reasonable Access (Section 312(a)(7))

Section 315 requires even-handedness, not access. Indeed, Section 315(a) specifically states that "No obligation is imposed under this subsection upon any licensee to allow the use of its station by any such [legally qualified] candidate." Technically, a station could avoid Section 315 entirely simply by refusing to allow any candidate to appear. But in so doing it would violate other sections of the Communications Act. Thus, with respect to federal candidates, Section 312(a)(7) of the Act specifically includes, as a ground for revocation of license, "willful or repeated failure to allow reasonable access to or to permit purchase of reasonable amounts of time for the use of a broadcasting station by a legally qualified candidate for Federal elective office on behalf of his candidacy." CBS, Inc. v. FCC, 453 U.S. 367, 101 S.Ct. 2813, 69 L.Ed. 2d 706 (1981). And although state and local candidates are not specifically mentioned under the access provisions of Section 312(a), the Commission has interpreted the general "public interest" standard of Section 307 of the Act to forbid any station from simply refusing to allow political candidates to use the station's facility in any way simply to avoid equal time obligations. Some access must be given to certain state and local candidates, although the rules in this respect are imprecise.

What represents "reasonable access" for federal and state candidates has not been precisely defined—the concept necessarily varies with the circumstances. But the Commission has set forth certain guidelines. If, for example, there are dozens of state or local candidates for state or local elective offices, the FCC has never required that every candidate for every office must be given access. A broadcast station is not a common carrier and access cannot be achieved on demand. A station can prune out election campaigns for minor offices and allocate time only for the major offices on the state and local level. This flexibility with respect to state offices arises because there is no specific requirement in the Act that all state or local candidates must be given access. See Political Primer, 1984, 100 F.C.C.2d 1476, 1525–26.

A station's discretion is much more limited with respect to federal offices. All federal candidates, under the strictures of the statute, must be given "reasonable access." But even here the station retains some discretion to determine the manner of access. Thus, even under Section 312, a station is not required to *sell* programming or advertising time to candidates. Stations can, and some do, take the position that they will sell no program time to candidates, but instead will meet their "access" obligations by giving candidates a reasonable amount of free time. Political Primer 1984, 100 F.C.C.2d 1476, 1523–24.

But, if a station does choose to sell time, its discretion is further limited by (a) the provisions of Section 315 which require that the time be sold on a basis at least comparable to that offered to commercial clients, and (b) the provisions of the Federal Election Campaign Act of 1971 which require that during a period of 45 days before a primary election and 60 days before a general election, the station may only charge a candidate the "lowest unit rate." The "comparability" requirement means, with respect to federal candidates, that if a station sells 60 or 30 or 5 second announcements during prime time to commercial advertisers, it cannot refuse to sell such announcements during prime time to federal candidates. Public Notice, 47 F.C.C.2d 516 (1974). Thus, it would be illegal for a station to take the position that political issues do not lend themselves to proper discussion in a spot announcement format and should be handled only in programs of five minutes or more. Similarly, a station could not legally relegate all of its advertising for federal candidates to non-prime time periods—this would violate "reasonable access" on a "comparable basis." Summa Corp., 43 F.C.C.2d 602 (1973). The Commission has held it improper for a station to limit political programs for candidates for President to no more than five minutes during prime time. The Commission found that such a limitation did not constitute "reasonable access," and that situations must attempt to respond to the individualized situation of a particular candidate rather than adopt "across-the-board" policies. CBS, Inc. v. FCC, 453 U.S. 367, 101 S.Ct. 2813, 69 L.Ed.2d 706 (1981).

4. Lowest Unit Charge

Prior to 1971, Congress required only that stations treat political candidates in ways comparable to commercial advertisers. Thus, no station could charge a political candidate whether federal or state a greater amount than was charged for a comparable announcement presented on behalf of a commercial advertiser. The obvious intent was to prevent stations from taking advantage of the necessity for political candidates to obtain advertising time during election campaigns. For most of the year, the comparability criteria still holds true. However, in 1971, Congress amended Section 315 to require that during a specific election period (45 days preceding the date of a primary election and

60 days preceding the date of a federal or special election) a station may charge a political candidate no more than the lowest unit charge for the same class and amount of time for the same period. 47 U.S.C.A. § 315(b) (Cum.Supp.1976). The station must, during this period, treat the candidate in a manner comparable to its most favored commercial advertiser. The difference between "comparability" and "lowest unit charge" may be illustrated in this way: if a station has an advertiser willing to commit itself to purchasing an advertising schedule which will run an entire year, the station might be willing to give that advertiser a quantity discount so that instead of paying a normal rate of, for example, $10 per announcement, the advertiser need only pay $6 per announcement. Under the comparability standard in effect during most of the year, the station need only give political candidates the $6 rate if the candidate also agreed to purchase a schedule of announcements for the entire year. Since both are being treated in a comparable manner, the terms of the Act have been met. However, under the lowest unit charge concept, enforced during the 45 or 60 day period prior to a primary or general election, a station would be required to offer the $6 rate, even if the candidate bought only one announcement, since this would be the "lowest unit charge" being made for the time in question. In other words, lowest unit charge requires a station to give a political candidate a quantity discount even if the candidate does not purchase the

same quantity as would a commercial advertiser receiving the discount.

Even under the lowest unit rate the station still retains some flexibility. It may make distinctions between classes of time so that a candidate seeking, for instance, to purchase prime time advertisements would be required to pay the lowest unit charge for prime time advertisements. Nevertheless, the lowest unit charge rule has given political candidates a significant price advantage in using broadcast facilities. But it must be emphasized that the lowest unit charge criteria is applicable only to a "use" by a legally qualified candidate. Appearances by spokespersons on behalf of a particular candidate would not fall within the lowest unit charge concept because, as discussed above, it would not involve an appearance by the candidate and thus technically would not be a "use." Political Primer 1984, 100 F.C.C.2d 1476, 1519.

5. Legally Qualified Candidates

"Equal time" obligations come into play only upon "uses" followed by demands by "legally qualified candidates for public office." The determination of whether or not a user (or demander) is a legally qualified candidate for public office is made by reference to the law of the state in which the election is being held. Political Primer 1984, 100 F.C.C.2d 1476, 1480–86. All elections are not for "public office." For example, the position of delegate to a party convention is not a "public office," even though the name of that person may appear on an election ballot. Russell H. Morgan, 36 R.R.2d 890 (1976). Conversely, a candidate can be legally qualified even if his or her name is not on the ballot if such a person, under state law, is making a bona fide "write-in" campaign. Political Primer 1984, 100 F.C.C.2d 1476, 1482. But in order to be a legally qualified candidate the person must publicly announce his or her candidacy, even if everyone expects the person to be a candidate. Thus, an incumbent president, for example, cannot be presumed to be a candidate for reelection until such candidacy is announced. Until that time, appearances by the incumbent president would not be considered a "use" triggering equal time requirements. Id. at p. 1480. And if a purported candidate is too young to serve even if elected, he or she could not demand equal time to respond to an opponent. Socialist Workers Party, 39 F.C.C.2d 89 (1972). The question of whether a person is "legally qualified" can be quite complex, and the Commission will follow the laws of the particular state wherever possible. Committee for Mayor Bergin v. Station WATR–TV, 90 F.C.C.2d 813 (1982). In cases of ambiguity, the Commission will be the ultimate arbiter of whether the person is a candidate. CBS, Inc. v. FCC, 453 U.S. 367, 101 S.Ct. 2813, 69 L.Ed.2d 706 (1981).

6. Censorship

Section 315(a) specifically provides that no licensee can have any "power of censorship over the material broadcast under the provisions of this section." Thus, a legally qualified candidate for public office is free to say anything, whether or not it relates to the candidacy, and whether or not the material is scandalous or in any other manner unsuitable for broadcast. The obvious intent behind this subsection is to allow candidates to use radio or television time free from the fetters of any other person or entity. As a quid pro quo for such freedom, the Supreme Court has held that no station can be sued for libel or slander arising from such use by a candidate, nor can it be acted against in any manner by a private person or by the government. Farmers Educational and Cooperative Union v. WDAY, Inc., 360 U.S. 525, 79 S.Ct. 1302, 3 L.Ed.2d 1407 (1959). This immunity from suit is, the Court declared, constitutionally required to insure free speech by candidates. The "no censorship" provision is so stringently interpreted that it would be considered improper for a station to request that a candidate provide it with a copy of the candidate's speech or other materials prior to broadcast, the Commission holding that such a condition might inhibit the candidate in his or her use of the facility. Western Connecticut Broadcasting Co., 28 R.R.2d 1091 (1973).

There is one caveat to the "no censorship" clause. Although there has been no direct adjudicated case on the point, the Commission's staff has concluded in a memorandum to Congress that the prohibition against censorship would not apply to the broadcast of obscene material forbidden by the criminal code. Legislation to this effect has been introduced into both Houses of Congress, but not yet adopted. Even without legislation, it is likely that the Commission would take this position if an actual case came before it since otherwise it would be requiring a broadcaster to violate the criminal law in order to comply with Section 315. See Political Primer 1984, 100 F.C.C.2d 1476, 1513.

It must be stressed that the "no censorship" provision applies only to a use by a candidate. It does not apply to a use by a spokesman on behalf of a candidate, and (as will be discussed below) it did not apply to appearances by non-candidates under the "Fairness Doctrine when the Commission was still applying that doctrine."

7. Necessity for Timely Demand

Equal time rights, though available, can be lost through inactivity or delay. A candidate must make a request of a station for equal time within one week of the day of the first use giving rise to the right to equal opportunity in the use of the broadcast facility. 47 C.F.R. § 73.1940(e) (1981). If the person was not a candidate at the time of the first prior use, he is entitled to equal opportunity with respect to uses made during the week prior to his announcement of his candidacy. Letter to Joseph H. Clark, 40 F.C.C. 332 (1962).

There is no obligation on the part of the station to inform all other candidates, for purposes of equal opportunity, that a particular candidate is appearing on the station. It is assumed, and in essence required, that candidates will be vigilant on their own behalf. The only exception to this rule would be where the candidate—or user—is the licensee of the station involved. Under these circumstances, the Commission has held that the licensee is under an obligation to inform his opponent of the specific days that the licensee would be using the station for his candidacy. Letter to Emerson Stone, Jr., 40 F.C.C. 385 (1964). Absent such special circumstances, however, a licensee is under no obligation to inform candidates of uses by other candidates.

8. Political Editorializing

The Commission's Rules (47 C.F.R. § 73.1930 (1981)) contain special provisions relating to editorializing by licensees. These rules provide that where a licensee in an editorial either endorses or opposes a legally qualified candidate, the licensee must transmit to the other candidates within 24 hours notification of the date and time of the editorial, a script or a tape and an offer of reasonable opportunity for the candidate or his spokesperson to respond. Where such editorials are broadcast within 72 hours of the election, the licensee shall transmit the material sufficiently far in advance of the broadcast to enable candidates to have a reasonable opportunity to present a reply. This obligation, however, only arises with respect to endorsements of candidates. It does not apply to editorials on issues not involving candidates such as, for example, municipal bond issues and referenda.

9. The "Zapple Doctrine"

Although the "equal time" rule applies only to uses by candidates, the Commission has created what has been termed a "quasi-equal opportunity doctrine," which relates specifically to appearances by spokespersons for candidates. As noted above, appearances by such spokespersons on behalf of candidate A are not "uses" and therefore do not vest any "equal time" rights in A's legally qualified opponents. However, under the "Quasi-Equal Opportunities Doctrine" (known as the "Zapple Doctrine") when a station sells time to supporters or spokespersons of a candidate during an election campaign, the licensee must afford comparable time to the spokesperson for an opponent. Letter to Nicholas Zapple, 23 F.C.C.2d 707 (1970). If the first group of spokespersons purchases time, then the opposing group can also purchase time if it wishes to respond. If the first group is given free time, then the second group must also be given free time. The Zapple Doctrine is, in essence, a type of hybrid between the "Equal Time Doctrine" and the "Fairness Doctrine." But although it contains elements of the "Equal Time Doctrine," there are, nevertheless, important distinctions. Thus, the Zapple Doctrine does not apply to all parties and all candidates. A station may choose not to provide "fringe candidates or minor parties" with broadcast time under "quasi-equal opportunity." First Report, Docket No. 19260, 36 F.C.C.2d 40 (1972). The Zapple Doctrine does not apply outside of campaign periods. And the Equal Opportunities Doctrine is mutually exclusive with the Zapple Doctrine. If a legally qualified candidate appears in the broadcast with his supporters, then the broadcast is a use under the Equal Time Doctrine and the Zapple Doctrine does not apply.

For further elaboration of the now quite complex evolution of political broadcasting, see Political Primer 1984, 100 F.C.C.2d 1476 et seq.

B. THE "FAIRNESS DOCTRINE"

Perhaps nothing better illustrates the deregulatory thrust of the present Commission than its recent repudiation of one of the fundamental pillars of broadcast regulation: The Fairness Doctrine.

The Fairness Doctrine arose out of a series of FCC rulings which for over two decades were thought to have been codified by Congress in its 1959 Amendments to Section 315(a) of the Communications Act. P.L. 86–274, 73 Stat. 557. The amendments specifically make reference to the obligation of a broadcaster "to operate in the public interest and to afford reasonable opportunity for the discussion of conflicting views on issues of public importance." This language was traditionally construed to be a type of legislative shorthand which enacted into positive law a dual licensee obligation: (a) to devote a reasonable amount of broadcast time to the discussion of controversial issues, and (b) to do so fairly, i.e., to afford reasonable opportunity for the presentation of opposing view-points. Red Lion Broadcasting Co. v. Federal Communications Commission, 395 U.S. 367, 377, 89 S.Ct. 1794, 1799, 23 L.Ed.2d 371, 381 (1969). See also 47 C.F.R. § 73.1910.

The entire "Fairness Doctrine" area was thrown into confusion by a 1986 United States Court of Appeals decision, Telecommunications Research and Action Center (TRAC) v. FCC, 801 F.2d 501 (D.C.Cir.1986), rehearing denied 806 F.2d 1115 (D.C.Cir.1986) cert. denied ___ U.S. ___, 107 S.Ct. 3196, 96 L.Ed.2d 684 in which the court held that the Fairness Doctrine was not, in fact, codified in the 1959 amendments. The court held that, rather than being a congressionally mandated statutory obligation, the Fairness Doctrine was the Commission's creation and its enforcement was left by Congress to the Commission, which was free either to apply the doctrine or eliminate it. The court decision was in one sense not surprising. The Commission itself had begun to question its long-standing interpretation of the 1959 amendments and, in a 1985 "Notice of Inquiry," had stated its belief that the Fairness Doctrine, as traditionally interpreted, was no longer necessary and was constitutionally infirm because of the increase in the number of broadcast stations and the emergence of new communications technologies, which assure the public access to a variety of viewpoints. See Notice of Inquiry Concerning General Fairness Doctrine Obligations of Broadcast Licensees, 102 F.C.C.2d 143 (1985).

The confusion was compounded when, in response to a court mandate (Meredith Corp. v. FCC, 809 F.2d 863 (D.C.Cir.1987) that the Commission specifically consider the constitutionality of the doctrine, the FCC overturned decades of practice to hold that, in its present view, the Fairness Doctrine "contravenes the First Amendment and thereby disserves the public interest." In re Syracuse Peace Council, Memorandum Opinion and Order, 2 F.C.C. Rcd. 5042 (August 6, 1987) at paragraph 98. The Commission reasoned that the Fairness Doctrine both chills speech and is not narrowly tailored to achieve a substantial government interest. It based its decision to no longer enforce the doctrine in part upon the growth of the electronic media which, in its view, removed the "scarcity" rationale of Red Lion. The Commission acknowledged that there still exists so-called "allocational scarcity" in that there are still more applicants for stations than spectrum space to accommodate them. However, the Commission now feels that this allocational scarcity cannot alone justify controls upon program content, with their chilling effect on editorial discretion.

The Commission decision caused sharp reaction from Congress, which immediately passed legislation enacting the Fairness Doctrine, as traditional-

ly understood, into law. This legislation was vetoed by President Reagan. At the time this book is
being written Congress was threatening to again
legislatively reenact the doctrine, this time attach-
ing it to other legislation felt to be veto proof.

Because the last word appears not to have been
written on the doctrine, we will discuss it as it
traditionally had been applied prior to the recent
Commission repudiation.

1. The Traditional Concept of "Fairness"

The traditional notion of "fairness," simply stated, is the obligation to afford reasonable opportunity for the presentation of opposing viewpoints on
matters of public controversy. On its simplest
level, it means that the broadcaster cannot use its
facilities to promulgate only one particular point of
view on a major issue. In practice, however, the
doctrine becomes quite complex and involves a
mixture of government pressure and licensee discretion.

The first point to note is that a station need be
fair only with respect to issues of public controversy. There never has been a fairness obligation
with respect to matters which, though of interest
to a particular listener, are not matters of important public controversy in the community. Cattle
Country Broadcasting, 58 R.R.2d 1109 (1985). For
example, a particular viewer may be quite firm in
his or her conviction that there is no God. The
viewer may also be quite upset with a station that

presents substantial religious programming affirming the existence of God. Yet the presentation of such religious programming would not impose upon the station a Fairness Doctrine obligation to present an agnostic or atheistic point of view, unless the existence of God was at that time a matter of major public controversy. See David S. Tillson, 24 F.C.C.2d 297 (1970). On the other hand, the fact that a religious issue is involved does not necessarily mean that the controversy is one of private morality alone. Presentation of an anti-abortion viewpoint, held for the most devout religious reasons, would nevertheless trigger a fairness obligation if the abortion issue were a matter of local controversy involving, for example, the passage of pro or anti-abortion legislation. Whether or not a particular matter is one of public controversy is, as the Commission admits, susceptible to no easy determination. It involves such matters as the level of public debate, the appearance of the issue in local news media, the existence of an election question on the point, and the like. Fairness Report, Docket No. 19260, 48 F.C.C.2d 1, 11–12 (1974).

Assuming that a matter of local public controversy has been covered on the station, what, specifically, are the obligations of the licensee? Is it obligated, for example, to devote "equal time" to the coverage of both sides of the issue? The answer is no. The "Fairness Doctrine" does not operate with the precision of the "equal time" rule for political broadcasting. Indeed, this is one of the basic differences between the two doctrines. The licensee need merely demonstrate that he has afforded a reasonable amount of time (not necessarily equal) to proponents of varying points of view. "Applicability of the Fairness Doctrine in the Handling of Controversial Issues of Public Importance," 29 Fed.Reg. 10415, 10419 ¶ 12 (1964) (hereafter referred to as "1964 Fairness Primer").

The Fairness Doctrine vests a broad discretion in the licensee not only as to the amount of time to be devoted to the controversy, but to the issues to be covered, the viewpoints to be presented, the appropriate spokespersons, the format of the programming, and other similar programming decisions. With the exception of the personal attack aspect of the Fairness Doctrine (discussed below), the "reasonable access" rights of Federal candidates, and the specialized rules covering political editorials, no particular person or group has a constitutional or legislative right of access to the facilities of a broadcast station. The Supreme Court in Columbia Broadcasting System, Inc. v. Democratic National Committee, 412 U.S. 94, 111, 93 S.Ct. 2080, 2090–2091, 36 L.Ed.2d 772, 788–789 (1973) rejected the "right of access" theory and reaffirmed the rule that a broadcast station is not a common carrier which must open its facilities on demand, even if the demand is made on behalf of a worthwhile cause. Additionally, there is no requirement that a licensee internally balance a program or series of programs; rather, the Fairness Doctrine requires a balanced presentation of controversial issues in the licensee's overall programming, not in any single broadcast. American Security Council, 94 F.C.C.2d 521 (1983). The United States Court of Appeals has held that the Commission's role in reviewing Fairness Doctrine judgments of a licensee is akin to the role played by the courts in reviewing the actions of an administrative agency. The Commission cannot substitute its judgment for that of the broadcaster and penalize it because the Commission disagrees with the broadcaster's exercise of judgment. Only when the broadcaster's judgment is of such an egregious nature that no reasonable person could doubt that it is an abuse of discretion can the Commission step in and order a particular course of action by the broadcaster. Straus Communications, Inc., v. Federal Communications Commission, 530 F.2d 1001 (D.C.Cir. 1976); Syracuse Peace Council, 57 R.R.2d 519 (1984), remanded sub nom. Meredith Corporation v. FCC, 809 F.2d 863 (D.C.Cir.1987), vacated by Order of Aug. 6, 1987, 2 F.C.C. Rcd 5042.

There are certain imposed limits to licensee discretion, even in Fairness Doctrine situations. As part of its public interest obligation, a broadcaster must affirmatively encourage the presentation of opposing views even to the point of itself seeking them out. 1964 Fairness Primer, 29 Fed.Reg. 10415, 10418, ¶ 9. A broadcaster cannot defend its refusal to present varying points of view on the basis that no one asked to reply. If the licensee has reason to believe that there is an identifiable group or person which would speak out on an issue had it been informed of the broadcast, the licensee must seek that group out. Columbia Broadcasting System, Inc., 34 F.C.C.2d 773 (1972). And the licensee is required to present contrasting viewpoints even if it receives no consideration. Thus, under the doctrine enunciated in Cullman Broadcasting Co., 40 F.C.C. 576 (1963), if one side of a controversial issue is broadcast on a sponsored basis, the licensee must broadcast contrasting viewpoints even if those with contrasting viewpoints cannot afford to purchase the time. But there is no required ratio of time to be given to the various sides. The Commission has rejected as inappropriate such a "mechanical" approach. Fairness Report, 48 F.C.C.2d 1, 17 (1974).

It must be emphasized that the Commission's role in Fairness Doctrine situations is not that of a continuing monitor to insure that licensees adhere to the tenets of the Doctrine. Rather, the Commission's role essentially is to enforce the Doctrine upon the filing of appropriate complaints by members of the public. This is critical because the Commission has listed certain prerequisites to an appropriate Fairness complaint which, in fact, limit the practical impact of the Fairness Doctrine upon broadcasters. In its 1964 Fairness Doctrine Primer the Commission stipulated that it will act only where a complainant includes in his or her complaint to the Commission:

> . . . specific information indicating (1) the particular station involved; (2) the particular issue of a controversial nature discussed over the air; (3) the date and time when the program was carried; (4) the basis for the claim that the station has presented only one side of the question; and (5) whether the station had afforded or has plans to afford, an opportunity for the presentation of contrasting viewpoints. 29 Fed.Reg. 10415, 10416.

The last of these elements is particularly significant because it places upon the complainant the burden of prima facie demonstrating that the licensee has failed to present varying viewpoints on the point at issue. This includes the necessity of showing that the complainant is a regular viewer. Unless such a prima facie case is made, the station need not even respond because, in the Commission's view, forcing stations to respond to less than prima facie showings would place too great a burden upon licensees and might force them to eschew coverage of controversial issues entirely. Wilderness Society, 41 F.C.C.2d 103 (1973).

In order to meet this last element, the complainant, prior to contacting the FCC, is required first to contact the broadcaster and to provide it with all the information necessary to make the prima facie showing of violation. Irving Gastfreund (Neighbor to Neighbor), 59 R.R.2d 1070 (M.M.B.1986).

The burden imposed on complainants of making such a prima facie showing may be one explanation for the fact that while the Commission receives thousands of Fairness Doctrine complaints (4417 in 1979 alone), only a very few of these are ever followed up with demands upon licensees for further information (approximately 45 in 1979). And an even smaller number of complaints ever becomes the basis for a Commission decision. In only a minuscule number of cases has the Commission ever reached the determination that the broadcaster in fact breached his responsibilities under the Fairness Doctrine. Some commentators have even suggested that the Doctrine exists only because of the infrequency of its use by the Commission. A more vigorous enforcement might well doom the Doctrine as having an improper "chilling effect" on freedom of licensee speech. See Robinson dissent to Opinion and Order on Reconsideration of Fairness Report, 58 F.C.C.2d 691, 703 (1974); Bazelon dissent in Brandywine-Main Line Radio, Inc. v. Federal Communications Commission, 153 U.S.App.D.C. 305, 473 F.2d 16, 63 (1972).

The Doctrine has raised some interesting problems with respect to the presentation of commercial spot announcements and news programs. When the question of whether cigarette smoking was dangerous was under investigation by, among others, the Surgeon General of the United States, cigarette companies continued to advertise their product over radio and television. In response to a complaint, the Commission, rather surprisingly, held that the mere presentation of product advertising was itself a statement of a "point of view" on the "controversial issue" of whether cigarettes were damaging (even if, as was invariably the case, the product advertising never mentioned the controversy). Thus, stations that presented cigarette advertising were under an obligation to present "anti cigarette advertising" in some reasonable proportion to the amount of cigarette ads presented. WCBS–TV, 8 F.C.C.2d 381 (1967). This ruling, affirmed by the Court of Appeals (Banzhaf v. Federal Communications Commission, 132 U.S.App. D.C. 14, 405 F.2d 1082 (1968), cert. denied 396 U.S. 842, 90 S.Ct. 50, 24 L.Ed.2d 93 (1969)), ultimately led to demands by environmentalists and others to respond to product advertisements for, among others, automobiles, gasoline engines, and public utilities on the grounds that advertisements of these products and companies were statements on the controversial issue of pollution, whether or not the controversy was mentioned in the commercial announcement. After some confusion and litigation the Commission ultimately ruled that its earlier cigarette holding was erroneously based. Fairness Report, 48 F.C.C.2d at 26 (1974). The present rule is that product advertising per se is not a statement on a controversial issue so long as the advertising merely extols the virtues of the product and takes no explicit position on matters of public controversy. Ibid.

With respect to news programs, the charge is often made that a particular news program is "slanted" or "biased." The Commission has recognized that direct intervention into the thought processes of broadcast newspersons could well have an extremely "chilling effect" in an area explicitly protected by the First Amendment. Thus, the Commission has held that absent some direct, extrinsic evidence of deliberate news slanting, the Commission will not entertain complaints concerning the "fairness" of news presentations. Hunger in America, 20 F.C.C.2d 143 (1969); Central Intelligence Agency, 58 R.R.2d 1544 (1985).

2. Personal Attack Rule

The Personal Attack Rule (47 C.F.R. § 73.1920) is an aspect of the Fairness Doctrine relating to the right of a person attacked to gain access to the broadcast facility to defend himself or herself. The Personal Attack Rule is quite precise and specific. It holds that when, during the presentation of views on a controversial issue of public importance, an attack is made upon the honesty, character, integrity or like personal qualities of an identified person or group, the licensee shall, within a reasonable time and in no event later than one week after the attack, transmit to the person or group attacked (1) notification of the date, time and identification of the broadcast; (2) a script or tape of the attack; and (3) an offer of a reasonable opportunity to respond over the licensee's facilities. The rule does not apply to:

1.   attacks on foreign groups or foreign public figures;

2.   personal attacks made by legally qualified candidates, their authorized spokesmen, or persons associated with them; and

3.   bona fide newscasts, bona fide news interviews or on-the-spot coverage of bona fide news events.

The key features of the rule are that the rule does not apply to every personal attack carried on the station, but only to a personal attack broadcast during the presentation of views on a controversial issue of public importance.   Galloway v. FCC, 59 R.R.2d 587 (1985).   A person attacked at some other time will have no redress from the Commission but must look to the law of defamation for remedy.   Straus Communications, Inc. v. Federal Communications Commission, 530 F.2d 1001 (D.C. Cir. 1976).   Moreover, the attack must be as to the person's honesty, character, integrity or like personal qualities if the rule is to be invoked.   An attack, for example, upon a person alleging that a person's ideas are "stupid" would not be considered a personal attack for the purposes of the rule. Mrs. Frank Diesz, 27 F.C.C.2d 859 (1971).   Additionally, a complainant must show that the person or group attacked was identified with sufficient specificity that the listening or viewing public would have been able to discern the specific person or group.   Fairness in Media, 58 R.R.2d 1633 (M.M.B.1985).   Finally, if the Personal Attack Rule applies, the person attacked has an absolute right to appear in his or her own defense. The station has no discretion to require that the defense be made by another person. This is in contrast to practice under the Fairness Doctrine generally by which the licensee is not required to choose any particular person or group to present the contrasting point of view.

Paradoxically, the Commission did not overturn the Personal Attack Rule in its August, 1987 repudiation of the Fairness Doctrine. Because the Personal Attack Rule is really only an aspect of the Fairness Doctrine, there is little logic in continuing the rule once the doctrine has been abandoned. It is likely that the Commission will soon repeal the rule. Whether or not Congress will then move to reenact the rule is more unpredictable.

3. Present State of the Fairness Doctrine

The very recent Commission repeal of the Fairness Doctrine, coupled with Congressional agitation to enact the Doctrine specifically into positive law, has caused significant uncertainty. The confusion is beneficial, however, in the sense that it properly raises for reexamination the basic tenets of government media regulation. At the very least, courts, the Commission and the media must revisit the First Amendment rather than merely allow regulation to continue through inertia. The prime thrust of the attacks on the constitutionality of the Fairness Doctrine lies in the premise that government regulation of any kind of media content is inherently improper and can be countenanced, if at all, on a showing of overwhelming need. If the "scarcity" of broadcast frequencies (in terms of absolute number) is the element that supplied that need, the emergence of new types of telecommunications capabilities (e.g., cable television, satellite broadcasting, computer communication, teletext) has attenuated the need to the point where any government regulation of content can no longer be countenanced. If, on the other hand, the need for government regulation arises irrespective of the absolute number of non-broadcast technologies, and continues because at any given time the number of persons who wish to use a broadcast frequency is greater than the available spectrum, then the Fairness Doctrine may be properly viewed as the constitutional price one must pay for being allowed monopoly use of a scarce resource. Ultimately, only the Supreme Court can tell us which of these theories will prevail.

C. OBSCENITY AND INDECENCY

Although not contained in the Communications Act of 1934, the Criminal Code of the United States (18 U.S.C.A. § 1464) contains a specific prohibition against broadcast stations presenting any material which is "obscene," "indecent," or "profane." Although rarely invoked, the "obscenity" section of the statute has been held constitutional under the prevailing theory that obscenity is not protected by the First Amendment. Illinois Citizens Committee for Broadcasting v. Federal Communications Commission, 515 F.2d 397 (D.C.Cir.), rehearing denied 515 F.2d 407 (D.C.Cir. 1975).

With respect to "obscenity," the general standard is that followed in the normal "obscenity" case, i.e., whether or not the material taken as a whole is patently offensive and appeals to an average person's prurient interest without serious literary, artistic, political, or scientific value when considered in connection with contemporary community standards. Miller v. California, 413 U.S. 15, 93 S.Ct. 2607, 37 L.Ed.2d 419 (1973). In practice, the courts have applied a more expansive concept of prurience to broadcasting than that applied to other forms of media. But there are few reported cases and the outlines of such standards for broadcasting have not yet been fully delineated. The courts have approved Commission prohibition of explicitly sexual programming where, during daytime hours, listeners freely discuss their sexual practices, in a normal "disc jockey" format readily accessible to children. See Illinois Citizens Committee v. Federal Communications Commission, supra. Beyond this, the line between protected programming and "obscenity" is far from clear. In recent years, the Commission has evidenced a reluctance to become involved in obscenity determinations. While recognizing its concurrent jurisdiction to enforce federal anti-obscenity statutes, it has nevertheless determined to leave to local prose-

cutors the responsibility of identifying and prosecuting violators of such statutes. Video 44, 103
F.C.C.2d 1204 (1986).

The "indecency" standard has also been upheld
as a constitutionally proper exercise (under certain
circumstances) of the state's police power. FCC v.
Pacifica Foundation, 438 U.S. 726, 98 S.Ct. 3026, 57
L.Ed.2d 1073 (1978). Significantly, however, the
Supreme Court has allowed the Commission to give
the concept of "indecency" a broader definition
than that of "obscenity." Material which is "patently offensive," "sexual" and "excretory" may, if
broadcast during times when children are presumed to be in the audience, be punishable even if
not "obscene." Pacifica, supra. The case is instructive because the Court had previously defined
the concept of "indecency" to be coextensive with
"obscenity" if presented in books and films. Pacifica is an excellent example of the court applying
different statutory and constitutional standards to
broadcasting, primarily because of broadcaster's
ease of access to children and the difficulty of
parental supervision.

For almost a decade after Pacifica, the Commission, in practice, limited its definition of "indecency" to the specific "seven dirty words" at issue in
that case. In 1987, however, it gave notice that in
the future it would apply the standard more broadly and take action if such material was broadcast
at a time of day when there is "reasonable risk"
that children were in the audience. The Commis-

sion gave no guidance as to what would be considered "reasonable risk" and it warned broadcasters that adult programming after 10 p.m. might not be safe. 52 Fed.Reg. 16386 (May 5, 1987). It gave no indication of how broadcasters were to determine "community standards." Apparently, even "marketplace" advocates at the FCC have their limits of tolerance. Constitutional challenges to the Commission's new policy on indecency are all but certain.

D. LOTTERIES

The federal criminal code generally prohibits any station from broadcasting any information concerning a lottery. 18 U.S.C.A. § 1304. Section 73.1211 of the Commission's rules essentially follows this criminal code section. A lottery is any game or contest which contains the elements of prize, chance and "consideration." These elements are construed in terms of a type of federal common law of lotteries followed by the Federal Communications Commission, the Post Office Department and the Department of Justice. Because of the varying state law definitions of these terms, it would be impossible to rely upon often conflicting state definitions to prohibit lotteries by radio transmission, which is, by statute, an interstate activity. See Federal Communications Commission v. American Broadcasting Co., 347 U.S. 284, 74 S.Ct. 593, 98 L.Ed. 699 (1954). This area of the law can become quite complex particularly in determining whether "consideration" is present. The federal common law of "consideration" has been established to mean a monetary or other detriment to the participant in the contest rather than merely a benefit to the contest operator. For example, the requirement of the listener mailing in a post card to a station would not be considered "consideration," even though the station may thereby "benefit" by obtaining a list of members of its audience or by the contest enlarging the station's audience. Federal Communications Commission v. American Broadcasting Co., supra; cf. Caples Co. v. Federal Communications Commission, 100 U.S.App.D.C. 126, 243 F.2d 232 (1957).

There are two exceptions to the general lottery ban. A station is now allowed to broadcast any information it wishes about a state authorized lottery in its own or adjacent state so long as the station is located in a state which has its own official lottery. 18 U.S.C.A. § 1307, 47 C.F.R. § 73.1211(c)(1). Additionally, a station may broadcast information concerning a fishing contest if such contest is not conducted for profit. 18 U.S.C.A. § 1305; 47 C.F.R. § 73.1211(c)(2).

E.   PRIME TIME ACCESS RULE

The Commission, over the years, has evolved a series of policies which have specific impact upon the material presented by a network affiliated broadcast station. Networks are, generally speaking, organizations which have been created for the purpose of producing and distributing programming to individual stations and also to act as advertising clearance centers for all network affiliated stations. Although networks can (and do) act as licensees of individual stations, the networks themselves are not regulated by the Commission and the Commission has no power directly to regulate their operations. But the Commission can and does indirectly regulate the networks through its power over the licenses of individual stations. This regulation is apparent in the so-called "Network Rules" which prohibit any individual station from entering into contracts with networks which contain certain provisions that the Commission finds offensive to the public interest. 47 C.F.R. §§ 73.132 (AM radio); 73.232 (FM radio); and 73.658 (television) (1981). These prohibitions forbid network contract clauses that would prevent the licensee from broadcasting the programs of any other network, or that would prevent another station in the affiliate's area from broadcasting a network program if the affiliate declines to broadcast it. The Rules also require that television network affiliation terms be no longer than two years (§ 73.658(c)), and that the television affiliate be granted the right to reject network programs that it believes unsatisfactory (§ 73.658(e)). Among the most important of these rules are provisions covering television prime time programming. These rules, referred to as the "Prime Time Access Rules," reflect a concern with the lack of local programming activity among network affiliates.

They provide (§ 73.658(k)) that television stations owned by or affiliated with a national television network in the 50 largest television markets shall devote during the four hours of prime time (7–11 p. m. Eastern Time and Pacific Time and 6–10 p. m. Central Time and Mountain Time) no more than three hours to the presentation of programs from a national network, including programs which formerly had been presented on national networks. The only exception is that certain categories of programs need not be counted toward the three-hour limitation such as (1) programs designed for children, public affairs programs or documentary programs; (2) special news programs and political broadcasts; (3) regular network news broadcasts up to one-half hour when immediately adjacent to a full hour of locally produced news programming; and (4) run-overs of sporting events and network broadcasts of national sports events or other programs of a special nature. In practical effect, the Prime Time Access Rule means that three hours of the four-hour-prime time period will be devoted to network produced or distributed entertainment programs, one-half hour will be devoted to network news programming and the remaining one-half hour will consist of either non-network produced entertainment programs or special documentary or public affairs features. The Prime Time Access Rule represents as definite a restriction on program content as the courts have countenanced. It has been justified as appropriate regulation in the public interest and not program censorship otherwise prohibited by Section 326 of the Act. Mt. Mansfield Television, Inc. v. Federal Communications Commission, 442 F.2d 470 (2d Cir. 1971).

Other rules prohibit television networks from engaging in "syndicating" non-network programming, or from having an ownership interest in broadcast programming produced by others. 47 C.F.R. § 73.658(j) (1981). There has been some pressure to relax the restrictions upon networks in the syndication and ownership interest areas and this entire question is being revisited by the Commission and Congress.

F. SPONSORSHIP IDENTIFICATION RULES: "ANTI–PAYOLA" AND "ANTI–PLUGOLA" REQUIREMENTS

Congress and the Commission have expressed concern that broadcast frequencies not be used by "hidden persuaders." Although most sponsors purchase time specifically to identify themselves and/or their products, there are occasions when persons wish to use programming time anonymously to further their own purposes. Such use can occur in a number of ways. Record promoters may offer money to disc jockeys to induce them to play their records ("payola") or to advertise certain activities ("plugola") without the public being aware that such material is being broadcast for pay. Other examples include broadcasting paid political matter or material concerning controversial issues without identifying the person or group presenting the material.

Because it is believed important that the audience be aware of the person paying the piper, Section 507 of the Communications Act and Section 73.1212 of the Commission's Rules stipulate that any person who pays or receives money or other valuable consideration for including any material as part of programming to be broadcast over a station must report that transaction to the licensee or licensees over whose facilities the program is aired. In turn, under Section 317 of the Act and Section 73.1212 of the Rules, the licensee is required to identify over the air, clearly and concisely, the person making the payment, and the fact that payment was made.

The sponsorship identification rules have caused some particular anomalies in the public broadcasting field where sponsorship, per se, is prohibited, while identification of sponsors is required by Section 317 of the Act. The Commission has resolved this anomaly by holding that a public broadcaster is required to identify the name of a donor, and may even refer to the donor's product or service, but may not "promote" the product or service in the sense of urging viewers to purchase it. See Educational Broadcasting Stations (Promotional Announcements), 90 F.C.C.2d 895 (1982); Educational Broadcasting Stations, 97 F.C.C.2d 255 (1984). Admittedly, the line between "identifying" and "promoting" becomes rather thin.

Further, Section 73.1212(d) of the Rules require that if any material or service is given to a station as an inducement to use such material or service in the broadcast of political matters or during the discussion of controversial issues of public importance, an announcement must be made indicating the material or service that was received by the station and identifying the person or entity which provided that material or service.

G. CONTESTS

Both Congress and the Commission have adopted standards of conduct governing broadcast contests. Section 73.1216 of the Rules mandates that a station must fully and accurately disclose the material terms of any contest which the station presents and the contest must be conducted in the manner advertised. The material terms include, inter alia, entry qualifications, eligibility restrictions, deadline dates, prize information, basis for valuation of prizes and tie-breaking procedures.

Section 508 of the Communications Act provides that, in contests of "intellectual knowledge, intellectual skill or chance," it is illegal to supply any contestant with any special or secret assistance, to persuade or intimidate a contestant from refraining from using his knowledge or skill or to engage in any prearrangement or predetermination of the outcome.

CHAPTER XII

CABLE AND NEW TECHNOLOGIES

A. TELEVISION BY CABLE

CATV (cable television) arose because of inherent limitations in commercial television. Television is merely the wireless transmission of visual and aural material over the air. Because of its physical characteristics, the distance that the television signal can travel over the air is limited. This fact, together with the Commission's television allocation policy whereby only a limited number of frequencies were assigned to designated cities throughout the country, posed significant reception problems for many residents of outlying areas, or areas on the fringe of larger cities. The problem was exacerbated by the fact that even some of the larger cities to which frequencies were assigned were only assigned three VHF channels, and some only two; thus there were large areas of the country that could receive no more than two or, at most, three signals. Because television signals only travel a line-of-sight path, there were some communities located in mountainous terrain that could not even obtain adequate reception from the two or three stations that they theoretically should have been able to receive over the air.

The solution to the problem for many of these communities was to erect extremely tall receiving towers at the highest point in the area to pick up the off-the-air signals and then retransmit the signals over wires run from the tower to various homes (subscribers). Typically, the home subscriber would pay a one-time installation fee for the wiring and a monthly fee for the service.

Although the original CATV systems were intended mainly to fill in the blanks within stations' normal coverage areas, it soon became apparent that CATV could also bring in service from distant cities which, under the Commission's allocation plan, were never intended to render service to that particular cable community. Thus, for example, a city such as Kingston, New York, located 90 miles from New York City, was never intended by the Commission to receive off-the-air service from the New York City television stations; the Commission intended Kingston to be served by the closer Albany, New York, facilities. However, cable television could bring in all of the New York stations, an obvious benefit to the residents of Kingston, but also a possible economic detriment to the Albany station, which could have its "natural audience" in Kingston fragmented. Moreover, CATV system operators could offer other communications services, including programming services such as sports events and feature films. This latter capability caused many to begin referring to CATV as "cable television," implying that the new service was much more than merely a community antenna.

Cable television also posed legal problems:

(a) Was cable television subject to FCC jurisdiction? It was not in existence when the Communications Act was passed, and might be considered merely a receiving rather than a transmitting unit, thus not "broadcasting."

(b) If the Commission did have jurisdiction, did the federal government preempt the field of regulation so that state or local governmental bodies were deprived of jurisdiction over such systems? This question was particularly important since cable television systems required local construction of wire lines and thus had a significant effect on the local citizenry;

(c) If jurisdiction was to be shared between a federal and local agency, how should the power to regulate cable be allocated?

(d) How was the Commission to reconcile the new technology of cable and its potential for carrying distant signals over the entire country with the existing Commission policy of station allocation?

(e) How did cable television comport with the copyright laws?

1. Jurisdiction

a. History

At first, the Commission refused to take jurisdiction over cable on the grounds that its power to do so was in question and that it did not feel the impact of cable television at the time was sufficient to invoke discretionary jurisdiction. Frontier Broadcasting Co. v. Collier, 24 F.C.C. 251 (1958). In 1966, the Commission changed course and adopted the first general federal regulation of cable systems, asserting that some overall comprehensive federal regulation was necessary to meet the Commission's responsibility to promote, maintain, and supervise an effective television service throughout the country. Second Report and Order, 2 F.C.C.2d 725 (1966). The Commission's power to assert jurisdiction under its general grant of power from Congress and in the absence of specific legislation concerning cable television was affirmed by the Supreme Court in United States v. Southwestern Cable Co., 392 U.S. 157, 88 S.Ct. 1994, 20 L.Ed.2d 1001 (1968). The Commission's jurisdiction was limited, however, "to that reasonably ancillary to the effective performance of the Commission's various responsibilities for the regulation of television broadcasting."

Some clarification of what the Court meant by reasonably ancillary came in United States v. Midwest Video Corp., 406 U.S. 649, 92 S.Ct. 1860, 32 L.Ed.2d 390 (1972) when, by a 5–4 vote, the Court upheld regulations that required specified cable systems to originate local programming. But the Chief Justice (who voted with the majority) took pains to point out that in making such a requirement the Commission appeared to be reaching the limits of its authority under the Communications Act. Actually, the Commission had voluntarily stepped back from its position during the course of the Midwest litigation. It suspended the mandatory program origination rule and never reinstated it.

The Chief Justice's remarks were prophetic. The mandatory program origination rules appear to have been the high water mark of Commission cable regulation. Not long thereafter, the court of appeals struck down Commission rules restricting the ability of cablevision systems to present certain feature films and sports programs, holding that such regulation was beyond the power of the Commission because it was not "reasonably ancillary" to the Commission's long-term regulatory goals and responsibilities. Home Box Office, Inc. v. FCC, 567 F.2d 9 (D.C.Cir.1977), cert. denied 434 U.S. 829, 98 S.Ct. 111, 54 L.Ed.2d 89 (1977). And in 1979, the Supreme Court struck down the Commission's rules requiring that cablevision systems offer channels to the public on a lease basis (so-called "access" channels) on the grounds that these provisions also went beyond the Commission's regulatory powers. Federal Communications Commission v. Midwest Video Corp. (Midwest Video II) 440 U.S. 689, 99 S.Ct. 1435, 59 L.Ed.2d 692 (1979).

In cable, unlike in broadcasting, the Commission accepted a bifurcated jurisdictional scheme that also allowed state and local authorities regulatory authority over cable. Under this scheme state or local authorities issued the franchise or license for the specific cable operator, imposing whatever obligations they thought necessary. For example access channel requirements, similar to those held beyond the Commission's jurisdiction in Midwest Video II, were common in franchising agreements. The franchise agreements were, however, subject to certain minimal FCC limitations, such as a ceiling of 5% of gross revenues on franchise fees.

By the early 1980s, there was a great deal of controversy over the jurisdictional scheme that had developed. Cable operators felt that some franchising authorities were making excessive demands. Of even greater concern was the question of renewal. With no renewal standards or guidelines and no specific requirement of renewal expectancy, cable operators were worried about what would happen when initial franchise agreements expired.

Meanwhile, the FCC was becoming more aggressive in asserting its jurisdiction at the expense of the state and local authorities. For example, the Commission preempted rate regulation of premium cable services (pay services such as HBO). The preemption of franchising requirements for SMATV was seen as a foreshadowing of even more preemption in the cable area. See New York State

Commission on Cable Television v. FCC, 749 F.2d 804 (D.C.Cir.1984).

Then in 1984, the FCC received strong support for its authority to preempt state and local regulation of cable in Capital Cities Cable, Inc. v. Crisp, 467 U.S. 691, 104 S.Ct. 2694, 81 L.Ed.2d 580 (1984) (application of Oklahoma ban on alcoholic beverage advertising to out-of-state signals carried on Oklahoma cable systems held preempted by FCC signal carriage regulations). Further limitations on state and municipal franchising authority seemed inevitable.

b. The Cable Communications Policy Act of 1984

Cable operators, represented by the National Cable Television Association (NCTA), and state and local authorities, represented by the National League of Cities (NLC), sought legislative relief. Eventually a compromise bill was drafted and, in late 1984, enacted into law as the Cable Communications Policy Act of 1984 (P.L. 98–549, 47 U.S.C.A. § 151 et seq.).

The Cable Act created Title VI of the Communications Act, 47 U.S.C.A. §§ 521–559, setting explicit rules for cable that clearly delineate the jurisdictional division between the FCC and state and local authorities. Franchising authority still rests with state and local authorities. They cannot, however, regulate cable as a common carrier, nor can they require specific video programming services. Specific guidelines for franchise renewal are set out, giving extensive protection to the incumbent franchisee. There are also guidelines for franchise modifications that permit an operator to appeal the denial of requests for modification.

Franchise fees are limited to five percent of gross revenues. Rate regulation is prohibited except where there is a lack of effective competition. The FCC has subsequently defined effective competition as the presence in the market of at least three off-the-air television signals. Even where there is a lack of effective competition only basic cable rates may be regulated.

Franchising authorities may require cable operators to designate a portion of their channel capacity for public, educational and governmental use. Other than the right to prohibit obscene or otherwise constitutionally protected programming, cable operators have no editorial control over these "PEG" channels. The Act also requires cable operators to set aside a specified number of channels (based on the total number of channels available) to be leased for commercial use. No editorial control over the leased access channels is permitted.

Earlier Commission rules prohibiting a television broadcast licensee from owning a cable system within its signal coverage area or a common carrier from owning one within its telephone service area have been codified in the Act. State ownership restrictions have been preempted.

The full impact of the Act is still to be seen. In addition, as we will discuss later, serious questions concerning the constitutionality of some of its provisions or even the entire Act have been raised.

2. Signal Carriage Rules

The potential impact of cable television upon the Commission's television allocation scheme has two aspects: first, the importation of distant signals might fragment the audience of the local television station since the local station would now be required to compete with "outside" signals not originally anticipated in the Commission's allocations policy. This is the so-called "distant signal" problem. Second, unless the local cable system is required to carry the signals of the local stations, viewers who choose to subscribe to the system usually would not be able to receive the signal of the local station because they would probably disconnect their regular antennae.

To complicate matters further, the cablevision impact upon independent, non-network and UHF television stations is paradoxical. To the extent cablevision systems carried local, non-network, UHF stations, the cablevision system helped them since it eliminated most of the technical advantages which off-the-air VHF reception possessed over UHF reception. On the other hand, to the extent these systems carried distant signals, they tended to fragment the audience and, therefore, harmed local non-network UHF facilities.

The Commission, in 1972, attempted to resolve these issues and integrate cablevision in the television scheme by enacting a series of rules aimed at protecting local stations. These rules essentially fell into two categories: "Must Carry"—rules requiring cable systems to carry local stations—and "May Carry"—rules limiting the number or type of competing signals cable systems may carry.

The must-carry rules were designed to ensure that cable subscribers would still receive the local broadcast stations and that these stations would have the same signal quality as competing signals. We will return to these rules later in this chapter in our discussion of cable's First Amendment rights.

The may-carry rules took several forms. One was a limit on the number of signals from distant stations that a cable system could transmit. This limit varied according to market size and the number of available over-the-air signals within the market.

A second restriction on distant signals involved syndicated programming. Generally, syndicated programming is sold on a market-exclusive basis, but the importation of syndicated programming made it impossible to guarantee market exclusivity. The Commission responded by requiring cable systems in major markets to black out distant syndicated programs when local commercial stations owned the exclusive rights to the broadcast of these programs.

In 1980, as part of its cable deregulation effort, the Commission abolished both the distant signal limitations and the syndicated exclusivity rules. See Malrite T.V. v. FCC, 652 F.2d 1140 (2d Cir. 1981). However, as an outgrowth of the new must-carry proceedings discussed below, the Commission has issued a combined Notice of Inquiry and Notice of Proposed Rule Making proposing the reinstitution of some form of syndicated exclusivity rules. 2 FCC Rcd. 2393 (1987).

One may-carry rule that remains is the network nonduplication rule. It is aimed at the problem that arises when the same cable systems carry "local" and "distant" stations which may both be broadcasting the same network program. Because such duplication through the use of cable television could have a detrimental economic effect on the local station that had obtained exclusivity for the program under its network agreement, the Commission has enacted rules which require that cable systems with more than 1000 subscribers delete the network programs of duplicating distant stations under certain circumstances. See 47 C.F.R. §§ 76.92–76.99 (1985). The deletion is made in accordance with certain priorities set forth in the Commission's Rules: a "local" television station has the right to require the deletion of a duplicating network program from the signal of a lower priority station. See 47 C.F.R. § 76.92. In order to invoke such protection the station requesting deletion must formally notify the cable system.

3. Content Regulations

In addition to the so-called carriage and nonduplication rules discussed above, the Commission has imposed upon cable systems certain operating requirements similar to those imposed upon broadcast stations. Thus, despite the fact that cable may not be considered "broadcasting" in the usual sense, nonetheless, to the extent cable systems originate their own programs, the Commission's Rules require that these systems follow all of the "equal time" and "lowest unit rate" political broadcast regulations promulgated pursuant to Section 315 of the Communications Act, adhere to the rules concerning the Fairness Doctrine, Personal Attack and Political Editorial Rules, forego broadcasting lottery information except that concerning a state-run lottery and only then under certain conditions, not transmit obscenity, even on the so-called "access" channels, identify all material that is sponsored, and maintain certain records.

4. Copyright Problems

One of the earliest legal problems to be faced with the advent of cable television was whether a cable system, by the act of receiving a program broadcast over the air and then sending the program by wire to various subscribers, was undertaking a "performance for profit," thereupon subjecting itself to liability either to the television station whose program it was re-transmitting, or to the copyright holders of the work being presented on the station. It was argued by the cable interests that cable systems were not "performing" in the sense contemplated by the copyright laws since they were merely receiving material sent out over the air by stations which had already paid a copyright fee. Imposing liability on the cable system would, the argument ran, result in double payment to the copyright holder. Others argued that whether or not copyright fees should be paid depended upon whether the cable system merely filled in the blanks within a station's normal service contour or whether the cable system extended the range of a station's service beyond the normal service contour.

The Supreme Court dealt with the issue in two landmark cases absolving cable systems of copyright liability for material picked up over the air and then sent through wire, on the ground that this was not a "performance" but merely a mechanical, passive act no different in quality than the erecting by a single person of an extremely tall receiving antenna to improve his or her own reception. Because such an act did not subject the individual to copyright liability, the provision of such a service for profit did not change the quality of the act for copyright purposes under the then existing copyright act. Fortnightly Corp. v. United Artists Television, Inc., 392 U.S. 390, 88 S.Ct. 2084, 20 L.Ed.2d 1176 (1968); Teleprompter Corp. v. Columbia Broadcasting System, Inc., 415 U.S. 394, 94 S.Ct. 1129, 39 L.Ed.2d 415 (1974).

The Fortnightly and Teleprompter decisions led Congress to enact significant revisions of the copyright statute. Under the Copyright Act as it now reads, cablevision systems are free to retransmit television signals containing copyrighted materials without obtaining permission of the copyright holder, but the systems must pay a compulsory license fee. The amount of that fee, and the manner in which the fee is to be disbursed, are determined by the Copyright Royalty Tribunal (CRT), a statutory body created by Congress for this purpose. See 17 U.S.C.A. § 111.

The compulsory license has proven quite controversial. Broadcasters have been extremely dissatisfied with the CRT's distribution formulas. The Motion Picture Association of America (MPAA), which represents those holding copyrights in televised motion pictures and syndicated programs, has consistently been awarded the lion's share of the license fees. Broadcasters have received very little by comparison.

The distribution proceedings have also become more complicated. As a result of the elimination of the syndication exclusivity rules and distant signal limitations, the CRT imposed two new license fees. The first is a charge of 3.75% of gross revenues for systems carrying distant signals prohibited by the old rules. The second is a surcharge on all cable systems in the top 100 markets. The surcharge is designed to compensate for the loss of syndication exclusivity. See National Cable Television Association v. Copyright Royalty Tribunal, 724 F.2d 176 (D.C.Cir.1983) (upholding the imposition of the new fees). The result of these new fees is three separate distribution funds: the basic fund, the 3.75% fund, and the syndex fund. Broadcasters have not fared any better in the distribution of the new funds.

In sum, the only programming restrictions that still remain upon the type of material that can be presented on cablevision systems relate to the non-duplication protection afforded network programs (47 C.F.R. §§ 76.92 thru 76.99 (1981)), and those portions of the Commission's rules placing a blackout upon the cablecasting of sports events taking place locally (See 47 C.F.R. § 76.67) (1981).

5. Constitutional Protection for Cable

Probably as a result of the early decisions linking the FCC's jurisdiction over cable to its jurisdiction over broadcasting, as well as the essentially identical nature of the product distributed by cable and broadcasting, cable was considered to have First Amendment rights no greater than those accorded broadcasting. The few First Amendment challenges to cable regulation were quickly dismissed with references to Red Lion and the scarcity rationale.

The only exception was Home Box Office, Inc. v. FCC, 567 F.2d 9 (D.C.Cir.1977), cert. denied 434 U.S. 829, 98 S.Ct. 111, 54 L.Ed.2d 89 (1977). HBO had challenged a series of regulations which prohibited cable systems from presenting certain film or sports presentations which were available on "off-the-air" or "free" television. In addition to finding the rules both beyond the FCC's jurisdiction and arbitrary and capricious, the court found them unconstitutional. The court held that Red Lion was inapplicable because cable was not limited by the physical scarcity of the electromagnetic spectrum. Viewing the anti-siphoning rules as regulation where the restriction on speech was incidental to the purpose of the regulation, the court chose to apply the O'Brien test: "If such regulations 'further an important or substantial government interest; . . . and if the incidental restriction in alleged First Amendment freedoms is no greater than is essential to the furtherance of that interest,' then the regulations are valid." See United States v. O'Brien, 391 U.S. 367, 88 S.Ct. 1673, 20 L.Ed.2d 672 (1968). Under this test the rules were found to be grossly overbroad.

In its first two opportunities directly to address the issue the Supreme Court avoided it by striking down the challenged regulations on nonconstitutional grounds. See Federal Communications Commission v. Midwest Video Corp., 440 U.S. 689, 99 S.Ct. 1435, 59 L.Ed.2d 692 (1979); Capital Cities Cable, Inc. v. Crisp, 467 U.S. 691, 104 S.Ct. 2694, 81 L.Ed.2d 580 (1984).

Then in 1985 a series of appellate court decisions recognized First Amendment rights for cable in cases involving such disparate issues as the must-carry rules, franchising regulations, and indecency statutes. A year later the Supreme Court finally addressed the issue in City of Los Angeles v. Preferred Communications, Inc., 476 U.S. 488, 106 S.Ct. 2034, 90 L.Ed.2d 480 (1986).

a. The "Must-Carry" Rules

In Quincy Cable TV, Inc. v. FCC, 768 F.2d 1434 (D.C.Cir.1985), cert. denied sub nom. National Association of Broadcasters v. Quincy Cable TV, Inc., ___ U.S. ___, 106 S.Ct. 2889, 90 L.Ed.2d 977 (1986), the court declared the must-carry rules, as written, unconstitutional under the First Amendment. The case involved two petitions. Quincy Cable, located in Quincy, Washington, was appealing an FCC order requiring it to carry some Spokane, Washington, television stations as well as a $5,000 forfeiture for its failure to comply with the Commission's order. Turner Broadcasting System (TBS) was appealing the Commission's denial of TBS's petition to have the must-carry rules eliminated.

The court began by stating that the more limited scope of First Amendment protection enjoyed by the broadcast media as a result of Red Lion is not appropriate for cable. The court rejected any application of the scarcity rationale noting that cable does not use the airwaves to deliver its programming to its subscribers. The court also rejected an economic scarcity argument based on the idea that cable is a natural monopoly. Not only was the court skeptical of cable's status as a natural monopoly, suggesting that the pattern of one cable system to a market was primarily a result of municipal franchising policies, but the court observed that economic scarcity had been rejected as a ground for infringing First Amendment rights in Miami Herald Pub. Co. v. Tornillo, 418 U.S. 241, 94 S.Ct. 2831, 41 L.Ed.2d 730 (1974).

The court found it unnecessary to decide whether the rules should be examined under the O'Brien test or some more exacting level of scrutiny, because in the court's analysis the rules failed even the more relaxed O'Brien test. Thus, it is not yet clear what test will be used to evaluate the constitutionality of future cable regulation—including any revised must-carry rules. The Supreme Court has yet to decide this issue although there is some suggestion that the Court will adopt O'Brien. See discussion of City of Los Angeles v. Preferred Communications, Inc., infra, pp. 499–501.

The court held that the Commission had failed to prove that the rules served an important government interest. Although the Commission asserted that the interest served by the rules was preserving free, locally-oriented television, it failed, at least in the court's eyes, to prove it. Even though substantial deference to the Commission's expertise is required, the court concluded that after twenty years of regulation, something more than unsubstantiated assumptions and speculations was needed to support the Commission's conclusions.

The court went on to state that even if it assumed that the rules served the asserted government interest, they would still fail the O'Brien test
as overinclusive. In the guise of protecting local
broadcasting the rules were protecting local broadcasters regardless of the quality of their service or
the number of stations in the market. The rules
imposed no requirement that a station offer at
least a minimum amount of local programming or
demonstrate that its programming was not completely duplicative of another already in the market.

Finally, the court of appeals majority indicated
that it had "not found it necessary to decide whether any version of the rules would contravene the
First Amendment" leaving the door open for the
Commission to draft new rules.

The Commission ceased enforcement of the old
rules on September 10, 1985 and later the Supreme
Court denied certiorari. National Association of
Broadcasters v. Quincy Cable TV, Inc., ___ U.S.
___, 106 S.Ct. 2889, 90 L.Ed.2d 977 (1986). In the
meantime, under pressure from Congress the Commission started proceedings to write new must-
carry rules. Negotiations between various elements of the broadcast and cable industries resulted in a proposed compromise, but the Commission
decided not to accept the compromise in its entirety.

In August, 1986, the Commission announced a
new set of must-carry rules. Under these rules a

maximum number of must-carry stations is established, the number to be dependent on the size of the system. Must-carry status is limited to full-power stations located within fifty miles of the cable system's head end that deliver a good quality signal to the head end. Commercial stations on the air for more than one year are also subject to minimum non-cable home viewership requirements. Where the number of must-carry stations exceeds the maximum number a cable system is required to carry, the cable system is allowed to choose which stations to carry.

The most controversial aspect of the proposed rules was a requirement that cable systems provide an A–B switch (a device that allows the subscriber to easily switch between an antenna for broadcast reception and the cable feed) free to each new subscriber and either free or at cost to each existing subscriber requesting one. Upon reconsideration this requirement was modified. Cable systems need only offer a switch to new subscribers and can charge for the switch. In the case of existing subscribers, the cable company can charge for both the switch and its installation. 62 R.R.2d 1251 (1987). The modified rules did retain the requirement that cable companies educate their subscribers as to the existence and use of these switches.

The purpose of the new rules, according to the Commission, is to ease the transition from a regulated to a market environment. Consistent with this market approach is the requirement in the new rules to make available to consumers equipment that allows them to switch easily between competing services and to educate them as to the availability of that choice. Reinforcing the transition concept, the Commission included a five-year sunset provision in the rules.

The new rules have come under heavy attack. Even with the modification in the A–B switch requirement, several groups have already announced their intention to file a challenge with the court of appeals. Meanwhile, broadcasters have discussed asking Congress to codify the rules in the Communications Act and to eliminate the five-year sunset provision.

b. *Franchising*

For many years cable companies were loath to challenge franchising regulations—probably because of fear that such an action would damage the challenging company's chances of obtaining the franchise. Then, in 1984 Preferred Communications Inc., sought to bypass the City of Los Angeles' franchising regulations by asking various utility companies to provide space on their poles for the express purpose of constructing a cable system. The companies refused because Preferred had not obtained a cable franchise from the city.

Preferred then brought an action seeking to have the cable franchising regulations declared unconstitutional under the First and Fourteenth

Amendments. Los Angeles' successful motion to dismiss for failure to state a claim upon which relief could be granted was appealed by Preferred. In a strongly worded opinion, the court of appeals reversed the district court's grant of the motion to dismiss. The court defined the issue as whether the City could, "consistent with the First Amendment, limit access by means of an auction process to a given region of the City to a single cable television company, when the public utility facilities and other public property in that region necessary to the installation and operation of a cable television system are physically capable of accommodating more than one system?" The court, noting that economic scarcity had been rejected in Miami Herald as grounds for restricting First Amendment rights, concluded that the city could not so limit access and seemed to stop just short of declaring First Amendment protection for cable to be the same as for the print media.

Although the Supreme Court affirmed the appellate court's decision, it did so on narrower grounds. Justice Rehnquist's majority opinion stated that the activities engaged in by cable television companies clearly implicated First Amendment activities but then noted, consistent with the Court's new hierarchical approach to the Amendment, that "[E]ven protected speech is not equally permissible in all places and at all times." He also noted that the construction and operation of a cable television franchise involved a mixture of speech and conduct thus presenting special questions regarding the right of the state to regulate the non-speech elements involved. The Court was unwilling to decide the appropriate degree of First Amendment protection to be afforded cable without the more complete factual record that an actual trial could provide. Justice Blackmun concurred to emphasize that the proper First Amendment standard for cable was still undetermined. City of Los Angeles v. Preferred Communications, Inc., 476 U.S. 488, 106 S.Ct. 2034, 90 L.Ed.2d 480 (1986).

Although it may be dangerous to draw too many conclusions from what is really a very limited opinion, it appears as though the Court is leaning toward granting cable less protection under the First Amendment than is enjoyed by the print media. Whether the cable operator's rights will be restricted as much as broadcaster's is much more difficult to predict, especially with the Court's suggestion in League of Women Voters that broadcasting may soon find its First Amendment protection increased.

Rehnquist's opinion also suggests that the Court may adopt the approach used by the United States Circuit Court of Appeals for the District of Columbia in HBO and Quincy, viewing cable as a mix of speech and conduct that requires the application of the O'Brien test.

c. Content Regulation

Most of the constitutional challenges to content regulation of cable have involved laws aimed at limiting the carriage of indecent programming. Supporters of such indecency restrictions argue that they can be constitutionally applied to cable for the same reasons that the Supreme Court held similar restrictions are constitutional when applied to broadcasting. See FCC v. Pacifica Foundation, 438 U.S. 726, 98 S.Ct. 3026, 57 L.Ed.2d 1073 (1978). Opponents contend that the Pacifica rationale is only applicable to broadcasting and that the appropriate precedent is Erznoznik v. Jacksonville, 422 U.S. 205, 95 S.Ct. 2268, 45 L.Ed.2d 125 (1975) in which a local ordinance banning all nudity on drive-in movie screens visible from the street was held unconstitutionally overbroad.

In Cruz v. Ferre, 755 F.2d 1415 (11th Cir.1985), a Miami ordinance banning the distribution of obscene and indecent programming over cable was struck down on overbreadth grounds. The court distinguished Pacifica on the basis of differences between broadcasting and cable. Cable requires the affirmative decision to subscribe and juveniles can be protected through the use of lockboxes that permit parents to lock out channels and put them out of reach of their children.

Even if these differences did not exist, the court would still have found the ordinance unconstitutional because it banned indecent programming outright. In Pacifica the U.S. Supreme Court had indicated that indecent programming might be permissible in appropriate time periods or programming contexts. No such allowances were made in the Miami ordinance.

Similarly, in Jones v. Wilkinson, 800 F.2d 989 (10th Cir.1986) the court of appeals affirmed a lower court decision striking down the Utah Cable Television Programming Decency Act. However, one member of the court argued in his concurrence that Pacifica was the appropriate standard by which cable indecency regulations should be judged. He then found that the Act could not even meet the more relaxed Pacifica standard. The U.S. Supreme Court affirmed without issuing any opinion. Wilkinson v. Jones, 480 U.S. __, 107 S.Ct. 1559, 94 L.Ed.2d 753 (1987).

Except for the clear authority of Miller v. California, 413 U.S. 15, 93 S.Ct. 2607, 37 L.Ed.2d 419 (1973), chapter IV, supra, to ban obscenity over cable, it is not yet clear whether any other sexually oriented programming may be proscribed.

B. HIGH DEFINITION TELEVISION (HDTV)

While a plethora of new systems for delivering television programming (cable, MDS, DBS, and SMATV, all discussed later in this chapter) have been developed, one thing has remained constant— the television picture itself. The last major change was the advent of color decades ago.

All this could change with the development of High Definition Television (HDTV). The key difference between HDTV and the current U.S. broadcast standard is that HDTV has approximately double the number of scan lines (1100–1200 as opposed to 525). The result is a sharper, brighter, clearer picture with deeper, more vibrant colors. In addition HDTV uses a five-to-three aspect ratio as opposed to the four-to-three currently in use. Proponents of HDTV claim that its quality approximates that of 35 mm. film.

However, before HDTV can become a reality in the United States, several major problems have to be solved. The first is compatibility. If the HDTV standard is incompatible with the television sets currently in use, its development could be seriously hampered. How many people will be able to afford two television sets, one for regular television and one for HDTV? Imagine for example, what would have happened if the FCC had chosen a standard for color that was incompatible with black and white television sets.

A second problem is delivering the picture to the home. A regular broadcast signal requires six mhz of spectrum space. In contrast HDTV can require as much as 30 mhz. Even though some proposed HDTV systems have reduced the spectrum requirement to as little as 8.1 mhz, there is still a major delivery problem. Current broadcast stations have only been allocated 6 mhz. Because of the allocation scheme adopted by the FCC, VHF stations could only expand their space by infringing on someone else's.

The UHF band is not as saturated. In 1986 an experimental HDTV broadcast was transmitted over channels 58 and 59 in Washington, D.C. But the use of excess UHF spectrum for HDTV is far from assured. Representatives of other services, primarily land-mobile radio, have applied to have some of the unused UHF spectrum reallocated for their use. The Commission is faced with the choice between accommodating an existing service with a current need or reserving the space for a new service that may or may not develop.

The HDTV spectrum question is a serious one for broadcasters. If HDTV becomes a reality, but no method of broadcast delivery is feasible, those services that do not have the same delivery problem will acquire a tremendous competitive advantage. Foremost would be cable which, because it does not use the spectrum, will have no difficulties accommodating HDTV's increased frequency demands.

C. MULTIPOINT DISTRIBUTION SERVICE (MDS)

Despite the emergence of cable television and pay television, and despite the nationwide saturation of receivers, there are still approximately 1.2 million households that have no access to television service and there are approximately 4 million households that receive only one or two channels (see 47 Fed.Reg. at 1967, Jan. 13, 1982). There are additional millions of households that receive only three or four channels. Technologies have been developing to attempt to alleviate the shortage.

The multipoint distribution service (MDS) is one such technological alternative. This service typically consists of a microwave transmitter and antenna at the transmitting site broadcasting over a microwave frequency omnidirectionally covering a line of sight area of approximately 10 to 20 miles. The signal is then received by a receiving antenna at a particular site. The signal is converted from the microwave frequency to a lower frequency compatible with the customer's television set. The signal is passed from the downconverter through a cable to the customer's set on a VHF channel which is vacant in the community (see 45 Fed.Reg. 29350 at ¶ 24 (May 2, 1980)).

Economically, the arrangement is as follows: the transmitting equipment is licensed to an entity which acts as a common carrier. The licensee as a common carrier does not have control over the programming presented on the channel. Persons wishing to present programming over the system (called "subscribers") lease air time on the transmitter and make the programming available for transmission. Time is usually sold to a programmer on a block basis. The subscriber also typically owns the receiving antenna and the downconverter. The subscriber then contracts with the customer for delivery of the program to the customer's set. In essence, the transaction is very close to a point-to-point transmission, using the air waves rather than a wire.

Originally, most markets had only one or two microwave channels available for MDS service. They were allocated via the comparative hearing method with all its attendant delays and expenses. Then in 1983 the Commission reallocated eight of the 28 instructional television fixed service (ITFS) microwave channels to MDS. ITFS (MDS Reallocation), 48 Fed.Reg. 33,873 (July 15, 1983). At the same time, the FCC authorized MDS operators to lease extra channel capacity from ITFS operators and changed its method of allocating MDS channels from the comparative hearing to a lottery system. The expanded service created by the rule changes is called multichannel multipoint distribution service (MMDS). It is often referred to as "wireless cable."

Because the service is called a "common carrier" service neither licensees nor subscribers (i.e., programmers) are subject to the equal time or fairness rules, the access rules for political candidates, or the other doctrines which control broadcast operations. Unlike cable system operators MDS operators do not have to obtain a franchise grant from a state or town because the FCC has preempted state and local regulation of MDS. See New York State Commission on Cable Television v. FCC, 669 F.2d 58 (2d Cir.1982).

As a competitor of cable, MMDS has several advantages. Installation is much less expensive, especially in urban areas where cable must be placed underground. Because there are no franchising requirements, MMDS does not have to provide expensive community services such as access channels and studios. Long expensive franchising battles are not required and an MMDS operator can offer service to all the surrounding communities.

On the other hand, even with the new channels made available, MMDS is limited to less than thirty channels, whereas some urban cable systems have the capacity to provide 100 or more. Perhaps more important, cable is already established in many communities and it may be difficult for MMDS to convince existing cable subscribers to switch. The best opportunities for MMDS appear to be in those communities that either have no existing cable service or have old, limited-capacity systems.

D. SATELLITE MASTER ANTENNA TELEVISION (SMATV)

One of the earliest alternatives to cable, satellite master antenna television (SMATV) is really a cable system that does not cross a public right of way. A SMATV operator sets up one or more earth stations on an apartment building or residential complex. The programming received by these earth stations is distributed throughout the building or complex by wire.

In 1983, the FCC preempted state and local entry regulations for SMATV. The Commission's decision was affirmed in New York State Commission on Cable Television v. FCC, 749 F.2d 804 (D.C.Cir. 1984). As a result SMATV is an essentially unregulated industry.

Because a SMATV system cannot cross a public right of way, SMATV is limited to large apartment buildings, hotels and private residential complexes. In those areas it has several advantages over other services. The absence of any franchising requirements allows immediate entry into the market. Like MMDS, SMATV cannot be required to provide access channels and studios, thus reducing the cost of operation. However, unlike MMDS, SMATV has no limit on channel capacity.

E.   DIRECT BROADCAST SATELLITES (DBS)

As satellite communications technology improved, both the cost and size of earth stations capable of receiving satellite transmissions decreased. As a result direct transmission to individual homes appeared to be both technologically and economically feasible. In 1980, the Commission began conducting inquiries into how best to initiate such a service. See Notice of Inquiry, 45 Fed.Reg. 72,719 (Nov. 3, 1980).

Among the questions that needed to be addressed were the type of service to be offered (pay or advertiser-supported), the number of satellites and channels to be used, and the frequencies to be allocated to the service. Permanent answers had to await the decisions of an international conference allotting frequencies and orbital slots to the Western Hemisphere nations.

However, in an attempt to hasten the development of this new service the Commission in July, 1982 issued interim guidelines for DBS operators. Licenses would be granted for five years, and licensees would be required to meet international guidelines. DBS services with broadcast characteristics would be subject to the broadcast sections of the Communications Act, but not subject to non-statutory Commission policies with the exception of the Commission's equal employment opportunity rules. DBS operators offering common carrier-type services were to be subject only to the common carrier sections of the Act. The interim guidelines were challenged in National Association of Broadcasters v. FCC, 740 F.2d 1190 (D.C.Cir.1984) and were upheld except for the exemption from the broadcasting sections of the Communications Act of programmers leasing DBS channels.

The 1983 international conference set aside 12.2 to 12.7 GHz for DBS and awarded orbital slots. Other allocation questions were left for a 1985 conference which in turn left them for another conference scheduled for 1988.

In 1983 United Satellite Communications, Inc. (USCI) became the first company to offer DBS service. Less than 2 years later, after huge losses, USCI discontinued its service. Meanwhile a number of the other companies that had originally applied for licenses to offer DBS service have abandoned their DBS plans.

The advantages of direct broadcast satellites had appeared obvious. A single satellite could provide programming to a large area of the country. Most importantly, satellites offered a way to serve those areas of the country (primarily rural) where cable cannot be profitable due to high per-subscriber installation costs.

Unfortunately, less immediately apparent were some of the key disadvantages. DBS service turned out to be very expensive because of the costs involved in putting satellites in space. There were not enough potential subscribers to make advertiser-supported service feasible. Instead subscribers had to pay several hundred dollars to buy a receiving dish in addition to a monthly charge of more than $20/month for a limited number of channels. Thus, in those areas where cable was available DBS could not compete. The uncabled areas were insufficient to support DBS by themselves.

The future for DBS appears doubtful. However, high-powered satellites will become operational in 1988. These satellites will permit the use of smaller, less expensive, receiving equipment. Whether this will improve the economics of DBS service to the point where it can survive is difficult to judge.

F. HOME SATELLITE DISHES (TVRO)

Still another competitor for cable spawned by developments in satellite communications is the television receive only dish (TVRO). As the size and cost of these dishes dropped, people began buying them for their backyards. With a dish it became possible to pick up a seemingly endless number of programming feeds. The two most important types of signals available were cable programming services and network television feeds.

Earlier purchasers of these TVRO systems were mostly those who lived in remote areas. Unserved by cable or in many cases even by conventional broadcasting, these people had no other way to obtain video programming. However, as the prices of the equipment dropped, people in more populated areas became increasingly interested. The large number of available signals as well as the lack of any cost beyond the initial purchase price made them an attractive alternative to cable.

As the number of backyard dishes increased, cable operators, cable programmers and television network executives all became concerned. The cable operators and cable programmers had obvious economic concerns—dish owners were not likely to subscribe to cable and they were not paying the programmers for their services. The networks had a different concern. Much of what the dish owners were receiving was raw programming material, for example, news reports being sent back to the network studios or programs being transmitted from the network to the local affiliates without the local commercials inserted.

These concerns were addressed in The Cable Communications Policy Act of 1984 which amended section 605 of the Federal Communications Act specifically to prohibit unauthorized reception of any *encrypted* satellite cable signal, as long as there is a marketing mechanism available for those who wish to purchase the service.

In 1986 various cable programming services began scrambling their signals and more announced their intention to do so in the future. The industry did agree on a standard for scrambling, which means a dish owner only has to buy one converter no matter how many programming services are desired.

A great deal of controversy still surrounds scrambling. Many of the services initially designated local cable companies as the only ones authorized to market their programming to dish owners. The prices set for these services were almost always as much or more than the cost of the service when delivered by cable, even though the cost of delivery is less.

The Society of Private and Commercial Earth Stations (SPACE), a trade association for dish owners, has claimed that the cable programmers set prices artificially high and used cable operators as marketers in order to protect the cable operators, who are, of course, their largest customers.

As a result, Congress held numerous hearings on the scrambling controversy in 1986 and 1987. Several bills designed to protect dish owners have been introduced, particularly by Congressmen representing rural areas.

There are several difficult questions involved here. Although it is obvious that the dish owners shouldn't be able to obtain the programming free, neither should the price be prohibitive. If TVROs are to provide a competitive alternative to cable, how can cable operators be the sole distributors of satellite delivered programming? What about network programming? Why should dish owners have access to programming other than the finished product aired by network affiliate? And what about the rural dish owner who does not otherwise have access to network programming? It will be the job of Congress to resolve these questions and recognize the conflicting interests involved.

G. ELECTRONIC PUBLISHING
(TELETEXT)

Another new technology whose promise has far exceeded its performance is electronic publishing. It is possible, utilizing previously unused portions of television signals (the Vertical Blanking Interval (VBI) or the space between frames) to transmit textual information. A decoding unit can take the information in the VBI and display it on the television screen. Closed captioning for the deaf is a simplified version of this process.

Original proposals for this service often known as teletext or videotext analogized it to an electronic newspaper. Viewers would be able to call up news, sports, and weather, as well as restaurant reviews, airline schedules, and concert ticket availabilities at the touch of a button. They could then make plane reservations, and order concert tickets or merchandise by phone. Interactive cable versions of the service would even allow the entire transactions to be done by cable.

In 1983 the FCC authorized the use of the broadcast VBI for teletext. Teletext service would be regulated as either broadcast or common carrier depending on the nature of the service. No specific teletext standard was set. The Commission declined to apply the equal time or fairness rules to broadcast-like teletext services and also refused to require cable systems to carry the teletext portion of stations, even when required to carry the stations themselves under the must-carry rules.

The equal time and fairness aspects of the ruling were appealed. In Telecommunications Research Action Committee v. FCC, 801 F.2d 501, reh'g denied, 806 F.2d 1115 (D.C.Cir.1986) the court held that because teletext was a broadcast service, it had to be subject to § 315 of the Communications Act. However, the court found that the fairness doctrine was not codified in § 315 as many had thought and therefore, the Commission had the authority to exempt teletext from its application.

The court's holding may well be the only important aspect of teletext or the overall field of electronic publishing. So far there are no major teletext operations in existence and a similar service supplied via telephone (Viewtron) was shut down after several financially unsuccessful years. Only if VBI decoder circuitry were included in new television receivers at reasonable cost would electronic publishing have any likelihood of succeeding in this country.

INDEX

References are to Pages

References are to Pages

†